Cuba 1933:
Students, Yankees,
and Soldiers

North-South Center
UNIVERSITY OF MIAMI

Cuba 1933:
Students, Yankees, and Soldiers

Justo Carrillo

DISTRIBUTED BY

LYNNE RIENNER PUBLISHERS

1800 30TH ST., SUITE 314, BOULDER, CO 80301
TEL: 303-444-6684 · FAX: 303-444-0824

This book is an edited version of the Spanish volume, *Cuba 1933: estudiantes, yanquis y soldados*, originally published in 1985 by the Institute of Interamerican Studies, University of Miami, ISBN 0935501-00-2.

Mario Llerena, *translator*.

Elizabeth D. Posey, *manuscript editor*.

Library of Congress Cataloging-in-Publication Data

Carrillo, Justo.
    [Cuba 1933, English]
    Cuba 1933: students, yankees, and soldiers / Justo Carrillo: foreword by Luis E. Aguilar: translated by Mario Llerena.
        p. cm.
    At head of title: North-South Center, University of Miami,
    ISBN 1-56000-690-0: $15.95
    1. Cuba -- History -- Revolution, 1933. 2. Cuba -- Politics and government -- 1909-1933. 3. Cuba -- Politics and government -- 1933-1959. 4. Directorio Estudiantil Universitario (Cuba) 5. Carrillo, Justo. I. Title.
    F1787.5.C2813   1994
    972.91'06'2--dc20   93-38233
                                                      CIP

English edition © 1994
ISBN-1-56000-690-0
Printed in the United States of America

CONTENTS

Dedication i
Apologies iii
Acknowledgments v
Foreword vii

CHAPTER 1: PRELUDE TO REVOLUTION
The Thirtieth of September, 1930 1
The Military Pay Homage to Machado 6
The Directorio Develops Political Consciousness 8
Anti-Machado Activities of the Politicians 13
Political Formation Behind Bars 16
Fraternizing with Anti-Machado Military Prisoners 19
Change of Government in the United States
    and the Mediation Process 23
The Directorio Vacillates 33
The Directorio Rejects Mediation 38
Machado's Fall — Céspedes' Government 49
The Céspedes Government — Its Character and Its Fall 53
The Treason of Soler 56
The Atarés Discoveries and Consequences 60
The ARPE Idea 70
The ARPE Program (The DEU Document) 75
August 22: The Day of Confrontation 82
The DEU Challenges the Government 84
Conversations with the Military Sector 89
The DEU Pressures the Mediation Government 91
Agony of the Céspedes Government 98

PHOTOS: PRINCIPAL PERSONALITIES AND DOCUMENTS

CHAPTER 2: THE FOURTH OF SEPTEMBER REVOLUTION:
             FROM THE PENTARCHY TO PRESIDENT GRAU
The Beginnings of the Sergeants' Movement 113
Causes of the Sergeants' Movement: A Synthesis 117
Welles and Menocal 121

The Young Officers Corps of the National Army 126
Military Causes of the Sergeants' Coup: Detailed Exposition 132
Reaction of the Directorio 137
The Directorio's Psychological Transformation on September 4 139
The Events of September 4 — Dialogue Between the Author
    and Juan Antonio Rubio Padilla 142
The Events from September 5 to 10 152
Batista from September 5 to 10 177
Welles from September 5 to 10 182
Carbó from September 5 to 10 186
Welles and the Plattist Officers 189
How Things Stood on September 10 195

CHAPTER 3: THE REVOLUTIONARY GOVERNMENT I:
    FROM SEPTEMBER 10 TO NOVEMBER 30, 1933
President Grau 205
The Government Legislates I 209
The DEU-Welles Interview on September 15, 1933 214
The Government Legislates II 217
Welles and Batista Conspire 220
The Government Legislates III:
    Confrontation with the Communists 228
The Drama at Hotel Nacional 232
The Welles-Batista Pact Is Strengthened 237
The Meeting at the Carbó Home and the Dissolution of the DEU .. 244
The November 8 Insurrection Fiasco 261
Welles and the Nonrecognition Policy — The Growing Enmity
    between Cordell Hull and Sumner Welles 274
Revolutionary Legislation: October and November 1933 285

CHAPTER 4: THE REVOLUTIONARY GOVERNMENT II:
    DECEMBER 1933 AND JANUARY 1934
Montevideo: Triumph of the Revolution,
    End of the Platt Amendment 297
Women and the Directorio 310
Legislative Depth in December 1933 311
January 1934: Legislative Fervor and Genuine Revolution 317
Caffery Accelerates the Conspiracy Against Grau 330
How Mendieta Came to Be President 336
The New York Times Serves U.S. Colonialism 346
The Batista-Castro Parallel: Why Did Cuba Fail to Achieve
    Genuine and Permanent International Individuality? 350

CHAPTER 5: A REVIEW OF THE 1930S MOVEMENT

The 1930 Directorio: Final Synthesis 361
The DEU, the 1930 Generation, and Political "*Autenticismo*" 371
Appendix I: The Platt Amendment 403
Appendix II: Microbiography of Carlos Manuel de Céspedes 405
Appendix III: Microbiography of Sergio Carbó 411
References 415

DEDICATED TO

Angel (Pío) Alvarez

Rafael Trejo

Carlos M.
Fuertes Blandino

Félix Ernesto Alpízar

All were members of the 1930 University Student Directorate who became martyrs in the struggle against tyranny and in pursuit of liberty.

APOLOGIES

To write about a particular period of history in which one was personally involved, even after fifty years have elapsed, can be a truly painful effort. Inevitably, there will be cases in which the narration of the facts, together with their — in my judgment — appropriate interpretation, will touch critically upon the conduct of many dear people already gone, others still alive, and even their respective descendants. And that causes me no little emotional distress, since it can affect existing human relationships. In my particular case, based on bitter personal experiences, the situation can be compared to the loss of someone close to my heart with whom I had serious differences in ideas and positions, but whom, nevertheless, I loved just the same; or with a tearing divorce that would separate me from a beloved person for unsurmountable causes that made life together impossible.

Those are the sentiments that motivate these words, now that I have written this book, with the intent of presenting my most heartfelt apologies to a number of people.

First of all, to the descendants of Major General Mario G. Menocal y Deop, of whom my forebears were followers, but with whose political conduct I never agreed. This apology goes to the general's children, Raúl and Georgina, and even to my own daughter, Madeleine Carrillo Menocal, a grandniece of the general, who, by the way, was himself a descendant on his mother's side of four other Menocal Deops who were officers of the Independence Army. To their memories, I pay my sincerest respect.

Next my genuine regrets go to the academy officers who in 1933 were ousted by the Sergeants' Coup. My respect for them will be apparent throughout the narration of events in this book as well as in the references of Juan Antonio Rubio Padilla, a fellow member of the

Directorio Estudiantil and active participant in that historic event. From among those officers, I would like to stress my contrite feelings to Carlos Montero, Rafael Galeano, Carlos Valdés Fauli, and Manuel F. (Freddy) Goudie. I hold the last, for instance, in such high esteem, for his deep Cuban devotion, pristine military vocation, and commanding aptitude, that I would have gladly accepted him at any time as Chief of Staff of the Cuban Army.

In the same manner, I extend my apologies to the two daughters of former President Carlos Prío, the most gracious ladies María Elena and Marianne, with whose acquaintance I have been honored. And also, of course, to the late president's brothers Paco (who died after these lines were in print) and Antonio, with whom I always shared the greatest friendship.

Lastly, but by no means with less emotional intensity, I must extend my apologies to Polita Grau, who was like a fifth lady accompanying the four who were part of the Directorio Estudiantil. She took active part in the heroic struggle and later married the most purehearted of the DEU men, Roberto Lago Pereda, who left this world prematurely. Perhaps her ambivalence during the struggle caused Polita to suffer a contradiction of sentiments between family loyalty to her uncle, President Grau, and deep identification with the student group whose history is retold in this book. I would even venture saying that Polita was more pro-Directorio than she was pro-Grau.

ACKNOWLEDGMENTS

First and foremost, to the University of Miami, to its Institute of Interamerican Studies, and to its director, Professor Jaime Suchlicki, for having sponsored the publication of this book — something that would otherwise have been impossible.

To the great Spanish maestro Julián Marías, whose study on the role of generations made it possible for me to write the last and most difficult of the chapters of this book. Many thanks, maestro.

To banker José R. Garrigó, Argentine sociologist Alberto Calvo, and Luis Aguilar León — who wrote the Foreword — for having been the ones who most heartily insisted that I should write about the 1930-33 period of Cuban history.

Next, to Juan Antonio Rubio Padilla, whose invaluable eyewitness information greatly enhances the historical contents of this book, and to Carlos F. de Armenteros, who provided the author with exclusive insights regarding the case of traitor José Soler, who was tried and sentenced precisely on the Fourth of September, the day of the epoch-making military shake-up at Columbia Camp.

Acknowledgment is likewise given here to Carlos Manuel Alvarez Tabío, a decent and patriotic gentleman, who successively knew persecution under Machado, Batista, and Castro. He offers in these pages exclusive information on the three-man meetings in which Ambassador Caffery, Colonel Batista, and Colonel Mendieta decided upon the designation of the last as president.

Special mention should be made here also of Hugh Thomas, Antonio Jorge, and Octavio Paz, whose respective scholarly analyses present a clear and devastating view of the communist Castro regime.

And to Cuban political scientist Andrés Suárez, professor emeritus of the University of Florida, whose qualified suggestions were taken into account in the preparation of this study.

To Gerardo and Isabel Canet, from the old Washington group, who so kindly responded to my continuous consultations.

Special mention and recognition to Guillermo Rubiera for providing me valuable historical information through the years, and to Horacio Ledón, who assumed the difficult task of placing the footnotes of this book when Rubiera was suddenly and unexpectedly disabled.

To Fermín Peinado, for his contribution in arranging and titling the chapters.

To Julio César Fernández, former chief editor of the 1930s student paper *Alma Mater*, for providing a sample of the bonds issued by the Directorio and the paper's front page from 7 November 1933. And to Jorge Beato Núñez, who provided the Soler "Wanted" poster.

To Rosa Abella and Hortensia Rodríguez, from the University of Miami and Florida International University libraries respectively, for giving me efficient assistance in the research for this book.

To Heriberto Cerdá, who transcribed the taped conversations and assembled and reassembled the various texts of this book - frequently.

To José I. Zárraga (Fral) and Jorge Figueras, as well as Max Lesnick and Rafael Menéndez, who provided dozens of the photos that illustrate this book.

To Gerardo Canet, who designed the cover, and to Margarita Carrillo, who gave it the colors of the Cuban soul.

To my wife, Ofelia Carrillo, who for years had to wade among mountains of paper that disrupted her exquisite penchant for domestic tidiness but who, nevertheless, always encouraged me to keep going.

And to all those — kinsmen I love as friends and friends I love as kinsmen — who contributed financially to my dues in the cost of this edition sponsored by the University of Miami. Their help made it possible for this book to reach the reader at a low price.

As will be realized, the final product has been the result of the joint effort of many, even if the ultimate responsibility for publication falls on the author. To all, therefore, thanks, many thanks.

FOREWORD

To be a writer of history is a relatively easy task; to be a maker of history is something else, an engagement reserved for a few rare individuals — hence, the importance of books written by members of that elite that Ortega used to refer to as "history makers." Instead of the cold analysis of academic narrative, such works vibrate with pulsations of lived and living history; in their pages one can sense the vitality of entire eras. This book by Justo Carrillo belongs in that notable category. In the case of Cuba, sad to say, that kind of literature, so vital for the historian, seldom sees print. Most of the actors in our political scene have preferred to keep silent or produce some occasional work that adds nothing to the collective vision. Former President Carlos Prío Socarrás, to cite the best-known example, who could have thrown light on so many aspects of Cuba's unrecorded history, especially his relations with Fidel Castro, postponed giving his testimony until it was too late. His silence, which his death made permanent, has left Fidel Castro's distorted version without a valid reply. A historic contribution such as this one by Justo Carrillo is, therefore, worthy of being received with gratitude.

Significantly, the life of Justo Carrillo y Hernández is rooted, both chronologically and by active participation, to the most dynamic and decisive period of contemporary Cuban history: the one that begins with the Revolution of 1933 and culminates with that of 1959. Should one wish to look for an explanation for Justo Carrillo's revolutionary vocation, one could go beyond his own chronological enclave to the deep roots of his Cuban ancestry. His father, Justo Carrillo Morales, was a colonel during the War of Independence, and his uncle, Major General Francisco Carrillo, likewise a veteran of that war, figured prominently in the early political life of the republic. Three other uncles, Andrés, Sixto, and Vicente Carrillo Morales, fought in each of the three independence wars and died fighting for the liberty of Cuba. With such background weighing on him as a spiritual gravitational force, it was no wonder that Justo should enter the Cuban political arena quite early. His youth coincided with the first great political storm to rock the foundations of the young republic: the Machado dictatorship. At sixteen, Justo joined the *Directorio Estudiantil Universitario* (University Students Directorate) and actively participated in the struggle against the Machado regime. From then on, his life, interspersed with risks, prisons, exiles, and successes as well, would be guided by an immutable ideal: the vision of a free, democratic Cuba. It has been this unremitting nationalistic conviction that led him to fight Machado, then Batista, and finally Castro when the "maximum leader" betrayed the cause Justo had supported and sold it to the totalitarian conspiracy. These pages are eloquent proof that the struggle has not ended, nor has Justo Carrillo abandoned it.

This book, however, is far more than the documented account of an honest revolutionary who participated fully in the events of 1933 — whose effects on the history of Cuba are so amply known. The solitude and time for reflection that life in exile provides have given Carrillo the opportunity to read abundantly and meditate seriously on the violent period in which it was his lot to live. As a result of this study, he has felt moved to propose answers to certain questions that arise from the process itself. What were the aspirations of the 1930 Directorio Estudiantil? Why did it dissolve precisely at the most critical moment of the revolutionary struggle? What is the relation between the "*Auténtico*" movement and the so-called "1930 Generation?" What did the Sergeants' Movement, ultimately headed by Batista, mean for Cuba? How should the figure of Eduardo ("Eddy") Chibás be situated in Cuba's national panorama?

In search of answers for these and many other questions, the author, who was personally acquainted with almost every one of the important characters of that period, lets us in on fascinating revelations. The reader learns, for instance, about the main books from which the revolutionary youth of the 1930s absorbed their ideological preoccupations; who were moved by idealism and who by personal motives; what intimate reasons affected the decisions of many a principal actor; the successes as well as the essential frustrations of the revolutionary quest that galvanized his generation. Throughout all this, the author simultaneously combines his personal perspective with the honest intent of being objective, of granting consideration to the reasons even of those with whom he flatly disagrees or evidently despises.

It must be stressed that this book is not, nor does it attempt to be, a history text, measured and didactic. From a strictly formal viewpoint, the author sometimes stretches the note in detailing situations or in remembering marginal episodes. Judged as literature, the style of the book tends toward vibrant narrative rather than cultivated prose. And throughout the text, it becomes obvious that the author can hardly control his own personal political feelings. None of this detracts from, but rather adds to, that peculiar charm that seeps out of the pages written by the "makers of history," for whom evoking battles is to fight them all over again. In this regard, it is always good to remind those, in particular, who are devoted to "historical objectivity" of the irritated rejoinder of the usually calm Leopoldo Ranke when certain critics accused him of partiality. "To be objective," he said, "doesn't mean being a eunuch."

Personally as a reader, but also as a historian of the period he describes, I believe that the best tribute I can offer to Justo Carrillo's work is to encourage him to continue in this endeavor. For exciting as this book is, its closing remarks, in which Carrillo scarcely touches upon the existing connections between the 1933 and 1959 revolutions, whet the appetite for more, for learning how the two revolutions interweave or separate. An in-depth study of the causes that led from the revolutionary process of 1933 to the "socialist deviation" of 1959, taken from the experienced vision of Justo Carrillo, who in both left visible traces of his participation, would be highly illuminating.

For all its recognizable merits, or precisely because of them, this book leaves the reader with a melancholic note of unfinished symphony. While applauding with all my heart, therefore, the effort involved in the publication of this work, praising it for its intrinsic worth, I pray that my recognition will become a spur that will prod the author to continue the journey on which he has so brilliantly begun. We Cubans trudge along without good guides to light the way of our national process. It wouldn't be fair for Justo to leave us at the threshold of the most transcendent chapter of our contemporary history. As the ghost of Virgil transformed by Dante into the immortal guide of lost souls used to say, "Hoc opus, hic labor est," which freely translated means, "Here is the assignment; here is where we must work." And I dare add, here is an author capable of fulfilling the task.

Luis E. Aguilar

Chapter 1

PRELUDE TO REVOLUTION

September 30, 1930 to September 4, 1933

THE THIRTIETH OF SEPTEMBER, 1930

An individual's role in public life can be enlarged by many factors, especially when one begins young and has the opportunity, through circumstances and decisions, to take advantage of options and important events presented by fate. An individual's prominence is, thus, as much a product of his personal capabilities as it is the result of the opportunities destiny places in his path.

This is my story, as I gaze over a half-century and retrace my steps across history. Some of my footprints have become indiscernible, yet others have left permanent marks both upon my soul and, like successive waves, upon the currents of history.

Historic importance dictates the recognition of certain events while obscuring others that, though fruitless, nevertheless held the potential to alter the course of history. That same requirement of history, while drawing the imagination away from failed efforts, nevertheless presents evidence that those vain efforts still resonate with their own historic consequences and should, therefore, not be disregarded.

One such case is the Fourth of September, 1933. I was not quite eighteen, and I had just become a participant in the overthrow of the Machado dictatorship by signing the declaration of takeover (Adam Silva 1947, 484-85; Ferrer 1950, 354-55; Padrón Larrazábal 1975, 173-75; Soto 1977, Vol. III, 35-36) made by the *Agrupación Revolucionaria de Cuba* (Revolutionary Association of Cuba, ARC) — in which the 1930 *Directorio Estudiantil Universitario* (1930 University Student Directorate, DEU) comprised the obvious majority. The ARC had thrown its support to the movement of lower-ranking soldiers of the

1

National Army, the uprising which eventually became known internationally as the Sergeants' Coup.

Because of the historic prominence of that event, from which emerged the sinister figure of Fulgencio Batista and, in the grand finale, the dire figure of Fidel Castro, I consider it the single most important event of my life.

But in order to arrive at a correct evaluation of the full significance of the Fourth of September, 1933, the facts and the circumstances that led to it must be carefully examined. Above all, specifically, it is necessary to examine the reasons the *Directorio Estudiantil Universitario* (DEU), the most popular civilian force then supporting the "Sergeants' Movement," decided to do so based on the sudden intuition of a few individuals, rather than on the basis of discussion, consensus, and formal agreement. Such an evaluation requires, then, a review of the political development of the organization during the three years of struggle against the Machado regime.

To any observer of political affairs, it is intuitively obvious that historic events, in their proper perspective, are determined beforehand by a series of preceding circumstances which shape them. Likewise, the outbreak of a political battle produces, in the revolutionary himself, the hardening of character, the development of a personality — formed in battle — with the characteristics of leadership, and the ultimate attainment of a true revolutionary conscience.

Over that period of three years, the leaders of the student organization developed a maturity which transformed them into an elite group with an ideological and political definition totally distinct from that which they had espoused when they had originally entered the struggle. Through literature and, eventually, through the doctrinal preparation and guidance acquired through discussion and debate, the leadership honed the contours of their individual and collective political consciences. Through contact with all strata of society, including the poorest, and especially when we found ourselves involved in the clandestine revolutionary world, both in travels and in exile, we gained a greater understanding of social problems. Finally, through reciprocal influences that the process and the individual exchange over the course of years, we inevitably endured circumstances that forced the evolution of attitudes distinct from those which originally would have been considered the logical result of our political development.

In order to prove this assertion, it is necessary to analyze the five different positions adopted by the DEU, each a distinct political attitude, each progressively further from the original, each a response to the changing political events and conditions as they occurred from 1930 to 1933.

General Gerardo Machado Morales was inaugurated president of Cuba on May 20, 1925, after winning the previous November's election with the slogan, "Water, Roads, and Schools." The people, anxious to overcome twenty-three years of frustration in the toils of the Republic, had elected him nearly unanimously. They expected a change from the customarily corrupt activities and conduct of the government and its elected officials, a reform that would encourage a return of confidence in the country's future.

Instead, within four months of the inauguration, the people were dismayed to realize that political crime had not been eliminated. The assassination of dissenting journalist Armando André Alvarado, chief editor of the daily newspaper *El Día*, followed soon after by those of labor leader Enrique Varona and syndical-anarchist José Cuxart Falgons, clearly demonstrated that Cuba was in the grips of a cruel, despotic government. Shortly thereafter, a sinister political trend dubbed by Cuban political commentators "policy of cooperation," or *cooperativismo*, emerged. The top leadership of the *Partido Conservador Nacional* (National Conservative Party), headed by Senator Wifredo Fernández Vega and Congressmen Santiago C. Rey González and Manuel Rivero de la Gándara, literally abstained from opposition and adopted instead a policy of unconditional cooperation with the Machado regime. That policy enabled Congress to pass legislation designed to grant Machado powers beyond the limits of his constitutional mandate.

Without *cooperativismo*, which silenced all opposition in Congress, Machado's plans to remain in power could not have been carried out. The first step in fulfilling his ambitions was the Law of December 16, 1925, which proscribed both the (constitutionally mandated) reorganization of the existing political parties and the creation of new ones.

Then, on March 28, 1927, in a session that lasted nearly twenty-four hours, a sweeping reform bill was presented to the House of Representatives. The enactment of this bill would extend Machado's term in office and legalize consecutive presidential reelection, thus guaranteeing the president would serve ten years in office instead of the original four. Government legislators achieved the necessary tampering with the Constitution with the full cooperation of the "opposition." Their own terms in office, of course, were also extended in the process. The legislative body both approved and enacted the constitutional changes that same day.

In the November 1, 1928 elections, Machado, as the sole candidate for *all* the existing parties — Liberal, Conservative, and Popular — was, naturally, reelected. His new six-year presidential term began on May 20, 1929. The president would, therefore, remain in power until May 20, 1935 — "Not one minute more, nor one minute less," as he himself put it.

All the regular legal channels for opposition had been effectively blocked. The democratic process was paralyzed. Cuba was forced to submit to the will and caprices of the President of the Republic.

Immediately, demonstrations exploded at the University of Havana. The *Asociación Unión Nacionalista* (National Union Association, AUN), whose members were generally respected opposition politicians, also voiced their protest and condemnation. All protests, of course, were dealt with harshly. Dissenting students were summarily expelled from the university, and the AUN leaders were subjected to harassment and persecution. Most found no choice but exile. The seeds of student rebellion, however, had been planted.

That was Cuba's political climate when I entered the University in 1929. Anti-government activities had resumed during that academic year, and students had begun to organize in small, scattered cells. At that time, however, there was little or no connection among those cells, and little if any conspiratorial activity. Nevertheless, the following year, as the school term in October drew near and the students began gathering after the summer recess, those little cells of protesters began to join together and organize. That was the birth of the *Directorio Estudiantil Universitario* (DEU). The official consolidation of the various cells took place on September 28, 1930, at a private school on San Rafael Street, close to Trillo Park in Havana. In that formative meeting, we also decided to stage a demonstration two days later, on the thirtieth. We planned a rally at the Patio de los Laureles, a plaza on the university campus, after which we would march to Enrique José Varona's residence on Eighth Street in the Vedado district. Varona was an elderly philosopher, writer, and highly respected public figure whose dislike for Machado was discreet but obvious. We planned to retrace the route followed by the students who, on March 30, 1927, had protested Machado's term extension. We also discussed future activities and appointed an executive committee. Upon me fell the honor of being named to that committee, just days before my eighteenth birthday.

On September 30, the scene changed radically. The previous night police detachments had cordoned off the campus. A company of soldiers took over Quinta de los Molinos, an academic building on campus, and military posts in the city and at Camp Columbia were reinforced. Despite all the display of force, the involved students still managed to filter onto the university campus. In view of the circumstances, though, plans obviously had to change. We decided to gather instead at the Eloy Alfaro Park on Infanta Street and from there march to the Presidential Palace; this would be a more effective itinerary than the planned march to Varona's residence, since it would identify President Machado as the direct object of our public rejection.

When the group started moving from the plaza, we were about eighty or a hundred in number. The police wasted no time in harrying the marchers, who began splintering into smaller groups. One of our number, Rafael Trejo González, a fearless individual who always seemed to lead the way, found himself suddenly engaged in a wrestling match with a policeman. Another student, Antonio Díaz Baldoquín, who had been expelled in 1927, ran to aid Trejo. For a few seconds, the three were locked together in combat. Then, the policeman pulled out his gun and fired. Trejo collapsed on the pavement, fatally wounded. Rafael Trejo, thereby, became the first student martyr in an event that set off a new historic era.

On that same date, September 30, 1930, an anonymous document appeared, signed only, "*Patio de los Laureles, septiembre de 1930.*" The document had been penned not by the DEU as a group, but by one of the original members of the Directorio, Raúl Roa. Until then, the Directorio and its members were completely unknown. Only eight days later, their names would appear, for the first time, on the public invitation to Trejo's funeral.[1]

The members of the infant organization expounded in that first, unsigned declaration a series of general considerations which referred to the "Machadocracy that exploits us and decimates the people through financial blows, taxation and *perdigonazos* (wasteful spending, or bird-shot)" and stated that they were "prepared to give new meaning to the word sacrifice," adding that "we are, from this moment on and forever, a pure force that will not be determined by foreign influences, nor colored with partisan hues." The students demanded "the termination of the present regime and the immediate resignation of the President of the Republic." This, they affirmed, was not just the sentiment of a minority, but the "unanimous cry of the whole country, which is ready to achieve this end by whatever means may be necessary and at the cost of whatever sacrifices, including that of life itself."

THE MILITARY PAY HOMAGE TO MACHADO

The Spanish Academy of Language does not differentiate between the words *acontecimiento* and *suceso* (event, occurrence, incident). We as users of the language pretend to do so, however, attributing to the former the concept of certain historical consequence, a high degree of positive or negative endurance, as deeds and perhaps as roots of essential changes in a socio-political process.

Thus, I count as an "*acontecimiento*" the homage that the rank-and-file soldiers from Camp Columbia rendered to President Machado, who by then was executing the duties of his office unconstitutionally, his original term having been due to expire on May 20, 1929. This particular homage was rendered just eight days after the burial of the first student martyr of the struggle, Rafael Trejo.

At the time, the Directorio was deeply engrossed in recruiting new activists and, above all, in the selection of new members. Of the eighteen that had signed the invitation to Trejo's funeral, seven had disappeared as if by magic.[2] We also worked feverishly to organize delegations in each province capital. There was, to put it succinctly, a climate of national anguish because of the crisis provoked by the student movement and Trejo's death, and public opinion openly condemned the conduct of the Chief of State. Against this somber backdrop, the rank and file of the army, in absolute contradiction to popular sentiments, displayed their loyalty to President Machado.

This display occurred on October 10, a national holiday, and just ten days after Trejo's death. It was organized by a group of sergeants led by Sergeant Pablo Rodríguez Silverio, chairman of the camp's enlisted men's club. The organizational committee included Sergeants Gonzalo García Pedrosa, Otilio Rojas, Ladislao Suárez, Pedro Rojas, and Aquilino Guerra. The event was a declaration of unconditional support for Machado, as author Ricardo Adam Silva stated in two separate books. He pointed out that no officer was included in the organization of this banquet, an obvious breach of the most elemental principles of respect for authority.

The event itself was a gala feast, which began in the traditional manner with the national anthem played in salute to the arriving president. Each of the enlisted men and noncommissioned officers present received a leather wallet with one peso inside and an inscription that said, "Compliments of General Gerardo Machado y Morales. 10 October 1930." According to *Diario de la Marina* the next day, the members of the cabinet and the leaders of the political parties were also among the guests.[3] This obviously contradicts Adam Silva's assertions that no officers were included.

In his keynote speech, Sergeant Aurelio Torrente Escudero said,

> Mr. President, this act in your honor has been organized and prepared by soldiers of the army. This fact is of tremendous importance. This is the first time that a tribute such as this is offered by the military rank and file to a President of the Republic. It is inspired by two capital truths: admiration and gratitude. This alone is enough for us to erect a monument to the President in our hearts.

The rest of the speech continued in the same vein, full of flatteries and adulation, as reported in the newspapers that day and the next. Sergeant Torrente went on, at one point, to say,

> As for ourselves, the sergeants, I can state that it is an absolute truth, that we have the option to gain promotion to officer rank, that we can attend school, because the Army takes care of capable men.

He closed by saying,

> Finally, honorable President of the Republic, a toast to your health; to the health of your generous and beloved family; a toast to the country, that shall always be protected; and if you should ever have any doubts, return to this camp, where [former president] Estrada Palma lived, here where a group of men commanded by Colonel Castillo and General Herrera would know how to defend you, for in so doing we would be defending our free country.

Of course, Machado, in answering Sergeant Torrente Escudero's speech, addressed almost exclusively the factional spirit of the occasion. As if to underline a reciprocal solidarity with the lower ranks of the army, he prided himself on having promoted more sergeants to officer status than any of his predecessors. An extended standing ovation greeted his words and continued long after he had left the hall.

Among those cheering the president were a few whose names would later gain various degrees of public notoriety, including Fulgencio Batista, High Command Sixth Military District (Camp Columbia);[4] First Sergeant José Eleuterio Pedraza, First Company Second Infantry Battalion; Sergeant Ignacio Galíndez, Tactical Corps; and Sergeant Quartermaster-General Manuel López Migoya, Third Company Second Battalion.[5]

But this historic event, even though reported in the newspapers, was hardly noticed by the Directorio Estudiantil Universitario, who had already begun to lead the battle against Machado's government. I never heard much about the event at the time, nor did I hear, either within nor outside of the Directorio, any comment at all about the significance of the banquet at Camp Columbia. To be exact, however, there was an occasional satirical remark referring to the sergeants' "little wallets" with the peso, and so forth. But the members of the DEU did not know anything about the event beyond the occasional comments, inasmuch as that would imply full knowledge; we did not examine political content or impact, analyze possible consequences, acquire a list of participants, collect their biographical data, or in any other way evaluate the event. Only when in the course of subsequent events some of us landed in prison at the Modelo Penitentiary on the Isle of Pines, and there came in contact with military men who had been at the banquet and had later been caught conspiring against the regime, did we have reason to ponder the significance of the homage rendered to Machado at Camp Columbia.

THE *DIRECTORIO* DEVELOPS POLITICAL CONSCIOUSNESS

Some 60 days after its first public pronouncements against the government, the Directorio, with the dawning realization that it could become an influential force against the Machado regime, produced a list of demands. Though still somewhat vague, this manifesto insisted upon fundamental changes that represented a distinct departure from the Directorio's original position as expressed on September 30.

This second major document was a response to negotiations with official Machado representatives: Army Major Alberto Barreras, a veteran of the Wars of Independence, and Dr. Lucas Lamadrid. In it, the DEU declared the following:

> It should be made known that if there are similarities between our program and those of other citizen groups also under persecution, those likenesses indicate no less than that in Cuba there already exists a common front of public opinion that clamors for the recovery of fundamental rights and fights for sacred principles, and that the stubbornness of the administration and the suppression of liberties that were won on the battlefields of the Revolution [War of Independence] affect equally all sectors of the national conglomerate, which unanimously clamors for not just a mere clever change of subordinates but for a TOTAL AND DEFINITIVE CHANGE OF REGIME (González Peraza 1933, 267-69).

From the simple renunciation of Machado, demanded in the original statement on September 30, to this other, adopted a few weeks later, the difference is intuitively profound, though still lacking in political or ideological precision. From the appeal for Machado's resignation, stated simply as his removal from the executive office, to the rallying cry of "total and definitive change of regime," there is an obvious and intrinsic transformation.

True, the Directorio did not spell out at the time whether and how the "total and definitive change of regime" might include or affect the legislative and the judicial branches of government. However, where the DEU had originally alluded only to the individual who *was* the president of the Republic, it now seemed to imply a purge of both the legislative and judicial powers as well as additional and fundamental innovations that might be defined in or derived from the broad concept of "total and definitive change of regime."

Before analyzing the significance of the declaration itself, four key words must be studied within the context of this sweeping phrase, "total and definitive change of regime." To begin with, the word "total" indicates both depth and reach and has the peculiarity, when inserted in this phrase pregnant with content, of indicating both substitution and replacement. The term "definitive," in turn, adds a tone of finality and termination to the idea. Termination of what? Nothing less than all that existed: the institutions, contaminated from their beginnings, and their representatives. The third concept, that embodied in the word "regime," is understood as being the whole, not just the classic powers in balance within the State. To apply the fourth concept, "change," to the regime, a change that would be "total and definitive," implied changing absolutely everything: the Constitution of 1928 (already abrogated legally and popularly), the form of government, its means, methods, and procedures. What it meant was that, in essence, the structure of the government, the entire "establishment" required changing — the confluence of laws, ordinances, regulations, statutes — all that had been established. In terms of people, a "mere clever change of subordinates" would not serve — it required nothing less than a true change of regime, and it must be total and definitive.

Immediately before that demand appears the phrase "public opinion . . . clamors for the recovery of fundamental rights." In that phrase rests the totality of the revolutionary interpretation — to recover, to regain that which already belonged to the people; to claim, to demand, that to which one already had the right — and, by extension, it included the concepts of liberation, rescue, redemption, vindication. This undoubtedly represented the launching of a radical call to arms, on the level of a revolutionary populist movement. Sadly, conditions within the Directorio, as we shall see, would not permit them to go any further. They would not be able to state openly and directly that what they pursued was the complete overthrow of the existing order and outright replacement of all the people who ran the "establishment."

My personal testimony, then, is of utmost importance for its intrinsic historic value.

The Directorio, at the chronological moment of this declaration, was ready to assume leadership of the anti-Machado struggle. It already had a revolutionary program that would, no doubt, rapidly gain popular support, but we had to proceed cautiously. We had to avoid being accused before the student body of overstepping our boundaries by carrying the battle out of the academic arena and into the political arena. One false step would cost us the confidence of the student body, providing a significant moral victory for Machado and his "normalcy policy." The DEU had, therefore, issued a minor document on October 23, listing exclusively university-related demands. Of course, this was strictly a diversion preceding the frontal assault which would follow in the form of the November 18 declaration (González Peraza 1933, 264-69; Padrón Larrazábal 1975, 106-9).

The October 23 demands included, among other things, an investigation to determine responsibilities for the events of September 30; the expulsion of Professor Octavio Averhoff and his resignation as Secretary of Public Education and Fine Arts; the expulsion of Dr. Ricardo Martínez Prieto as university rector; the demilitarization of all the schools (which Machado had established); the right among student groups to assemble; student representation in the governing of the University; amnesty for students expelled from the University in 1927 for protesting against Machado's term extension; and finally, autonomy for the University. This list of demands apparently limited to the student environment was, in reality, a pause before the tremendous leap forward on November 18.

There were within the Directorio's executive committee three outstanding leaders, Carlos Prío Socarrás, Rubén León García, and Manuel Antonio (Tony) Varona Loredo. They were a little above the average age of the rest, and Carlos Prío, the eldest, naturally had the greatest influence. They all had prior political experience, specifically as members of *Juventud Universitaria Nacionalista* (Nationalist University Students). This group was an offshoot of the *Asociación Unión Nacionalista* (AUN), whose most notable members were Colonels Carlos Mendieta, Roberto Méndez Peñate, and Cosme de la Torriente, all nationally known public figures. Because of their previous excursions into politics, Prío, León, and Varona had been the target of some criticism from both within and outside the Directorio, particularly Prío.[6] It is possible that the three young men, at that time, did not yet perceive the revolutionary function for which the DEU was destined. For one reason or another, they instead adopted an extremely *apolitical* position quite at odds with the spirit of the November 18 declaration.

It was at this juncture that there began to emerge within the committee one Juan Antonio Rubio Padilla, whose following included Rafael Escalona, Marcio Manduley, Raúl Ruiz, Augusto Valdés Miranda, and myself, joined shortly thereafter by Roberto Lago Pereda. This subgroup advanced a radical position that, though still lacking ideological precision, openly advocated two elements that were only suggested by the November declaration: total renovation of the system and intransigent rejection of any compromise. This select group had drawn up the declaration and submitted it for review and revision to journalist Sergio Carbó. Our sheer audacity gained us the victory of approval for this document which had been presented, fully prepared, to the entire Directorio. The DEU's true historic baptism by fire occurred almost immediately as a result of this call to arms.

The response was overwhelming. The various university faculties, as well as those of secondary, vocational, and professional schools; civic organizations, nonpartisan public figures, and feminist associations; labor unions and economic groups; columnists in the daily papers; even social clubs and their members; all hastened to voice their support for the students' manifesto. At the same time, from the international intellectual community came messages of support: from student federations all over Latin America; from the Venezuelan intellectuals, and from the University Federation in Madrid, Spain; from a conference of eight hundred Spanish-speaking professors, writers, and students meeting at the Hispanic American Historical Association in Boston in December 1930; and finally, from a public manifesto of support entitled *"Mensaje de los Intelectuales Españoles"* ("Message from the Spanish Intellectuals"), which included thoughts from Miguel de Unamuno, José Ortega Gasset, Luis Jiménez de Asúa, Luis de Zulueta, Gregorio Marañón, José Martínez Ruiz (Azorín), Ramón del Valle Inclán, Gustavo Pitaluga, Roberto Hoyos Santos, and several dozen more (González Peraza 1933, 274-75).

The call to arms penetrated deeply and became the ideal and battle cry of the Cuban public. We felt we had the support of Spain and Latin America. Peaceful solutions that did not represent a total and definitive change of regime were summarily rejected. Our revolutionary line was drawn. The historic charisma of the DEU was emerging to take command.

A few weeks later, on February 3, 1931, the Directorio published its third major document to elaborate on some of the integral changes that made up the whole of the fundamental transformations it was proposing. In support of an effort made by the *Directorio Radical de Abogados* (Radical Lawyers Directorate), the DEU — comprised at that moment only of those who had not been captured in a meeting raided by the police one month earlier — launched fourteen demands, five of which dealt with political and juridical reforms; five of a strictly academic and educational character, including, of course, university autonomy; and four devoted to defining the ideological and political orientation of the movement. We shall examine them and compare them with demands that were realized some thirty months later, immediately after the takeover on September 4, 1933.

The first of those demands was civil, political, and economic equality for both men and women. This was followed by the workers' right to strike; next was rights of laborers to present demands and to organize unions. The next was an unusual demand for the era — it called for a maximum workday, minimum salary, free transportation for the unemployed, suspension of undesirable immigration, unemployment compensation, accident insurance, and a workers' retirement plan. These seven demands, embodying the overall concepts, truly signified a total and definitive change of regime in terms of social and economic practices. The complete list of demands, including women's suffrage, was eventually attained through the implementation of the Directorio's program by the first Grau administration, which the DEU carried to power.

Now in the forefront, the Directorio only fought in a revolutionary manner. Its manifestos would be stinging and painful expressions in the face of the deaths of its members: Félix Ernesto Alpízar (December 21, 1931), Angel Pío Alvarez (January 4, 1933), and Carlos Manuel Fuertes Blandino (April 7, 1933).

The next ideologico-political pronouncement would be against the North American mediation, in June 1933. In order to understand this fourth major pronouncement fully, it is necessary to review the events that led to the publication of the document.

ANTI-MACHADO ACTIVITIES OF THE POLITICIANS

We have seen the formation of the DEU's principles and observed the following it had gained among the general population. But we in the Directorio, because of our own confrontation in the struggle, our natural student environment, and, perhaps, our conviction that we must organize the disorder, did not realize, could not imagine that we might need to construct a secret organization incorporating both action and support groups comprised of our followers to develop revolutionary militancy and civil collaboration.

We did not know at the time that in every struggle there were people from all walks of life and all ideologies, who, because of their circumstances, sympathize and provide resources — sometimes financial aid, sometimes refuge, and at times intelligence information — and that the influence of these supporters can at times be more decisive than violent actions. Neither did we know that there are other revolutionary collaborators whose contribution to the process cannot be measured solely in terms of time dedicated to the cause. Stated bluntly, we did not know how to organize militants and sympathizers; therefore, we failed to take advantage of them.

At the same time, the traditional political forces opposing Machado also underestimated our political revolutionary power. These *caudillos* fell roughly into three primary groups: the *Asociación Unión Nacionalista* (AUN), whose chief leader was Colonel Carlos Mendieta; the *Partido Conservador* (Conservative Party), under the leadership of former President General Mario G. Menocal; and followers of Dr. Miguel Mariano Gómez (son of late President General José M. Gómez), who had been a very popular and able mayor of Havana. Even though these *caudillo* groups underestimated us, they also identified within our movement basic inconsistencies among various factions, mostly in our aspirations for a Cuban future totally distinct from its past identity.

When it became obvious that Machado could not produce a peaceful solution to the national crisis, these three political groups began to plan an armed insurrection to overthrow the government.

Each of these groups ultimately depended in some form or another on General Menocal for leadership. He was thought to have personal influence within the armed forces, a belief that would prove unfounded in the course of the insurrection. Dr. Miguel Mariano Gómez, because of his admitted popularity in the city of Havana, was placed in charge of operations there so that, at the proper moment, he could lead the action in the capital. As for Mendieta, who at the time basked in an aura of apparent personal honesty and patriotism, he and Menocal would lead the conspiratorial activities as well as the insurrection itself. Little was expected of the Directorio because it was supposed to operate within Havana; furthermore, we were not provided arms or any other kind of resources.

August 1931 produced the catastrophic insurrectional attempt. Menocal and Mendieta had tried to enlist the assistance of the Cuban navy and the complicity of the commander-in-chief of the First Military District and his troops. Unfortunately, the gunboat *Baire*, which was supposed to transport the two commanders to Oriente Province, failed to make the rendezvous, and the whole operation fell apart. Nevertheless, the conspirators still managed to launch a minuscule operation in

Pinar del Río at the other end of the island. They camped with their staff in a place called Río Verde, where they and their staffs were quickly surrounded by a government patrol and taken prisoner. In Havana, meanwhile, Miguel Mariano Gómez found himself unable to mount any kind of action either. He decided to go underground.

A few days later, however, on August 17, an armed expedition commanded by Lieutenant Emilio Laurent landed in the port city of Gibara in Oriente province and took the city with little resistance. Laurent then commandeered a train and headed for the city of Holguín, some 25 miles to the south. Of course, the expedition fell apart when the train derailed and Laurent's detachment came under attack by the government's combined land, sea, and air forces. The expeditionary group was soon rounded up and taken prisoner. The few conspirators who managed to escape had been travelling separately. Among those lucky few was a man who would have been considered a key prisoner — Sergio Carbó, chief editor of *La Semana*, and a key figure in the eventual organization of the Sergeants' Coup.

During this insurrection, the Directorio was unable to mount a single revolutionary action, not only because we had been sidelined by express orders from Menocal and Mendieta but also because we had absolutely no resources with which to function.

The complete failure of the political *caudillos'* military attempt ended the apparent domination they had maintained in the revolutionary process. With the mystical power of the *caudillos* broken, the doors of history opened to the younger generations.

The events of August 1931 had actually been a frustrated attempt to turn back the clock of history. During that period, only two events besides the attempt at Gibara stand out for their heroic qualities. The first was the action that unfolded at Loma del Tor in Pinar del Río, under the leadership of the AUN General Francisco Peraza. General Peraza launched an extraordinary attempt at military coup, which cost him and a group of his subordinates their lives. Among those who fell were the former officer Miguel de Miguel and one of the better men in the student group, former athlete Eusebio "Chacho" Hidalgo. The other outstanding act of heroism was committed by Arturo del Pino, a captain from the War of Independence. Del Pino was discovered by the police while guarding a cache of arms in a Havana suburb. Completely surrounded and alone, he still fought back until he ran out of ammunition. When he could no longer defend the cache, he committed suicide rather than allow himself to be captured.

Enrique Fernández, an active participant close to the Directorio and a prominent figure in the subsequent revolutionary process, later summarized and appraised the events of the Río Verde disaster in a treatise entitled *La razón del 4 de septiembre* (*The Reason of the Fourth of September*):

> There, in the swamps of that Pinar del Río inlet, the old legend evaporated. When Menocal and Mendieta ascended the pilot ladder of the navy gunboat as prisoners, they carried with them, in abject defeat, the prestige and dominance of a whole generation. What the popular hatred for Machado had seen in Menocal and Mendieta was only reprieve, not redemption. The classic opposition and restorationist camp was defeated. When in the city of Santa Clara the dictator celebrated his ephemeral triumph, he didn't realize that on that same day the Cuban Revolution had begun: a new era of reform represented by the Directorio (Fernández 1950, 20-21).

POLITICAL FORMATION BEHIND BARS

The derailment of the *caudillos'* insurrectional movement spawned two occurrences that would radically alter the course of the revolution. The first was the appearance of the ABC, under the direction of such distinguished professionals as Doctors Joaquín Martínez Sáenz, Carlos Saladrigas, Ramón Hermida, Alfredo Botet, Juan Andrés Lliteras, Jorge Mañach, and Francisco Ichaso, to name a few. These men and other professional agents directed the task of reuniting nontraditional opposition forces within the Cuban political arena who wanted to participate in the fight against Machado. The second occurrence was linked to this new organization. The Directorio, whose members were suffering increasing oppression, had begun to change its battle tactics, shifting from methods of simple protest, agitation through the press and in the street, public outcry and the method popularly known as student *tángana* (free-for-all), to overt actions, including dynamite terrorism and supporting and assisting in political assassinations.

The leaders of the ABC lacked the prestige of having been involved in the struggle, since not one of the founders had participated in the effort as had both the students expelled from the University of Havana in 1927 and the political opposition headed by the *Asociación*

Unión Nacionalista. The organizers, therefore, considered it necessary to seek the DEU's support to attract all those elements and forces that supported the Directorio's demands for a total and definitive change of regime. These forces had never been properly organized because of persecutions, exiles, and the murders of those who had been identified as revolutionaries by the government's various repressive bodies. It ended up being highly advantageous, though, to have unknown figures initiate, secretly and anonymously, the recruitment of those who wanted to participate in the battle.

In response to the ABC leaders' interest, the Directorio designated two representatives, supposedly completely loyal to the DEU, to become members of the *Célula Directriz* (Directing Cell) of the new organization, and who thus became two of the seven supreme directors of that organization. These two delegates were Juan Pedro Bombino and Orestes Figueredo.

The ABC produced a totally revolutionary manifesto-program, containing precise objectives that reflected the radical position toward political groups that the Directorio had developed. Thus, the ABC began to outline a logical alliance of the truly reformist forces. The ABC hoped, as well, to attract the independents whose ideals had been repeatedly frustrated, beginning with the deceptive outcome of the War of Independence as executed through the Treaty of Paris and the Platt Amendment, and as continued by the administrations that had followed in the Republic since 1902.

In its return to the battle, the Directorio suffered the greatest adversities, because its leaders were known while those of the ABC succeeded in remaining incognito. Many of its members were imprisoned and submitted to the infamous *Causa 13*, which covered military treason. Others were assassinated by police, and a few were forced into exile. Of course, a small and very select nucleus of acting members, unknown to the police, continued to function completely shrouded in anonymity.

In addition to the original martyr Rafael Trejo, out of the total of 36 members that eventually comprised the organization, three other members were assassinated. The first case was the treacherous death, on December 21, 1931, of Félix Ernesto Alpízar, who disappeared after extensive police persecution and imprisonment. His body was discovered months later, buried in the slopes of the hill on which stands Atarés Castle, the domain of dreaded Captain Manuel Crespo Moreno, the most sinister torturer of Machado's repressive apparatus.

Two years later, Angel Pío Alvarez himself, born in Spain and one of the most valiant and intrepid figures of that period, was arrested at the home of Doctor Gustavo Cuervo Rubio, a prestigious physician and member of the political opposition. Although Alvarez identified himself as Doctor Hernández, he was later properly identified and subsequently executed.

And finally, the third member of that era, Carlos Fuertes Blandino, was likewise assassinated after informant José Soler, the only traitorous member of the Directorio, tipped off the police concerning his whereabouts.

Meanwhile, seventeen members of the actual Directorio were in prison. They developed a particular ideological understanding during their incarceration, through reading, culturization, and living together with and debating leaders of the extreme left. Their position, strictly democratic and anticommunist, was fed by works available in the prisons, such as *Crónicas de la guerra* (*War Chronicles*) by General José Miró Argenter, a Catalonian who joined the Cuban Liberation Army and became chief of staff for legendary Lieutenant General Antonio Maceo. Naturally, everything that had been published by or about José Martí, the most revered hero of Cuban independence, was avidly read and discussed. Another favorite book was *Azúcar y población en las Antillas* (*Sugar and Population in the West Indies*) by Ramiro Guerra, a study of political and economic developments in the Caribbean under the shadow of American interests. There were also books on agrarian reform in Europe after World War I. Of course, no student failed to read *El hombre mediocre* (*The Mediocre Man*), a very popular essay by Argentine leftist philosopher José Ingenieros. Four texts we considered basic, three of which were written by American authors: *Our Cuban Colony* by Leland H. Jenks; *Our Bankers in Bolivia* by Margaret Alexander Marsh; *Yankees in Santo Domingo* by Melvin Knight; and *La agonía antillana* (*The West Indian Agony*), by Luis Araquistain, a Spanish Republican. These works constituted the politico-ideological anchor of the DEU. We acquired a sense of ideological balance and direction, however, through reading Rumanian author Panait Istrati's *Russia in the Nude*, a voluminous essay containing severe criticisms of the Soviet system. Istrati's arguments helped us to shape our own orientation and fundamental politics. These general principles and ideas included such concepts as a deep sense of Cuban identity and patriotism (*Cubanía*), elimination of North

American hegemony in Cuba, ample assurance of civil rights, elevation of living standards for workers and peasants, guaranteed function of the democratic electoral system, and social justice. These ideals were underlined by a solid anticommunist stance, which, joined with a strong sense of *Cubanía*, had generated the history of the Independence. Our concepts rejected the classist interpretation that the Communist Party falsely directed toward us, both because of the negative conclusions we drew from *Russia in the Nude*, and because of the continued attacks that the *Ala Izquierda Estudiantil* (Student Left Wing), a communist faction, directed at the DEU throughout its heroic battle against the Machado regime.

I must pause briefly at this point for a necessary digression. I feel I should make it very clear that I do not propose to write a historic study of the entire struggle against the Machado dictatorship. That would be a titanic undertaking demanding years of arduous work and research, although several separate works have been published. Neither has it been my intention to produce what might have turned out to be, perhaps, a very interesting project: the group biography of the 1930 Directorio Estudiantil Universitario.

This book is no more than a personal testimony meant as a memoir covering the three most intensely lived years of my life. That is why I will record here only those historic facts that in my judgment will contribute to an understanding of what took place in Cuba in 1933 and, more specifically, an understanding of the DEU's still unexplained backing of the "Sergeants' Coup" of September 4, 1933.

FRATERNIZING WITH ANTI-MACHADO MILITARY PRISONERS

Now, I digress. In previous pages, I described the banquet in honor of President Machado given by the rank and file of Camp Columbia in October 1930. The leaders of that group of military men were the same that, interestingly enough, would turn up again in September 1933. As a whole, that sector of the Cuban military could be considered definitely pro-Machado. In order to secure their most unflagging loyalty, the president had exalted them precisely for becoming partisan and politicized. The assumption of their loyalty, however, was not completely watertight. The saying that "a country's armed forces are still part of its people" remained true in Cuba, even then. Even if they could have been kept in strictest isolation, confined to their barracks most of the time and with virtually no leave days, total insulation from the public environment was still impossible. Soldiers and their officers are still compatriots of the civilians; they read the same newspapers and magazines, and their families come from the same popular stock. There still exists, even in isolation, an intellectual permeability which is despised by ironclad discipline; and in totalitarian systems, the percolation of ideas results in bloodbaths and terror against those who dare to conspire.

So, even in Machado's Cuba, the supposedly impermeable solidarity of the soldiers had sprung a leak. By the middle of 1932, a group arrived at the Modelo Penitentiary on the Isle of Pines, consisting of some thirty sergeants, corporals, and privates from the army relieved of duty and imprisoned for conspiring to rebel. Never before during that struggle had there been so many members of the armed forces behind bars. Besides the enlisted men and non-commissioned officers, a total of six officers were also incarcerated: Colonel Julio Aguado and Lieutenants Emilio Laurent, Feliciano Maderne, Manuel Villada, Pedro Luis Díaz, and Edmundo Nin. This is strictly incidental, but I do not want to imply that there were more rank-and-file soldiers than officers opposed to Machado. There were just fewer officers in prison. There was also another difference; while we lived together with the soldiers and sergeants within the prison, such was not the case with the officers. They were isolated from the other political prisoners. Only toward the end were the leaders of the unsuccessful Gibara expedition, Lieutenants Laurent and Maderne, allowed to live among the rest of us.

Strings of convicts arrived on the Isle of Pines aboard the gunboat *24 de Febrero* on May 25 and July 21, 1931. The soldiers, all classified "ex-military," included Adolfo Antonio López Tomey, José María Martínez Martínez, Timoteo Sinforiano López Paz, Arcadio Nicolás Pérez Ruiz, José Morales Velázquez, Juan Rodríguez Ortega, Francisco Melitón Alemany Rivero, Daniel Blas Barreras, Florentino Julio Bienvenido Ortega, Sandalio Bombino Aguila, Manuel del Valle Marrero, Juan J. Fernández, Ignacio Hernández Flores, Eduardo Márquez Rizo, Santiago Valle Rodríguez, José A. Rodríguez Fierro, Antonio Armenteros Linares, Narciso Romero Borrego, Francisco Gómez García, Tomás Ortiz Barboza, Eladio Llano Morejón, Donato Vázquez Vázquez, and Emilio Jacobo Manso. There were also two sailors, Juan Ramírez and Miguel Angel Cruz Rodríguez, and one railroad security guard, Ramón Casales Rizo. Also in the group were several sergeants and corporals, namely, Cecilio Nápoles Hidalgo,

Rutilio Ramos, Carlos Mesa, Antonio Santana Macías, José Zambrana Alvarez, and Antonio M. Tabares. Except for the two sailors and the guard, all these men belonged to units from Camp Columbia and the Cabaña Fortress, that is, the Sixth and Seventh Military Districts, both within the Havana area.

When these military convicts arrived at the Isle of Pines penitentiary, they joined or were soon joined by seventeen members of the 1930 Directorio there. Also among us were ten members of the 1927 *Directorio Universitario contra la Prórroga de Poderes* (University Directorate against the Extension of Powers). Among the 1927 Directorio members, there were two permanent delegates who remained in the 1930 DEU — Eddy Chibás and Reinaldo Jordán. Furthermore, there were eight members of the Directorio of the Institute of Havana and no less than thirty other fighters who were dedicated followers of the 1930 DEU. Among them, three eventually became members of the Executive Commission, or Pentarchy: Ramón Grau San Martín, Guillermo Portela, and José Miguel Irisarri.

All together, students, professors, sergeants, corporals, and soldiers comprised a group of about a hundred people. This group established a certain sense of community that prison generates: companionship, fraternity, camaraderie . . . .

But why the understanding among these one hundred and not between them and "the rest?" Among the flow of political prisoners being sequestered, transferred, and released during that period, those that passed through the Modelo Penitentiary numbered some 538 men. One reason for our rapport, in my judgment, is that we were, despite intellectual and social differences, still very close in age. We were also all men of action, with vast reservoirs of spiritual energy. Furthermore, within the military there soon developed a sense of cohesion similar to what already existed within the Directorio and among our followers. These factors all contributed to mutual respect and rapport.

It can also be said that almost every one of the Directorio men was held in high regard by the other prisoners. Most were serious yet jovial individuals, open to communication. They were studious but always willing to share their knowledge and their education with those soldiers of a generally lower intellectual level. The young university fellows were blessed with a certain openness and sincerity that sharply contrasted with the bearing of certain other political prisoners, who read romantic novels while wearing silk pajamas and smelling of

Guerlain cologne. It was not strange, therefore, that the Directorio should enjoy within the prison walls the same recognition it had already won in the streets (Embade 1934; Torriente Brau 1969).

That camaraderie transcended all social boundaries and would leave its mark in upcoming developments. Looking back into that empathetic interrelation, I can detect today an undercurrent of subtle influences, an array of hidden psychological forces of which nobody was then aware. That unspoken understanding in which the student came out about a notch above the soldier, the man of letters above the unlettered one, the civilian above the military, unconsciously caused the student leaders to look upon those sergeants, corporals, and soldiers with a sort of paternalistic feeling. In the same fashion that the therapist listens while his patient relates the memories of his early life, the perspective of history gives me the vision to assert that there, in the penitentiary on the Isle of Pines, an embryonic subconscious principle developed that would later lead us to support the coup that "other" sergeants, corporals, and soldiers would stage on September 4, 1933.

As it happened, those "other" sergeants, corporals, and enlisted men, quite distinct from those who lived among us in the prison, organized a movement to defend their positions through the appearance of recovering "class" (or group) rights and privileges. The DEU's affinity with them — explicable in part by the aforementioned psychological factors and in part by historical determinism — arose simply because of our lack of understanding of their true identities and background. Our mistake, derived from friendship with the soldiers imprisoned with us, was the generalized attribution to an entire low-ranking military population the same attitudes we had discovered in a few with whom we had struggled for liberty. Our lack of understanding and insight at the time drove us to consider as equals those who, in fact, favored a very different political direction.

I stress the "others" concept here. Normally, when a rebel group takes power, those who were displaced or imprisoned by the previous regime are restored to their previous positions. The triumphant "other" sergeants of the September 4, 1933, coup apparently ignored their fellow soldiers who, in 1932, had landed in prison precisely for dissident activities against the Machado rule.

Contrary to all spirit of rectification or recovery, the "revolutionary" military high command of August 12, 1932, in its scant twenty-three days of power, had not even managed to reinstate displaced officers at the military district level. In their short regime, they could scarcely free and reinstate the "rebel" soldiers who had been imprisoned.

The common soldiers who had organized the homage to Machado in October 1930 were even less disposed to expedite the reinstatement of their "dissident" companions. Later, the DEU in its turn would be unable to promote the reinstatement of their military companions in prison because they were already fighting against the new regime. They were struggling in a fierce battle against the government produced by the Mediation and peopled by representatives of the old Machado opposition, all of whom were puppets of the United States Ambassador Benjamin Sumner Welles and against the armed forces, who had remained exactly the same — with the sole exception of the Army Chief of Staff, who as commander-in-chief had ordered the dictator deposed.

CHANGE OF GOVERNMENT IN THE UNITED STATES AND THE MEDIATION PROCESS

Meanwhile in the United States, Franklin Delano Roosevelt had assumed the presidency after winning the November 1932 election. His country was in the midst of the Great Depression, the most dramatic economic crisis of modern capitalism.

As a bold stroke against the crisis, President Roosevelt launched two novel policies that would have far-reaching repercussions: the "New Deal" in the domestic sphere and the "Good Neighbor Policy" in inter-American relations. These policies, especially the latter, of course, touched off a wave of optimism throughout Latin America in general and Cuba in particular. The island country had suffered because of the Hoover administration's unrestricted support for the Machado government, and Cubans naturally expected Roosevelt to rectify that situation. It was presumed, with obvious lack of maturity and even naiveté, that Roosevelt would immediately withdraw all American support for Machado and that a new Cuba, symbolically represented by the DEU and the ABC, would emerge triumphant in spite of the Platt Amendment. (The text of that amendment, imposed on Cuba during the Treaty of Paris, appears in Appendix I.)

Since life in Cuba had become virtually intolerable for leaders of the cause, national opposition leaders and several members of the Directorio had gone into exile. In Cuba there remained the leaders of the ABC, relatively safe under their cloak of anonymity, and some DEU members who, precisely in anticipation of such circumstances, had purposefully kept their names off any manifesto or other public document. Because of that precaution, they were able to continue operating incognito while audacious action groups from both movements continued to undermine the regime.

This solidarity in Havana couldn't help but be influential; the leaders of the new, powerful reformist movement, in which the DEU and the ABC were the vanguard, would naturally move ideologically closer. A good sociologist would have considered this phase the birth of the new Cuba that José Martí had envisioned. But this possibility, contrary to such high hopes, was totally frustrated.

The optimism evaporated when in due time it became apparent that neither was Roosevelt the hope of the Americas nor was the ABC the hope of Cuba.

First, a contradiction arose between the ABC and the DEU; if that rift had been prevented, the two movements united would have constituted the most powerful political force in the history of Cuba.

As we shall see later, the two organizations joined with the leaders of "traditional" politics in early 1933 to form a junta to coordinate efforts against Machado. This junta was supposed to be permanent but, as it turned out, had only an ephemeral life. Both groups had fallen into an historic trap: the belief that it was necessary to "unite" at all costs all the anti-Machado elements so as to present the American government with both a reason to withdraw its support of Machado, and a solid, unified group, a "*con quien tratar*" — someone "with whom to deal," a phrase that soon found itself on everyone's lips. In truth, it was rather an advantageous attitude as far as Washington was concerned, inasmuch as it invited unofficial suggestions from that powerful neighbor, the acceptance of which invariably implied concessions.

So it was done — the suggesting, the setting of conditions — which inevitably led to the bending of the inflexible position. That, in turn, weakened the determination to exercise sovereignty that by now was demonstrated more by the opposition than the government, since the government itself lacked an established regime, much less a constitutional basis by this time, and had absolutely no apparent popular support. In this specific instance, those who felt most pressured to reunite with the old politicians were the DEU. The

Directorio had entered the fray a full year before the ABC and had never once signed any document in conjunction with representatives of "old Cuba." They had, after all, entered the insurrection against Machado in 1931 with the demand for a total and definitive change of regime. Nevertheless, in this historic moment, with the accusation that their isolation from the other groups was impeding unity, the DEU was persuaded that the union of all the adversary forces against the regime would be equivalent to its downfall.

The DEU acceded, therefore, to incorporate itself into what came to be called the *Junta Cubana de Oposición de Nueva York* (Cuban Opposition Junta of New York, or the New York Junta). It is necessary to examine what led to this new alliance.

We have already seen the derailment of the caudillos' insurrection in 1931 at the hands of the Machado regime, an insurrection in which the DEU played absolutely no part. Now we will watch the birth, development, and frustration of what was a powerful, secretly organized movement that called itself the ABC after its alphabetically designated cellular structure. Logically, the ABC filled an historic vacuum created, precisely, by the absence of an expansionist program from the DEU. The Directorio committed this grave error near the end of 1930, when all segments of Cuban society were behind their rallying cry of total and definitive change of regime. They did not know how to exploit this advantage to organize a militant apparatus with backing capable of carrying out the revolution; instead, the Directorio chose to remain hemmed in to a strictly academic sphere.

It was this great error that led the DEU to back the ABC, as it organized in autumn of 1931, and which led it to send two delegates to the ABC's *Célula Directriz*, delegates who later would convert to the new cause and become important members within the ABC. In remaining as leaders of the new instrument of battle instead of abandoning it and returning to the Directorio, these two individuals betrayed the fundamental principles that had prompted their nomination as delegates to the ABC in the first place.

But since I want to support this statement in a more obvious way, I shall now review two divergent positions. The first is expressed in the ABC's own Manifesto-Program of November 1932. The other is the Directorio Estudiantil Universitario's declaration withdrawing its representatives to the ABC, the two who would betray their origins after having signed (as DEU representatives) two ABC documents in March and April 1933.

Said the ABC in its manifesto under the heading "The Offensive against Culture:"

> When still public opinion, fearful or deluded in the face of the first excesses of the tyrant, had not reacted against him; when still no single voice of protest against the dictatorship was heard coming from the political sectors; when the ill-advised extension in office was being hatched; when the university professors, either in cowardice or servility, for which they have not yet completely redeemed themselves, conceded, grotesquely, to a semi-illiterate despot the honorary title "*Doctor Honoris Causa*;" only the Directorio Estudiantil of 1927 dared voice their protest. And ever since, the combative attitude of the students, oriented and maintained by the 1930 Directorio, has been extraordinarily effective in raising the popular spirit; and their valor, their enthusiasm, and their self-denial have won for them forever the gratitude of the people of Cuba. *And of that civic vanguard, the majority have already joined the ranks of the ABC* [emphasis added] (Padrón Larrazábal 1975, 118-52; Soto 1977, Vol. II, 126-32; Organización Abecedaria del Exilio 1977, 11-54).

What did the ABC mean when they said that "of that civic vanguard, the majority have already joined the ranks of the ABC?" Simply that they had obtained the Directorio's backing with its appointment of two delegates from within its ranks as a predominant organization in the battle, to act as members within the ABC *Célula Directriz*. Whether through oversight or by intent, the ABC left undefined the role these two individuals would play in the emerging organization, as well as how they, as delegates of the DEU, would fit into the leadership structure.

Obviously, the ABC should have made it clear that when enlisting the DEU's cooperation and assigning two of its members to their leadership committee, it was not just entering into a political pact but also into an ideological understanding of the highest level, one that could signal the fusion of both organizations. Instead, the ABC simply created the impression that of that civic vanguard, the majority, the DEU, had just transferred to the ABC. The equivocal wording would lead to much greater recruiting successes, as it led to the assumption that the "1930 Directorio," now just a limited number of leaders, had already joined the ABC cells.

Aside from this political, semantic juggling, their obvious intent was to absorb the DEU's followers. In spite of the enrollment of fighters gathered for the ABC by the Directorio, there was manifest bad faith in ABC's action, an attitude that would be proven a few short months later when Benjamin Sumner Welles, the ambassador of the United States and envoy extraordinary of the president of that country, arrived to initiate the Mediation Process.

In spite of the fact that the ABC had specifically rejected North American influence in Cuba in its Manifesto-Program, it is obvious from the following texts what position the organization adopted in practice. In the Manifesto, the ABC declared, in reference to the Treaty of Paris:

> The Cuban economic drama arises from the fact that at the time, the problem of the peace was not resolved. Owing to last-minute North American intervention, Cuba was not able to protect its natural authority as the winner of her own War of Independence, nor was it a party to the Treaty of Paris that put an end to [that war]. Spain did not have to pay any damages or compensation to Cuba, and the United States was satisfied with the geographic and economic booty of Puerto Rico and the Philippines.

And elsewhere in the same document:

> The Cuban state, in apparent subservience to the will of its producers, has docilely followed the directives of foreign capitalism. . . . Our government administrations have allowed the foreign banks to lord it over our land, while neglecting even the elementary provision of regulating their activities and overseeing their operations. . . . The invasion of foreign capitalism with the acquiescence of the Cuban state has completed the process of displacing the natives from the national resources. . . . The sugar mill enclaves develop into townships of greater economic, sometimes demographic, importance than the surrounding municipalities. There are Cuban cities, like Banes in Oriente, literally surrounded by the property of the United Fruit Company, where the law is that imposed by the North

American administrator and the Cuban authorities are his
vassals; where all the city benefits are reserved for the
Yankee residents; where the Cubans are treated as serfs of
a plantation; to the point that Cubans are denied access to
downtown areas at certain times. Conditions are analogous
in the enclaves of the big Yankee sugar mills. The American
general manager is a sovereign chieftain; the native population are his subjects. . . . *This description can and must be
applied to all those who, by force of their circumstances, find
themselves obliged to serve the agents of foreign capital in
Cuba* [emphasis added]. Even those companies which are
less dependent on political favor to carry on their operations do not look favorably on and at times prohibit their
employees from engaging in civic activities. Although those
companies are generally neutral in political matters, their
interests are usually contrary to Cuban interests. Intuitively,
therefore, they go along with corruption in government
circles, which assures them of virtual impunity to [commit]
abuse, and they distrust, therefore, any attitude of political
nonconformity on the part of their employees. Equal with
their official bureaucrats, the foreign capital employees find
themselves obliged to accept the imposition, less directly,
for the difficulty it would cause them to substitute with
other ways of life, the post which they occupy. . . .

After denouncing these negative realities of Cuban life, the ABC
propounded radical solutions that practically coincided, though without saying so expressly, with the total and definitive changes advocated
by the Directorio.

Nevertheless, in a later stage of the process, the ABC and the DEU
joined hands with those to whom the ABC referred when it said,
". . . appreciation can and must be extended to all who, by force of their
circumstances, find themselves obliged to serve the agents of foreign
capital in Cuba . . ."

And who were those to whom the ABC alludes here but the
professional politicians? The ABC and the DEU were able to unite with
these servants in what turned out to be a temporary success for
American policy in Cuba.

In this I refer to the Junta formed by the various opposition groups
in the United States. The Directorio joined, in spite of the fact that many

of its members were the same individuals who figured prominently in the traditional Republican history of Cuba.

There were only two documents during the entire anti-Machado period which the Directorio Estudiantil Universitario appeared to back in conjunction with the traditional opposition sectors. They were also the only declarations in which the Directorio appeared to sign a declaration along with the representatives of the ABC. The first one was dated in Miami on March 27, 1933. It said:

> The various sectors of the Opposition, forever united in the fundamental purpose of overthrowing the illegal and tyrannical regime of those who inserted themselves through a coup d'état as unlawful holders of the government, and with misery and death are annihilating the nation, have realistically constituted themselves in a Central Junta in which all those sectors have representation and which will be, from now and forever, the supreme agency which shall direct and execute, in complete solidarity and harmony, all that may be necessary to accomplish the goal of the constitutional restoration and the dominion of the right of a just and democratic administration.
>
> For that purpose, we, the cosignatories, looking for the people of Cuba to support and assist the organization we represent, in the assurance that, far from [seeking] personal ambitions or partisan interests, crave only to make way for the establishment of a provisional government that will grant *campo de derecho* [equal or uniform rights] for all citizens, regardless of their previous political convictions, so that Cuba can choose, in completely untainted electoral proceedings, their legitimate representatives, who will in turn decide, as unimpeachable trustees, the future course of the Republic under those principles of sovereignty and democracy consecrated by the endeavors of heroic generations.
>
> In requesting the aid of all Cubans, this Manifesto, which is a cry of Patriotism, refers to the assistance that we hope will be understood as giving the country the tranquility and calm it so badly needs. In times like these, faced with a government that persists in maintaining a state of illegality and tyranny, force is indispensable as the only means of bringing about the rule of law, and with it the state of

civilization that may take the place of the anarchy and savagery that is the actual state of Cuba today.

To all Cubans, without distinction, we request your assistance in this quest for dignity and justice in which we have struggled for more than five years already, engaging the Opposition against the official elements that have made of the Nation a private pleasure ground, and of the Republic an instrument of persecution and death for all those who will not docilely bow to the yoke of tyranny. Miami, 27 March 1933.

(Signed) General Menocal; Dr. Pedro M. Fraga; Dr. Santiago Verdeja; Colonel Carlos Mendieta; Colonel Aurelio Hevia; Colonel Roberto Peñate, Vice President; Dr. Miguel Gómez; Dr. Juan Espinosa; Carlos Peláez; Dr. Carlos de la Torre, President; Dr. Ramón Grau San Martín; Dr. Ricardo Dolz; Luis Barreras, Guillermo Barrientos, Secretaries; Dr. Carlos Saladrigas; Carlos Hevia; Dr. Juan A. Lliteras (González Peraza 1933; Soto 1977, Vol. II, 46).

There is a strong belief that there was a hidden hand behind this declaration. Many believed that it belonged to Colonel Cosme de la Torriente, diplomat and former president of the League of Nations, who maintained close contact with both the political opposition leaders and with the American government. He was certainly in a position to make the necessary secret arrangements for such a united declaration from the opposition.

On April 15, the United States government announced the designation of Undersecretary of State Benjamin Sumner Welles as envoy extraordinary to Cuba. Mr. Welles would replace Harry F. Guggenheim, who as U.S. ambassador had subscribed to the interventionist policy laid down by the Sixth International Conference of American States (1928). In high society circles, Guggenheim had been awarded a prize for distinction in dancing the *son*, a typical Cuban dance. Of course, the honor was not a genuine recognition of the ambassador's expertise as a dancer but rather a political act of flattery in the U.S. government's favor.

The spirit of harmony expressed in the document of March 27, 1933, continued well into April. The Directorio had participated indirectly in the drafting of that document through its delegates, Luis

Barreras and Guillermo Barrientos, who were secretary and vice-secretary of the Junta, respectively. In that same harmonious mood, the coalition group published its second declaration in late April, describing its plan of action:

The Cuban Opposition Junta of New York makes public its program of action.

The Cuban Opposition Junta of New York, at the end of April, published its program of action, which was the following:

First: The Junta declares itself in favor of revolution, understanding that only by this means can Cuba's political system be radically changed and the legitimate aspirations of the Cuban people be realized.

Second: In view of the realities of the situation, *the Junta declares its disposition to accept the mediation of the American government* in order to achieve the solution to the crisis, *if the Junta should be officially invited to negotiate; and would fulfill the political, social, and economic program* [emphasis added] that said group would accord, which program would be submitted by the representatives of the Junta designated to deal with the Washington government, as a basis for the solution of the political, social, and economic problems of Cuba.

The document approved by the Junta put on record that

. . . constitutionally it was unable to organize its own government to succeed that of Gerardo Machado, which it sought to overthrow.

Later the document continued the political statement of the Junta, which lay down the following conditions:

1. Resignation of Machado and all the members of his cabinet.

2. Dissolution of the Congress.

3. Creation of a Provisional Government made up of nine persons designated by the Junta, one of whom would act as Provisional President. This Provisional Government would function in a collective way, assuming both executive and legislative functions.

4. Dissolution of the existing political parties in Cuba.

5. Removal from office of all the mayors, governors, city councilmen, province councilmen, and members of boards of education who were elected in the election last November [1932], who would be replaced by persons designated by the Provisional Government (González Peraza 1933).

These five conditions constituted no less than the total and definitive removal of Machado's regime, but not necessarily a change in the nature of the government itself. The document did not go on to define what it meant by a "political, social, and economic program."

It is possible to substitute one regime for another that would be its equivalent. That was the case in the sequence Machado-Herrera-Céspedes, as we shall see. There was not a total and definitive change of regime, as we can now see from the box seats of history.

The conditional demands would be abandoned almost immediately by their own proponents in their haste to sit with Welles at the North American mediation table and construct the Céspedes government. Only the Directorio Estudiantil Universitario would hold fast to those ideals. Four months later, the DEU alone still supported the position that the rest of the signers abandoned.

However, the DEU's influence is actually quite evident in the Junta's pronouncements. The suggested collective administration was already incorporated in the DEU's own program for government, as I shall soon prove. In fact, all the conditions were proposed by the DEU, shaded with a certain political radicalism carried by the Directorio's representatives within the Junta. Nevertheless, we cannot ignore that the general content of the demands, even though powerfully influenced by the thoughts of the DEU, were diminished in their historic importance for having been signed in the company of traditional political agents and diffused by the declaration that they "would accept the mediation of the American government in order to arrive at the solution to the crisis."

In spite of the fact that the DEU delegates obviously carried the initiative in the Junta enclave, notwithstanding also that the representatives of that same DEU promoted the demands in the document, the DEU nevertheless fell into the trap that had been set for it. The DEU had insisted that none of its members aspire to any position within the government that would succeed Machado, while at the same time demanding, once again, a total and definitive change of regime. The traditional politicians rightly felt, therefore, that it was necessary to carry this stronger propulsive force to a position which would neutralize ". . . the dangerousness in you, of which you yourselves are not aware," as one of the caudillos told me as we were boarding a ship to Costa Rica to attend the Second Ibero-American Congress of Students as a representative of Cuba.

And in order to neutralize us, there was no better way than to get us to join them. Recognizing beforehand the current lack of any documented proof that supports me, I might add that the possibility that the Junta as a whole would accept the American mediation was first suggested by Washington to Colonel Cosme de la Torriente, the maximum behind-the-scene arbiter of that affair.

THE DIRECTORIO VACILLATES

The United States is often wrong in its foreign policy stands; still, Washington has always maintained basic "plans" of action ready, both strategic and tactical, to deal with revolutionary situations as they may arise. It was not accidental, for instance, that Víctor Raúl Haya de la Torre, a continental figure, never had a chance to reach power, despite being the leader of APRA, for half a century the majority party in Peru. Surely the United States would, likewise, have policies and alternatives for the replacement of Machado.

While the dictator's blunders had certainly brought discredit and unpopularity to the state, its public institutions, and the political parties — in a word, the entire system operating in Republican Cuba — the "establishment" still recognized the imperative to avoid the implications of the slogan "total and definitive change of regime." To derail the revolutionary movement, the regime found it necessary to place its opponents on the *red* (rosters, rolls; **net**) of its organization. Once inside, they wouldn't be able to get out.

We shall see later how the Directorio did escape this historic trap and remove itself from those rosters, and how, while the other sectors of the Junta one by one joined the American Mediation, the Directorio managed to take the opposite direction and again become the only organization that acted deliberately. First, though, we shall examine how the DEU arrived at the unique political position contained in the Cuban Opposition Junta's document published at the end of April 1933.

In order to explain the student participation in this grave contradiction, it is necessary to understand at this point that to come to a consensus over important decisions, the Directorio usually consulted its members, who fell into four distinct categories based on their personal circumstances. First, there were those in prison, divided among the penitentiaries of Príncipe Castle, La Cabaña Fortress, and Modelo on the Isle of Pines. The second group was in exile; the third group consisted of members of the Directorio who found themselves living underground and constantly pursued by the police. Finally, there were those who had entered the organization as proxies and replacements for assassinated or imprisoned members and who had a larger degree of personal freedom precisely because the government had not yet identified them.

Of course, measures adopted through these consultation procedures could still not express a general consensus with absolute certainty. If opinions were solicited *en blanco*, or requesting individual feelings on a subject without advancing or suggesting any particular point of view, surveys frequently resulted in at least as many responses as there were groups asked — if not a separate idea from each individual. For example, we might receive the opinions of every Tom, Dick, and Harry from Príncipe Castle, versus the opinion of the entire Isle of Pines group or the exiles in Miami.

On the other hand, if we sent out a plan of action already approved by the acting (Surrogate) Directorio — which was always the most respected, being the group in charge of orders and the actual center of operations, and whom the other members expected to have the most information with which to deliberate and decide — then the referendum became simply a yes or no question. Furthermore, communications difficulties increasingly delayed the final results of surveys and referenda. Nevertheless, the Directorio finally developed a means of self-determination of such nature that, after the initial blunders during the early stages of basic program development, the functional and operative decisions — strategies and tactics, positions on distracting the government — were practically adopted by unanimous consent. Never was there a schism that could have led to the development of secessionist groups, new organizations, or public or private conflict among the leaders of the DEU, as had occurred within the ABC, who had offshoots such as the Organización Celular Radical

Revolucionaria (Revolutionary Radical Cellular Organization, OCRR) and the ABC Radical.

The reader, however, might be confused at this point, having heard or found in some other text, that in the Modelo Penitentiary on the Isle of Pines there existed a definite separation between the Right and Left, and that the Directorio belonged to the Right. This is true, but, paradoxically, it is also false. A separation certainly did exist, unfortunately, but it would be termed today the difference between Social Democrats and communists. The later physical separation within the prison hospital building became necessary after daily confrontations between the two extremes. Nevertheless, it must be said that no official member of the Directorio ever converted to communism.

Another historical reference that is frequently cited erroneously concerns the Ala Izquierda Estudiantil (Student Left Wing). Contrary to this common misconception, the Ala Izquierda was not an ideological offshoot of the DEU. Several members of the old 1927 Directorio against the Extension of Powers, led by Gabriel Barceló Gomila and Aureliano Sánchez Arango, organized the Student Left Wing in 1931 as an independent, Marxist-oriented group. But the bulk of the 1927 Directorio did not follow them. Instead, they attached themselves to the DEU of 1930 under the leadership of Eduardo ("Eddy") Chibás and actively participated in the struggle. Their activities ranged from helping develop political stances to actual participation in the revolution itself. Thus, the 1927 Directorio earned a permanent representation among the leadership of the 1930 Directorio Estudiantil Universitario.

In spite of the fact that the Ala Izquierda Estudiantil certainly constituted a vigorous and capable group of leaders, it concentrated its forces on fighting the DEU instead of Machado. Although none of its members were assassinated, they suffered persecution, exile, and prison like the militants of other antigovernment groups, though not as principal targets, as the 1930 Directorio did. And no official member of the Directorio ever joined the Ala Izquierda Estudiantil, either.

Even without these clarifications, it is still apparent that the interior unity of the DEU, even in the midst of adverse and changing conditions, never suffered the slightest division. That is why Carlos Prío Socarrás, one of the most popular Directorio leaders (later elected president of Cuba), said in his political testament, "The DEU was the purest and most cohesive group of that revolutionary period. Within their ranks, envy or deleterious intrigue was totally unknown." This testament was published posthumously by José Ignacio Rasco in the *Miami Herald* on April 26, 1977.

When the Directorio was functioning under normal circumstances, that is, when we could meet with all or at least most of our members, we as individuals gradually melded in ideals and goals, anticipating ideas later advanced by George H. Mead in his treatise on interrelationships, *Mind, Self, and Society.* We became a group so unified that the continued growth process itself aided in the further unification of our thoughts and ideals and encouraged tolerance and harmony among ourselves.

The complete list of DEU members, including the few who quit along the way, reached thirty-six. We were born between 1898 (Guillermo Cancio Sánchez, "Maco") and 1912 (Felipe Pazos Roque and myself, Justo Carrillo Hernández). We came from all six of Cuba's provinces and represented all three of the then-existing schools of the University — Law, Medicine, and the Arts and Sciences. Socioeconomically, we were all from the middle class.

In our inner circle, we expressed passionate opinions, but not a single meeting became confrontational. When differences of opinion did arise, we openly discussed those differences, seeking the best conclusion. No one ever tried to prevail upon the rest or gain a majority by resorting to maneuvers, intrigue, tricks, or sheer forcefulness. Our understanding — more fraternal than merely human — of the real common danger we faced had led us to the purest and most free play of individual opinions. When we came to an agreement, then our agreement would be total and our decisions immediately executed in military fashion. We would go out to accomplish our mission with a sense of sacred commitment, as a solemn vow to the Cuba of our dreams.

But in the unusual circumstances, when the members of the Directorio found themselves scattered to the four winds, the benefits of collective decision making were lost, and good intentions, poorly directed, led to a serious blunder. Because the arguments used in the first phase of program development had lacked counterarguments during their formation, the conclusions reached lacked the group political philosophy of a homogenous revolutionary group.

And then, when the process of establishing positions demanded speed because of urgency, the rudimentary verbal computer of the consultative process could provide a quick, quantitative response, but not a qualitative opinion based on rigorous ideological analyses and true determination of the correct historic position.

So it was a most grievous mistake for us to join the "traditional" politicians — for just over two months, from March 27 to early June 1933 — and to accept, through them and with them, the possibility of North American mediation. The extenuating circumstances under which we adopted that decision explain but do not justify the decision to join the Junta. There existed a break, a sidestep, a rupture in the maturation process of the Directorio as the directing group of a revolution, when we committed two simultaneous errors: first, to meet, even temporarily, with the representative figures of the frustrated traditional Republican scene; second, and more grave, to declare publicly with them that we might accept American mediation in the resolution of the internal Cuban conflict.

It was a bona fide error, born out of revolutionary political naiveté, of immaturity, in which we agreed to concede to the argument that complete unity would speed the fall of Machado's dictatorship. When the national desires are deep and extensively felt, the vibrations filter through the most diverse and unexpected means of expression. We were aware of it while riding the bus, in the café, in one's usual social group; while waiting at the doctor's or dentist's office, while reading a magazine or newspaper, while waiting at the barbershop; everywhere the same expressions and clamor were heard. In those times, the distinctions of leader, director, charismatic messenger, and man of the masses were lost. Everyone wanted the same thing, and the very atmosphere carried the message: "Machado's got to be toppled! By whatever means! *No matter who comes afterward!*"

The Directorio finally conceded to popular clamor and gave in to pressure from the other leaders of the opposition who blamed us for delaying and obstructing the regime's fall. Worse still, the Directorio did not perceive then that the presumed acceleration of the process would not necessarily facilitate our ultimate revolutionary objectives, especially if it came as the result of a change of ill-fated, though temporary, alliances and the acceptance of the foreign mediation principle. Nor did the Directorio perceive that this was rather a time to stand alone, if necessary, and fight for decisive victory over the Old Cuba.

The Directorio Rejects Mediation

Now we shall see how the Directorio escaped the *red* (net) in the course of May and June of that stormy year 1933.

Late in 1932, two DEU members, José Morell Romero and I, Justo Carrillo Hernández, were released from prison — on the condition that we go into exile. A little later, in the same way, Carlos Prío Socarrás and Manuel A. Varona Loredo were released, too. Shortly thereafter, on May 6, 1933, Juan Antonio Rubio Padilla was released. We all went to Miami. Even though the so-called Second Directorio — that surrogate organization of proxies and replacements that had risen through time and attrition to full membership — continued to function in Cuba and lead the political development (through consultation, of course, with the dispersed members), those of us in exile were, in reality, among the founders of the organization. We were the ones who had gained the greater public recognition, the ones who had the opportunity, in prison, to acquire the greater political culture through reading and study. In other words, one could say, in typical local jargon, that outside Cuba were gathered those who were capable of "inventing" it.[7]

In Miami at that time, moreover, were two other dedicated DEU activists, Clara Luz Durán and Sarah del Llano. The group was further augmented by the arrival of Luis Barreras and Guillermo ("Willy") Barrientos, who not only had an impressive record of revolutionary action, but who had the additional advantage of having been members of the self-styled Junta Central (precursor of the New York Junta), as we shall see in the documents from March and April 1933. It is interesting to note that Barreras and Barrientos lacked the political formation acquired by those who had been in prison, since, even though they had been sought, they were never captured. However, they had lived closely with the "traditional" politicians for two months and knew them well. They were aware of their overly flexible policies, their subservience to Washington, their tortuous maneuvering, their secret little memos to the U.S. State Department. They had been radicals in revolutionary action; they did not delay in becoming radicals in thought and behavior as well. As was to be expected, the group of student leaders accepted them as like-minded comrades-in-arms at their first meeting.

So the Miami DEU — to give some designation to the group that would return to be decisive — decided to break with the New York Junta by simply denouncing the Mediation. This transcendentally historic decision and the simultaneous ideological definition of the correct historic position belonged, once again, to Juan Antonio Rubio Padilla. It was he who called me in Mexico, as I was returning from the Second Congress of Ibero-American Students held in San José, Costa Rica, to consult me on the problem. I supported the antimediation stand, thereby completing the unanimous consensus of the DEU Miami cell.

Several closely linked occurrences culminated in what I consider the fourth ideological position of the DEU. First, the Miami DEU reached the decision resolutely to denounce the Mediation; meanwhile, the Havana DEU received an invitation from Ambassador Welles for a get-acquainted chat. As this contact did not necessarily mean joining the Mediation, some of the students were inclined to go and see what the ambassador had in mind, even though the majority in their group opposed that move.

It was at this transcendent juncture that the Miami-Havana phone call alluded to in the Padilla letter occurred. This handwritten note by Rubio Padilla was reproduced in facsimile in the now-defunct magazine *Pensamiento Crítico* (Number 39, April 1970). The text was as follows:

> The session is suspended in order to telephone fellow student Miranda in Havana. Rubio talks with Miranda and informs him of the decisions taken in connection with their attitude regarding the ambassador. Miranda answers that the interview hasn't yet taken place and that he will make known to the council of the Directorio our opinion and decision to break with them for the variation of their political line. Prío speaks with Martínez Arango and also insists on the error of the decision of the students in Cuba and the desirability of ignoring Welles.

Ambassador Welles had left New York aboard the *S.S. Petén* of the United Fruit Company and arrived in Havana on Sunday, May 7, 1933. Police prevented the public from getting near the man who came to the island as President Roosevelt's personal envoy. Orders were that only reporters and government officials could have access to the pier area. Meanwhile, the American diplomat, jealously protected by security guards, conducted himself in a relaxed way, with serene gestures of a purely British style — which caused a press commentator to remark that Mr. Welles "looked more like a graduate of Cambridge than of Harvard" — a very subtle observation, indeed. The ambassador took residence in the newly inaugurated Hotel Nacional at the entrance of the Vedado suburb. Coinciding with his arrival was the report, spread by that most rapid means of clandestine communication — the rumor — that there had been an insurrectional uprising in San Luis, Oriente. In effect, government sources confirmed it while minimizing the importance of that enterprise led by the great soldier Antonio Guiteras Holmes.

The newsmen wasted no time attempting to approach the ambassador. But he, with diplomatic skill, sidestepped the reporters and, with good humor, let slip the comment that "the Cuban people are very impulsive and impatient, and even more so when they should be more calm concerning the future of their national destiny."

Following the telephone exchange between the Miami and Havana DEU groups, the Directorio came out solidly unified on the antimediation position at the same time the ABC resolutely decided to involve itself in the American intervention, a position which the Célula Directriz adopted on June 14, 1933, (*Pensamiento Crítico* April 1970, 173-79; *Foreign Relations of the United States* 1933, Vol. V, Welles Cable 85, June 16, 1933, 308-309).[8]

Meanwhile, only five days after the publication of that decision, the *Miami News* published a statement by Juan Antonio Rubio Padilla that stated in part:

> Despite reports published in Havana to the effect that the student organization in Cuba had accepted the Mediation of the American ambassador between the Machado regime and the Opposition, that information was based on totally erroneous data (*Miami News*, June 19, 1933).

The statement added that

> The Directorio neither has accepted nor will ever accept foreign mediation for the purpose of resolving Cuba's internal political affairs.

The statement continued, stating that in assuming this position against the Mediation, the Directorio

> was being faithful to the true sentiments of the Cuban people, who, like the students, were not interested in

personal political gains that might lie behind the proposed compromise with Machado.

The prevailing mood when the Directorio acceded to Opposition pressure to accept American Mediation was radically reversed when the Miami cell assembled. Its more seasoned leaders immediately began to develop a new policy.

Those who had had the opportunity in prison to mature intellectually were basically men of action. André Maurois pictures the man of action at the edge of a dark abyss where he cannot yet discern the future that is his to mold. Nonetheless, he relies on his own strength and knows that he will be able to accomplish his goals and reach his objectives. His self-confidence is part of his success. We were, likewise, poised.

Once a unanimous consensus was achieved within the Directorio, as a result of the agreement of the Miami DEU cell, the directing Havana group, along with some like myself who had carried on independently, proceeded to define the fourth basic ideological position of the DEU. This is the position which finally achieved, in the course of events, a retuning of public opinion, which can be so easily persuaded along determined lines of thought until presented with a superior principle, the guiding light to their true and proper destiny. The DEU at this point, during this totally mediocre phase of Cuban history, distinguished itself historically by defining this beacon, the fourth ideological position, and simultaneously defining its view of national destiny. In a document printed by the *Miami Herald* on July 16, 1933, which was nearly identical to the text being clandestinely circulated throughout Cuba (Padrón Larrazábal 1975, 153-56),[9] the DEU declared that it had begun to comprehend the role that it must play in the struggle against Machado. It went on precisely to define four principles:

First: The DEU was against all United States intervention in the Cuban national life and, for that reason, it absolutely refused to participate in any way in the Mediation, which they considered

> a tacit intervention advanced by the coercive force of the American government — for only in that way could it have any virtual power to achieve its purpose. The Mediation, therefore, made light of the right of the Cuban people to self-determination and tends to inculcate in the populace, once again, that our internal problems can only be solved by foreign collaboration.

The manifesto elaborated further on this point:

> We cannot overlook the fact that the Platt Amendment —
> a "bilateral" treaty that binds only one of the parties, the
> weaker one — grants the American government the right
> to intrude in our internal problems. But it is also no less a
> fact that acceptance of that treaty was imposed on the
> Cuban people as a requisite condition for recognition of
> their independence. If in 1901 the members of our first
> constituent assembly preferred a mortgaged republic to no
> republic at all, that does not prevent us from rebelling
> against that negation of our sovereignty and against what-
> ever action might be based on that negation. If our fight for
> tomorrow must count among its primary objectives the
> repeal of that treaty, it would be immoral for us to hide
> behind it [the treaty] in order to obtain a momentary
> solution to an immediate problem.

Thus, the DEU put in clear terms its position not only in opposition to the Mediation and any other form of intervention, but in opposition to the Platt Amendment itself.

Second: The manifesto declared further that

> The student movement did not come into existence solely
> to fight and overthrow Machado, but for the purpose of
> bringing about a total purification of the system, seeing to
> it that the political machinery shall be adjusted to its true
> function within an authentic democracy.

It is interesting to note, incidentally, that this is the first appearance of the concept of *authenticity* that, beginning just a few weeks later, would be applied to the process of recovering the frustrated objectives of the movement.

But the political line thus expounded in this manifesto reveals further that the Directorio was indeed envisioning *that it would still exist and function after the overthrow of Machado, and pointed out, perhaps unconsciously, that it might have to assume power at some point after the end of the dictatorship.* It did not aspire only to annul the Platt Amendment (for which they would have to be in power), but also to effect a purification of the system, in order to adjust the political machinery to its true function and establish an authentic democracy.

And it added:

> The Student movement endeavors to strengthen all the
> positive forces of moral order that operate in our society
> and one of those positive forces — perhaps the principal
> one — is the consciousness of being a free and sovereign
> people. This is absolutely necessary in order for a free social
> group to be able to maintain its individuality in the concert
> of nations, nurturing and realizing its collective goal and
> thereby effectively fulfilling its mission among those other
> peoples of the earth.

Thus, the Directorio waded deeper into what it believed was its
essential function for the future. Even though it had not yet fully
explored the concept, as later would be done in the last pronouncement before the Sergeants' Coup on September 4, it had already
isolated itself from all the sectors that had gone along with the
Mediation process. At the same time, the DEU declared itself as the only
faction promoting the establishment of an authentic democracy and
the strengthening of all the positive forces within our society, which
would lead to the development of a consciousness of a free and
sovereign republic, indispensable for an international individuality and
the realization of the collective ideal.

Third: Up until that time, the Directorio had not defined precisely
— to sustain and defend the battle cry for a total and definitive change
of regime — a new concept that crept into the document at this
particular time:

> If we do not rise up today and rescue the maltreated
> consciousness of national identity, we will have neither the
> strength nor the dignity to give our country economic and
> political independence, nor ever again will we have the
> right to feel ourselves and call ourselves a free people.
> When a people does not consider itself free, it does not
> consider itself responsible; and an irresponsible people is
> incapable of carrying out any historic role.

In making this statement, the Directorio was expressing far-
reaching goals: it envisioned Cuba fulfilling a historic role, through
consciousness and strengthening of national identity; in order to
achieve political and economic independence, it began by announcing
the annulment, in due time, of the Platt Amendment which it rejected.

Fourth: Interpreting correctly the Mediation process, the Directorio felt that these Cuban leaders who would sit with the Ambassador of the United States at the negotiating table, beside the supposedly revolutionary sectors, were tacitly exempting the governing individuals from judgment and punishment for their constitutional violations and the crimes they had committed, simply by allowing their participation in the Mediation. In due course, the DEU also declared that the simplistic acceptance of this Mediationist effort would, in effect, be conceding to the usurping regime a status of legitimacy that had been popularly rejected. The Directorio defined this position with the following phrases:

> . . . and if foreign circumstances or pressures create a favorable atmosphere for the removal from those governing persons the penalties of law and of justice, not by this will they be absolved from their crimes nor will they be held less in contempt by honorable and dignified persons. We cannot, therefore, enter into negotiations, even by proxy, with our assassins and executioners, nor recognize — condition imposed by Mr. Welles on the "Mediationist" sectors — a legal status that we continue to consider illegitimate, since it originated in the transgressions of constitutional principles until now held as inviolable.

Thus, synthesizing the demands of this new document, we might put them together in the following form:

First: Rejection of any kind of American intervention in Cuban affairs and the emphatic demand for the future annulment of the Platt Amendment.

Second: Purification of the current political system and establishment of an authentic democracy.

Third: Independence of Cuba, both political and economic.

Fourth: Recognition of the illegitimate nature of the regime and reiteration of the demand for punishment of those in governing positions for their violations of law and justice, and the executioners for their crimes.

Thus, they clearly defined certain specific nuances of that somewhat diffuse battle cry from the November 18, 1930, declaration for a total and definitive change of regime.

Taking this irreversible stand, the DEU declared its opposition to all intervention by the United States government into Cuban affairs and aligned itself against all the Opposition sectors which had accepted that mediation. Apparently, the Directorio stood alone — alone on the side of righteousness and with the people of Cuba. "The strong are stronger when they stand alone."

To sit at the table with representatives of the Machado regime and leaders of the supposed Opposition assumed three fundamental principles: first, that the people gathered at the meeting respected the intervention of the powerful neighbor in resolving a truly national problem; second, that both sides, the oppressors and the oppressed, were at the same moral level, historic category, and political hierarchy, implying legitimate recognition of the Machado regime; and third, that both sides were, in turn, disposed to reciprocal transactions of a special kind in ideological respect to the United States, beneath whose aegis they gathered to put together the transactions entailed in all negotiation.

That the traditional politicians should come to sit at the table there, under the direction of the American ambassador Benjamin Sumner Welles, was no great surprise. But that they should respect the intrusion and submissively give in to and serve it, as had the ABC — held at the time to be pure and uncontaminated — would seem to imply that the measures developed should be considered truly just and, in a historic sense, the correct solution to the larger process of arduous battle, of bloody encounters, of unique repressions on the part of the oppressive regime.

The ABC, in whose foundation the DEU had collaborated by designating two of its members to the seven-person Célula Directriz of the new-born entity, bowed to the political power of the United States and agreed to accept a process that would obviously frustrate all the spirit and the net gains of the revolutionaries. There was absolutely no doubt that in acting thus, the ABC committed treason against the principles that it had expounded in its very own Manifesto-Program barely two months before (Welles Cable 85, June 16, 1933, 308-9).

The United States should have feared such suspicious slogans as for a total and definitive change of regime and the transformational postulates of the ABC's Manifesto-Program. They represented the long-term danger that the revolutionary process, the nearly exclusive objective of which was the restoration of political liberties, would continue to evolve into a genuine revolutionary movement that would clandestinely carry out an authentic socio-economic transformation capable of illuminating the entire path of Cuban future.

At the beginning of the Mediation, not only were representatives of Machado's government and its "Opposition" present; the most important delegation, though officially invisible, was the United States of America. After having unreservedly backed Machado, the U.S. now agreed to impede, this time as mediator, all possible revolutionary realization.

Later, on the third of August that year, the huge abyss between the two historic positions was made public with the Directorio Estudiantil's declaration that it would withdraw its representation from the Célula Directriz of the ABC.

The text[10] of that declaration, which was brief, to be sure, stated the following:

> The Directorio Estudiantil Universitario, in fulfillment of a resolution, makes known that it has withdrawn from the ABC organization the delegation this Directorio had within its Célula Directriz and Technical Committee, through which means we were collaborating.

> The irresistible force of events has compelled us to make this decision, its principal motivation being the growing ideological divergence between said ABC organization and this Directorio, which has become manifest in the face of the present Mediation.

> We wish to make clear, however, that this Directorio shall as always cooperate with whatever organization — including the ABC itself — in any type of energetic and effective action conducive to the victory of our ideals (González Peraza 1933, 315).

The kind of "energetic and effective action" to which the Directorio thus invited the ABC was no longer within the capabilities of the alphabetic organization. It had already vowed not to act against the government as of 15 June. On that day, in a memorandum to Ambassador Welles, the ABC *formally committed itself to "refrain from all forms of agitation directed against the constituted authorities in Cuba"* [emphasis added] (Welles Cable 85, June 16, 1933, 309). This commitment was not without rewards; from July 7 on, there would be no arrests, no house searches, and no restrictions on their travel either within the country or abroad. However, these guarantees would not apply to members of the DEU, since they had rejected the Mediation. Of the only two organizations that had been actively engaged in the revolution, the ABC bowed to the United States, while the DEU issued an invitation to energetic and effective action. One became exempt from all police persecution (Rosell 1973, 225; González Peraza 1933, 313); the other remained vulnerable.

I now return to the withdrawal of the DEU representatives from the ABC to suggest that piqued interests generally have more influence than ideological principles and even more than the loyalty that one owes to organizations one represents. Upon receiving word of the DEU decision to withdraw them, the two Directorio representatives in the ABC Célula Directriz, whose names were never mentioned in the document, but who were, in fact, Juan Pedro Bombino and Orestes Figueredo, both chose to abandon the loyalty owed to the Directorio and remain as leaders with the ABC. They paid no attention whatever to the fact that they owed their status within the organization in the first place to a Directorio decision and that an elemental sense of decency and duty required them to respect the revocation of that decision.

And to terminate the analysis of the historic contradiction between the DEU and the ABC, that perhaps prevented the due and natural transformation of the history of the Republic of Cuba, I turn finally to the last Directorio statement concerning the alphabetic organization, issued in its manifesto to the people of Cuba after August 12 (when Machado fell) at the reinitiation of the battle, now directed against the Céspedes administration. By then, the DEU had resolved to organize its own force and, rejecting the ABC, made a call to enlarge the ranks of the new movement.

Following is the text of the DEU's analysis of the ABC and the new call to arms.

> Public opinion recognizes the treason of certain opposition sectors which have tried to make profit — for personal gain — on their popular exaltation provoked by the Tyranny. Their treason has had a triple effect: on the REVOLUTION, for having stooped to validate essentially void directives and to recognize, more or less explicitly, the legitimacy of a government that used crime and systematic robbery as political instruments; on CUBA, for shamelessly declaring the incapacity of our people to govern their destiny; on

LATIN AMERICA, finally, for encouraging Yankee intrusion and the penetration into our America of interests that for the past one-and-a-half centuries have shown themselves to be hostile to the development of our peoples. But we Cuban students are on WATCH; we are on watch for the Revolution, for Cuba, and for Latin America. And, not satisfied with limiting our gestures to words of protest, we CLAIM from this day forth, the initiative and the direction of the struggle for the LIBERTY of the Cuban citizen in his own land and for the LIBERTY of Cuba — which is also that of Latin America — in the concert of all civilized peoples.

The situation is unique. For the first time in [our] History, the student undertakes a task of such magnitude. Moreover, the Cuban student would fall under the harshest criticism should he be indifferent to the historic circumstances that place in his hands this most difficult and noble mission. Let this not be mistaken as immodest pretension of youth. Our commitment is the mature fruit of reflection, fertilized by the blood of martyrdom of our most worthy. Ten years ago Cuban students initiated their protests against the political degradation our country has been suffering, and the students were the first to raise their voice against the barbaric system set up by Machado. . . . And at the hour of sacrifice, they offered their self-abnegating phalanxes with such splendor that there is hardly an alley or a square in city or town, or spot in the Cuban countryside that has not been spattered with the blood of students. There is no prison nor dungeon where students have not lived in anguish and deprivation. Machado has not the henchman nor the lackey who has not satisfied his savagery or excited his rabidness with student flesh. Nevertheless, the students have behaved always with discipline. Not without misgivings, they accepted that, in order to put an end to the MONSTER[11] and reform Cuba's political system, the action would be better conducted by the men [the Opposition] whose experiences would provide some sort of useful means. They could not imagine that the supreme interests of the people could be subordinated to petty rivalries or personal ambition; now they know better. And when "new" groups [the ABC] emerged with seemingly sincere yearnings for reform, the students hastened to join their ranks. Now they realize it is impossible to trust those who were with Machado until yesterday or have defended imperialist interests until today.

That cruel lesson fills our souls with bitterness, but it does not cause our faith to flounder. On the contrary, in the midst of material ruins and moral debris, upon the tombs of our sublime martyrs, the Directorio Estudiantil Universitario, in the name of all Cuban students, voices a FINAL APPEAL to all YOUTH.

Young men of Cuba: enroll for action under our banner! We are the ones who will carve our own world! Let us unite in order to create! Young men of Latin America: lend us a hand in the task of rebuilding our nation. Our glory will be your reward.

And you, men of good will who perhaps are a step ahead of us in years, you are not old, for your soul is forever young and in love with lofty ideals. Help us! The nation we envision is the same one you love (Padrón Larrazábal 1975, 157-72).[12]

MACHADO'S FALL — CÉSPEDES' GOVERNMENT

Less than a month after the Directorio's pronouncements against Welles and the U.S. Mediation, several events occurred that set up the collapse of the Machado government.

Without any such suggestion coming from the Mediation table, a strike was begun on one of Havana's bus routes during the last few days of July. Like the successive ripples caused by a pebble thrown in a pond, the strike began to spread until, four or five days later, a general strike had evolved. It was decidedly revolutionary in nature, in spite of having been perhaps the most spontaneous strike movement ever to take place in history. Without any sort of instigation or encouragement from anyone, but with the enthusiastic backing of the working class, and eventually the employers (who cooperated in the effort) as well, the country came to a standstill. Not even the Cuban Communist Party could stop it, even though in negotiations with Machado, the Party had put together an arrangement to end the strike, wanting to interpret it as a simple labor dispute. The total suspension of activities throughout the nation culminated in a military coup d'état on August 11. The rebellion began with the First Artillery Battalion from the Máximo Gómez Barracks, which occupied the street floor of the later-demolished Department of Agriculture building near the Havana docks. The movement was quickly joined by the rest of the Seventh Military District based at Cabaña Fortress, as well as by the air corps. A few hours later, Camp Columbia itself refused Machado the support he requested (Ferrer 1950; Welles Cable 152, August 12, 1933, 358-59). The next day the dictator left the country in a rush, flying to Nassau in the Bahamas. Before he left, however, Machado took time to sign his own leave of absence notification.

I must sidetrack here a moment. When Machado found himself surrounded, he, with extraordinary courage, went to Camp Columbia to coalesce his military following and with it crush the First Battalion insurrection. He was relying on his long-standing friendship with Colonel Castillo, the Sixth Military District commander, and the promises made by the rank-and-file soldiers at the October 1930 banquet. But Colonel Castillo either would not or could not assist him, and Machado, knowing perfectly well that the military chain of command was still intact, did not appeal directly to those sergeants, corporals, and enlisted men who had offered him unconditional support with the empty words, "If you ever are in doubt, come . . . here . . . [we] would know how to defend you, for in so doing we would be defending our Homeland." Machado indeed went, but those who had promised him support — Batista, Galíndez, López Migoya, Pedraza, Rodríguez Silverio, Torrente Escudero — cowered in silence while the voice of the people raged outside against their master. Consequently, the homage and the "political force" of this armed sector remained untapped.

The armed forces had been, up to that point, the object of severe popular criticism, and the successful coup that exploded at noon on August 11 was not the positive result of a prevalent consensus among the officers as a group. Other conspiracies that had arisen between 1930 and 1933 had been the product of individual initiatives, in which neither the high command nor the majority of the officer corps had ever been implicated. In October 1930, Colonel Julio Aguado and four young officers — Pedro Luis Díaz, Emilio Laurent, Feliciano Maderne, and Manuel Villada — had been court-martialed for conspiring to overthrow Machado. Colonel Aguado had been commander at the

Cabaña Fortress at the time. It is also a fact that there was an elite group of young officers who were ready to side with the Cuban people if the Supreme Court declared the Machado regime unconstitutional. But neither one nor the other manifestation of military discontent — both meriting the highest historical respect — was able to crack the apparently solid monolith of support that high officers and the rank and file would offer Machado. That solidarity encouraged the people to consider the National Army responsible for maintaining the regime. I must specifically exclude the limited number of academy officers and their students because we recognized then that they suffered with us the depredations of Machado and because — as we shall shortly see — that part of officialdom never had any decisive influence over the control of troops. But the Army, as an historic whole, was the true support for the oppressive regime.

Finally, Sumner Welles arrived, and with his belief in the simplicity of intervention to achieve a peaceful resolution, he inadvertently precipitated the crisis he was supposedly trying to avert. His very presence implied a decrease, a deterioration of the all-embracing power of Machado. This leaching or loss and deterioration of the power of the "establishment" indicated a hidden rupture in the solidarity of the whole, and Welles's presence alone was destructive enough to facilitate the disintegration. But on top of that, the Cuban people had declared a general strike — and several key sectors of that very same crumbling "establishment" joined in the protest. The result was a definitive demonstration of popular force.

Into this situation, which degenerated into a caricature of the true power Machado had enjoyed for eight years, exploded the decisive military rebellion led by Lieutenant Colonel Erasmo Delgado Alvarez, who had been a tool of the regime as special prosecutor in the "barracks assault" case of December 1930. I don't intend to minimize the resolved courage with which this particular military man, and more especially his group of young, idealistic officers, undertook the task of the overthrow, but neither do I believe that an action carried out by a handful of men could possibly remove the guilt of hundreds of officers.

Nor do I believe that the members of this small group, who attempted and achieved the fall of the dictator, acted at the suggestion of Ambassador Welles. On the contrary, the sudden military eruption severely damaged his mediation plans. So simple as to be ingenuous was the action that, at that time, it may not have occurred if the Welles

Mediation had not undermined the solidarity of the regime and if the general strike had not ultimately carried it to the precipice. Furthermore, contrary to what generally occurs with military coups, the rebellious officers of August 11 did not retain the power they had seized but immediately turned the political command over to the Mediation itself. This, in my opinion, was why the Directorio, in the manifesto of August 22, 1933, voicing almost unanimous public opinion, assumed that it had been Welles's intervention with the officers that had impelled the military coup against Machado in the first place. (According to Horacio Ferrer [1950, 331], Machado attributed the coup to General Alberto Herrera.)

Never during Machado's overthrow and replacement did the small group that produced the final downfall make the slightest effort to consult with the Directorio Estudiantil. A mental pattern, settled in the subconscious of the men in uniform through decades of programmed behavior and conditioning, prevented them from associating with the young and rebellious group who had already denounced the American Mediation.

While all this occurred, the Mediation was working to put together a "mediated" formula by which they could "legally" replace the deposed president. Their plan designated the Secretary of War, General Alberto Herrera, who had up to that time also been the Chief of Staff of the Army, as President of the Republic. Of course, this designation was a mere formality. Because of the resulting opposition from the officers who orchestrated Machado's fall, Welles and his associates were forced to make another selection. In great haste, the Mediation determined that power should pass to Doctor Carlos Manuel de Céspedes y Quesada, former colonel of the Liberation Army, former representative in the Congress, and former ambassador of Cuba. In order to collect this last title, there had been a measure of "legal cunning" with respect to normal formalities that contend with historical fact. His microbiography appears in Appendix II.

Machado had violated whatever legitimacy his regime might have had, not only through forced constitutional reform and his term extension but also by gaining reelection for a longer period than that which had been established in his own constitutional reform. It was, therefore, quite a task to mediate a "legitimate" successor. In order to accommodate a "legality" that in the practical sense did not exist, the Mediators cobbled together a series of three distinct steps to be taken in order to provide a "legal" succession. First, President Machado would accept the resignation of all the members of his cabinet, except the Secretary of War, General Alberto Herrera, who would countersign the decree as acting Secretary of State; second, that same General Herrera, acting now as provisional president, would appoint Doctor Carlos Manuel de Céspedes as Secretary of State; and third, in a supposedly constitutional move, certain articles of the Constitution would be reformed in such a way that they would modify and supersede other articles requiring a thirty-day minimum incumbency before any cabinet official could assume the presidency. These manipulations were essential to provide an appearance of legality to Céspedes when he, through decree by Herrera, became President of the Republic after a nominal "term" as Secretary of State.

THE CÉSPEDES GOVERNMENT — ITS CHARACTER AND ITS FALL

President Céspedes proceeded, then, to select members for his cabinet, which, except for the inclusion of ABC representatives, would look like what later was recognized as a typical "Emergency Cabinet." This pattern, typical of cabinets formed during public opinion crises, generally dictated the inclusion of one or more individuals of note from private life, and, perhaps, some one or another representative of the party or political group that caused the public opinion crisis as well. Céspedes included in his cabinet politicians of the old school: Federico Laredo Bru, Rafael Santos Jiménez, and Raúl de Cárdenas. Further following the pattern, he included four men, all with no previous experience in public affairs: Joaquín Martínez Sáenz de Abascal and Carlos Saladrigas Zayas, both key organizers of the ABC; Nicasio Silverio Saínz, and Guillermo Belt Ramírez. Then he appointed two figures of high personal prestige, Eduardo J. Chibás (father of Eddy Chibás) and José Antonio Presno. Finally, to round out the "old guard" requirement, he found some old relic, forgiven for past political peccadillos and totally unconnected with the struggle, one Demetrio Castillo Pokorny. He, a typical "Platt" man, was named Secretary of War. Although well-rooted in Cuban society, Castillo Pokorny, graduate of West Point, was doubly steeped in the Cuban Colonialism mentality.

On August 14, Welles said that the cabinet was a "new deal" for Cuba and added at the same time that "there is not a man appointed to the Cabinet who is not of high personal integrity and of individual ability" (Welles Cable 159, August 14, 1933, 364). Needless to say, "the new composition of the Executive Power" amounted to a restoration of the old patterns of pre-revolutionary political leadership in which — illustrating exactly what I have said — the occasional new "young" element was incorporated in order to assimilate into the status quo someone who could have been a representative of the rebellion or some other minor disquietude. But this time the restoration comeback was implemented in the midst of severe social unrest as a youth movement, with powerful backing by the great majority of the people, was not only vigilant but also participatory and militant about the "option for changes" as opposed to the other national alternative of regression, through the collective anguish that had marked the stormy period of eight years, to the frustrating traditional past.

This cabinet, fruit of the Mediation table, had absolutely no moral authority. In consequence, it came as no surprise, then, that public disorders erupted and that the violence of the masses was carried out with impunity as a direct result of the regime's lack of authority.

As the chaos advanced, Ambassador Welles, who just five days earlier had contentedly praised the Céspedes cabinet, now lamented, "I am now daily being requested for decisions on all matters affecting the government of Cuba." Those men of "high personal integrity and of individual ability," according to his earlier evaluation, now constantly accosted him for "decisions that range from questions of domestic policy and . . . questions involving appointments in all branches of the government" (Welles Cable 172, August 19, 1933, 368).

The Céspedes government had not issued a single directive that could be considered revolutionary. It had not dissolved Congress; it had not convened a Constitutional Assembly; it had not expedited a single judicial action against those responsible for crimes during the Machado regime. Except in the city of Havana, where City Commissioner José Izquierdo Juliá fled popular justice, the Céspedes government tried to leave most of the mayors elected in the spurious Machado elections in their positions throughout the island. Neither did the coalition government make any move toward reorganization or purge of the armed forces. Furthermore, it was rumored with reliable signs of credibility that there were plans to have the same Machado congress hold a session, although with a limited number of members, to solicit an urgent loan from the U.S. government in order to meet the precarious current financial crisis, the worst in the Republic's history.

What should have been a revolutionary government turned out to be, as a result of following Ambassador Welles's instructions to the letter, "a Machadato without Machado." Indeed, not only had there failed to be a "total and definitive change of regime," but not even a "mere clever change of subordinates" had occurred, something the Directorio had also repudiated in November 1930. They tried, rather, to reduce everything to an opportunistic change of tenants of the Executive Office, while maintaining the entire political structure of the deposed regime intact.

During the twenty-three-day period between August 12, the date of Machado's fall, and September 4, the date of the Sergeants' Coup, several episodes occurred that had profound historic impact. There were five key events in all: 1) the discovery of documented proof of treason against student leader José A. Soler and his subsequent pursuit, capture, and execution by firing squad; 2) the discovery of the remains of four revolutionary leaders in the hillside of Atarés Castle in Havana and the burial of three of them on August 19; 3) the release of the DEU manifesto entitled "To the People of Cuba," on August 22, in which the Directorio more clearly defined its ideological position and articulated a program for a provisional government; 4) the reappearance of Sergio Carbó's highly popular political weekly *La Semana* on August 26, containing the fiery editorial Carbó had prepared for that premier edition; and 5) the conspiratorial conversations between members of the Directorio and young officers of the army who not only denied supporting the Machado regime but were, to the contrary, dedicated to its overthrow. Meanwhile, members of an improvised militia that had ties with the Directorio and called itself "*Ejército Pro Ley y Justicia*" (Army for Law and Justice) were having similar talks with sergeants and soldiers of the army.

These five events, among other concurrent circumstances, accentuated the general atmosphere — the revolutionary climate, the crisis of authority, and the "power vacuum" that finally begat the conditions for the September 4 military coup. These concatenated events, entwined and interwoven ever so tightly, presaged a revolutionary upheaval. Their inevitable result was the takeover by all those who disagreed with the political regime established by the American ambassador and the Mediation, the so-called "Céspedes-Welles government."

The aforementioned intertwining of historic factors is what permits me to begin the analysis of the chronological period with the most prolonged and dormant of the mentioned: the pursuit, capture, and execution of the traitor Soler.

THE TREASON OF SOLER

Chronologically, the Soler case is the first among the series of significant events that developed during the lapse of twenty-three days between Machado's fall and the military coup that toppled the Céspedes government. The discovery of Soler's treason was almost synchronous with the dictator's fall, as it came to light with the occupation of the archives of the various police departments. Still, the episode was the first to begin, and it continued to unfold until that very September 4. The Soler case came to form part of the great agitation that directed the unexpected unraveling because of the lack of realizations and, above all, because of the lack of authority of the regime that knew not how to fulfill the destiny that belonged to the victors of the bloody battle against the Machadato.

It just so happened that within seventy-two hours following the fall of the Machado tyranny, long-held suspicions of treason were confirmed. José Soler had been an activist in the revolutionary process, particularly in the student movement, even though he had not been a member of the 1927 Directorio against the Extension of Powers. He was, to be sure, a most unusual character, extremely strange in the Cuban picture of his times. He was, unquestionably, a man with a very lucid mentality and who possessed a great political awareness. He came from a respectable family that lived according to the most revered Cuban traditions. Possessed of clear intelligence and being an indefatigable reader, he could be considered a natural-born revolutionary. When Soler joined the battle against Machado's term extension, he and other students who took part in those activities were barred from the University of Havana, where he had been studying law, for ten years by the General Disciplinary Council. He chose to flee the country and stayed abroad for some time. When he returned to the island, Soler rejoined the ranks of the anti-Machado activists — which meant once again running the gamut of police persecution and all the rest.

This public image made his double life as a vulgar, unprincipled informer entirely incomprehensible. It is no small wonder many of his fellow activists refused until the end to accept the fact that he had betrayed the revolutionary movement and, in his moral degradation, had descended so low as to provide the police with written and signed reports filled with confidential and important information concerning activities being planned or proposed against the government in power.

In his incredible lack of scruples, Soler even went to the extreme of informing on one of the Directorio members most deeply involved in clandestine operations in the city of Havana, Carlos Manuel Fuertes Blandino, in whose death Soler played a decisive role. Unfortunately for him, it was eventually proven beyond a doubt that he was the only informant to the repressive government and the one individual who made possible the location, identification, and arrest of the unfortunate Fuertes.

The night immediately before the discovery of Fuertes Blandino's body near the now long-gone Hermitage of the Catalanes in Havana, the two men — Fuertes and Soler — found themselves together, in complete secrecy, in the house of a mutual lady friend on Animas Street between Crespo and Amistad in Havana. The house belonged to a prostitute known as Carmelina, who had concealed various fleeing revolutionaries from the police. (The two men had been long-time rivals for the favors of one of the ladies who worked there.) After a brief conversation with Fuertes, Soler excused himself on the pretext of having something important to do nearby; he would be back soon. Fuertes agreed, and Soler walked briskly to the National Police Headquarters on the corner of Monserrate and Empedrado Streets, less than five blocks away. Just moments later, he returned and invited Fuertes to leave with him. This was apparently so that the occupants of a car that had just parked down the block could identify Fuertes. His mission accomplished, Soler quickly disappeared, and Fuertes was immediately detained by members of the dreaded *Sección de Expertos* (Section of Experts) of the Special Police Corps. Taken to headquarters, Fuertes was subjected to severe interrogation under torture and finally murdered. In this way, Pedro Aincart and his hired assassins avenged the death, a few hours before, of one Lieutenant Pau, the military supervisor for the city of Guanabacoa, who had been assassinated for his criminal activities against revolutionary elements. (Fuertes had opposed the attempt on grounds that it would provoke harsh retaliation. However, he had collaborated by oiling and cleaning the weapons to be used in the execution. Fuertes was discussing the assassination when Soler arrived, causing Soler to believe that Fuertes was the mastermind of the whole operation.)

What is most interesting is that all these suggestive coincidences later were completely confirmed in reports found in the files of the National Secret Police, all signed by Soler himself. He had periodically sent reports to the second in command of that entity, Saúl Herrera, a brother of General Alberto Herrera Franch, Chief of Staff of the Army. In reports Soler sent from Modelo Penitentiary on the Isle of Pines through the prison warden, Major Pedro Antonio Castells, he had detailed the existing DEU battle plans and even allowed himself to advise the Machado regime on measures he thought would adequately thwart the revolutionary movement and, in particular, all that proceeded from the university student faction, whose constant action was uncontainable. Since Soler had given up his militancy in the Communist Party, he was unable to provide such specific details about their activities as well. However, since the communist faction was the best known revolutionary group, he didn't find it difficult to "sell" the quality of his biographical sketches of the most notorious communist leaders of that period, including Jorge A. Vivó, Joaquín Ordoqui, Sandalio Junco, and José Chelala Aguilera.

Once Soler's consistent character as a traitor was amply confirmed and documented, the DEU made a decision of extraordinary significance, considering its unique position within Cuba's social and political framework immediately after the fall of Machado. The Directorio felt obliged to establish itself as a revolutionary tribunal while it was still alone in terms of organizations and national and/or traditional leadership that could have existed. Most of the other opposition sectors or groups that had battled Machado had participated in the Mediation and, in one form or another, found themselves represented in the Céspedes government. Even supposedly revolutionary organizations, such as ABC and OCRR (*Organización Celular Radical Revolucionario*), had members in the Céspedes cabinet. Consequently, the Directorio was practically alone — I repeat — against the Mediation government, against all the political groups that it had absorbed, and against the government of the United States that backed it. If one could name a single other high personality of politics or organization or revolutionary faction not directly represented, one could only consider former president General Mario G. Menocal. But the once-powerful conservative caudillo had long since lost any vestige of popular support and, apparently, only intended to capture power through some kind of sleight-of-hand coup that never materialized. (Nevertheless, even Menocal himself had representatives in the Cabinet, such as lifelong loyal follower Raúl de Cárdenas, the Chief of the Executive Staff, no less.)

With the discovery of documented proof of Soler's treason, the Directorio felt obligated to start at the beginning, judging that the most elementary revolutionary duty demanded the application of punitive actions to those who were oppressing the people as well as to those who chose to serve the oppressors, especially those who chose to inform on their comrades, delivering to death the bold champions of the revolutionary battle.

Facing a national chaos in which the great majority of the people darkly considered the total inaction of its new officials, without ever consciously or responsibly making up its collective mind concerning its impact, and without considering the transcendence of its decision, the DEU created what today would be considered its own governmental jurisdiction. This jurisdiction still could not be extensive nor complete, since the DEU did not actually possess any power, but it could certainly begin to exercise one of the duties of the State by attributing to itself a judicial role and authorizing the leaders of the university student body to judge a companion turned traitor in the battle against the tyranny. Thus, the Directorio commenced by establishing a revolutionary court of its own.

First, they printed up announcements calling for the pursuit and capture of the traitor Soler, a copy of which is reproduced in black and white in this book. It is certainly the only document signed by both the *Ala Izquierda* (Student Left Wing) and the Directorio. The announcement did not directly state that its goal was to try and sentence Soler, once captured, but it was taken for granted that this was the only and real purpose of the search. Not only did the citizens of Havana distribute these handbills; they guarded them against removal so vigilantly that even the uniformed police of the capital did not dare to take down a single one of those "Wanted" posters. The Directorio daily received hundreds of phone calls offering tips that produced false trails. Finally, one day, one of the many groups who eagerly sought the betrayer Soler found him in the Vedado district and took him to Casuso Clinic on the corner of Calzada de Jésus de Monte and Santo Suárez, in Havana. From there he was transported to the trial site, a small estate thirty minutes from the capital belonging to Pepe Plasencia, co-owner of the Vieto-Plasencia laboratory.

THE ATARÉS DISCOVERIES AND CONSEQUENCES

The second episode in the fateful string of events during that "power vacuum" was the discovery and burial of three victims of the Machadato: a student, a laborer, and a sergeant.

Atarés Castle,[13] in whose foothills were discovered the remains of the assassinated revolutionaries, was also where Captain Manuel Crespo and his team of assassins had tortured them. They had tortured innumerable political prisoners during the Machado dictatorship (Crespo 1934).

As mentioned earlier, it was an odd coincidence that the torturer Crespo contributed indirectly to the historic, political, and philosophical motivations of the September 4 Coup. He unknowingly, of course, did so by ordering the burial in the fortress's surrounding hillside of the bodies of assassinated leaders from the three factions that ultimately would become the mortar of the revolutionary regime that followed the military coup.

A student, Félix Ernesto Alpízar, a member of the Directorio Estudiantil Universitario, captured on December 21, 1931, and later assassinated, was among those whose remains were unearthed there. The second victim was Margarito Iglesias, a blue-collar worker who had been one of the leaders of the anarchic-sindicalist faction within the Anarchist Party of Cuba. He was quite well known through his campaigns for an industrial workers' union. He had been interrogated and subjected to torture, but he never yielded even the slightest information that might compromise anyone else. The third corpse was that of an Army Corps of Engineers sergeant, Miguel Angel Hernández, the most audacious individual of those who, from such a modest rank, conspired against the Machado dictatorship.

The remains of Alpízar, Iglesias, and Hernández were found by a revolutionary committee sent to Atarés with the intent of locating victims of the dictatorship who had been assassinated and buried in the hillsides below the fortress. It should be added that on the day following these findings, the grave of a fourth victim was located. He was identified as Alfredo López Arencibia, an active labor leader and general secretary of the Labor Federation of Havana.

As I have already explained, we lived together for a number of months at the Isle of Pines Modelo Penitentiary with a number of sergeants and corporals from the army and ensigns from the navy who had been caught in diverse conspiratorial activities of a minor nature, but which had placed them in extreme danger. Nevertheless, Miguel Angel Hernández, who was registered as the last political prisoner to enter that penitentiary, with no further information listed — no next of kin, no place of birth, or date of incarceration — was not involved in the conspiracy that led to the incarceration of the other sergeants and corporals. His own revolutionary doings were of a more discreet yet bolder nature — and, one could add, riskier.

The discovery of the remains of Alpízar, Iglesias, and Hernández reinforced the popular indignation. Their skulls had been fractured, a grisly proof of their assassins' cruelty.[14] Furthermore, the triple discovery led to the decision to hold a common funeral and that the funeral celebration would take on revolutionary characteristics. That spectacular demonstration of collective mourning occurred Sunday afternoon, August 19, and embodied the general rejection of the incapable, week-old government. The governmental weakness was accentuated by the multiplying factor that the very burial itself and the victims buried represented.

In order to appreciate this new state of affairs, we must take into account that on that very day, when the funerals were held, there appeared on all the lampposts and telephone poles, on every tree and wall, placed in the window of every shop, on the sides of buses and at the theater entrances, in every school, public and private, elementary and secondary, on every possible surface, "Wanted" posters advertising the search for the traitor Soler. These posters, so widely distributed that they seemed to flood even the most outlying district and corner of the capital city, encouraged the citizens of Havana, or at least a great majority of them, to become involved in the matter. This involvement can be explained by the total support of the people who believed that the sensational case would indeed result in the imposition of punishment for treason, only if real evidence, examined and analyzed with care, led to a reasonable and certain determination of guilt of the accused. Obviously, that popular participation would consequently cause the revolutionary wave to grow.

Of course, the events of the common funerals must be examined. The student Alpízar's body first lay in state in the assembly hall of the university, as would dozens of other fallen students in the continuing struggle for liberty in months to come. But in spite of Alpízar's procession, most representative of the terribly bloody struggle in which the self-same Directorio Estudiantil had already lost four of its known members, the greatest result was not to be the huge turn-out for the funeral, nor the massive presence of spectators lining the streets all the way from the University to the Colón Cemetery in Havana, as we shall see.

The funeral of labor leader Margarito Iglesias had its own peculiar characteristics. Iglesias had been missing since early 1926, right after his arrest by Machado's police. Since his body had never been found, it was presumed that the unfortunate prisoner had been tossed to the sharks from a certain rampart of the Cabaña Fortress, as was known to be the case with at least three other prisoners before.[15] However, investigations shortly after Machado's fall revealed that the labor leader had actually been placed in the custody of the chief of the Fifth Squadron of the Rural Guard, part of the presidential guard, who put him through ruthless interrogations and horrible tortures, during which he never wavered in his determination to resist, until death put an end to his sufferings. None of those who had been involved with Iglesias was ever bothered by the police, thanks to his heroic silence in spite of torture. Even though he had never been a militant in the Communist Party in Cuba, his martyrdom was appropriated by that group to try to compensate for the fact that in the last days of Machado's government, the Party had entered into grave complicity with the dictatorship.

The Communist Party and the *Confederación Nacional Obrera de Cuba* (National Laborers Confederation of Cuba, CNOC) then just an instrument in the Communist Party's hands, tried to resuscitate "Cuba, the dead island" through an agreement with Machado in exchange for a few simple concessions to the unions for the working class and for official recognition of the Party itself and for the labor union. Of course, as we have already seen, their efforts were in vain, and the spreading strike was a major factor in the ultimate downfall of the Machado regime.

When the nation looked down upon a certain class, the Communist Party would raise that class over the nation; but not even this class, the working class, which was considered "theirs," would submit to the Party's will. Such were things when the Labor Confederation (CNOC) gave the order to return to work (immediately after the connivance with Machado); the general strike, which had evolved into a political strike, not only continued but actually spread. After having tried hard — even with the Port of Havana stevedores, where they had influence — the communists failed in their attempt to stop the strike. One of the

Party members was even pushed into the water during a heated argument with the stevedores.

On the afternoon of August 7, 1933, throngs had gathered in the streets to celebrate the alleged fall of the dictatorship, which had erroneously been broadcast that afternoon by radio. A new massacre was perpetrated by the Section of Experts of the National Police and members of the *Porra*[16] on the celebrating populace. Twenty died and nearly a hundred were injured, provoking an even greater support for and silent participation in the strike by the people of Cuba.

The communists completed their agreement with Machado just a few hours after that massacre, at the very time that funerals of some massacre victims were beginning, and as other victims' families still kept vigil over the bodies of their loved ones.

Despite the fall of Machado at the hands of the Cuban people, the party which had attempted to maintain the regime was able to revive a scant seven days later. The discovery of the remains of Margarito Iglesias was providential for the Red leaders.

Having discovered the perfect device, and exploiting the selfsame liberties gained by the people who disregarded the return-to-work order, the communists themselves, in the hours following the Atarés discoveries, presented themselves with the duty of providing an honor guard at the common funeral procession for Iglesias, Alpízar, and Hernández. Even though there were actually three separate funerals resulting from the dramatic discoveries, the demonstration of pain would provoke a type of popular reaction that supported a combined procession.

There is no room for the slightest doubt that the Communist Party in Cuba produced for the people of Havana on August 19, 1933, a grand proof of organization, discipline, and force, surprising the multitude who were present at the spectacular funeral. The demonstration, it is clear, was covertly impregnated with the characteristic maneuverings of the communist movement. In the first place, it was the product of the appropriation of an unaligned victim, since Margarito Iglesias had never been a communist; and in the second place, the itinerary of the funeral procession presented another opening for opportunism. In effect, the wakes of Iglesias and Hernández were being staged primarily from the steps of the University, and the three funeral processions marched together, from whence it was difficult to distinguish which group was following which cortege. However, the very short delay at the bottom of the steps to wait for the Iglesias procession was of particular importance to the Party, since, through its incorporation into the student martyr's cortege, it implicitly received the DEU's absolution from guilt, and through the Directorio, from the Cuban people, who otherwise would not so easily forget those sinful arrangements with Machado just a few days before. Ultimately, the communist group was not the largest of the three entourages. Nevertheless, it was certainly that which marched with greatest order, manipulating appearances so that it seemed to be the largest group. By happily singing the *Internacionale*, it demonstrated the greatest enthusiasm for the struggle. The communist display left hundreds and thousands of Cubans who participated in the common procession or watched the funeral caravan with a very strong impression. (One of those deeply impressed individuals happened to be Sergio Carbó, as we shall soon see.)

Finally, the funeral cortege of former Sergeant Miguel Angel Hernández, too, was distinctive in its own way. The remains of Margarito Iglesias were accompanied by a small but spectacular parade, orderly as well as combative, demonstrating enthusiasm more as if entering a battle than leaving one. Hernández' cortege had a singular characteristic; though not so well-attended as Alpízar's or Iglesias's, it relied, nevertheless, on the opportunistic apparition of a man who had been considered up until then well entrenched with Machado. From that moment on, he would become a prominent figure. Three weeks later he would be incorporated into the history of Cuba with a notorious reputation after once again opportunistically manipulating a situation to his great advantage.

Miguel Angel Hernández is an exceptionally rare case in the revolutionary process of 1930-1933, since military men of all ranks may conspire, but they seldom participate in those actions. As such, the concept of maintaining order may have been planted in the very cells of the military brain, so that those men cannot even conceive the use of violence out of uniform. They are completely different from the revolutionary civilian, who in rebellion against the law that Congress produces, desecrates it, fails to follow it, and nonchalantly violates it. He is a typical transgressor of the law. Thus is generated the civilian's danger during normal periods, which can encourage common delinquency. More dangerous, even, is when, already corrupt, one of these civilian individuals finds himself in a legislative position, or when he rises to the presidency — the most serious risk for his country, his region, even his continent, and quite possibly the whole world. These types are not so unusual in Latin America. We have very good examples of this in Cuba's Fidel Castro and Venezuela's Carlos Andrés Pérez. The former, having trampled the most elemental principles of public ethics, both in the national and international fields, came, nevertheless, to lead the nonaligned world, and would have captured for Cuba a seat in the Security Council of the United Nations if the Soviet invasion of Afghanistan had not split the unity of that group, which originally consisted of seventy-seven countries and later exceeded a hundred. And as for Pérez, for personal gain he exhausted the Venezuelan public treasury and was, nevertheless, called to account only for the smallest of his malfeasances, the so-called Sierra Nevada case. Yet, despite his turbid background, Carlos Andrés Pérez became one of the "liberators" of Nicaragua, using foreign funds which he had already appropriated; later he was one of the leaders of the *Internacional Socialista* (International Socialist), which mustered support for both the Salvadoran guerrillas and the Sandinistan government of Castro's comrades.

Of course, these historic examples represent the most obvious cases. There are, also, various revolutionaries who have achieved the presidency of their countries and left office with no blemish on their records. To cite only a few of the Latin American presidents of recent times, we could mention Juan José Arévalo, Guatemala; Rómulo Betancourt and Rafael Caldera, Venezuela; Eduardo Santos, Colombia; Eduardo Frei, Chile; and that very important individual from Puerto Rico, Luis Muñoz Marín.

Neither was Miguel Angel Hernández a man of direct revolutionary action. He was a sergeant in the Corps of Engineers, headquartered on Third and Second in the Vedado district of Havana, who joined in the most audacious revolutionary activities.

Arsenio Ortiz, a commander of the National Army, had accumulated an extensive criminal record and earned the title "Jackal of Oriente." He had been sentenced to death in a joint action by the Directorio and the ABC on December 6, 1932. When the team assigned to carry out the sentence, consisting of Argelio Puig Jordán, Luis Orlando Rodríguez, and Domingo Cañal, closed in on Ortiz, a policeman by the name of Cepero warned him of his imminent danger, and Ortiz immediately turned about and shot back, fatally wounding Puig Jordán and seriously wounding Rodríguez and Cañal.

In retaliation, the ABC and DEU condemned the police officer Cepero to death en absentia. He was executed a few days later in the city of Marianao, while bragging of having saved Ortiz's life. Among his executors was Sergeant Miguel Angel Hernández, dressed as a civilian.

When Captain Crespo, the master of repression, was informed by a former corporal of the same Corps of Engineers unit of Hernández's participation in the plot, he ordered his detention. After his arrest, Hernández attacked his custodian with an ax, but another corporal shot and wounded him as he attempted to flee. As he fled, he left a telltale trail of blood to a private hospital in the Vedado district, where he was found and detained again.

He was treated in the Military Hospital and discharged upon his recovery to the lair of Captain Crespo, the Atarés Castle. There he was tortured while Crespo consulted with General Alberto Herrera about whether Sergeant Hernández should be court-martialed.

Since he had already been released from the Army, Herrera decided to leave Hernández at Atarés until the order to execute him arrived. When the order arrived, in Captain Crespo's own words, it "*was complied with immediately, according to the established norms*" (Crespo 1934).

After his assassination, it was made to appear that Hernández had previously been a "political prisoner" in the Modelo Penitentiary where he was registered as "No. 538" and later released. According to the official version, he had been declared a deserter for failure to present himself regularly to the High Command.

While all these events were developing, another sergeant, Fulgencio Batista, a privileged stenographer serving in the military court convened to try the accused revolutionaries, was selling copies of the transcripts of the courts-martial to defense lawyers for some twenty pesos (approximately the equivalent of $200 in current terms). Of course, logically, the defense lawyers tried to obtain as much information as possible on the accused they represented, and Fulgencio Batista, the stenographer in the courts-martial, clandestinely passed them transcripts of the judicial sessions, for what was then considered a rather high fee. Here was a speculator in stenographic clandestinity!

I remember having spoken with Eduardo J. Chibás, father of the Eddy Chibás who later became a famous political combatant and remained a national figure until his death. He [the father] told me once, when we were both political prisoners at the Modelo Penitentiary, that he had paid that sum to Sergeant Batista for the transcripts of his own trial. But not only was it Chibás who knew of this enterprise, but all those who passed before the courts-martial in 1932 and 1933. This fact does not necessarily mean that Batista was an ardent sympathizer within the Machado regime, but the facts to which I refer do demonstrate two very personal characteristics. First, Batista enjoyed a great deal of privilege within the regime, since he was not the only stenographer in the army, but nevertheless, he was the only one selected to serve as stenographer to all the courts-martial convened to deal with military procedures in the Fifth (Dragones), the Sixth (Columbia), the Seventh (La Cabaña), and the Eighth (Pinar del Río) Military Districts [in and around Havana]. The second of these characteristics to which I allude was the fact that, betraying the confidence that the regime had placed in him, and making a mockery of his oath sworn at the beginning of his first session in the council, he made the most of his advantageous situation in order to effect the commercial sale of documents pertaining to those individuals who had been summoned. This characteristic was even more damning than the fact that he enjoyed great preferential treatment within the Machado regime, to the point of being sinful.

Well, then, this was that same Batista who had been a background participant in the October 1930 banquet and never forgot to carry with pride, during that age of "crimes and horrors of the regime," the "little wallet with the peso inside." This same Batista was among those who organized that demonstration of lackeyism and support, but who failed to fulfill their promise when Machado went to Columbia on August 11, 1933, to call on the support of the encampment offered in 1930. It was this same Batista who, up to the very last hours of the Machado regime, had been one of the most privileged individuals, and now was, through his own opportunistic appointment, the speaker at the funeral of Miguel Angel Hernández, who typified the revolutionary sergeants' corp. He who, neither as a sergeant nor as a soldier, ever saw himself persecuted or thrown in prison on the Isle of Pines, as were the sergeants and corporals arrested for conspiracy; he who did not participate in heroic actions, like that which cost Miguel Angel Hernández his life, is the individual — now that Machado had fled — who presented himself to give the eulogy as a representative of the "revolutionary" sergeants, among whom he never belonged. Such incredible cynicism would have to be ultimately profitable and productive.

Directly linked, then, with the common funeral demonstration was another occurrence during that twenty-three-day lapse between August 12 and September 4. It was the reappearance of Sergio Carbó's magazine *La Semana* after a two-year hiatus. For several years, but particularly following the death of student Rafael Trejo on October 1, 1930, *La Semana* had been the instrument of the most vigorous civilian battle against the Machado dictatorship. Wednesdays the public practically snatched copies out of the hands of the street vendors, and each issue further consolidated its prestige and increased circulation, until the failed Gibara expedition in August 1931 forced Carbó to flee into exile. Regardless of whatever critical reservations one may have concerning its creator, one thing must be made clear about *La Semana*; it was one of the most decisive driving forces in the battle against the Machado government. Its historic function of coalescing a nonconformist, nontraditionalist population to oppose the Machado regime will never go unrecognized or underestimated. The true marvel is that it obtained those results thanks to the use of a particular brand of Cuban humor known as "*choteo*" (mockery or teasing). That grand accomplishment was attained, not simply through Carbó's editorials, but also with the particular grace with which the revolutionary message was delivered through the power of irony and good humor contained in almost the entirety of every single edition.

Chief editor Carbó had made plans to resume weekly publication on August 16. However, various unfortunate obstacles and difficulties presented themselves to make that date impossible. Carbó, therefore, had to wait until August 26 to publish the first edition after the fall of the dictatorship.

Sergio Carbó, deeply impressed by the triple funeral he had seen, decided to explore the possibility of a military plot in which he, perhaps, might assume leadership. Did he have the necessary aptitude? It is worth the trouble at this point to engage in a little "psychoanalysis." We must realize, above all, that when he was encouraged to return to his theater of operations, Carbó still waited four days before returning to Cuba to take the first step toward taking command — evidently, an excess of caution.

Once in Havana, three days after his arrival, he was present for the triple funeral and its multitudinous attendance. Right away he could see with his own eyes the frustration of the popular power, conscious of itself and unsubmitting: the human mass that accompanied the remains of a student, a worker, and a soldier. The enormous demonstration of grief, along with other minute details he noted, would signal the sinking of the Mediationist power of Welles and Céspedes. He realized immediately that what was demanded by that same student message that he had helped to polish — "for a total and definitive change of regime" — had not happened. He could see that the masses not only knew it, they lived it. Right away, yielding to his thirst for power, he decided to launch a new call to arms that would unite those three factions that were already participating in History. He sat down at his old typewriter.

Of course, that call had to have a title, for which he had been searching since observing the funeral. He was a journalist of long-time experience, but he had only written a single book, a work in which he described a visit to Soviet Russia, a trip that had left in him indelible impressions. And buried deep within his memories and his most intimate reactions, he discovered the title for which he had been searching so anxiously. He leaped to the memory of a question that a factory worker had shot at him unexpectedly: "When is the social revolution going to explode in Cuba?" (Carbó 1928, 170). He applied that unexpected question to this Cuban event almost verbatim. That is why, on the front page of *La Semana* on August 26, there appeared in full colors, arm-in-arm, a student, a worker, and a soldier, with the title below that said, "*¿A qué se espera para comenzar la revolución?*" — "What are you waiting for to start the revolution?" His regular editorial inside, "Two Words in Earnest" contained the call for the students, workers, and soldiers to unite. This harangue was a true exhortation to battle so that these factions would instigate — within the course of the frustrated struggle by the Mediation and by the Céspedes government — a new wave of agitation and combat. With coordination of the three factions and their efforts, the entire people of Cuba could apply pressure for a change in the revolutionary process that was coming to nothing. It is also possible that Sergio Carbó had discovered that both the Directorio and other similar elements were sustaining clandestine conversations with members of the armed forces, and he, among whose characteristics was also that of political opportunism, possessing a huge revolutionary sensibility, and believing his "moment" had arrived, took advantage of the extraordinary force of the resurgence of *La Semana* in order to situate himself immediately in the first row of the revolutionary opposition against the Mediationist government of Céspedes.

Carbó's call to arms, then, was perhaps the most important direct result of that massive funeral procession on August 19, 1933.

The interesting Carbó personality was to play a transcendent role in the next fifteen days of Cuban history. Only by understanding this personality can one find the thread of the intricate developments of those days. This brief biographical sketch appears in Appendix III of this work.

THE ARPE IDEA

As the national feeling expressed in *La Semana* carried Carbó to the peak of popularity, the Directorio was becoming the hegemonic center of the revolutionary struggle. The DEU had consulted Carbó from the beginning; it was he who created the 1930 slogan, "for a total and definitive change of regime," and it was his brilliant pen that gave form and substance to the memorable text that contained that battle cry. Furthermore, after his first exile, the Gibara fiasco and his second expatriation, Carbó finally reappeared in the center of the vortex with his weekly publication and his call to arms directed toward the students, workers, and soldiers. It is a widespread belief that probably at some time during the nine days after the August 26 edition of *La Semana* hit the streets, and before the September 4 rebellion of the rank-and-file soldiers, some soldier may have approached Carbó to give him a pat on the back and whisper something in his ear. Even Batista himself, perhaps, could have done that. But while his star was rising, perhaps Carbó forgot that climbing heights requires greater courage and sense of balance than just walking comfortably on the plains.

While his revolutionary message, and specifically the calls to action to students, workers, and soldiers filtered through the general public, the DEU announced its political program for government and its determination to seize power.

It would be difficult for the historian today, for contemporary observers of those developments, for those who might be antagonistic toward the DEU or even, going still further, for the Directorio members themselves, to discern precisely the various transitions the DEU had undergone since the publication of that manifesto-program of October 23, 1930. It had advanced steadily, then tactically retreated, fearing that the student body would not back it in the revolutionary battle and limited itself to strictly academic pronouncements until the manifesto of August 22, 1933. Now, in this new transcendentally historic document, the DEU expounded its programmatic ideas in order to bring about their implementation upon assuming the government of the country. The abysmal difference between the two positions could only be interpreted as maturity; the Directorio had hardened its collective character through suffering the loss of companions in the hard and heated battle, through persecutions, imprisonments, and deceptions, after watching as the ABC appropriated members from its multitude of followers, aided by two of its own representatives in the ABC's Célula Directriz. After this slow but immense change of focus, the Directorio found itself alone against the Mediation process directed by the United States and including, on both sides of the negotiating table, the representatives of the Machado regime and the opposition sectors, some of whom, such as the ABC, were only revolutionary in name.

After all these changes in the political landscape, the Directorio decided to create a broader organization, oriented toward itself. This organization would create an army of soldiers from professionals, from workers already tied in some form to its agenda, from middle-class men and women who had sustained vigorously, perhaps more than any others, the DEU's efforts. It would involve the people of the countryside who until that time had never participated militantly in the process but, nevertheless, knew precisely who were their adversaries and who were their allies. They made up the so-called silent majority (*masa neutra*, "neutral masses") who longed for the power and the means to produce the economic, political, and social liberation of Cuba. This organization would be named *Agrupación Revolucionaria Programa Estudiantil* (Revolutionary Student Program Association), better known in the small circle that conceived the idea by its acronym, ARPE.

The programmatic document was actually drafted in July 1933, when neither the general strike, nor the Communist Party's deal with the dictator, nor the military putsch that finally toppled Machado, had occurred. By then, the Directorio felt that it had enough time to be able, by its own means and at its own risk, to topple the regime, but this time under the ideological doctrine defined in the very document that they themselves had presented to Cuba.

First of all, though, it is important to note that this Manifesto Program has two dates. The first, of course, is July 1933, when the Directorio's objectives were determined; the other is August 22, 1933 (Padrón Larrazábal 1975, 157-72). Why should the same document have two dates? Simply, because the initial section of the document, that extensive portion which includes the Program, was adopted in July 1933; but since the members of the Directorio were still scattered across the country and abroad, the process of obtaining signatures was prolonged. Then, the printing which should have occurred in secret was delayed by the general strike and the other events that followed. The document, therefore, appeared openly ten days after the fall of the dictatorship, rather than earlier in clandestine form, and gave due credit to the printer, Imprenta Marta Abreu 37, in Havana.

The fact that those difficulties delayed the publication of the document allowed the DEU time to evaluate the developments and, overall, appraise what had not occurred. This permitted the members then to express an opinion concerning the huge gaps in terms of unfulfilled expectations produced by the Céspedes government, and at the same time allowed them to call on the government to adopt the DEU's recommendations that lacked nothing more than their implementation.

In order to analyze the programmatic aspect of the document properly, I must provide the actual text of the Directorio's "first objective:"

> Organization of the armed insurrection against the Tyranny, until the hordes of unprincipled politicians on which it rests are beaten and annihilated. With that aim, such procedures and methods shall be implemented as they opportunely present themselves.

In those two simple sentences, the DEU declared that it would organize the insurrection and announce the implementation of procedures and measures as they presented themselves; namely the organization of the *Agrupación Revolucionaria Programa Estudiantil* (ARPE). The DEU never got around to doing so, though, since the precipitous fall of the tyranny impeded implementation of those proposals, as we shall see shortly.

I submit that there are circumstances that probably must be experienced by all peoples; circumstances that are given with certainty within all the twists of history; circumstances in which they who, with a careful eye to the future, map out routes and, in some cases, go so far as to encourage means in order to reach the best ends. Sometimes, those intentions are frustrated upon the convergence of the routes, means, and objectives, or because totally unforeseen factors arise to confound the plans. Thus, the accomplishment of the optimum results are impeded by events previously set into motion.

That was, precisely, the case with the Directorio and its projected ARPE. If the DEU could have detained history, or perhaps delayed it a little, the unchaining of the Cuban destiny could have been different. If Machado had remained in power only a few months more, the DEU might have been able to group together beneath its banners or, more precisely, under its ideological slogans, the great majorities in the nation that openly identified with its ideological program.

If by some magic power the Machado government could have held on a little longer, then it would have been the Directorio itself, under its slogans and with the open support of the Cuban populace, that toppled the tyranny. Perhaps the victory would have been accomplished in alliance with the young officers of the army, with whom there was, if not a complete ideological affinity, at the very least complete agreement in their vocation to serve their country and in their recognition of the need to purify the Cuban public arena. If this young group of officers had "gotten on board" with the aforementioned proposals, the popular backing would have given them such spiritual satisfaction that they could have overcome the ingrained conservativism of their military training and career indoctrination.

Unfortunately, the Mediation process and the decision of the Cuban populace to carry forward the total and absolute general strike unleashed the events, precipitating them in an accelerated form.

As I mentioned before, I was abroad at the time of change in the tempo of the process, and under the inspiration of Emilio Laurent, the principal inventor of the ARPE concept, we had decided to embark clandestinely for Cuba and produce an event that would alone be capable of provoking the fall of the regime. Emilio Laurent planned that we would embark for Cuba with all the arms and equipment that we could collect. Once within our national territory, we would occupy the University of Havana. Once there, we would sequester several prestigious professors and would entrench ourselves, creating a center of subversion and rebellion. Emilio Laurent understood that if we could pull it off, the army officers who would be ordered to destroy our center of rebellion would simply have to disobey the orders, and in that juncture the understanding between students and military officers would inevitably become a determining factor in the downfall of the dictatorship. With that objective, we were able to stockpile in Miami some thirty thousand .30-caliber bullets, five thousand .45-caliber bullets for Thompson machine guns, five Browning machine guns, four Thompson machine guns, eleven automatic rifles, five regular rifles, two special rifles, and an assortment of cartridge belts and other war accessories. This was the largest and most effective war matériel cache to arrive in Cuba since the 1931 Gibara expedition.

Separate cars carrying all this matériel left for Key West in the early morning of August 10, 1933, and on that same morning Laurent dispatched a special courier to Cuba bearing a secret document to his former fellow officers of the army. With everything arranged, we set out at intervals starting late on August 10 and continuing through the morning of August 11, filtering down to Key West, from whence we were to embark immediately for Cuba. The group included Emilio Laurent, his brother Delfín, José Morell Romero, Manuel Rogelio Alvarez Bacallao, Edgardo Buttari, Rafael de Jesús Iglesias, Juan Antonio Rubio Padilla, Emilio Fernández, Cándido (Pu Yi) Durán, Gonzalo de Varona, and myself, Justo Carrillo.

Before leaving Key West, we spent a few hours trying to familiarize ourselves with that variety of armament and learn how to use it all. Laurent, meanwhile, studied maps of the University campus to determine the best sites for emplacement of the automatic weapons. While Emilio was planning the assault operation — since at that point we did not know that the troops occupying the University had been withdrawn a few days before — a small plane arrived to pick him up and return him to the seditious labors that were under way in Havana and which set up the fall of the Machado government. But Laurent arrived too late. The rest of us — that is to say, those who immediately set out in a motorboat laden with all the arms and equipment — unfortunately ran adrift in sight of the coast of the island, and when we finally made it ashore, the dictator was already a fugitive and our action, consequently, would not take place.

THE ARPE PROGRAM (THE DEU DOCUMENT)

With the fall of Machado, the warlike ARPE project ceased to exist, even though the program itself did not. The Directorio now had a different adversary: the Mediation government of Sumner Welles. We shall see how that was addressed in the historic document of August 22, just four days before Sergio Carbo's call to arms in *La Semana*.

In order to understand clearly the scope of this penultimate document published before the DEU seized power — a power they themselves did not know awaited them just fourteen days hence — I will summarize as superficially as possible the three most important aspects of the most transcendental pronouncement during the interregnum from August 12 to September 4, 1933. Those three aspects were as follows:

1. Ideological definition;
2. Pressure on the Céspedes government to become a de facto government and analysis of the deceptive solution given to the national crisis on August 12; and
3. The appeal to the armed forces to embrace the revolutionary program of the young people of Cuba.

I shall begin, then, with the analysis of the ideological definition, which would have to be orchestrated in the provisional government the DEU then aspired to implement. In that aspect of the document, the DEU listed as its second objective the establishment of a provisional government,

> formed of persons that the Directorio Estudiantil Universitario shall select and nominate for the purpose of carrying out its program. . . .

In this very text, the DEU already committed a philosophical and historic error. The DEU was both more self-assured and more sure of its historic function within Cuban destiny. It believed it must augment its power and that, as it became more powerful, its influence on the process of change within the State inevitably would grow.

At the same time, the Directorio had evolved from a purely student organization into an instrument of the revolutionary battle which aspired to provoke no less than an essential change in the direction and quality of the Cuban political system, through transformations that we are about to study. But, even from the beginning of its activities, the DEU was branded as "political" by the sympathizers of the regime and by the columnists and reporters aligned with Machado who defended that regime.

Also, Mediation supporters harshly criticized the members of the DEU, calling them "perturbers by duty, with whom it is not possible to reach an agreement." It is logical, therefore, that the Directorio would want to guard against all possible vulnerability in respect to its true intentions.

Because of those considerations, the Directorio incurred the tremendous error of aspiring to power so that, upon assuming it, the DEU could promptly delegate it. It is clear that the Directorio aspiration to establish a provisional government, staffed by people that it itself "shall select and nominate," proved authentically that the Directorio did not want to exercise the power directly. This statement makes clear that the members of the DEU did not aspire to any public office, as they would later demonstrate in the period during which they indirectly became the "power," and that the purpose that drove them was that of passing on the exercise of power to people that they would select. With all that, the Directorio was falling into self-exclusion in terms of its aptitude for governing directly, in order to interpret and bring about the very program it had devised and written. In this political philosophy error were sown the seeds of the penance the DEU would later suffer. It is a fine example of selflessness and, at the same time, it is the abandonment of the responsibilities that historically belonged to the Directorio. The phrase from the document, ". . . *the student body of Cuba, which from the first moment manifested its intention not to occupy positions in the new government . . .* " encourages the highest regard, but also permits the interpretation that they failed to assume the minimum — as well as the maximum — role that history demanded of them: that of exercising power instead of delegating it.

Now entering the study of the program, and to limit my remarks about it, I shall try to summarize the titles and contents of its distinct chapters.

In regard to the Executive Power, the DEU maintained that this should be exercised by five commissioners equal in function and authority. The Directorio had been influenced in this proposal by the experiment of the Eastern Republic of Uruguay, a country that had come to be regarded as an example among the other republics of the continent, and which the Cuban people considered a symbol of democratic beauty and functionalism. This attitude was determined by the fact that what the Directorio feared most was the effects of *caudillismo*. The members had learned of the evils of *caudillismo* through their Ibero-American readings, which contained such salient quotations as "The independence of Latin America was the last day of despotism and the first one of the same." They were also well aware of the evils that Cuba had undergone at the hands of José Miguel Gómez, Mario García Menocal, and Gerardo Machado. The DEU found no better formula to avert that menace than to create a collective Executive Power. This proposal, born exclusively in the sanctum of the DEU, had already been suggested by its members before the Cuban Opposition Junta of New York. This body, in the third condition expounded in its document of April 1933, had suggested the constitution of a provisional government consisting of nine persons.

In regard to the Legislative Branch, the DEU proposed a council of twenty-five citizens whose function would be to elaborate projects and laws on bases formulated by the Collective Executive Commission. The councilmen would receive a compensation of $20 per session, but in no case were their emoluments to exceed $300 monthly.

In regard to punishment of those guilty of crimes committed during the ill-omened era of the tumbled regime, the Directorio favored the establishment of a Court of Punitive Sanctions, whose five members, like those of the Legislative Council, would be selected from a list presented by the Directorio Estudiantil. Among the duties of this Court would be that of determining the guilt or innocence of authorities, functionaries, and public employees; it, thus, assumed the governmental functions of the Supreme Court. They would judge and remove from office even the Executive Commissioners, the legislative councilmen, and the delegates to the Constituent Assembly whenever there should arise a case against them. Finally, they would organize the judicial aspects of the transition until the end of the Transitional Government. The magistrates of the Court of Punitive Sanctions were themselves answerable to the Constituent Assembly.

In regard to the Constituent Assembly, the DEU proposed that this body should be convened within ninety days following the promulgation of the Electoral Law, which was to spell out all the requisites concerning the election and duties of the delegates. It specified that no member of the Constituent Assembly could accept a nomination for any public elective office until six years after the end of his post in the

Assembly. The delegates to the convention would only receive remuneration for their attendance at the sessions, and that could in no case exceed $300 monthly. The assembly would approve whatever laws were deemed necessary to complete the reforms the Constitution itself would establish. The delegates' terms would not exceed a year and a half, and they would be answerable to the Court of Punitive Sanctions.

Later in its program, the Directorio would establish the immediate goals of the Constituent Assembly as well as the means to achieve them. It went further into a number of other aspects, but there is no need to detail them here.

In regard to Agrarian Policy, the Executive Commission was obligated to implement legislation establishing land distribution and ownership rights. Among the proposed legislation was to make Cuban citizenship a requirement for the acquisition of rural property in excess of five *caballerías* (some 165.8 acres). It would, likewise, require that from then on companies and corporations could not acquire rural property unless they were based in Cuba and registered under the laws of the Cuban state. Thus, foreign enterprises that had been operating without restrictions would finally be subject to Cuban sovereignty and law. A progressive tax of 10 to 50 percent was to be imposed on rural estates larger than five *caballerías*. Anyone owning more than one hundred *caballerías* was prohibited from acquiring more property. Expropriation for public utility use was authorized in the case of owners of more than five hundred *caballerías*. A survey was to be made of all public lands and of expropriations realized in order to determine future reclamations. The Executive Commission would also create a Land Redemption Fund, specifying the distinct source of resources with which the new institution would be funded. The ultimate goal of this measure was to create a law of land distribution to Cuban citizens in lots not exceeding five *caballerías,* with fixed limitations and conditions of use. The properties would be bought at low interest and in no less than thirty annual installments. The Executive Commission was at the same time required to produce a law creating the Agricultural Bank, whose main purpose would be to provide financial resources to farmers for the exploitation of their lands and the acquisition of agricultural tools and equipment.[17]

The program further stated that the Executive Commission was to declare illegal, as being contrary to the national interest, all those contracts for sugar cane processing or plantation farming known as "by administration," and penalties were to be established for violators. With this particular measure, the Directorio intended to put an end to the total monopoly imposed by big companies throughout all phases of the industrial sugar cane process.

During that time, the North American sugar-processing enterprises were not only owners of the factories and all related industrial facilities but, in order to increase their profit margins, they also owned the cane that these facilities would process. This meant that these foreign companies absorbed every cent of profit from the entire process: they produced the raw sugar cane, thus deriving profits normally spent on the purchase of the raw material; then, upon producing the sugar, they derived profits from the conversion of the agricultural product into an industrial product. Furthermore, the American companies also owned and controlled all commercial activities on the sugar cane plantations as well. Agricultural and industrial workers had to buy their necessities in company-owned stores at prices fixed by the companies. Moreover, salaries were paid not in cash or checks but in tokens valid only at these company-owned stores at rates fixed by the companies.[18] It can easily be understood that this was a closed circuit of goods and maximum exploitation of the sector that these North American companies exercised. The system held a likeness to the employers in some other South American countries, where they called it "the screw" or "the nut."

This legislation completed the agrarian reform by addressing the regulation of cane pressing contracts in the cases of the individual cane growers known historically as *colonos*; thus, in reference to agricultural restitution, and with the object of protecting the interests of the farmer, it declared unattachable minimum lots of land, the homes, and the farming implements and the draft animals of the *campesinos* (farmers and other rural workers).

At the same time, the Executive Commission was directed to initiate studies concerning the establishment of a National Bank, the money itself, a National Mint, and the Institute of Currency Issuance. This section ended with considerations about the possible nationalization of the sugar industry as well as the mining industry ". . . and others that should be essential to national development." It was, as always, taken for granted that the public utilities of electricity and telephone service would have to be nationalized.

Even though it will seem to some people — probably to the landowners still living and the big foreign sugar tycoons of that time — that some of the Directorio's programmatic pronouncements were too moderate and others excessively radical. The reality is that now, through the perspective of history that time offers, no one of either opinion nowadays can deny that a program such as this, in terms of agrarian policy fifty years ago, was one of the most advanced and far-reaching of those which could have been adopted under those circumstances. If only those recommended provisions had been put into effect at least in the course of two successive administrations, we could have realized — then — the dream of the Chilean Christian Democrats thirty years later; that is, the creation and settlement of one hundred thousand farmers as proprietors of their own lands. One hundred thousand farmers, when the total Cuban population was barely three million, would have given way to a later agrarian policy that would have created permanent pressure for the land distribution program and, as a result, in a quarter of a century, the disparities in land distribution would have been minimal in comparison with the rest of Latin America.

In regard to Public Finances, the Directorio favored the adjustment of the tax system according to the contributing capacity of the population. The income tax was to be determined on scientific criteria, reducing or altogether eliminating tariffs on articles of vital necessity, and in general imposing a fiscal policy of social programs.

In regard to Social Programs, the Directorio commissioned the provisional government to exert itself toward the rapid reduction of illiteracy, with preferential attention to the rural schools; and toward the implementation of technical secondary education so that those without the means or the opportunity to pursue a superior education could avail themselves of a craft or professional preparation in other fields. It proposed also the elevation of the obligatory school age to eighteen years and the adaptation of the buildings and grounds of Modelo Penitentiary on the Isle of Pines for technical and compulsory education. Also in this section, the DEU proposed the modernization of prison facilities, demanded that the direction of those facilities be placed in the hands of individuals with recognized competence in psychiatry and criminology, and provided for the creation of a Jails and Prisons Commission.

Special care was to be taken for the protection of the working woman, and child labor would be prohibited. Immediate steps were to be taken toward the enactment and enforcement of the eight-hour workday, minimum wage, overtime payment, accident insurance, unemployment insurance, and a workers' pension plan. (It should be pointed out that all retirement and insurance pension funds created between 1940 and 1950 were inspired by this pronouncement.)

Immigration would be regulated in accordance with Cuban interests, and special attention was to be given to the improvement of sanitary conditions of the needy classes, the reorganization of hospitals, asylums, nursing homes, and orphanages and the creation of new dispensaries, clinics, and sanitariums, hygienic assistance to the peasant population, and the elimination of urban slums and shantytowns. Finally, as one way to alleviate the problem of unemployment, an extensive public works plan was contemplated. This plan would include sewage systems, canals, irrigation projects, public buildings such as new penitentiaries, schools, hospitals, asylums and refuges, and whatever other projects should prove to be of public benefit or urgency.

In regard to Foreign Policy, the Directorio stated that one of the basic functions of the Constituent Assembly was to annul the so-called Platt Amendment. It is interesting to note that, both in the documents against the Mediation and in this document several months later, the Directorio never considered any alternative to the annulment of the Platt Amendment. It was as though the DEU had assumed that, if an opinion poll were taken, 100 percent of the interviewed would support this requirement which, I permit myself to repeat, was more than an arbitrary imposition. This conviction was based on the opinion that, since there were no coercive groups capable of requiring the "amendment" imposed by the United States in 1901, there would not be a Cuban delegate to a Constituent Assembly elected by the people who would be capable of defending it.

Later, the DEU would go further in this position and demand that the Provisional Government denounce the Reciprocity Treaty with the United States, suggesting in its place a more equitable mutual agreement and the intensification of economic relations with Canada. As for Latin America, looking ahead at least two decades to what became the concept and policy of integration of communities of common origin and destiny, the Directorio proposed the stimulation of a greater identification of moral, cultural, and economic interests with Latin American countries.

AUGUST 22: THE DAY OF CONFRONTATION

B efore continuing with the analysis of this historic manifesto, I would first like to describe the mental state of the country on the day this document was published — this day of confrontation between highly contradictory forces — so that we may place ourselves in the general scene of this special historic crossroad.

Ten days had passed since President Machado's flight to Nassau. On this day, August 22, two men, Colonels Carlos Mendieta and Roberto Méndez Peñate, arrived in Cuba. They had been, along with the 1927 Directorio Estudiantil, the first antagonists of the Machado regime; they founded the *Asociación Unión Nacionalista* (Nationalist Union Association, AUN). Now they were the last to return from exile. They had participated in the Mediation and their political organization had ministers representing their aims in the Céspedes cabinet; consequently, they had returned to support the Mediation government. Their reception, because of the general discontent with traditional politicians and the Mediation government, had been extremely poor. I went to observe it: there were two hundred people to greet them.

Also on the morning of this fateful day, President Céspedes corresponded with Ambassador Welles, upon whom he planned to confer the highest decoration of the Republic of Cuba, which just happened to carry the name of Céspedes' own father, after whom he himself had been named. That name had produced, perhaps, the psychologically understandable impression that the award was also a little bit "his." He had awarded it profusely when he was Secretary of State for presidents Zayas and Machado. Now, as president of the Republic, he signed Decree number 817, on August 22, which stated:

> I CARLOS MANUEL DE CESPEDES, President of the Republic,
>
> LET IT BE KNOWN THAT:
>
> In accordance with the powers vested in me by Article 111 of Decree Number 486 of 18 April 1926, I have the pleasure to bestow on His Excellency Mister Sumner Welles, Ambassador Extraordinary and Plenipotentiary of the United States of America, the degree of the Great Cross of the "Carlos Manuel de Céspedes" National Order of Merit.

Ambassador Welles, who already had similar Latin American medals and decorations, felt the exhilaration and the satisfaction that is naturally experienced by those who enjoy showing off with multitudes of miniature medals on their evening jackets at diplomatic functions. Nevertheless, and perhaps to his surprise, the decree had not been sent for publication in the *Official Gazette*. Considering the frontal assault proposed by the Directorio Estudiantil Universitario document published on that very same day, as we are yet to see, President Céspedes preferred to "cubbyhole" the decree. Later, neither the Pentarchy nor Grau San Martín considered it proper to make it official. It was only reconsidered, a bit late, when Carlos Mendieta assumed the presidency. In the end, the award decree would be published in the *Official Gazette* on March 23, 1934, seven months later.

Also on that very same date, August 22, 1933, Ambassador Welles informed his government:

> I have repeatedly emphasized in all my conversations with these leaders and with the leaders of the groups and parties represented in the present Government that only through the maintenance of a constitutional form of government in Cuba until the next national elections would it be possible for the Government to make effective the urgent measures required to improve economic conditions here as well as the financial situation of the Government itself and in addition thereto to take steps to ensure the satisfactory result of the next elections through the enactment of a new electoral code and through the passage of constitutional reforms to be submitted to a constituent assembly (Welles Cable 180, August 22, 1933, 370).

If this was the opinion the North American Ambassador held on August 22, what was Céspedes thinking? The President of the Republic on that same day made the following declaration, which was published in that day's edition of *El País*:

> I need a Congress in these moments, since it is necessary to consider the laws that must be approved promptly, such as those of Constitutional reform, electoral reform, university autonomy, the "American" loan, and the conversion of the debt, among other laws.

This sounded like a carbon copy of what Welles said, but the president's declaration was more concrete and precise. The Mediation government proposed to carry out an "American" loan and consolidate the debt with the United States. Welles had disguised it in his declarations as the need "to improve . . . the financial situation of the Government itself." Those plans would be impeded by the revolutionary coup on September 4.

And finally, on that fateful day, the Mediation government published its plan to prevent military coup. In Decree 1262 of August 22, President Céspedes ordered that retired army and navy personnel be recalled to service as the Secretary of War and the Navy deemed necessary during any time that constitutional guarantees may be suspended, or if there existed a state of public unrest. With the Chief of Staff of the Army, Colonel Julio Sanguily, sick, with various lieutenant colonels imprisoned because of grave accusations of crimes and repressions against the people, and debilitated by the popular rejection of other high-ranking officers, the transition government could neither retire nor promote anyone without recalling retired officers who had absolutely no ties with the body of soldiers. Ultimately, however, this policy actually assisted the sergeants' insubordination and facilitated the Sergeants' Coup.

To sum it up: on August 22, ten days after General Machado's departure for the Bahamas, Colonels Mendieta and Méndez Peñate returned from exile; they, receiving a minuscule reception, "felt" more than "knew" that they were too late to be a part of the "historic moment." Also on August 22, President Céspedes awarded his protector, Ambassador Welles, the highest rank of the Great Cross, a medal that carried the name of the Father of the Country, President Céspedes's father. Also on August 22 — a day of seemingly definitive positions for the transitional government — Ambassador Welles, on the one hand, and President Céspedes on the other, declared that it was necessary to maintain the Congress, and also on August 22 a decree was signed to return retired officers of the land and sea forces to active service.

THE DEU CHALLENGES THE GOVERNMENT

Now I return to the Directorio Manifesto issued on that ominous historic date to show how, in its demands to the Mediation government, the students' leadership organization began to govern even before assuming power.

In this document the DEU declared:

> After the military coup perpetrated the past 12 August, at the suggestion of Ambassador Welles, the Republic still has not recovered as had been hoped and demanded by the needs of the nation, to a truly revolutionary juridical status.
>
> On the contrary, the Provisional Government, a product of the Mediation with the assistance of the Army, persists in giving to its situation and to all its actions a legal character that is far from being real or legitimate, and manages to ignore all who try by revolutionary means to replace the old with the new.
>
> If we ignored that the Provisional Government was a product previously manufactured in the diplomatic recesses of the American embassy, we would be quite surprised at this acquiescent attitude in terms of Machadist pettifoggery — incompatible with the revolutionary ideology displayed in their respective programs — of certain groups that until now had been held as extreme radicals.[19]
>
> But since we know of all that, and recognize, furthermore, the yankees' scruples at acknowledging revolutions and likewise their disinvolvement in sponsoring them, it explains to us this strong urge of the President and his cabinet to act only within the Constitution, even though they themselves have so many times declared this Constitution to be a product of a *de facto* regime.[20] On the other hand, can this government in truth boast of carrying on its duties within the frame of the law? In a transfer of power like what has taken place these last days among Machado, Herrera, and Dr. Céspedes, in an inauguration ceremony with less than half the quorum, is there any room for speaking of constitutional compliance?
>
> The provisional regime shies away from becoming a revolutionary *de facto* government and lets Congress, the judiciary, the governors, and the mayors remain in their positions. The coup d'etat, therefore, has overthrown Machado but, because of constitutional scruples, has refused to demolish the Machadato, and is waiting for it to fall on its own (Padrón 1975, 157-72).

The Directorio immediately went on to make the following pronouncements:

> The high commanders that used to issue orders, protected by the favor of the mediator Welles, have been able to leave the country unmolested, carrying in their coffers portions of the Public Treasury and only leaving behind, well-safe-guarded by the authorities, the sumptuous mansions they built with the people's money.

> The way this Cabinet of concentration has been formed . . . leads one to think that the basic program of the opposition representatives that now form the Government has been the distribution and enjoyment of positions in the new Administration.

> We, the Cuban students, who from the very first moments of the struggle have maintained our goal of not accepting positions in the new government, . . . demand the total· extirpation of the Machadato.

> The bases on which the new government has been built do not satisfy the aspirations of the Youth, which demands in the affairs of public life changes more substantial than those proposed by the provisional regime constructed . . . representing a political system that, even as it tolls its end, still remains dormant and willing to demonstrate all the defects of the past.

And in the final paragraphs of the extensive document, the Directorio states:

> If the Armed Forces of the Republic, who have rebelled against the Machado tyranny, limit their action to the single purpose of overthrowing a despotic Government and ignore the civic demands of a young generation which has amply earned its right to accomplish an *authentically revolutionary program*, [emphasis added] that generation will consider itself defrauded in its dearest ideals.

Here, for the second time, appears the concept of revolutionary *authenticity*. ("Make way for the Authentic Revolution" quickly became a political slogan.)

If the National Army, for so many years marked by Public Opinion as the support and bastion of Dictatorship in Cuba, does not adopt a truly revolutionary attitude, bringing about the fulfillment of the program of the new generation, their labor until this very moment can be considered less than nothing. If the men of arms do not embrace the revolutionary program of the Youth, they will feed the belief that their attitude in these moments responds to the same motivations that until yesterday were imputed to their conduct. If they do not tear down what is obsolete nor cooperate with the Youth to establish the republic on a solid foundation, then they will not be able to elude their responsibility for all the abuses that until a short time ago they continued to commit.

The men of arms of our Homeland until a few days ago were the object of popular rejection.

To what extent each member of the Army is responsible for this condemnation on the part of the Public Opinion is a point that for the moment we do not propose to determine.[21] But it is fitting that we put on record that the exculpation of the Armed Forces can only occur when they prove by their deeds that they are not some mere supporters of whomever might be at the top.

If the rebellion carried out by the most distinguished military commanders at the friendly injunction of Mr. Welles, backed in good faith by the sound and pure portion of the Cuban Army, is not supported by a dignified and valiant revolutionary attitude, the National Army will remain before history with the graceless role of those who support, right or wrong, those who represent power at a given moment. The Army, if it does not even take the first step of the action to which it is morally obligated, will remain marked by the finger of today's Youth as a body of individuals ready to serve only whomever may come along backed by the power of the North.[22]

The Directorio, therefore, makes an appeal to those sound and pure elements within the present military movement, in order to gain for themselves the exculpation and the sincere applause of the Youth, and being true interpreters

of popular expectations, to demand the immediate implementation of the revolutionary student program, the only
one called, by virtue of the principles in which it is
sustained, to mold in reality the free Republic, prosperous
and happy, to which aspire those who love Cuba with all
their hearts.

Now, having signed the document of power seizure on September
4, 1933, together with the other nine members of the Directorio that at
that time signed public pronouncements, attempting now, after fifty
years, to analyze this process in which I participated, I can now see that
the dramatic appeal to the armed forces offers a certain inherent
philosophical contradiction. This contradiction appears specifically in
the phrases, ". . . backed in good faith by the sound and pure portion
of the Cuban Army" and "The Directorio, therefore, makes an appeal
to those sound and pure elements within the present military movement."

When interpreted revolutionarily, the appeal to the young officers
to unite with the civilian youth who heroically battled for public
liberties and launched a program in favor of the great masses of the
nation implied, for right or wrong, the most difficult of ideological and
democratic choices. Is this call to the armed forces, to the most "sound
and pure elements," to subscribe to a determined ideological agenda
not in conflict with the principle of apoliticism of the armed forces, with
its obligatory respect for popular decisions? To respond to this question
would require a separate book because of that profound essence of the
democratic concept of military professionalism, the nondeliberative
and nonpolitical character of the armed forces of a nation.

In spite of my own antimilitarism, and not expecting their favor,
I offer as the best positive example none other than Ataturk of Turkey;
I believe that most countries intuitively understand the ideological
routes to their well-being and that their military officialdom must rely,
within their own academic formation, on the intimate knowledge of the
economic, political, and social problems whose solutions are the
essence of their very national identity. An optimum national ideal, with
international and democratic objectives above and beyond sectarian-
ism and partisanship, must permanently develop a supreme program
that would seek to reach the ultimate destiny of a nation, even though
this program might come to be supranational in its advancement
toward the goals of integration that could supersede limiting nationalisms.

CONVERSATIONS WITH THE MILITARY SECTOR

I have said earlier that during this period of only twenty-three days there had occurred five episodes that filled it with historic gravity; I have examined four of those episodes, leaving only the conversations that occurred between young army officers and several members of the DEU. Those conversations more or less involved a very few Directorio members, some fighters with common ties with the DEU, and members of the recently arisen organizations *Pro Ley y Justicia* (For Law and Justice), who also carried on with several army sergeants and soldiers.

When I pointed out certain phrases from the highly accusatory Directorio text, I did so to emphasize that it was the express will of the DEU to realize an alliance with the officers from the military academy. That same determination will stand out again in the analysis of the September 4 coup. Nevertheless, at this point, I must underline that the Directorio was very conscious that there existed, within the armed forces, officers with the same type of personal conviction felt by the majority of the DEU's members; simply stated, it was their will to serve the country that went above and beyond personal interest, shaded by the true technical professionalism of their military career, after having suffered personally the tragic scenes enacted during the dictatorial regime.

Likewise, the Directorio, in working with the pro-Directorio Lieutenant Emilio Laurent, recognized the existence of this exemplary type of officer. Since some of us were close friends with some of those officers, the result, of course, followed logically: conversations occurred and possibilities were considered involving the joint realization of some kind of historic decision. Retrospectively analyzing this aspect, I would now add that the sense of obedience to command, perhaps subconsciously, would always impede the execution of what some of us proposed. Unfortunately, there existed another — now identifiable — incompatibility that then neither they nor we perceived. Even though these officers wanted to serve Cuba, as much as would the best member of the Directorio, they lacked within themselves two basic requirements for absolute integration with the sensibility and the ideological program of the DEU: on the one hand, the emotional force of an ardent struggle, converted to passion, carried into a cause; and on the other hand, the political formation evolved toward an ideological radicalization that, lived daily through analysis and reading, had converted the Directorio into a solid historic antagonist of the government of the United States, the most firm supporter in its time — at least, until Roosevelt took office — of the Machado regime.

Two essential differences, then, made very difficult a true understanding at heart: the different emotional tensions felt by the revolutionary fighter and the purely military officer who, through his own sense of professionalism, has maintained himself expressly distant from the public agitation; and our different levels of political culture. Furthermore, these political levels, although limited in the members of the Directorio to monothematic understandings based on shared events, had gained special force as the student leaders enjoyed the advice of men given to daily study of social and political issues, such as the jurist José Miguel Irisarri. On the other hand, professional officers had not received in the Military Academy of Morro any other cultural formation beyond the strictly technical training of the militia. But that does not stop me from giving historic testimony to the extraordinary good faith of those men and at the same time recognizing the honor they merit for the difficulty that the contradiction between personal conviction and military discipline caused them.

Of course, these meetings never were of an official nature, nor did they count on the presence of all the DEU members. They were of the most unofficial nature on our part, inasmuch as those conversations signified the recognition of the existence of distinct moral hierarchies within the armed forces. These men were exactly the "sound and pure portion of the Cuban Army" to which we referred in the document of August 22, the same as those "pure elements within the present military movement" whom the Directorio excluded personally and specifically from responsibility for the actions of the army as a whole.

Those meetings, of which there must have been two or three, took place during the second half of August at the residence of Doctor Gustavo Cuervo Rubio at the corner of Twenty-First Street and O in Vedado, Havana. The officers who participated in those meetings were Captains Carlos Montero, Enrique Varona (son of the philosopher Enrique José), Lieutenants Carlos Valdés Fauli Montagú, Manuel Federico (Freddy) Goudie, Miguel Angel Gonzales Parra, Pedro Morfi Linares, Rafael Galeano Herrera, Raúl Suárez Bermúdez, and Ricardo Adam Silva. They were new men who, against their true feelings of military loyalty, met with the most radical wing of the revolutionary democratic movement against Machado, to try to articulate a joint action of service to the country. In those meetings we never got to the point of adopting an agreement or a decision, but it was understood that there existed basic elements for a possible identification in common efforts that, unfortunately, were not accomplished in the historic order of things, because of the aforementioned reasons and the precipitous events that later occurred.

At the same time, in several of the many Directorio meetings that occurred during that tempestuous period, someone (naturally, a member of the Directorio) made reference to conversations with some sergeants of the army. It could have been Ramiro Valdés Daussá, or "Pepelín" Leyva (José Leyva Gordil), or perhaps Juan Febles Secretal, the only members who maintained close contact with the *Pro Ley y Justicia* group, although without having requested nor much less obtained authorization officially to join that rebellious group that arose scant days before the fall of Machado. Nonetheless, it is necessary to mention that undoubtedly, for the DEU, true importance was attached only to the conversations with the young officers rather than to the conversations that could have been conducted between the elements of *Pro Ley y Justicia* and some sergeants of the army whose extremely limited educational and political formations we had recognized in prison, where many members of the DEU had lived together with the only truly revolutionary enlisted men that had conspired against Machado.

Of course, none of the members of that group of sergeants and soldiers had the least knowledge of the political existence of Sergeant Batista, who, at that time, was nothing more than the privileged stenographic sergeant who served in the courts-martial against those persecuted by the Machado dictatorship.

THE DEU PRESSURES THE MEDIATION GOVERNMENT

While these two sets of conversations were taking place, neither of which would come to terms on a single formality, the agitation in the streets continued until Welles himself, who on August 13 had told Washington that the situation in the cities was much more satisfactory, now recognized — on August 24 — that on the Island "a general process of disintegration is going on" (Welles Cable 184, August 24, 1933, 371).

And on this very same date, the Céspedes government, pressured by the Directorio's demands just forty-eight hours before, came to realize a little too late what had already happened. Céspedes issued a decree which in appearance only satisfied the demands of the DEU, still the only revolutionary organization not included in the power structure and still challenging that structure. As always in traditional politics, though, Céspedes conceded (with a pair of cards up his sleeve — one to serve the interests of the North American financial capital, and the other hidden within the call for general elections within six months) in order to assure eventually the total and indefinite control of power for the members of the provisional government.

The Directorio triumphed 48 hours after the confrontation, when the caretaker of the official arena, Ambassador Welles, communicated to his government on August 24 that "my original hope that the present Government of Cuba could govern as a constitutional government for the remainder of the term for which General Machado had himself elected must be abandoned" (Welles Cable 184, August 24, 1933, 371).

A year later, the Foreign Policy Association, after nine of its members had spent several months in Cuba, said this about the decree:

> The adoption of the 1901 Constitution, combined with the effects of the composition of the Céspedes government and the circumstances in which it was born, did not satisfy the revolutionary sentiment that had spread throughout the Island, not only in the intellectual and political elites of Havana but in the masses of workers in the country as well, where radical strikes began to sprout. The revolutionary spirit appeared to demand more drastic and exciting changes that would do away with the brutalities of the Machado regime and the misery and the corruption produced by the old political system. And that same revolutionary spirit, dipped, too, in hot-headed nationalism, was protesting also against the United States mediation, of which the Céspedes government was a product (Commission of Cuban Affairs 1935, 15-16).

Professor Peter Frederick Krogh commented: "The decree abolishing the 1928 Constitution was a major step toward the elimination of the old regime that the political opposition to Machado, the young generation in particular, had been demanding since the outset. The decree was evidently a concession to the popular clamor. But this concession was granted at the cost of a fatal breach in the dam of constitutional government and without the compensating assurance that the breach would close in by itself once the popular clamor for sweeping reforms had died down" (Krogh 1966, 287).

Obviously, the Foreign Policy Association and Professor Krogh agreed that the decree was not popularly satisfying, nor did it pacify the agitation, even though they did not analyze the continued rejection the Directorio voiced in its own decree. The Directorio, in turn, echoed of the opinion of nearly all of Cuba and had maintained the agitation prior to the decree.

I intend, therefore, to analyze that continued rejection, starting from the decree itself. The preamble of Decree 1298 interprets in a practical manner, though from a unique political and constitutional point of view, the arbitrarinesses the Machado regime had exercised.

The Decree itself read:

Whereas the Congress of the Republic in the exercise of the powers established in article 115 of the constitution re-solved by the law of June 21st, 1927 to amend certain provisions of the constitution;

Whereas in the call of the election for delegates of the constitutional convention the laws by virtue of which the reorganization of political parties had been prohibited remained in force as well as that prohibiting the organiza-tion of new parties and other laws were enacted prohibiting the presentation of independent candidatures all of which legal provisions had no object other than to carry into effect the amendment to the constitution with absolute disregard of the popular will inasmuch as *the electors opposed to said amendment were not able to elect delegates to aforesaid constituttonal convention* [emphasis added] in manifest infringement of article 38 of the constitution which recog-nized the right of suffrage to all Cubans over 21 years of age;

Whereas, the constitutional convention elected to that effect did not limit its acts to the approval or disapproval of the amendment voted by Congress in accordance with the provisions of article 115 of the constitution above-cited but overstepping its authority proceeded to change certain provisions of the law which contained the amendment;

Whereas, one of the provisions which was the one of modification was that by virtue of which the presidential term of office which should have expired on May 20, 1929, was extended for two years to May 20, 1931, and which, furthermore, prohibited the reelection of the President of the Republic then in office, the change consisting in permitting said chief executive to be reelected for the next presidential term;

Whereas, on May 11, 1928, the amendment of the constitution was promulgated by the President of the Republic, the same containing as has been said important changes in the text of the law which had been voted and passed by Congress;

Whereas, in the emergency electoral law of July 20, 1928, a series of provisions were included tending to assure the reelection of the person who at the time held the Presidency of the Republic and at the same time to prevent the presentation of other candidates for the same office which objects were achieved with absolute disregard of the popular will;

Whereas, the Supreme Court of Justice *en banc* in several decisions handed down in writs of unconstitutionality has recognized that the constitutional convention in altering the text of some of the provisions of the amendment law infringed the provision contained in article 115 of the constitution so often cited;

Whereas, all the illegalities and overriding of authority which have been mentioned constituted a coup d'état *against the popular sovereignty* [emphasis added] and gave rise to an intense revolutionary agitation which obliged the Government constantly to maintain in suspense the individual guarantees and to appeal to all class of violence in order to appease the protests of the people;

Whereas, the good offices of the Ambassador of the United States of America to procure a solution to such an intense political crisis having been offered and accepted *and the President of the Republic having refused to give performance to the essential obligations acquired by the parties within the negotiations which were being carried on, the revolutionary state became more acute* [emphasis added] to such an extent that he was forced to resolve the abandonment of the power and withdraw from the national territory in use of a leave of absence at the same time leaving a full resignation of his office;[23]

Whereas, by virtue of said leave of absence I have provisionally assumed the Presidency of the Republic;

Whereas, a large number of Senators and Representatives have presented the resignation of their offices and others have left the country without requesting a leave of absence;

Whereas, in view of everything that has been set forth above and with the object of reestablishing constitutional legality and restoring tranquility to the country, interpreting the popular will which is clearly manifested at this time throughout the country, conscious of the national conventionalities and of the transcendency of the measures I am adopting, with my thoughts placed on the founders of the nation and on the welfare of the Republic, and having heard the opinion of my Cabinet, I proceed to issue the following decree:

1st. The text of the constitution of 1901 is reestablished in its full force and effect and consequently the constitutional amendment promulgated on May 11th, 1928, remains null and without any value or effect.

2nd. Therefore, the mandate attributed to citizen Gerardo Machado y Morales as President of the Republic is hereby terminated.

3rd. The present Congress is declared dissolved and as a consequence the mandates of the Senators and Representatives as well as the rights of their substitutes to take their places are terminated.

4th. The offices of Justices of the Supreme Court filled after May 20th, 1929, are hereby declared vacant.

5th. The mandates of all the other officials of popular election are hereby declared at an end, nevertheless, those holding such offices at the present time shall remain in the discharge thereof until the Government shall order what it deems proper in each case.

6th. On February 24th, 1934, general elections shall be held for the filling of all offices which have their origin in popular suffrage, the new Presidential term of office to be inaugurated on May 20th of that year.

7th. An advisory commission shall be created charged with the proposing of the modifications considered indispensable to carry into effect the measures contained in this decree, and the recommendations of the said commission once approved in whole or in part shall be promulgated by the Executive.

8th. The Government shall respect and give fulfillment to all international obligations contracted in the name of the Republic even though they may be dated after May 20th, 1929.

9th. All the Secretaries of the Cabinet are entrusted with the fulfillment of this decree insofar as it may be pertinent to each of them (Translation from Welles Cable 185, August 25, 1933, 374-75).

The first wile of the decree can be found in section six, referring to the convocation of general elections, and the second trap is located in section eight, announcing the decision to recognize the debts contracted by the tyranny since May 20, 1929.

In regard to the first trick, the maneuver is simple omission. The Decree does not dissolve the existing political parties, in spite of the role they played in sustaining the dictatorship through a misbegotten formula known as *cooperativismo*. Furthermore, reorganization of the existing political parties, formation of new parties, and the presentation of candidates supported by groups of independent voters were prohibited. That meant that the internal reorganization process, which might have permitted younger individuals to enter the electoral arena and rise within the existing political hierarchies, was forbidden. All possibility of change through the power of the ballot box had been eliminated, and with it the potential for change from within the opposition was capsized, since the government itself had turned revolutionary.

It is not just the announcement of general elections in a hundred eighty days — which was neither the demand of the Directorio nor the popular desire — that proved that those in command were trying to remain in power; there was another verification greater than this first stratagem in the preparation for electoral manipulation, with which the traditional political structure of the republican Cuba could be maintained indefinitely.

Within the Céspedes government were represented practically all the sectors that formed the Cuban Opposition Junta of New York. The exception was the Directorio, which fought the Mediation and which, through the August 22 document, made charges against the government that resulted from it. The government did not even exclude Menocal and his supporters; former president Menocal was, indeed, paradoxical though it may seem, both inside and outside the Céspedes government. He was inside by virtue of men he trusted, like Raúl de Cárdenas, who acted as chief of the executive staff; Demetrio Castillo Pokorny, first Secretary of War and the Navy, and later Secretary of Agriculture, Commerce, and Labor; and Horacio Ferrer, Secretary of War and the Navy after Castillo Pokorny. He was outside the administration inasmuch as, not having officially participated in the Mediation, those individuals in the cabinet did not *officially* belong to his camp, and outside, also, since he was already planning a coup against the regime, as I shall explain shortly. They had all met in the New York Junta and publicly declared as recently as April 27, 1933, that the dissolution of political parties was one of their five basic demands. It is certain that three of the five demands were satisfied in Decree 1298 of the Mediation Government, dictated under DEU pressure. First, the term of Gerardo Machado was terminated; second, Congress was dissolved; and third, all governors, province councillors, mayors, city councillors, and members of the boards of education were removed from office.

Jorge Mañach, the most cultivated and articulate mind of Cuba, after the grand men from the previous century were gone, and also a prominent leader of the ABC, maintained that Cuban political parties had not resolved the fundamental historic problem of transforming the unstable colony into a sovereign, self-sufficient republic.

The Directorio, in its August 22 manifesto, had emphasized that "the formation of political parties shall be free, but the used of the denominations *Liberal, Conservative*, and *Popular* shall be declared illegal, as shall also the emblems and insignias which represent the three current parties."

But two days later, in Decree 1298, the Céspedes-Welles government ignored the demand, since the continuation of those very parties would be necessary in order to hold elections in a scant one hundred eighty days.

Now, for the second trap: the deposed regime was given two distinct dates of virtual "legality." Officially, the regime ended on May 20, 1929, the last legitimate date of President Machado's term. But since financial commitments were illegitimately acquired after that date, the Céspedes government decided that "the Government shall respect and give fulfillment to all international obligations contracted in the name of the Republic even though they may be dated after May 20th, 1929."

First, the decree stated that May 20, 1929, was the last legal day for President Machado to function as president; here, only a few paragraphs later, the legitimacy of his term was extended indefinitely, as implied by the phrase, "even though they may be dated after 20 May 1929." This passage could be interpreted to mean that the legality of the Machado regime embraced not only that time until the day he fled the country, but until, twelve days later, his term was officially declared at an end. This only could have a single objective: to legalize the debts that the Republic had contracted with the Chase Manhattan Bank after May 20, 1929. God bless!

The Céspedes government had, for all practical purposes, bowed to the Directorio's demands when it said in that same decree that it was "interpreting the popular will which is clearly manifested at this time throughout the country." If all the factions that participated in the Mediation were in power; if the only organization that had openly confronted the Céspedes government was the Directorio Estudiantil Universitario; if the confrontation had consisted specifically in demanding that the government declare itself de facto, that it dissolve the Congress, that it reorganize the Supreme Court and that it terminate the terms of the governors, mayors, and other elected officials of the provinces and municipalities; who, then, represented "that clearly manifested popular will" throughout the country other than the only faction that expressed antagonism toward Machado, that was not in the government at the time, and that had challenged the ephemeral regime of Céspedes?

AGONY OF THE CÉSPEDES GOVERNMENT

The political atmosphere during those last few days before September 4 was tense. Sergio Carbó's appeal for the students, workers, and soldiers to unite, in the most widely circulated edition of *La*

Semana, was published only two days after the Céspedes decree. Furthermore, the search for the student traitor Soler had reached the peak of its intensity. It is obvious, then, that the Céspedes decree, forced by the revolutionary agitation led by the Directorio Estudiantil, did more than appease the will of the people; it exalted that will. The decree recognized the reason behind the growing wave of nonconformity, a nonconformity multiplied by the Directorio's position against the decree.

Permit me a sideline to point out that the position the Directorio adopted was not capricious, but, on the contrary, was perfectly justified, supporting what Welles knew implicitly. Remember that on November 18, 1930, the DEU had declared that:

> . . . the suppression of liberties that were won on the battlefields of the Revolution affect equally all sectors of the national conglomerate, which unanimously clamors for not just a mere clever change of subordinates but for a TOTAL AND DEFINITIVE CHANGE OF REGIME . . . (González Peraza 1933, 267-69).

The attitude the DEU assumed on August 22, challenging the Mediation government to assume a genuinely revolutionary role, was entirely a response to its own earliest aims formulated during the first months of the struggle. Justification for the Directorio's relative inaction until that moment toward achieving the true objectives of the revolution can be understood by reading the cable sent that very same day by Ambassador Welles to Secretary Hull, in which he stated:

> ". . . we had continued official relations with the present Government of Cuba in view of our belief that whatever the cause of the change in the Government the result had been *merely a change in the persons* [emphasis added] entrusted with the executive power of the Government through methods provided in the existing constitution . . . (Welles Cable 180, August 22, 1933, 370).

Returning to the analysis of Decree 1298, I must say that this state of affairs emerged contaminated with lack of authority, being as it was the product of popular pressure directed by the DEU; and, conversely, neither did it satisfy the desires expressed by public opinion. Thus, it can be stated that from August 22, when the Directorio published its manifesto-program, until September 4, there were thirteen days during which there was no national power except the Directorio itself. If Welles silently ordered the provisional government of Céspedes — as he did no less than a dozen times, and specifically to publicize with legal violation the debt to the Chase Bank — the Directorio publicly assumed the role of the highest public prosecutor, with the strong voice of command. At that point hundreds of thousands of small triangular lapel flags with the sports colors of the University appeared all over Cuba: *"Con el DEU"* (With the DEU), simply stated.

The Mediationist decree was expedited on August 24 and its publication produced the final confrontation between the world that was leaving and the world that was arriving. The old regime, of which Machado had only been the last representative, with its political, economic, social, moral, and psychological structure, with the United States as international support, had become a modernized secular colony more than a mediatized independence, and this modernization was reduced to little more than the substitution of the United States for Spain. Historically, the system could have continued, since the Mediation had arranged that, in addition to the old politicians, the "new" directors — representatives of the ABC and their offshoot, the *Organización Celular Radical Revolucionario* (Radical Revolutionary Cellular Organization, OCRR) — would also be shackled by the formula. These self-same groups had enjoyed popular sympathy in the continued struggle and, in a very special way, had revelled in the fall of the tyranny. Yet, *there exist rare situations in which it is the citizenry itself that decides its own direction.* This decisive popular force joined and backed the Directorio, which had evolved sufficiently to combat the decree openly, symbol of the regime that had been overthrown.

In concrete "Declarations," the Directorio repudiated the legal mess. The DEU characterized it as an "unfortunate consortium between Washington interests and domestic professional politicians of the past." It also denounced "plans to reform the Reciprocity Treaty and for a loan . . . which are ready to be promulgated in Cuba as soon as possible." These projects had been "outlined in the United States and finished in Cuba by Cubans writing under foreign guidance" (Pichardo 1973, 610-11).

The Directorio resolutely fought the creation of the advisory commission with the practical legislative attributes ordered in the decree; but its most vigorous assault was against the idea of holding general elections in February 1934, just 180 days off, saying that they

". . . are only to satisfy the desperate yearnings of the professional politicians . . . who look forward to taking hold of power as a means of fulfilling their secret yet shameful, disproportionate ambitions" (Pichardo 1973, 610-11). The Directorio advised that this election represented a snare from Washington and Havana against the people of Cuba. Or was it that Sumner Welles was not consulted about it? Was it that Welles, "political godfather of Céspedes since 1921," promptly lost his influence with his protégé, now Chief of State, he whom Welles himself had imposed? Was this the same Welles whom they had consulted, as we saw at the beginning, even down to the nomination of simple employees?

The general elections for president and vice president, senators and representatives, governors and mayors, provincial councilors and councilmen — were they legally correct when the Constitution that the Republic would readopt had been superseded by the Constituent Assembly of 1928, and when the Magna Carta approved in order to consecrate the reelection of Machado and the term extensions for the rest of the elected functionaries had engendered the entire revolutionary process?

Did not the substantial juridical reforms the process of agitated popular struggle demanded have to be considered prior to whatever electoral event? Did the Constitution of 1901 that the Céspedes-Welles government reestablished represent the aspirations of the youth, the professionals, the workers and the *campesinos?* The responses from Washington and Havana were categorical: the people would know how to elect their governing executives directly and rapidly, since the politicians had taken advantage of the fact that "only those of us who are in power can compete at the polls." (Dr. Rafael Santos Jiménez, Minister of Commerce in the Mendieta administration, and leader of the Miguel Mariano Gómez faction, said this to me.) Why run the risk that in a Constituent Assembly there might appear radicals like those that now propounded land distribution, maximum workdays, and minimum salaries?[24]

In precise terms, the Directorio demanded the cancellation of the call for general elections, while sponsoring an election "with a simple electoral procedure without acknowledging political parties, to elect people's delegates in a number proportional to the population, to convene a Constituent Assembly for the purpose of giving Cuba a new political regime in which the rising and thriving of tyrannies like the one that has just ended will not be possible" (Pichardo 1973, 612).

The Directorio understood that the Constitution of 1901, now obsolete, but restored by Decree 1298, "contained judicial roadblocks that impeded the political/economic independence of Cuba" and that its substance would be "the engenderment and nest of tyrannies, now that the economic control of the United States over Cuba will be complete and we will have failed to achieve our political independence" (Pichardo 1973, 612).

The DEU advocated an extremely simple election of members to its proposed Constituent Assembly. It would permit the presentation of candidates backed by independent groups of electors and by a determined number of signatures of citizens with the right to vote. The Directorio established, at the same time, two conditions, directed specifically against traditional political professionalism: first, no one who had been a candidate to elective posts after January 1, 1924 — the year Machado was elected President of the Republic — would be allowed to run for a seat in the Constituent Convention; and secondly, it prohibited all delegates elected to the Convention to run for any elective position in the following elections (Pichardo 1973, 613).

Upon constructing this Constituent Convention of delegates without complicity with the past, without aspirants to immediate and future gain, and without the authoritarian pressure of Washington, the most clean and fruitful of the republican Constitutions would have been drafted, in spite of the fact that the Directorio had committed a grievous error in defining the revolutionary qualifications of the members of the convention.

The students proposed, among their demands, a requirement that "every candidate to the Constituent Assembly must possess at least a professional degree that ensures his capacity," an elitist criterion that immediately excluded the students, workers, and *campesinos.* According to this exclusion, the labor leader of the strike of the sugar processing center at Punta Alegre (Happy Point), in the province of Camagüey, could not have run for a seat in the Convention. If anyone could best carry the message for a minimum salary and for the constitutional prohibition of salary payment by vouchers and chits, it would have to be the unknown leader from "Punto Alegre," a talented sugarman from that unhappy region.

In their declaration the Directorio authorized the Convention the power to "draft and enact the laws regulating the organic structure of the state as well as the electoral, economic and social laws, and the negotiation of those treaties indispensable to remedy the present situation of the country."

The Directorio had, in general terms, come up with the doubly correct solution. On one hand, it again suggested the development of a fundamental charter according to which the basic economic and social laws would be drafted as well as "those treaties indispensable to remedy the present situation of the country." But this "present situation" of the country — did it refer to everything listed in the clause, or specifically to the treaties? Probably to the entirety; concerning treaties, the self-same manifesto had repudiated "plans to reform the reciprocity Treaty," while a few days before, in its manifesto-program on August 22, it had indicated, with the authority of an entity that recognizes the sovereign will of the people, that one function of the Constituent Convention would be to annul the Platt Amendment and denounce the Permanent Treaty.

The second certainty of the proposed solution is even more evident. The Directorio proposed to eliminate the general elections because only the traditional political groups already represented in the provisional government would be allowed to participate. The only opposition to the rule of the established powers which Welles and Céspedes represented was the self-same Directorio Estudiantil Universitario, which was denied an electoral vehicle. The DEU, perhaps unconsciously, expressed then the same slogan that it had launched thirty-three months earlier, on November 19, 1930. By rejecting the general elections that Washington and Havana intended, and proposing a Constituent Convention "to draft and enact the laws regulating the organic structure of the state as well as the electoral, economic, and social laws, and the negotiation of those treaties indispensable to remedy the present situation of the country," the Directorio had simply repeated, in other sweeping terms, its battle cry, "for a total and definitive change of regime."

Its popular power was so strong that, at its simple statement that the Constituent Convention should be constructed first, there was no further need to encourage agitation. Neither did it have to coin the slogan that later would sweep Cuba: "Constituent first, elections later" — because its demand expressed a collective yearning that did not require promotion or propaganda. Immediately joining their position were the Cuban Bar Association, the Revolutionary Women's Group, the Teachers' Schools, the Havana High School Faculty, the *Alianza*

Nacional Feminista (National Feminist Alliance), and others. Even the Célula Directriz of the ABC in Santiago de Cuba, which had become a partner in the DEU's overall program, in a public announcement a few days before, stated in support of the student demands that they would only be satisfied by a government produced by an authentic revolution. (Oriente Province, and especially Santiago de Cuba, had developed a genuine revolutionary position during the anti-Machado period.) Furthermore, at least before the judgement of history, the ABC-Santiago de Cuba more accurately interpreted the necessary outcome of the Cuban revolution — at the time — than did the National Célula Directriz of the ABC.

The new tide of popular sentiment turned toward the overthrow of Céspedes and Welles, in the extremity of which the provisional president, upon dissolving the Cabinet on August 30, declared that "the Constituent Assembly will be an immediate reality." The Chief of the Executive Staff, Raúl de Cárdenas, informed the public on August 31 that the Cabinet, in a five-hour session the previous day, had heard the President express his opinion that a Constituent Assembly was the "yearning of the entire people."

For the second time the Directorio triumphed. On August 22, the DEU had charged the provisional government with failing to dissolve Congress, remove the governors, provincial councillors, mayors, councilmen, and members of the board of education, or even declare itself de facto. On August 30, only eight days later, the Directorio had imposed twice, from the trenches of the true opposition, its political will. What was left, then, to govern, except to seize power?

Overthrow of Machado. Lightning victory over the Mediation government, that had totally represented the interests of the United States. Bertrand Russell said that self-confidence is never superficial but penetrates deeply into the subconscious. That is what in this historic moment occurred within the DEU. Furthermore, after openly opposing a regime upon which it made demands and which it had forced to obey those demands, the DEU had suddenly become accustomed to command, making it easier to assume new responsibilities and adopt rapid decisions.

The Directorio had been conspiring with prestigious young officers, as we have seen, while some others of its members, without express approval, had been encouraging a group of "sergeants" to change the syndical and purely recovery-oriented direction of a movement they were organizing. It never occurred to anyone to ask those members in a loud voice, "Wouldn't those be the same sergeants who threw a banquet in Machado's honor when you were wearing black armbands of mourning for the death of Trejo?"

Weary of treasons and traps, the DEU advanced in the historic shadows, but confident in its own good faith and its support from the Cuban people who backed the organization and whose moods it felt. And since the power "was in the street," the DEU would seize it — knowing neither how nor when, though quite soon — and afterward, well, that was to be seen. With powerful faith that it would obtain the ends pursued, though with scarce consideration to the necessary means to obtain such ends, the DEU was ready to launch itself on the adventure. Struggles more difficult had ended without power. "Self-confidence had penetrated into the subconscious."

The headlines of the newspapers in the capital city registered the pulse of the Nation: "Power must by applied with full energy and authority if order is to be restored," declared the Secretary of War, Doctor Horacio Ferrer. "Judge Guillermo Montagú appointed special prosecutor in case against Machado and his henchmen." "Grave irregularities discovered in Treasury accounts." "One million pesos in Palace secret expenses." "Railroad board dismissed." "Students demand abrogation of Amnesty Law and punishment of criminals." Secretary of War Ferrer, again, with "The army shall use any means necessary to maintain order."

Unexpectedly, a hurricane whipped the northern length of Cuba, especially the provinces of Matanzas and Santa Clara, and news of the hurricane was interspersed with reports on the political crisis: "64 hurt and 3 dead in Havana." "The Mauritania unable to enter port." "Signs in the Supreme Court saying 'clean the temple' and 'the toga is not livery.'" "American investors in Cuba express confidence in the new provisional government." (Better if they had said, "Thank you very much," since this last headline was the note of gratitude for Section Eight of the Céspedes decree legally recognizing the debt to the Chase Bank of New York.) "30 dead and 100 injured by hurricane in Cárdenas." "Property damages reach 3 million pesos in Cárdenas." "Thousands of families in Sagua and Isabela left homeless." "Almost all Santa Clara province erased by storm."

In all these headlines from the *Diario de la Marina*, only the difficulties maintaining order, repeated in the course of short days, and the fateful hurricane, gained notoriety, while into the subsoil filtered Carbó's call for the students, workers, and soldiers to unite. A coup was rumored on part of former president Menocal, while the Directorio rejected the call to general elections and the reestablishment of the 1901 Constitution, advocating instead a free and sovereign Constituent Assembly. Thousands upon thousands of citizens continued wearing the triangular lapel pins declaring, "*Con el DEU.*" Colonel Ferrer had twice stated the necessity of energetic action to maintain order, a declaration he made and repeated from the beginning of his term, on August 30, when he replaced Castillo Pokorny. Scant hours later, he would repeat the same statement, perhaps in anticipated justification for a new program of force that would emanate from his own department. Since Horacio Ferrer had figured as a possible provisional substitute for Gerardo Machado as President of the Republic, a move backed by former president Menocal, it makes sense to suppose that the Secretary of War planned a more energetic and radical maintenance of order through the replacement of a practically nonexistent provisional power. Meanwhile, public opinion, a psychological observer which anticipated the best scientific investigative centers, and that at the same time can be the seed of the turbulence, was measuring unrest in the streets. That public opinion asked with anguish, breathed screams of protest and participated too late in the judgement of a discovered torturer. All this occurred with the indifference, at times, and the complicity, at others, of the most visible representative of authority, the soldier, who at that time was earning the insignificant wage of $13.80 a month.

In the pictorial section from the September 3 edition of *Diario de la Marina,* there appeared two photos: one, of Carlos Manuel Fuertes Blandino, member of the DEU assassinated through the betrayal of a supposed companion in arms, and the other, that of José Soler, the betraying figure, the counterpart of the martyr. They were the protagonists in the tremendous historic drama that compelled the Directorio to create its own judicial forum.

Thus, we arrive at September 4, 1933, on which date, and in that same *Diario,* in an unusual coincidence of historic detonation, appeared the headline, "Traitor José Soler captured early this morning." The article stated that Soler was discovered hidden in his uncle's house at 193 L Street in the Vedado district of Havana, by members of the *Pro Ley y Justicia* group, the DEU, and the *Organización Celular*

Radical Revolucionaria (OCRR). The photo showed Soler dressed in a white suit and smoking a cigarette.

Thus began Soler's last day of existence. Those of us who did not find out in time of his capture were unable to participate in his trial, sentencing, and execution. By that same token, those of us members of the Directorio who were not in the Summary Court and absent from the scenes in which this episode concluded were the first to arrive in Camp Columbia upon learning of the meeting of sergeants and enlisted men being held there. On this day, then, occurred the two events that represent for the DEU the most complete exercise of revolutionary judicial power in the celebration of the trial, sentencing, and execution of the captured traitor; for the Céspedes government, its last hours; and for Cuba, the events of a day in whose new dawning — pregnant with hopes and realizations — it would live exhilarated by the anticipated enjoyment of a liberty that as a nation it had not felt since Christopher Columbus set foot upon her shores nearly five hundred years earlier. Unfortunately, that day saw also the political birth of the most sinister personage of the epoch: Fulgencio Batista.

I emphasize the search, capture, trial, and execution of José Soler, betrayer at the service of the Machadato who was responsible for the assassination of student Carlos Fuertes Blandino at the hands of the minions of the dictator Machado. This event, as I have suggested before, demonstrates the DEU exercising an effective judicial power, and the actual search for Soler, in which nearly the entire city of Havana participated, gives evidence to the popular backing of the Directorio.

The trial was characterized by its great objectivity amid great passions, demonstrating the obvious desire to see justice done rather than to exercise revenge. It was a highly emotional event for the members of the Directorio, some of whom did not want to believe in Soler's guilt.

Suffice it to say that the DEU exercised, on this occasion, judicial power in accordance with objective norms. Soler was excellently defended by Doctors Lincoln Rodón and Alberto I. Alvarez. And only the incontestable weight of the accumulated evidence led to the sentence of death and the final execution, always with the greatest respect for the accused.

NOTES

1. Rafael Trejo's death notice was signed by the following members of the *Directorio*. School of Law: Raúl Roa, Carlos Prío Socarrás, Alberto Espinosa, Justo Carrillo Hernández, Augusto Valdés Miranda, Virgilio Ferrer Gutiérrez, Manuel A. Varona; School of Medicine: Rubén León, José Leyva, Carlos Guerrero, José Ramón Blanco, Fernando López, Jaime Urqui, L. López Luis; School of Arts and Sciences: Ramón Miyar Millán, Carlos Sardiñas, Carlos Fuertes, José Antonio Viego.

2. Those who vanished during the first three months were Raúl Roa García, Alberto Espinosa Bravo, José Ramón Blanco, Jaime Urqui, L. López Luis, and Carlos Sardiñas. Three or four others joined the group in October, but later withdrew from the struggle.

3. *Diario de la Marina*, in its October 11, 1930, edition, reported the banquet offered Machado at Camp Columbia under the heading: "The Army is for me the most beloved institution, said the President." On page 1, columns 6 through 8, the following officers were listed as present: Captain Martull, Colonel Rafael del Castillo, Captain Díaz Cía, Brigadier Lores, Captain Pío Alonso, Captain Raimundo Ferrer, Lieutenant Obdulio Herrera, Lieutenant Florentino Fernández, Major Báxter, Colonel Caballero, and all the captains in command of squadrons of the Rural Guard of the province of Havana, with the exception of Captain Suárez, who, being sick, sent Lieutenant Ducunjé, Lieutenant Colonels Guerrero, Benítez, and Cruz Bustillo, and "the whole cadre of officers of Columbia and La Fuerza Castle." This report contradicts what Ricardo Adam Silva declares in his books *La gran mentira* and *Cuba, El fin de la república*. In the former, he says that Machado "was not received by the superior officers of the military post" (58), and in the latter that "the celebration took place in Camp Columbia with express exclusion of the officers," and he adds the comment, "It was antimilitary to gather all those soldiers without officers" (8).

4. Fulgencio Batista was never a stenographer for the Army General Staff, as it has been erroneously stated. He obtained that title when he won the competitive exams called by the Seventh Military District (La Cabaña) to cover the vacancy produced when Pedro León Otaño was named to a position in the Department of Finances. Later Batista exchanged positions with his colleague Urbano Soler.

5. Pedraza and López Migoya both served as Army Chief of Staff; the former from 1939 to 1941 at the rank of major, and the latter from 1941 to 1945 with the rank of major general. Galíndez reached the rank of general and was retired from active duty by President Grau in 1944.

6. Among the leaders of *Asociación Unión Nacionalista*, besides War of Independence Army Colonels Mendieta, Méndez Peñate, and Cosme de la Torriente, were War of Independence General Francisco Peraza, Colonel Aurelio Hevia, and former senators Juan Gualberto Gómez and Aurelio Alvarez de la Vega. Prío, León, and Varona, several months before Trejo's death, had identified publicly with the political opposition to Machado. On April 10, 1930, a public manifesto was issued signed only "Patio de los Laureles" (a historical inner plaza of the university) calling the students and the people in general to attend a meeting scheduled for April 19 at the Central Park downtown. *Diario de la Marina*, on April 13, printed a detailed article describing the preparations for the meeting and those supporting it under the heading "The Nationalists will appeal Governor Barceló's [of Oriente Province] resolution" (12). Among the leaders of the Nationalist Youth were Rubén León, vice-president; Carlos Prío Socarrás, secretary; and Manuel Antonio Varona, for the School of Law.

7. "Inventing" Cuba, that is. This idiomatic expression thus used signifies in Cuban Spanish the idea of finding, through whatever means, the solution to very difficult problems which are considered nearly or totally impossible to resolve.

8. Hereafter, all references to communications published in *Foreign Relations of the United States* from the years 1933 and 1934 will simply be annotated "Author Communication number, date, page."

9. The original manuscript of the Manifesto is in possession of the author.

10. The original declaration by the Directorio is in the possession of the author. Further, in his book *Ocho años de la lucha* (1982), Gerardo Machado discussed the historic significance of the split between the DEU and the ABC with the following observations:

> All, revolutionaries and commentators, agreed that only Mr. Roosevelt's intervention could free Cuba from that most darkly painted government. And this, the only hope of my enemies, divided them even further. It divided them because the student sector, which was formerly in league with the ABC, rejected the idea of having foreigners dabbling in our affairs and claimed their right to operate freely and on their own for the purpose of overthrowing me. (65)

And further along the deposed president added:

> The students, who had already parted with the ABC, did not refrain from voicing their discontent, so that great expectations and profound unrest prevailed in everybody at the time of the ambassador's arrival. (71)

11. The Spanish word used in the original here was *vestiglo*, meaning "horrible monster," an allusion to dictator Machado. In various reproductions

of the document, however, it has been misspelled *VESTIGIO* (vestige), which, of course, does not make sense in the context.

12. The original of this manifesto is in author's possession.

13. As a lesson from the British occupation of Havana in 1762, consideration was given to the convenience of building a fortification on Soto Hill, overlooking the harbor, to protect the city and its neighboring areas. Atarés Castle was built between 1763 and 1767 under the direction of Engineer Agustín Crame. The castle was named by Conde de Ricla, governor of the island and promoter of the works.

14. This macabre evidence emphasized the chasm between Machado's strength and the subservience of the Céspedes government. That blunt contrast further aggravated the already explosive situation.

15. They were labor activists Noske Yalob and Claudio Bouzón, arrested when distributing leaflets against the visit of President Coolidge, who came to Havana to attend the Sixth Pan-American Conference in 1928; and the Venezuelan journalist Francisco Laguado Jaime, chief editor of *Venezuela Libre*, a newspaper published in Havana. His assassination was a special service of Machado to his colleague Venezuelan dictator Juan Vicente Gómez.

16. The *Porra* ("bludgeon"), Machado's paramilitary death squad, was organized in Havana by one Dr. Leopoldo Fernández Ros, lawyer and journalist (former chief editor of the daily *La Noche*) and a professor at the Institute of Secondary Education. The *Porra's* foundation took place at a meeting attended by some one hundred people on November 14, 1930. The given official name was *Liga Patriótica* (Patriotic League). Dr. Fernández Ros was designated president and War of Independence Lieutenant Colonel José Antonio Jiménez, vice-president. The *Porra* henchmen were on the public payroll, but they didn't have to work. In addition, the organization derived enormous profits from the exploitation of gambling houses. All of them were issued guns without licenses. The *porristas*, as they were known, had ID cards which they used for free access to theaters and restaurants. The *Porra* accumulated a dreadful record of assassinations, extortions, beatings, and other similar acts, all committed with impunity. A few months after founding the *Porra*, Fernández Ros was killed by revolutionaries and Colonel Jiménez succeeded him.

17. A twist of history: eighteen years later, I myself became the first president of the Agricultural Bank proposed by the DEU in 1933.

18. In theory, this practice had been abolished by the Arteaga Act of June 23, 1909. The law expressly prohibited the issuance of vouchers, chips, tokens, or anything else intended to substitute for actual cash in the payment of salaries or any other obligations. The affected employers, however, simply ignored the law. It later became, in principle, a part of the Constitution.

19. The reference is, of course, exclusively and directly to the ABC.

20. By virtue of the illegitimate procedure by which Machado extended his term in office, his regime must be considered *de facto* from May 20, 1929, on.

21. However, as Rubio Padilla will attest further on, the academy officers enjoyed general respect.

22. The Sergeants' Movement would provide the DEU an opportunity in its unexpected desire for power and its subordination to the hierarchy of young officers.

23. Machado's leave of absence and resignation and the decree by which he accepted the resignation of all members of his cabinet, except Secretary of War and the Navy Alberto Herrera, all appeared in the *Official Gazette* extraordinary No. 20 of August 12, 1933. That *Official Gazette* also contained a law modifying existing regulations in regard to presidential succession, all for the purpose of facilitating the designation of Carlos Manuel de Céspedes as provisional president.

24. As reported by *Diario de la Marina* in its August 25, 1933, edition seven days before the promulgation of Decree 1298; on August 17 the workers of Punta Alegre sugar mill had gone on peaceful strike because "the owning company continued paying the onerous salaries of 30 and 40 cents per day in vouchers for their own commercial department, and he who demanded to be paid in cash was summarily fired."

Photograph that served as a symbol of the Russian revolution in director Eisenstein's 1927 film "October."

The well-known photograph of the overthrow of General Machado: a soldier becomes the symbol of the popular revolutionary effort.

$1.000 POR SU CAPTURA!

TRAIDOR! TRAIDOR!

JOSE SOLER Y LEZAMA
¡A COGERLO VIVO O MUERTO!

JOSE SOLER LEZAMA, estudiante expulsado de la Universidad el año 27, exmiembro del Partido Comunista de Cuba, del Ala-Izquierda Estudiantil, amigo de absoluta confianza del sector Unión Nacionalista y militante también del A B C ha sido descubierto con pruebas abrumadoras como confidente de la Policía desde el año 1930. Sirvió a los asesinos Trujillo, Ainciart y Alberto Herrera. Preso, enviaba informe utilizando como mediador al ex-jefe de Presidio Castells.

Responsable directo de la mayor parte de los asesinatos cobardes cometidos en los revolucionarios Pio Alvarez, Sargento Miguel A, Hernández, Carlos Fuertes Blandino etc.

El Ala Izquierda y el Directorio Estudiantil lo buscan afanosamente.

¡Pueblo de Cuba, ayúdanos a capturar a este cobarde confidente! ¡No puede escapársenos!

LOS ENCUBRIDORES SERAN CASTIGADOS SEVERAMENTE

Poster offering a reward for information leading to the capture of Soler — thousands of copies were distributed in Havana and throughout the provincial capitals.

DIRECTORIO ESTUDIANTIL UNIVERSITARIO

AL PUEBLO DE CUBA

La opinión pública conoce la traición de ciertos sectores oposicionistas que han pretendido medrar—con miras personales—con la exaltación popular provocada por la Tiranía. Traición de efecto triple: a la REVOLUCIÓN, porque se han prestado a convalidar actos esencialmente nulos y a reconocer—más o menos explícitamente—la legalidad de un gobierno que instituyó el crimen y el latrocinio como armas políticas; a CUBA, porque declaran sin rubor la incapacidad de nuestro pueblo para regir sus destinos; a IBERO-AMÉRICA, en fin, porque dan pábulo a la ingerencia yanqui y secundan la obra de penetración en Nuestra América de intereses que, en el siglo y medio transcurrido, se han mostrado hostiles al desenvolvimiento de nuestros pueblos.

Pero el Estudiantado Cubano VELA; vela por la Revolución, por Cuba y por Ibero-América. Y no conforme con limitar su gesto a meras palabras de rebeldía, RECLAMA de hoy en adelante la iniciativa y la dirección de la lucha por la LIBERTAD del hombre cubano en su tierra y por la LIBERTAD de Cuba—que es, también, la de Ibero-América—en el concierto de los pueblos cultos.

El hecho es insólito. Por primera vez en la Historia, un Estudiantado asume tan magna tarea. Mas el estudiante cubano caería en la peor censura, si dejara pasar las circunstancias históricas que ponen en sus manos la difícil y hermosa misión. No se interprete por inmodesta pretensión de juventud. Tal resolución es fruto maduro de la reflexión, abonado por la sangre y el martirio de nuestros mejores valores.

Hace más de diez años que el Estudiantado Cubano inició su protesta contra la degradación política que Cuba venía padeciendo, y fué el Estudiantado quien—el primero—levantó su voz airada contra la barbarie que Machado entronizaba... Y a la hora del sacrificio, aportó sus falanges abnegadas con tal esplendidez que no hay callejuela ni plaza en ciudades, ni rincón en los campos cubanos que no hayan sido regados con sangre de estudiantes. No hay cárcel ni mazmorra en que los estudiantes no hayan vivido angustias y privaciones. No tiene esbirros ni lacayos Machado que no hayan saciado su salvajismo o estimulado su vesanía con carne estudiantil.

Sin embargo, el Estudiantado se comportó con disciplina. Aunque receloso, admitió que para acabar con el VESTIGLO y renovar la vida pública cubana, la acción iría mejor conducida por los hombres cuya experiencia procurabá algunos resortes útiles. No podía imaginar que los intereses supremos de la colectividad fueran subordinados a resquemores y ambiciones personalistas: ahora lo sabe. Y cuando grupos "nuevos" irrumpieron aparentando ansias sinceras de rectificaciones—el Estudiantado nutrió sus filas: ahora conoce que no es posible confiar en quienes estuvieron con Machado hasta ayer y hoy han defendido intereses imperialistas hasta hoy.

La dura lección llena de amargura nuestras almas, pero no hace flaquear nuestra fe. Por el contrario, en medio de las ruinas materiales y de los escombros morales, sobre los túmulos de nuestros mártires sublimes, el Directorio Estudiantil Universitario—en nombre del Estudiantado Cubano—hace una LLAMADA FINAL a la JUVENTUD.

¡Jóvenes cubanos! aprestaos a la acción bajo nuestras banderas. De nosotros depende que podamos vivir con la frente levantada. Somos nosotros los que hemos de labrar nuestro propio mundo. ¡Unámonos para crear!

¡Jóvenes de Ibero-América! prestadnos vuestro concurso para la empresa de afirmar nuestra nación. Nuestra gloria será honor vuestro.

Y vosotros—hombres de buena voluntad—que aunque nos adelantáis en años, no sois viejos, porque vuestra alma es perpetuamente joven y enamorada de generosos ideales, ¡ayudadnos! la nación que ambicionamos es la misma que vosotros amáis.

LA ACCIÓN A QUE INVITA EL DIRECTORIO ESTUDIANTIL UNIVERSITARIO TIENE DOS OBJETIVOS:

Primer objetivo.

Organización de la insurrección armada contra la Tiranía, hasta batir y aniquilar las hordas de politicastros en que aquélla se cimenta.

Con tal propósito, se pondrán en práctica los procedimientos y medios que oportunamente se conocerán.

Segundo objetivo.

Implantación de un Gobierno Provisional—integrado por personas que el Directorio Estudiantil Universitario seleccionará y nombrará—para el cumplimiento del siguiente

PROGRAMA
para el
GOBIERNO PROVISIONAL
I
ORGANIZACIÓN

El Gobierno Provisional se compondrá:
a) de la Comisión Ejecutiva.
b) del Consejo Legislativo.
c) del Tribunal de Sanciones y
d) de la Asamblea Constituyente.
De la Comisión Ejecutiva.

La Comisión Ejecutiva estará formada por cinco Comisionados de iguales funciones y jerarquía. Sus resoluciones para ser válidas deberán estar tomadas en junta y aprobadas por mayoría, excepto los casos en que se exija unanimidad.

La Comisión Ejecutiva ejercerá todas las facultades que correspondan por las leyes al Presidente y a los Secretarios del Despacho. Le corresponderá también la destitución de todos los que desempeñen cargos políticos o administrativos en el Estado, las Provincias o los Municipios, y su nombramiento según ternas que facilite el Directorio Estudiantil.

En tanto no se reúna la Asamblea Constituyente, la Comisión Ejecutiva asumirá, además, las funciones legislativas, pero sus leyes serán provisionales, a menos que la Constituyente las ratifique.

Para el despacho, los Comisionados instalarán la oficina en el Palacio Presidencial, pero no residirán en él.

Al tomar posesión de sus cargos, los Comisionados se declararán en junta y acordarán por mayoría:
a) la designación del Comisionado que ha de representar al Gobierno ante el Cuerpo Diplomático.
b) la persona extraña a la Comisión que ha de fungir de Secretario de ésta.
c) que se comunique al Cuerpo Diplomático la constitución del Gobierno Provisional y el acuerdo a).
d) cualquier otra resolución que las circunstancias aconsejen.

El Secretario de la Comisión llevará un libro de actas, será el Jefe del archivo, no tendrá voz ni voto, podrá ser removido en todo tiempo y deberá residir en Palacio.

Tanto los Comisionados como el Secretario percibirán emolumentos que en ningún caso excederán del sueldo usual de los Secretarios del Despacho, sin gastos de representación.

Ni los Comisionados ni el Secretario de la Comisión podrán figurar como candidatos a cargos electivos, ni desempeñar cargo público alguno hasta pasados seis años del cese en las funciones del Gobierno Provisional. Se exceptúan las plazas ganadas por oposición con anterioridad a la designación para el Gobierno Provisional: este impedimento se hará constar en la Ley Electoral y en las Leyes Orgánicas.

Los Comisionados responderán ante el Tribunal de Sanciones mediante querella firmada por cinco Constituyentes o miembros del Consejo Legislativo.
Del Consejo Legislativo.

Dentro de los ocho días siguientes a la constitución de la Comisión Ejecutiva, procederá ésta a nombrar de las listas que el Directorio Estudiantil Universitario

The DEU manifesto.

Supporters of the Directorate. Back row, from left to right, are Orlando Alonso, Ismael Seijas, Armando Machado, Manolo Arán, and Benito Fernández. Front row, from left to right, are Mario Fortuny, Orlando Castañeda, Arturo Galleti, Oscar Andino, Víctor Hugo Fernández, and Raúl Oms. Nueva Gerona prison, 1931.

Lieutenant Emilio Laurent

*Ideologist and advisor to
the Directorate,
Dr. José M.Irisarri.*

*Obituary of Rafael Trejo that appeared in Havana
newspapers on the morning of October 2, 1930.*

Rubio Padilla delivered the Directorate's program to the army.

Agriculture Minister Carlos Hevia, author of much of the revolution's legislation.

U.S. Secretary of State Cordell Hull (left) and U.S. Ambassador Sumner Welles, between whom there was great distrust.

Why did Jorge Mañach, leader of the ABC, go to Camp Columbia on September 4, 1933? Rubio Padilla reports the explanation given to him by Batista.

The wreckage of Captain Martull's plane from which he escaped uninjured.

Commentaries on the promotion of Sergeant Fulgencio Batista to Colonel: Guillermo Martínez Márquez: "If the popular and rebellious Sergio Carbó had not placed Fulgencio Batista at the head of the Army that was fragmented by internal rivalry, if he had not assumed the responsibility of authorizing the appointment that was published in the *Gaceta Oficial* with only Carbó's signature, perhaps history would have been different.

It will not be I who shall judge if Carbó's designation of Batista as Army Chief was a mistake, but there is one thing for certain: if it was incorrect, one must recognize that it was made in good faith. Otherwise, one would be obliged to place Carbó in a prestigious position, which everyone knows he has not held since the fall of Dr. Ramón Grau San Martín's revolutionary government."

At this time, Sergio Carbó said: "September Fourth inspired spirit, love of country, and the purest feeling of dignity. Perhaps, if events had been less tumultuous, the outcome might have been more measured and perfect, but possibly not as courageous. The deep impression that has been left, so lasting and strong that no one dares pursue a different course, are due mainly to the sincerity and spontaneity of the movement.

The appointment of Sergeant Batista to the rank of colonel, through my efforts alone, was in recognition of his powerful position in the military segment of the movement. Batista would not have been nominated to the post he occupies today had he not signed the *Proclama al Pueblo de Cuba de la Revolución* along with the civilian signatories on that historic evening at Camp Columbia."

On December 13, 1933, Sumner Wells left Cuba and concluded his assignment as President Roosevelt's personal representative. He was succeeded by Ambassador Jefferson Caffery on December 19.

Photographs of the officers' accusatory letters that were carried by Sumner Welles to the Hotel Nacional and appeared on the frontispiece of the newspaper Alma Mater.

Hundreds of civilian revolutionaries participated in the assault on the Hotel Nacional.

The facade of this hotel bore the evidence of numerous shelling attacks.

Justo Carrillo (top).

*Colonel Carlos Mendieta,
president following the fall of Grau
during the Caffery-Batista era (center).*

*Guillermo M. Cancio, oldest member
and permanent treasurer of the
Directorate (bottom left).*

Juan Febles and Mongo Miyar

On the roof of the Castillo del Príncipe (1932). Standing, from left to right, are Julio César Fernández, Ismael "Chino" Seijas, Emilio Laurent, Justo Carrillo, and Fernando Leyva. Seated, from left to right, are Carlos Prío and Casimiro Menéndez.

Front and back of the DEU bond.

Carlos Manuel Alvarez Tabío with the author in 1982, when they recorded their statements about the meetings at Enrique Pedro's farm during which Mendieta was named president.

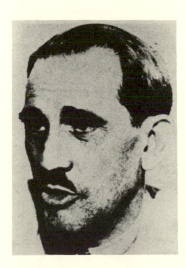

Grau, who represented the hopes of the Directorate and later betrayed it. Therefore confidence in the DEU declined and it was dissolved.

The creation of the Cuban Revolutionary Party (Auténtico) in 1934 was attended by the thirty-six founding members. Only a few had been members of the DEU in 1930: among those were Prío, Varona, and Laudelino González.

Departing the Presidential Palace, Grau is accompanied by Carlos Hevia and their respective assistants (Antonio Díaz Baldoquin and Rafael Menéndez); not appearing with him are any members of the Student Directorate who, on September 9, 1933, had chosen Grau as their candidate for president.

With a photograph of José Martí in the background, Batista and a group of his henchmen celebrate having gained control of Camp Columbia.

Chapter 2

THE FOURTH OF SEPTEMBER 1933 REVOLUTION: FROM THE PENTARCHY TO PRESIDENT GRAU

THE BEGINNINGS OF THE SERGEANTS' MOVEMENT
DATE: SEPTEMBER 4, 1933 — DURING THE DAY

On the first of September, a hurricane had struck the island with sufficient intensity to cause massive destruction in Matanzas and Santa Clara provinces, leaving thousands injured in its wake. Faced with this disaster, President Céspedes decided to travel to the provinces, taking with him the recently designated Chief of Staff of the Army, Armando Montes, recently promoted to the rank of temporary general because of his post. The objective of the trip was to verify the damage and decide what aid would be necessary in the course of the next several days.

That the President would ask the Secretaries of Public Health and Welfare, of State, or of Public Works to accompany him to assist in planning programs for aid and reconstruction would have been logical. He, instead, requested the company of his acting Army Chief of Staff, temporary general Montes, whose appointment was met with rumors of pay cuts and force reductions. Montes had been recalled from retirement to replace the ineffective bureaucrat, Héctor de Quesada, who had not held a command position for twenty years, yet had advanced to the post of Chief of Staff as the next eligible individual in the chain of command. Montes, on the other hand, had served as Secretary of War and the Navy under President Zayas (1921-1925) and was well, but not fondly, remembered in the military for reducing enlisted billets and salaries. His record naturally prompted rumors of a repeat performance. Céspedes' Secretary of War and the Navy, Horacio Ferrer, tried to "quell" the rumors with a statement that "salaries and emoluments will remain unaltered as they now stand." This statement, however, simply aggravated the Sergeants' Movement by scoffing at the real fears behind the rumors. When Céspedes took Montes to visit the disaster areas, de Quesada, that same ineffectual bureaucrat that Montes had replaced, was appointed to act as Army Chief of Staff in the interim. The stage was set.

So, on September 3, the president of the Enlisted Mens' Club at Camp Columbia, Sergeant Pablo Rodríguez Silverio, asked the chief of the Sixth Military District, Lieutenant Colonel José Perdomo y Martínez, for permission to hold a meeting in the Enlisted Club the following day. Perdomo immediately authorized the meeting without looking into the nature or true objectives of this unusual assembly.

Unbelievable authorization! Permission was granted to low-ranking soldiers of an institution whose essential characteristics are discipline and obedience and in which, as an essential factor of command and hierarchy, regulations specifically prohibited members from deliberating, to do exactly that!

The sergeants, corporals, and soldiers had assembled a committee dubbed the "*Junta de los Ocho*," or Committee of Eight, for its number of members. They were Pablo Rodríguez Silverio, quartermaster sergeant of the Third Company of the Second Infantry Battalion; Manuel López Migoya, quartermaster sergeant of the Second Company of the same battalion; Fulgencio Batista Zaldívar, stenographic sergeant assigned to the General Staff of the Sixth Military District; Juan A. Estévez Maymir, medical sergeant of the Military Hospital staff; José Eleuterio Pedraza, sergeant first class of the Second Company, Second Battalion; Angel Echevarría Salas, corporal of the Fourth Company, Fourth Infantry Battalion; and privates Ramón Cruz Vidal, also a medic, and Mario Alfonso Hernández, of the General Staff, Fourth Infantry Battalion.

Two characteristics of the group stand out: first, six of the eight members of the junta were mere staff workers, medical corpsmen, or other basic administrative types, and only two (Pedraza and Echevarría) were line troops; second, two of the members (Rodríguez Silverio and Batista) had been linked to the overthrown regime. Rodríguez Silverio had, among other things, helped arrange the banquet offered by the sergeants to the deposed president Machado. The other, Batista, had served as a stenographer for the military tribunals trying the revolutionaries and as an aide to the officer that acted as prosecuting attorney in the military procedures of the Sixth District.

That the majority of the "Committee of Eight" were office staff and that the two leaders had been attached to the deposed regime and had benefitted from that association is what accentuated the motivation of the group. As a movement it was originally syndical, proven by the development of demands "for no reduction in salaries; for the right to use leather leggings and flat caps like those of the officers; for no reduction in the number of enlisted personnel; for the abolition of assignments as aides to officers," (enlisted men who functioned as true servants), and so forth. Obviously, the demands were purely for the benefit of that group and constituted a defensive front more than an aggressive activity, even though neither type of activity had any place in the armed forces to begin with.[1] In addition to the merely classist and typically syndical demands, the very composition of the group — less militant than military — indicated clearly that such a meeting was not seditious in terms of its ultimate goals, nor was it secret, since it had the approval of the regimental commander, Lieutenant Colonel Perdomo.

Let's look a little more closely at the convolutions. Of the old commanders that wore the rank of colonel, twelve in total, only three remained in command position; nine others had been relieved of command for a variety of reasons; and three of those nine were imprisoned in the Cabaña Fortress awaiting trial before the military court on charges for various crimes and fraud. Helpless due to lack of support from their bosses and abandoned before the popular clamor demanding a purge of the military hierarchy that could reach even to them, the sergeants had created a defensive fraternity. It is surprising that a fraternity should be comprised of sergeants, corporals, and soldiers — men accustomed to obedience — but by now military objectives were no longer intrinsically combat-oriented.

The Sergeants' Movement was limited to Camp Columbia, the key army garrison in Havana. The meeting was public and open, not conspiratorial nor secret. The directors did not plan to take over machine guns, dominate the capital, or arrest the commanders, but simply continue adding demands. One of the ringleaders even proposed: "For a beach house for us at the Jaimanitas beach!" And the proposal was approved unanimously.

One more factor contributed to the hierarchical decay in the army. There had come to exist a *cuerpo extraño*, an "outside corp" or "odd group," consisting of technical officers who had graduated from the military academy. This group of officers demanded the removal of all the higher officers in the chain of command who had originally bypassed them for promotions and advancements into command positions. Moreover, that *cuerpo extraño* of academy officers demanded the elimination of all commanders with the rank of major on up. The sergeants' corps was further isolated in view of those demands and searched for protection from whatever means they could find. They discovered that they had been left alone, but not in the sense of being ignored; it was more the isolation of the weak and disabled.

"We aren't going against anyone. For now, we are going to take care of ourselves, and later we'll see." So said Batista in the course of the meeting on September 4, responding to observations made by the camp's Officer of the Day, Demetrio Ravelo.[2] It was the statement that best and most precisely expressed the circumstances. Certainly, the way the discussion proceeded that day, there was never a single indication of retribution, nor was their ever a point at which anyone ordered that the meeting be adjourned. And meanwhile, the men were feeling more and more bold and secure. The same sergeants — no less than six — that had continued to apprise Lieutenant Colonels Quesada and Perdomo of the course of the meeting by now had more or less joined the movement because they saw the possibility of reaping some benefit. One way or the other, they had, through their betrayal, "covered their retreat," so to speak, and furthermore, had discovered that the commanders did not consider the situation threatening.

On the afternoon of September 4, those of us who had missed the Soler trial began to hear rumors, echoed by some radio stations and by word-of-mouth commentary from individuals considered at the time to be well informed, to the effect that something unusual was happening at Camp Columbia. Even the afternoon edition of *El País* noted that in Columbia there existed a seditious event that seemed to have as its origin "the belief that the salaries of the enlisted personnel would be reduced starting with their next paycheck."

The Directorio was in a state of total alert. It had already confronted the Céspedes government and forced it to declare itself a de facto government, dissolve Congress and remove governors, councillors, mayors, councilmen, and members of the boards of education. Further, even after what we called "the confrontation of August 22," not only did the Directorio object to the general elections the transitional government proposed, but, moreover, the Directorio had made an appeal to the armed forces "to embrace the revolutionary program of the Youth."

Inasmuch as the rumor of sedition might be considered a response, so what if those who answered were not the same to whom they had appealed, "those sound and pure elements within the present military movement," the young academy officers with whom we had been meeting?

It became evident to the men of the DEU that if they were to be true to themselves and return to the people the decisive power that had been spirited away from them through the manipulations of the Ambassador of the United States, those young men had to pay more attention than anyone to the rumor of sedition, even if it was promoted by sergeants, corporals, and soldiers and for objective questions of pay and positions.

Historic determinism compelled the Directorio to repair to Columbia.

CAUSES OF THE SERGEANTS' MOVEMENT: A SYNTHESIS

If I were to employ some sort of subtitle for the first part of this chapter, I would use, with no hesitation at all, the concept of "approach to landing." This most graphic image of a pilot lining up with the runway aptly describes this particular moment in Cuban history.

First, I shall observe from the heights all the conditioning factors of the historic event. Later, I will measure opinions concerning those factors, and finally I shall enter the event itself.

While the trial of Soler unrolled, there occurred in Camp Columbia a gathering of sergeants, corporals, and soldiers, from which would develop the coup d'état *unplanned* by its own initiators. But before getting into the narration of the events that played out after the anguish of Soler's capture, trial, and execution, it is best to review the characteristics of the climate in which the historic event of Columbia would unfold.

After the chaos and anarchy described in the newspaper head-lines during the last days of August came the hurricane on the first of

September. On the heels of the natural disaster followed the political disaster that had been developing for months.

By August 12, all authority had disappeared. With the fall of Machado, order and hierarchy remained hazy. The power vacuum had not been filled, especially not by the provisional government; and its president, former diplomat Carlos Manuel de Céspedes, represented the negation of what the people had tried to accomplish: the punishment of the guilty. In its obligation to spirit away the power of the genuine revolution latent in the subsoil, Welles and Céspedes had no idea that what they were really doing was digging their own political graves.

If every historic date could be captured in a photograph from which could be deciphered what would befall later, we would have a living example of history in the making to analyze and interpret. The history of the Revolution of 1933 had that document. August 12 is identifiable by a photograph that is still published on every anniversary. It is not of any of the traditional opposition chiefs; they did not return to Cuba until many days later. Nor is it that of any labor leader, standing out as a standard-bearer for the political process; neither had there been leadership on that front. It did not show a student, whose class had, indeed, suffered like no other the rigor of an official policy of extermination. No; the symbol of August 12 is the photo of a modest and unknown soldier,[3] standing erect on the shoulders of the crowds after having killed Colonel José Antonio Jiménez, the feared chief of the Machadist *Porra*. This photo shows the initial moments of a hunting party looking for Porristas that lasted three days and resulted in some sixty deaths.

This photo, which is the one most reproduced in our contemporary history, portrays many facets: on the one hand, a certain predominance of the soldier that soon would exert even greater effect and, on the other hand, the sense of vengeance that the recruit had exercised. Completing the frame is the popular participation that exalts that simple soldier as leader of the vengeance. But the interregnum of those historic twenty-three days also produced the discovery of the remains of former sergeant Miguel Angel Hernández Rodríguez, together with those of a student and a worker, an event which would lead to the assumption that a class of sergeants had participated in the revolutionary struggle against the dictatorship in a significant manner.

The general populace, obviously, were self-congratulatory, acting for themselves. Even though they lacked direct power, they exercised it indirectly through association with the members of lower ranks of the armed forces, who approved the disorder and, in some cases, participated in it.

If there is a single factor in history that has proven to be the most direct formula against the state and toward the most rapid dissolution of the authority, it is the confraternization of the popular classes with the army. When the army feels itself an integral part of the great national majority, it unites with that popular majority in a confused identification of sentiments and intentions. The coercive power of the State disappears, and a new authority that will assume power begins to form, now in the name of the revolution.

As authority disappeared, national frustration grew, expressed sporadically by a multitude of demands, among which one prevailed: purge. This word, as differentiated from the concept of punishment, was basically applied to the high military commands, and to the repressive bodies of the State — then the National Police with its Section of "Experts," Secret National Police, and Judicial Police — that in one form or another had participated in persecuting the revolutionaries. While *punishment* implied arrest, trial, and condemnation of those responsible, *purge* implied a lesser tone than punishment, generally requiring the simple replacement of persons in positions of authority.

The concept of punishment within the military was applied narrowly to six or eight colonels and lieutenant colonels accused of having acted against the public welfare during the Machadocracy. Other officers of similar rank would only be caught by the concept of purge; they bore only guilt by association for having held command positions in the military districts during the Machado regime. The "purge" simply demanded their retirement from service, in some cases, and only removal from command in the rest.

Following the chain of command downward with the application of guilt, the concept of purge could have applied as well to those sergeants who offered a homage to Machado ten days after the death of the student leader Rafael Trejo. It was not important that one of them, Fulgencio Batista, stepped forward on August 19 at former sergeant Miguel Angel Hernández' tomb and, as if he had been one of those sergeants discharged and imprisoned for conspiracy, permitted himself, with manifest opportunism, to deliver the eulogy.

After August 12, there had been neither punishment nor purge in the armed forces. Only the leader of Machado's overthrow, Colonel Julio Sanguily Echarte, elevated to the temporary rank of major general upon assuming the office of Chief of Staff of the Army, had been replaced. When Sanguily became gravely ill, he was temporarily replaced by Lieutenant Colonel Héctor de Quesada, whom Secretary of War and the Navy Horacio Ferrer and military historian Ricardo Adam Silva both described in the same way. Ferrer said of de Quesada:

> For many years he was an excellent deskman who knew by heart all the laws, regulations, and orders concerning the Army. It was for that reason that they, unwittingly, insisted on keeping him in the general staff. But he lacked commanding aptitude (Ferrer 1950, 341).

And Adam Silva agreed that

> . . . he was more a deskman than a military man . . . (Adam Silva 1973, 28).

On August 22, three high-ranking officers were called back to active service after years of retirement. On August 29, upon assuming the post of Secretary of War, Horacio Ferrer recalled retired General Armando Montes after consulting with General Sanguily.

Montes' recall was the coronation of the policy of *status quo.* Selected for "having occupied nearly all the posts of greatest importance to the army in earlier years," he had against him the worst of records. As Secretary of War and the Navy under President Zayas (1921-1925) he had, for imperious reasons, reduced billets and salaries, according to Ferrer. Adam Silva added that for precisely that reason "the troops held a grudge against him." The staggering Céspedes regime placed at the highest level of command a military man retired from service for many years and of whom the troops harbored the worst memories.

Consequently, the rumor began to circulate that the number of billets for enlisted men in the army would be reduced, and speculation arose as well that there would be a salary reduction of such magnitude that the incomes of the lowest-ranking soldier would not exceed $13.00 a month. The very same High Command was forced to publish a circular on September 3, discrediting those rumors, and repeated that

... the Army enjoys the prestige that it has always enjoyed, and the salaries and emoluments of our institution will remain unaltered in terms of their computation and rank. Furthermore, when the economic situation of the country returns to normal and all the public salaries are restored to their previous levels, we the military, as servants of the nation, will also receive that which fairly belongs to us (Ferrer 1950, 347; Adam Silva 1947, 482).

Sumner Welles told Washington that "the Army mutiny was originally engineered by a few Communist leaders in Havana under the guidance of Martínez Villena, who got the soldiers to believe that their pay was to be cut and their numbers reduced" (Welles Cable 216, September 8, 1933, 405). But who could have known Montes' record better, Sanguily, the sick leader who would die a few weeks later, or the many sergeants and corporals who had escaped Montes' "pruning" a few years earlier?

Only five days passed between his designation and the Sergeants' Movement. How could the memory of the reduction of billets and salaries not filter like dust through the troops with any time in service?

WELLES AND MENOCAL

While all this was happening, what were Ambassador Sumner Welles and his military advisor, Colonel Gimperling, contributing to this phase of the process?

On August 14, two North American naval vessels, the *Taylor* and the *Claxton*, entered the port of Havana. Welles did not delay in explaining to the commander of the flagship that it was not necessary to land the marines. Later, though, among his commentaries to the Department of State, he stated that in one incident in Marianao "the [Cuban] enlisted men turned on the officers" (Welles Cable 158, August 14, 1933, 363). On August 15, he said that the Secretary of War, the Plattist Castillo Pokorny, had made clear to him that morning that

... if the Government insisted upon replacing the former officials in office by force, the Army in many districts would refuse to carry out orders (Welles Cable 162, August 15, 1933, 365).

He further added:

> . . . I feel that the prime necessity is to bring about at the first possible moment a restoration of discipline of the Army (Welles Cable 162, August 15, 1933, 366).

Three or four days later, he stated:

> . . . I am now daily being requested for decisions on all matters affecting the Government of Cuba. These decisions range from questions of domestic policy and matters affecting the discipline of the Army to questions involving appointments in all branches of the Government (Welles Cable 172, August 19, 1933, 368).

A few days later, he stated:

> . . . the military forces of the Government can only cope with the situation where the detachments are sufficiently large to inspire respect and as I have already informed the Department, the discipline within the Army, while improving, is not yet sufficiently good to give the Government assurance that its orders will be complied with in every instance (Welles Cable 186, August 30, 1933, 377).

And finally, on August 30, Welles informed the State Department that

> The President has appointed this morning Dr. Horatio [sic] Ferrer, Secretary of War and Marine in the place of Captain Castillo Pokorny, who has been appointed Secretary of Agriculture and Commerce to fill the vacancy created by the appointment yesterday of Dr. Rafael Santos Jiménez as Mayor of the city of Havana. Owing to the continued illness of General Sanguily, Chief of Staff, General Armando Montes, retired, has been brought back into active service to serve temporarily as Chief of Staff until General Sanguily is able to resume his duties.
>
> The changes made hold the promise of an immediate improvement in the discipline of the Cuban Army. Dr. Ferrer was until recent years Surgeon General of the Army and has the confidence and support of the great majority of the armed forces (Welles Cable 187, August 30, 1933, 378-79).

In other words, Welles and his military attache, Gimperling, believed that the appointments of Ferrer and Montes signaled an immediate improvement in the discipline of the Army. Before the week was up, it would become obvious that his prediction was completely wrong. But before exploring the consequences of this deterioration, it is worthwhile first to consider the developing conduct of the ex-president and former supreme commander of the armed forces, Major General Mario García Menocal.

There is an historic factor contributing to the Sergeants' Coup that has never been explored. I consider it necessary to incorporate this groundwork into the consideration of the events that developed during this period.

No one has ever explained the strange behavior of former president Menocal. He had always been solicitous of and complacent with the desires of the Chancellery on the Potomac. In January he had welcomed North American intervention into a Cuban problem. Almost immediately upon Sumner Welles's arrival in Cuba in May, he began to establish contact with various sectors and groups including exiled factions and their leaders who could not participate in the Mediation process. Then, suddenly and irrevocably, he shrank from the Mediation in June. Menocal did not express any opposition, nor did he make any statement, verbal or written, against the process as it began. He remained silently on the sidelines, trying to not align himself with the Directorio Estudiantil Universitario's revolutionary position against the Mediation.

Menocal had been protected by the United States from the insurrection against his government in 1917 by nothing less than a declaration from Washington that the Cuban rebels were to be considered, in the middle of World War I, as allies of Germany. This same Menocal, on January 13, 1933, had declared to the International News Service that "It would be sufficient for North America to threaten Machado with intervention — the opposition would do the rest. We would have Machado out of the presidency in less than 24 hours." Menocal added,

> The United States would have every right to intervene in all Cuban affairs because Machado has violated several clauses of the Platt Amendment. I have a government plan that would bring peace and satisfaction to millions in Cuba; but I will reveal this plan only to envoys of the American Government, in private, if they are interested (González Peraza 1933, 285).

This same Menocal, who was used to subordinating his actions to U.S. State Department policy, now became indifferent and shrank from serving the interests of the powerful neighbor again. There remained, then, one unique and ultimate alternative. Sumner Welles himself discovered it.

It was completely unfathomable that the former president, who had so benefitted from the meddlesome policy culminating in the acceptance of the intervention principle by the Sixth International Conference of American States, after having requested that Machado be threatened in January with that policy, should now in June of the very same year reject the Welles mediation.

It is necessary to ask why he adopted this antagonistic position. Brief analysis reveals that Menocal, had he accepted the mediation, would have dissolved as a decisive independent power within a conglomerate of sectors, public figures, and political groups, and he himself would have ceased to be the last real caudillo, since Machado, who had also represented that old political image, was sinking on the horizon.

Menocal was since youth a man of power. A graduate of Cornell University, by virtue of his heroism, he leaped to the grade of Major General of the Liberation Army. At the end of the war, he became chief of the Havana Police, a post he renounced two or three years later to administer a new and powerful sugar processing center. The *Partido Conservador* sought him out there in 1908 and 1912 to run for president on the conservative ticket. Victory favored him in 1912, and now as Chief of State and the armed forces, he immediately began to rid himself of the commanders and officers that had won their commissions in the army as reward for their activities during the insurrection of 1906. Convinced of the necessity of carefully purging the military ranks, he reorganized the Permanent Army and the Rural Guard in 1918 until he was sure that the uprising he had frustrated could not again develop. He had dominated the uprising in February 1917 by defeating former president José Miguel Gómez in Caicaje and making him prisoner, but Menocal was defeated in 1930 when he failed in his coup attempt against Machado and fell into the hands of the loyal troops who frustrated the Río Verde venture. The caudillo knew quite well that the current army was the historic offspring of the Liberation Army in which he had been Major General. He knew, as well, that its officer corps was even more so the offspring of the same origin, especially the older and higher ranking officers, among whom were many of his former companions from the War of Independence and men whom he had favored with promotions during his term as president of the Republic. It was a military class that, without partisan political leanings, had only had three military leaders: José Miguel Gómez, now dead; then Menocal himself, during his eight years as leader of the nation's destiny; and, finally, Machado.

Nevertheless, Machado was losing ground because of public pressure that would ultimately liquidate him when the United States retired its support of his regime. In the critical moment of deposing the last president from the ranks of the Liberation Army, that nonacademic military class would look toward Menocal as the only military caudillo remaining, not toward Mendieta, who had bowed to Menocal since 1931; not toward Miguel Mariano Gómez, whose image was that of the son of a caudillo; nor toward the secret organization ABC nor, much, much less, toward those "young perturbers" of the University. The key man of that military class was none other than Menocal, the old overseer of Chaparra, which was symbolized by that musical instrument called the *timbales.* Why, then, should Menocal dilute himself like all the other forces in the process of the mediation?

It was better and more noble to remain on the outside, not "together with," but in effect "on equal standing with" the Directorio Estudiantil Universitario. *Hands off!* Freedom to act! When he was ready to act, the givens would all be in his favor. It was a *sui generis* [unique] position that, though diametrically opposed, was parallel to that of the DEU. Both had been situated in isolated postures. Menocal followed the path of political calculation; the Directorio, through its radical political formation, had evolved a position diametrically opposed to Menocal. The DEU stood not only against the hero of Las Tunas but also against the ABC, against the Government of Céspedes, against the North American Embassy, and also against the Communist Party, which remained silent at this point in the historic process. Nevertheless, both extreme positions — that of Menocal and that of the DEU — were poles of attraction for power, magnets that would depend on political rather than metallic affinity, for the forces that were developing on all levels. Menocal acted in accordance with logical and deductive organization that, in terms of the old epochs and mechanics of power, would not have a single fault except that it was employed when the weather vane of the times indicated clearly that the banners of change would be hoisted. The velocity of the gusts seemed to show the winds blowing favorably for those who, two years before, had audaciously launched the battle-cry: Change, yes, but total and definitive!

When the worn-out colonial structure began to crack and everything indicated that the final rupture was imminent, it was then — paradoxically — that the two stanchions of that structure — Welles and Menocal — stood farthest apart.

Menocal had returned to Cuba in order to recover his power. Welles had the command in his hand and wanted to maintain the Céspedes government. Menocal had to appeal to the last of his resources: the old officers of high rank still remaining within the armed forces and the retired officers who could be recalled to active service. Welles, to whom it made no difference that those high ranking officers wanted the same as he and Menocal, nevertheless preferred the resolution already reached and that he had managed to impose. Nevertheless, as each works for his own, Menocal began to conspire with the high officers and Welles was vexed to the point that he informed Washington on August 24 that

> . . . The presence of General Menocal in Cuba is as always an exceedingly disturbing factor. His insatiable ambition and his unwillingness to recognize that he no longer can count on the support of any but a small group is causing him to attempt to undermine the authority of the Government, and I am reliably informed that he is trying to promote dissidence among the Army officers (Welles Cable 184, August 24, 1933, 371-72).

THE YOUNG OFFICERS CORPS OF THE NATIONAL ARMY

After reviewing the positions assumed in the course of those historic twenty-three days, and after learning Welles's opinions concerning military discipline, having reasoned over Menocal's motivations for opposing the Mediation that drove him to conspire, which the Ambassador himself denounced to Washington, it is now necessary to examine the attitude the young officers of the National Army had assumed.

An appreciable nucleus of those officers had participated decisively in Machado's overthrow through activities developed in the encampments. Afterward, a large number of those officers had held meetings with Directorio Estudiantil Universitario members, demonstrating their dissatisfaction with their position as a result of that military uprising.

These young officers, by virtue of their military careers, did retain some minimal political responsibility for helping maintain the Machado government. They expressed their dissatisfaction with that role in 1930 and 1931 by making it known that they would back the Supreme Court if it should declare Machado's government unconstitutional. The young officers felt totally disenfranchised within the military and demonstrated that they objected, not only to the abundant power of the old politicians but also to the reestablishment of the old colonial mold. At the same time, they understood that the reorganization of the military commands would only be achieved through the dismissal of the commanders who had proven themselves indifferent to the changing times. I venture to say that the young officer corps, without any great political training — that the DEU, by comparison, had continued to acquire — experienced an identification of historic contemporaneity and generational coincidence with the representatives of the university students' movement. Later, it will become apparent that, for motivational reasons, the final link between these two factors of Cuban society could not crystalize.

Horacio Ferrer, in his book *Con el rifle al hombro*, proves this point:

> There was contagion from the University where they campaigned against the old politicians, proclaiming it was necessary for the young generation to take in hand the destiny of the Republic. They went as far as considering useless all men over forty. They were also impatient for promotion. The officers of the Army, who at the beginning all proceeded from the Liberation Army, were replaced little by little, as I have pointed out, by young men, and probably in 1933 there did not remain more than some ten percent of the old officers. They, of course, occupied the highest posts, because they had twenty-five or thirty years of service, and because of their age they would remain on active duty for only a short while longer (Ferrer 1950, 340).

In continuation, he adds:

> The young officers proceeded unjustly trying to *eliminate all the commanders, from major upward.* The problem was not necessarily that they were led by commanders with insufficient knowledge of tactics and strategy, who from time to time would make disagreeable statements about the academy officers, who, when needed to fight revolutions, lacked sufficient knowledge to live on campaign. The grave problem for the young officers was stagnation in the ranks. Great numbers of cadets had been approved for promotion along with an even greater number of sergeants who had been approved for promotion to officer rank.

Through the previous lines of the man who was Secretary of War and the Navy for only five days, but who had been a decisive participant in the organization of the military coup against Machado, it is possible to determine without the least confusion what the policy of the directors of the established powers in military affairs must have been. It is necessary to remember that Welles already had commented in the message to the Department of State that he had been consulted concerning Army discipline. This leads to the assumption that the military attaché Gimperling, the secretaries of War and the Navy, Castillo Pokorny and Ferrer, and President Céspedes himself all followed the same policy dictated by the highest level of power in this chain of command: the Embassy of the United States.

This policy of *status quo* consisted, originally, in confirming in their positions the officers of the highest rank that had demonstrated their identification with the politico-economic structure of Cuba. It was impossible to retain all of these officers; out of twelve colonels and fourteen lieutenant colonels then on active duty in the National Army, no less than five were accused of serious crimes perpetrated during the Machado government. Another five had acted as commanders of the military districts, and inasmuch as a few had demonstrated excessive sympathy toward the deposed regime, even though they had done nothing criminal, they were, nevertheless, marked for purging.

The policy of *status quo*, then, had to be expanded to reincorporate retired officers of the old politico-economic leanings into the military. In order to implement that policy, Decree 1262 of August 22 was issued, recalling to active service "those retired from sea and land forces that the Secretary of War and the Navy may deem necessary during the time that constitutional rights and guarantees may be suspended or that disturbances of public order continue."

Who signed the decree, below the signature of President Céspedes? Well, no less than Demetrio Castillo Pokorny, graduate of West Point — the man most likely to have consulted Welles concerning the discipline of the Army, since he was the Secretary of War and the Navy on August 24, the day the Ambassador commented on that subject in Cable 184 (371-73).

This measure was the perfect bottleneck against the free flow of promotion among the young officers, who had to feel defrauded by the return to duty, a few days later, of three retired colonels. These three men had been called to serve as members of the Superior War Council of the Sea and Land Forces, but according to the decree recalling them, they could function in other roles as well. Specifically, the decree stated that they would be "appointed to the Court-Martial without affecting special commissions and services compatible with their ranks."

Emilio Laurent, my personal friend, had several reasons to be a qualified spokesman on this theme. He was born on a military post at Artemisa, where his father was commander of the unit. At seventeen he entered the Cadet School in Morro Castle, and at twenty-one he was a second lieutenant in the army. At twenty-five he was at the head of his class in Cavalry School. After a tour of duty in Oriente, he attended Artillery School, where he was also first in his class and won the Seventh Military District trophy. The Constitutional Reform and the Extension of Powers prompted him to turn conspirator. He participated first in Colonel Julio Aguado's conspiracy, aborted on October 5, 1930, and later in the failed attempt to assault the garrisons on December 24 of the same year. Absolved by the Military Court for the first conspiracy, his participation in the second was discovered and his arrest ordered. He was able to flee to the United States where, after a few months in exile, he assumed leadership of the *Ilse Volkmaner* expedition after Colonel Rosendo Collazo — who was originally designated to lead the expedition — was arrested in Atlantic City along with no less than a hundred people linked to the plan. Laurent led the expedition and, after taking the town of Gibara by assault with only 37 expeditionaries, he directed the party toward Holguín, one of the most important outposts of the army. Hounded by land, sea, and air forces loyal to the Machado government, Laurent and nearly all his companions were captured, and Emilio was sent under heavy guard to Havana. Later he was transported to Modelo Penitentiary on the Isle of Pines, where he spent two years.

That academy officer turned revolutionary expressed his opinions concerning the weak influence that the young military professionals exercised within the services in his book, *De oficial a revolucionario* (From Officer to Revolutionary):

> In the old Army of Cuba the highest echelon of command was occupied by a corps of officers which in its majority proceeded from the ranks of the Liberation Army. They lacked adequate technical preparation. The military commanders exercised real command within that army, almost exclusively through a direct understanding with the ranks, especially the sergeants, who in turn served to support their commanding officers.
>
> Between the top level of command and the sergeants, there appeared with time a *cuerpo extraño* [outside corps, "odd group"] formed by the technical officers. This group, instead of exercising leadership among the rank and file as was their duty as leaders of men, retreated to their exclusive ivory tower of cultural and social superiority, progressively distancing themselves from the rest. It should never be forgotten that an army is a mass of men organized and armed — the rank and file — commanded by a select minority: the officers (Laurent 1941, 132).

We have already seen why those that commanded in Cuba chose a policy of delaying history and perhaps even turning it back through their manipulations of the military. This already established policy impeded the development of the natural changes that would have prevented the Sergeants' Movement, even though those changes might not have been truly revolutionary.

After eight years of Machado government and the concentration of power in the hands of the Chief of Staff Alberto Herrera, after the fall of the regime and numerous military conspiracies, an elemental restorational policy was imposed that, in the military, would have required a fluid replacement of commanders. In face of the inevitable generational replacement, the four levels of command — Ambassador Welles and his aide Gimperling, President Céspedes, the Secretaries of War and the Navy Castillo Pokorny and Ferrer and Chief of Staff Major

Montes — committed the error of trying to shore up the old military structure with the same men with the same colonialist attitudes, all of whom lacked the capacity to command the troops that fraternized in the streets with the popular classes.

If a simple, fair formula had been applied, rather than recalling the old retired officers who had been on the sidelines during the revolutionary effort to overthrow Machado, the colonel and those lieutenants who had conspired against the dictatorship and had been court-martialed would have been reinstated and promoted. Those young officers with brilliant academy careers who had participated decisively in Machado's overthrow would have been promoted also. The thirty sergeants, corporals, and soldiers imprisoned in Modelo Penitentiary on the Isle of Pines for conspiring against Machado would have been returned to duty.

Of course, this reinstatement and promotion of young officers, sergeants, corporals, and soldiers would have constituted a truly revolutionary event. It would have ultimately reestablished the control of the Cuban Army at the service of the renovationist thought and with a totally modern internal homogeneity.

Without a doubt, these realizations would have produced some conflicts at the time. The military and political scene would clearly have changed. Furthermore, the sergeants, without true leadership over the masses — which Batista never had — would have been incapable of venturing the least attempt to present their union-like demands (their only real objectives in the first place), much less to subvert and overthrow the government.

Furthermore, these reinstatements would have created a chain of interior political unity during those inevitable, agitated days. A texture would have been created — based on the history of common struggle — a texture that would have engaged the machinery of the distinct elements that constitute the legitimacy of a young and genuine revolutionary authority.

Such reinstatements and promotions, updating the rank structure by promoting captains and lieutenants to colonel, lieutenant colonel, and major, would have generated a movement that would have carried many sergeants, now considered supernumerary officers, to the rank of lieutenant. Consequently, many corporals would ascend to sergeant, and a significant number of basic soldiers would move up to corporal.

Of course, such a broad reorganization could not have been completed in twenty-three days. Simply to set it in motion, nevertheless, would have altered the outlook of the participants in the process. The mental attitude and daily activity of those in uniform would have produced results quite different from those which occurred. A current of cooperation and accommodation would have been generated that would have overcome the stagnation in the ranks and the indefinite permanence, as supernumerary officers, of the approved sergeants. It would have created the bond among the academy officers and sergeants to which Laurent referred. Those promotions would have created among everyone, from the most recently promoted colonels and majors on down to the sergeants, corporals, and basic soldiers, a new structure of military command with an interior cohesion far superior to what then existed. Thus, the events of September 4 would have occurred in a completely different manner.

Of course, in order for all that to occur, a revolutionary president, resistant to the influence of the United States Embassy, would have had to be in power. That president would also have required a capable and revolutionary Secretary of War and the Navy who understood the signs of the times and was willing to live in the barracks of Camp Columbia and the Fortress of La Cabaña. Only then could the authority of the chain of command be effectively reestablished.

But even if the reorganization of the military had been undertaken by adequate men, the consequences of such changes would have been incompatible with the lack of spirit of renovation that characterized the political activity of the State. Thus, the goals pursued through those very necessary changes still would not have been fully realized.

In effect, until the day of confrontation, August 22, the government tried to maintain the Congress, retain the provincial governors and councillors, the municipal mayors and councillors, and to avoid any type of purge within the Judicial Branch. The government even began to arrange a loan with the United States. In other words, it remained firmly entrenched in the political apparatus of the Machadist power.

MILITARY CAUSES OF THE SERGEANTS' COUP: DETAILED EXPOSITION

Before going on with new considerations, I shall proceed — for the reader's benefit — to create a framework of the facts and events that contributed to the generation of the Sergeants' movement. This would equate to landing on the runway, in keeping with the aviation image. In so doing, I will include accounts by eye witnesses and active participants. These are testimonies, not journalistic reports.

This is my framework:

Critical period between the two coups:		23 days
Individuals holding title of Chief of Staff of the Army:		3

Time served by each:

Sanguily:	leader of the Machado overthrow:	*2 days*
Quesada:	more bureaucrat than military man:	*16 days*
Montes:	recalled after years of retirement:	*5 days*

In analyzing the events and decisions concerning this critical period, twenty significant causes emerge. Some were institutional; others, chance. Some were generated within the military institutions and were repercussions in the strictly military sense, while others were generated in the civil arena. Several led directly to the historic event called the Sergeants' Coup of September 4, 1933.

> 1. A soldier, not an officer, became the symbol of August 12, 1933, as captured in the historic photo reproduced in this book. The simple soldier became, more than a representative of the authority, a symbol of the popular demands for punishment, purge, liberties, and reforms.

Jorge Luis Borges has said, "what we call chance is our ignorance of the complete machinery of causality" (Borges [1980] 1984, 8). With that in mind, it no longer seems simple historic causality that six years before (1927) the famous Soviet film producer Eisenstein had, in his movie about the Russian Revolution, *October*, symbolically used an engraving amazingly similar to the real August 12 photo of the Cuban soldier. The explosive power that the photo expressed — the linking of the soldier with popular aspirations — remained undetected by the military advisors of the United States, by the Secretary of War and the Navy, and by the successive chiefs of the Cuban General Staff.

> 2. Ambassador Welles and his military aide Gimperling developed a policy to consolidate Cuban military authority in the older, higher ranking officers; the implementation of that policy began with decisions adopted by the Céspedes government.

Washington and its Cuban servants did not know then that, in certain historic crossroads, the solutions inherent in institutional or traditional norms cannot but encourage an irrational and deteriorating vicious circle.

> 3. This policy, in terms of the watchwords of punishment and purge, meant refusing to court-martial officers gravely implicated with the deposed regime; nor did it allow a purge of the Army by retiring older, high-ranking officers with responsibilities derived from exercising the commands of regiments during the fallen regime. Neither were the enlisted ranks purged, especially of those (including Batista) who had organized the homage to President Machado ten days after the death of student leader Rafael Trejo.

Even the extremely conservative Colonel Cosme de la Torriente noted the terribly grave error of President Céspedes, the military, and the commanders of the August 11 coup

> . . . upon not proceeding urgently to cleanse the Army of all those officers and enlisted personnel that had been docile and criminal instruments of the tyranny and despised by the Cuban people (Torriente, 1938; Soto 1977 Vol. III, 72).

> 4. Presidential Decree 1272 of August 23, 1933, authorized the Secretary of War and the Navy to call to active service retired officers, impeding the normal process of promotion to fill the seventy-nine slots of higher rank. No less than forty of those slots remained vacant as a result of this move.

> 5. Under the terms of that same decree, three retired colonels were recalled to service.

> 6. A colonel and four lieutenants discharged and imprisoned for conspiring against the overthrown regime were not reinstated into the army.

> 7. Young officers who played a decisive role in Machado's overthrow were not reinstated.

> 8. The sergeants, corporals, and soldiers discharged and imprisoned for conspiracy against the previous regime were likewise excluded from the reinstatements.

9. Major General Mario G. Menocal, the former president and commander-in-chief of the armed forces, was, according to Ambassador Welles, "trying to promote dissidence among the Army officers" (Welles Cable 184, August 24, 1933, 372).

Some of his followers remained in high command positions within the military, and others were recalled to service to fill additional command slots. The institutional policy created a vicious circle within the military, forcing the institution to regress more than a decade.

10. According to Colonel Ferrer, then Secretary of Defense, the high commanders, themselves with insufficient knowledge and training, at times expressed disagreeable statements concerning the actions and capacities of academy officers (Ferrer 1950, 340).

11. The young academy officers, guilty only by association for the crimes of the tyranny, requested the elimination of all officers from the rank of major on up.

Points 10 and 11 form part of the vicious circle generated by the institutional policy. The consolidation of high commands in the hands of old-style military men prevented the normal promotion of future military leaders. This is the counterweight in the vicious circle created by Menocal's cronies in command and their return to the army of the past.

The "chance" factors are, in turn, dependent on that same institutional policy.

12. The Chief of the General Staff who became ill 48 hours after the overthrow of President Machado and his Chief of the Army was replaced. Colonel Sanguily was temporarily replaced during his illness not by an officer such as Colonel Agaudo, convicted in October 1930 of plotting against Machado while serving as commander of the Military District of La Cabaña, but by an administrative bureaucrat (Quesada), who had not held a command position in years.

13. The Secretary of War and the Navy was replaced by a retired medical colonel, Doctor Horacio Ferrer.

14. The new Secretary of War and the Navy, upon the continued illness of the Army Chief of Staff, designated a

new Chief of Staff who had reduced billets and salaries years before as Secretary of War and the Navy. The designee, who would ultimately detonate the coup, was Colonel Armando Montes.

15. The new Army Chief of Staff, Colonel Montes, embarked with President Céspedes on September 2 for the province of Santa Clara to evaluate the damages caused by a hurricane. During his absence, he appointed Colonel Quesada, who had just served as interim Chief of Staff for Sanguily for sixteen days, to serve in that post again.

16. Lieutenant Colonel Perdomo finished his tour of duty as commander of Camp Columbia. His replacement was an old-style military man, sympathetic to the deposed Chief of Machado's General Staff, General Herrera. Until his arrival, Major Pineda assumed command of the encampment. Therefore, on September 4, the acting Chief of Staff was a military bureaucrat and the acting commander of Columbia, near retirement.

At this point, I must incorporate the authoritative opinion of Emilio Laurent, who in his book *De oficial a revolucionario*, described the situation this way: "The academy officers were a *cuerpo extraño* wedged between the high commanders and the sergeants, among those who were within the chain of command. But since the high commands were undergoing a process of investigation and accountability, the sergeants were practically left on their own" (Laurent 1941, 132-34).

17. The sergeants had no intention of doing away with their officers, but they were concerned that at the time there were 122 second lieutenants awaiting promotion, and they were to share half of the vacancies with those sergeants who had completed the Sergeants' School and had more than eight years in grade and twenty years in the army, (Perez 1976, 79)[4] in accordance with the basic law of 1926, which had reformed the so-called Law of the Sergeants.

We shall now see the facts that, though not strictly military in character, had a direct and profound impact not only on the so-called Sergeants' Movement but on the backing the Directorio Estudiantil would lend that movement as well.

18. Soldiers fraternized with the popular classes in the streets.

19. The remains of a sergeant, a student, and a worker were discovered in the hillside of Atarés Castle, which psychologically forged a potential link between students and soldiers.

20. Sergio Carbó's article, written after he attended the multitudinous wake of the three victims, containing his call for students, workers, and soldiers to unite, exacerbated the historically explosive potential generated by the Mediation process, by Ambassador Welles's continued manipulation of the policies of the Céspedes government, by popular frustration over the provisional government, by the failure of the North American policy that it followed to consolidate military commands in the older officer corps, and by the incapacity of the government to interpret the new signs of the times.

REACTION OF THE DIRECTORIO

This recapitulation covers strictly military factors without considering the existing revolutionary state, the sensation of instability, or the lack of control that the government itself had over its own decisions, causing it frequently to reverse itself on critical issues.

Therefore, the causes I cited as having led to apparently illogical consequences actually expedited the emergence at that exact moment from within the military institution in crisis of an individual to assume the role of the nonexistent natural leader. *Ersatz* it was called in Europe in the pre-war era of the 1930s, the synthetic products that substituted for those scarce or unaffordable essential articles. The armed forces, after failing to accomplish the normal generational succession in rank and hierarchy within what had been and must continue to be the backbone institution of the Republic, had no choice but to follow an *ersatz* leader who was far from being a natural military leader. Now another bureaucrat — not Lieutenant Colonel Quesada, who was at least a qualified bureaucrat — would arise to take charge of the General Staff; but this time it would be a sergeant, and not even a line sergeant. Worse yet, he would be a consummate politician.

As I said earlier, on the afternoon of September 4, the members of the Directorio who had missed the Soler trial began to hear rumors over the radio and through comments from well-informed people that something strange was going on in Camp Columbia.

In my case, I recall finding myself in the company of Rafael García Bárcena, another member of the Directorio Estudiantil Universitario. We went to the home of another companion, Juan Antonio Rubio Padilla, to find out how the trial of Soler had concluded since we knew, it being evening, that it must be over. At the same time, we were looking for further information about the rumor of the movement in Columbia. From that house in the Buenavista district in Marianao, we made a good number of telephone calls until we found out that Soler had been shot and that there was indeed a meeting of sergeants, corporals, and soldiers in Columbia, and they were composing a list of demands for presentation to the high military commanders. In view of this information, we decided to go to the camp. We were not reacting like recently graduated cadets from the Academy about to become officers; nor did we rely on the psychology and experience of a colonel with twenty years of service. To the contrary, we had, more so than the young officers, an allergy to colonels. We reacted like revolutionaries and not like students. (Recall the link between the students and the sergeants in Modelo Penitentiary on the Isle of Pines as described in Chapter 1, and note the interpretation provided by psychoanalyst Facundo P. Lima later in this chapter.)

We had gained a great deal of confidence; we were on the point of overthrowing Céspedes; and this movement at Camp Columbia might be the vehicle for that overthrow. These circumstances prompted us to get moving. We set out for Columbia to see what was going on, to figure out what we should do, and to see what we could accomplish.

When we left for Columbia, we did not even remotely consider — in spite of the psychological determinism that will soon become evident — that the sergeants would constitute the ultimate solution to the military conflict Machado had left behind. Perhaps — we felt more or less subconsciously — this might be an opportunity to bring down the Plattist regime Ambassador Welles had imposed and, after a very brief intermediate step, we might achieve an easy formula of happy adjustment to the apparatus of the State.

For us, in that historic moment filled with passions, the question of the instrument we were about to utilize was secondary — we believed, very transitional — to returning to the citizens of Cuba the right to rule their own destiny. Even though we recognized what was the optimum, final formula for the organization of the armed forces, we felt that the destruction of the colonial mold that represented equally the historic past of republican Cuba and the Welles-Céspedes government had greater priority. We wanted to lay the foundations of a solid and new structure that would permit the construction of a different Cuba, free, independent, and sovereign, so that its citizens would be able to develop for themselves their greatest achievements.

I must state that these speculations are strictly personal, and that in the vertiginous progression of events, we could not see any other alternative to what we assumed then. That said, I proceed now to the events that allowed the 1930 Directorio Estudiantil Universitario, without meeting beforehand nor making any relevant decision as a group, to back the Sergeants' Coup. That decision was made as much as a result of determining historic circumstances, which were oriented toward fundamental changes, as it was because of the inexplicable reactions of the human mind.

THE DIRECTORIO'S PSYCHOLOGICAL TRANSFORMATION ON SEPTEMBER 4

Before providing detailed information on the events that developed, I wanted to consult a psychoanalyst of the highest qualifications, Doctor Facundo P. Lima, graduate of the specialized academy of Topeka, Kansas, which has come to be the center of the world in that scientific discipline and in which practiced — among other great figures of this science — Doctor Anna Freud, daughter of the master Sigmund Freud.

I questioned the doctor about what psychological influence could have been exercised on the three members of the Directorio, and later on the rest of the members, that we should decide to converge on Camp Columbia, after having lived together in the Modelo Penitentiary with "other" sergeants, corporals, and soldiers.

I clearly framed the question in terms of determining if that cohabitation for several months with low-ranking military personnel could have subconsciously influenced us in the development of that conscious decision.

For the most exact understanding, as much of the question as of the answer, I think it opportune to transcribe our conversation as it was originally recorded on magnetic audio tape.

Carrillo: Do you think that the human relationship created in the Modelo Penitentiary a year before September of 1933 between the students and the sergeants, corporals, and soldiers could have influenced the nearly automatic decision of the members of the Directorio to converge on Camp Columbia on September 4, with only the knowledge that sergeants, corporals, and soldiers were in rebellion and were preparing a letter of demands? Please, in your response take into account that ten of us eighteen civilians that signed the proclamation of takeover that night in Columbia had cohabited with sergeants, corporals, and solders in the Penitentiary.

Lima: I believe that the link created in the prison was revitalized a few months later with the discovery in Atarés Castle of the remains of a worker, a student — as a matter of fact, a member of the Directorio — and a sergeant, according to what I have read and you have confirmed to me.

But furthermore, the common funeral procession of the three, headed by the student martyr, further cemented the newly revitalized bond. In a way we could say that there existed three antecedents instead of one, to add to your question concerning the influence that those events could have exercised in impelling you to direct yourselves to Columbia to learn the status of the subversion that existed there.

The Directorio was impelled by that which you yourself have called "historic determinism," that is, the series of circumstances that had led to the proposal of the overthrow of Céspedes. Now I am going to try to interpret the events in the simplest form and expression possible to, in turn, make my response more comprehensible.

I must begin by saying that one of the fundamental principles on which the psychoanalytical theory created by that great Viennese Sigmund Freud is based is that the greater part of our mental processes, be they in the form of thoughts, emotions, or actions, are, in great percentage, unconscious in nature; that is, we are not aware or conscious of what we are thinking, of what we are saying, or of the manner in which we act.

Of course, this that I have said has been the basis of extraordinary controversies in the scientific centers that deal with the psychology and functioning of the human mind. Nevertheless, for us psychoanalysts, in our daily practice, when we see time and again the actions, thoughts, or emotions that our patients bring to us, this principle of psychoanalysis becomes obvious and is demonstrable in a large percentage of the cases.

The other fundamental principle of psychoanalysis is the principle of psychical determinism; that is, that in our mind as well as in nature around us, nothing happens by *chance*, that a psychological event is in the majority of instances determined by those events which preceded it. Our work as psychoanalysts, as a part of the work that is ours to develop, is to demonstrate to the patients that many actions that for them seem inexplicable are, in reality, determined by thoughts and emotions that they have forgotten, or suppressed, as we say, of which they have no memory or did not consciously have, and that, nevertheless, existed.

Entering materially with respect to your query, it seems to me that there must have been other facts that would explain the presence in Columbia that early morning of September 4, 1933, of prominent leaders of the 1930 Directorio Estudiantil Universitario.

I have heard certain hypotheses, but the historic fact of the presence in the Penitentiary of another group of sergeants with you, members of the DEU, carries with it, in my opinion, a fundamental explanation of your presence at Columbia and the support you gave to the Sergeants' Coup.

Without a single doubt, you can confirm, Justo, that when you received the news that there was a seditious movement among the sergeants in Columbia, you could not in any way react in the same form as would have an officer of the National Army. No, among yourselves, there was present, in a latent or unconscious manner, if you like, the relationship that had been established with those sergeant companions in prison, recipients of the solidarity and the human warmth that you offered in the wards of the Penitentiary on the Isle of Pines. You reacted perhaps in an unconscious form but, as humans to the end, you went to Columbia to see what was happening, in order to repeat a phrase that you yourself have used.

It seems to me that the psychological forces, that in those wards of the penitentiary created a certain union between you and the imprisoned sergeants, assumed an evident manifestation in the early morning of the fourth of September, when you presented yourselves in Columbia to give a revolutionary character to that which possibly was not intended to be more than a mob of unionist [syndical] character. That is why I think that it is an extremely important and significant fact explaining your presence with the Septembrist Sergeants in that historic dawn in the summer of 1933.

Those events of that memorable September morning, in which the underlying psychological forces explained with ultimate clarity by Doctor Lima contributed greatly, will now be described by Doctor Juan Antonio Rubio Padilla in our dialogue which I reproduce here.

THE EVENTS OF SEPTEMBER 4:
DIALOGUE BETWEEN THE AUTHOR AND JUAN ANTONIO RUBIO PADILLA

Carrillo: The problem, upon recalling your participation and mine in the events that occurred on the night of September 4, 1933, is that I have gaps principally in respect to the hour at which we arrived at Columbia, even though I remember very well the various activities in which each of us was involved. In order to be a little more exact, I would commence by saying that neither of us was present for the trial and execution of Soler. I recall that because we had heard rumors that something strange was occurring at the camp, Rafael García Bárcenas and I went to find you at the house in the Almendares suburb and together we confirmed the rumors. That is why we decided to go to Columbia. We headed out in that direction, your wife Dania and the three of us. I recall quite well that upon arriving at Columbia, there were only two civilians, Ramiro Valdés Daussá and Santiago Alvarez. It would have been eight or nine at night. . . .

Rubio Padilla: Right now, I recall, for some reason that I cannot specify, that we believed originally that the center of the thing was in the Aviation [Branch], and we headed there intent on entering. Remember? But there was no way to persuade the soldiers on guard at the gate to let us pass. Then we decided to head for Columbia. We went in a European convertible automobile, a Dedione Butone that you had, and we travelled that night with the top down.

When we went to enter the camp by the entrance immediately at the end of the tramway, that is to say, where Avenida de los Oficiales ["Officers Row"] began, two soldiers with bayonets in place stepped out and told us that we could not pass under any circumstances since all entry there was prohibited. Then I began to try to convince them who we were, but all of it was useless. They had strict orders not to allow passage to absolutely anyone. Fortunately, at that moment we saw, coming down Avenida de los Oficiales from within toward the post where we were arguing, accompanied by two soldiers, our friend from the DEU, Ramiro Valdés Daussá, dressed in his red university letter sweater with the H on the back, that he had won in his sports contests. Upon recognizing us, Ramiro gave orders to the soldiers to let us pass. It was our first shock of the evening: to hear Ramiro speaking to the soldiers, not in a tone of persuasion, but on the contrary, in the tone one employs to give threatening orders when one has authority, and the soldiers obeyed, permitting our entry into the compound. From that moment on, we were aware that *the process of that day*, whatever it might have been, *had reached a level in which the students within the Camp already had authority.*

We went directly to the theater, which was a type of Enlisted Mens' Club and was situated beyond the offices of the commander of the Sixth District. The theater was full of noncommissioned officers and enlisted men, discussing what had occurred during the day, which was the course of that meeting and which was what moved us to present ourselves there. Thus, we could form for ourselves some judgment concerning how far the soldiers and the NCOs were disposed to go, not only in the military terrain, in which they had already consummated a rebellion, but also in the political aspect.

We confirmed that what the periodicals had published that afternoon and that those *enlisted men themselves had said, which was that the movement did not have the least political aim* and furthermore bore *the characteristics of some type of union strike with classist demands,* some of which were so mundane and superficial as the right to wear leather leggings and not the classic canvas leggings standard for the NCOs and enlisted personnel. Another demand referred to the "plate-shaped" [flat] cap used exclusively by officers. In the end, none of the ten or twelve demands enumerated in the formal list of the movement, including that which insisted on the end of the "aides" to the officers, had even the slightest political tone.

What had the greatest impact on me that night was my amazement at how all the classic military discipline of the National Army had completely fallen away to the point that soldiers met in an assembly to request or demand of their superiors, in a forceful manner, whatever demands came to mind.

Carrillo: Yes, but you cannot overlook the fact that the meeting was held with permission from the High Staff. The enlisted men had the authorization of competent authorities to hold the meeting. I remember that while the inquiries were being made over the course of the events, the poet Bárcena and I went to my house to search for some three thousand Directorio manifesto-programs, which had been printed and distributed only a couple of weeks earlier. The aim was to try to get the assembly to approve our program, remember?

Rubio Padilla: Yes, I remember it perfectly, and I was the one who made it happen. Look. Once there, because of the circumstances and because of the arrival of "Pepelín" Leyva, "Chino" Seijas, Labourdette, and others, I realized that it was the same conspiracy "of sergeants" of which Leyva, Seijas, and Labourdette had been informing the Directorio, since they had been authorized to remain in contact with the conspirators and keep us informed. But speaking personally, it was my first encounter with Fulgencio Batista, Pablo Rodríguez, Mario Alfonso Hernández, and the others in charge of the movement.

Concerning this conspiracy, I recall perfectly that the first news we had that some companions from the Directorio were in contact with it was when they told us [about it] shortly after a meeting we had with a group of young officers of the Army, among whom I remember Goudie, González Parra, Valdés Fauli, etc. The meeting took place in the dining room of Gustavo Cuervo's home on O Street at the corner of Twenty-first in Vedado, and when it ended, when the officers had already left, Leyva, Seijas, and Labourdette put before us the problem of the sergeants' conspiracy.

As you'll be able to understand, this episode in the dining room of Gustavo's house offers a *very clear idea of our state of mind and of our decision or will to precipitate the situation existing at that moment and seize power.* In fact, we were simultaneously involved in two parallel military conspiracies, but I personally had not had any contact with the conspiring sergeants. I venture to say that, in truth, *in technical capacity from a military standpoint, and in human quality as well as personally and morally, we trusted the young officers far more than we did the sergeants.* Later, the facts and their ultimate behavior would demonstrate that we were not misguided.

Carrillo: But we return to the historic narration of that night. . . .

Rubio Padilla: You had returned to your house with García Bárcena and brought something like three thousand manifesto-programs of the Directorio. When you arrived, a meeting was improvised in the doorway of the Enlisted Club in which members of the DEU who had already arrived participated and in which were included other members who arrived much later. In that *doorway meeting,* I repeat, the discussion with some of the sergeants that directed the movement — among them, I perfectly recall Pablo Rodríguez — *centered on how to transform all of that,* which up until that moment had no more than a strictly classist character, *into a political movement that would cement a military coup d'état overthrowing the government,* doing away with the juridical *status* created by the resurrection of the Constitution of 1901 and *establishing a de facto government in order to lead the nation toward a future theoretically framed in the Directorio's Program.* Once an apparent agreement was achieved on this basic and fundamental question, we decided that we would have to bring about within the assembly of corporals and soldiers the conversion of what had been done until that time into a coup d'état to seize power with a de facto government and a program, and that the Program of the Directorio Estudiantil, the only faction that was not involved in the government, would be proposed to the assembly. It was decided and it was I who would inform the assembly of the DEU Program.

It was then that we entered the assembly; we were presented as a group and received with visible signs of pleasure and encouraging applause, and I was announced to read the Directorio Program. I went up to the lectern and read the program, which was acclaimed at the end and supported without discussion by all those present; so automatically, in that moment, all that had occurred during the day was technically and in fact converted into a military coup d'état with a political orientation defined according to the text of the manifesto made public the twenty-second of August by the DEU.

As a natural consequence of the course events were taking, the next step was urgently to try to communicate with all the other military districts in La Habana province. This step required that contacts with the interior of the Republic be established from the staff offices of Camp Columbia that, incidentally, were located next to the Enlisted Club. Those offices were closed and dark, and no one had the keys. I recall that the entrance had to be forced by breaking some glass from a side window, through which one of the soldiers entered. He turned on the lights and opened the main door. Then we all went over there, the *group of members of the Directorio and the sergeants that had advanced the conspiracy, along with other civilians,* among whom I remember Sergio Carbó, Julio Gaundard, José Miguel Irisarri, Alejandro Vergara, and Gustavo Cuervo Rubio, who were among the first to enter the offices of the Staff.

The program the DEU presented to the assembly had been developed basically in a time period that coincided with our activities in exile, acquiring arms in different parts of the United States and moving them, first to Miami and later to Key West, in accordance with, I think, what you tell.

After we rejected the Mediation, the responsibility to produce a revolutionary movement capable of overthrowing Machado and seizing power was reduced to what we would be able to do, and the Directorio accepted the battle plan conceived and planned by Emilio Laurent based on the military takeover of the University Campus in order to fortify ourselves there and create a very difficult situation for the Machado government and the army, that we thought would lead to the crisis that would finally provoke a rupture between the army and the government. I recall that we reasoned that, given the degree of moral decomposition and the lack of authority in public power, *the army was not going to lend itself as the instrument to squash an insurrection promoted by the Directorio, especially if it considered the moral support the representative student organization was sure to have with the Cuban public.*

Parallel to all these belligerent activities, the portion of the Directorio in exile in Florida, that had maintained contact with the Havana Directorio, had decided that it was imperative to donate war resources to the organization because of all the defections to the North American Mediation. *Furthermore, they continued to add to the future responsibilities of directing the revolutionary struggle and the takeover of power, for which we lacked a specific program for the organization of a revolutionary government, the determination of the course of action to follow, and the goals that we proposed to reach, when that eventuality arrived.*

As usually occurred when we had to construct a document or program, which required discussions, precision of aims, and careful interpretations of concepts until then barely outlined in imprecise terms, several people intervened. Some of them were not members of the Directorio, although very directly tied to it, like José Miguel Irisarri. He, for the geographic circumstance of being exiled in Key West, maintained very close personal contact with the members of the Directorio in exile, who, because of the circumstances that I explained before in reference to the acquisition of arms and later translation to Key West, made frequent trips to that city.

Thus, there were *two simultaneous processes of great intensity: one, the purchase and conveyance of arms, and the other, in contrast, the study and deliberation of ideological points of view as a means of fixing with total clarity our position in terms of the seizure and exercise of power.* Of course, we maintained close contact with the Havana Directorio, and out of all that emerged the program that was read in Columbia the night of September 4 and was adopted as the official program of the revolutionary movement.

The Program had been published on August 22, a memorable day because it was the day of confrontation with the Céspedes government.[5] Upon clamorously approving the Program, the assembly of corporals and enlisted men expected all of us immediately to seize power and exercise it, constrained by the *limitations imposed by the program itself. Therefore, the first step was to establish the Executive Commission,* which the national press — with markedly pejorative intent — called from the first moment "The Pentarchy."

Carrillo: At what time, more or less, *was the military agreement achieved to give support to the program?*

Rubio Padilla: Well, I don't recall exactly, but it must have been *around eleven or twelve that night.*

Carrillo: What civilians participated in the events at that moment?

Rubio Padilla: The civilians mentioned before, a few names more or a few names less; but it must be said that at that moment in which the agreement was adopted, all or nearly all of them remained in the doorway of the Enlisted Club. *The only one that entered the assembly and read the program in representation of the Directorio was I, and it was I who required of the assembly that at the end of the reading they should decide on the document. The response, unanimous and clamorous, was of support and backing of the program.*

The first point of the program to put into immediate execution was the creation of the Executive Commission. Once we moved to the District headquarters, as I explained earlier, the first thing we did was to select the personalities that would make up the Commission. Then, in fact, a small group was formed by the Directorio members present there, and we began to shuffle names and make decisions. We were surprised that *some of the sergeants already had an opinion concerning one of the persons that, in their judgment, should form part of the new and important executive organ.* That did not cease to surprise us, since we had no idea of the popularity of that individual among the military. *It was no less than Sergio Carbó.* I doubt that, without the presence of this factor, the Directorio, allowed to select freely, would have selected Carbó, not because we had any particular prejudice against him, but because his relations with the DEU and our knowledge of his political activity would not have moved us to select him. But since we did not have any grave prejudice against him, there did not exist sufficient reason to veto him. Carbó's election was the logical consequence of a spirit of collaboration with the military that, in fact, was what produced the juncture that permitted us to seize the power and the future of Cuba.

The popularity Carbó enjoyed in the seat of the armed forces at that time evidently derived from the article he published in the August 26 edition of *La Semana*, exactly eight days before his designation to form part of the Executive Commission. At that time no one enjoyed greater support among the troops.

Upon advancing other names, one of the first to be cited was Ramón Grau San Martín, who was accepted by every one of the DEU members present. After that José Miguel Irisarri, Guillermo Portela, and Carlos de la Torre were also nominated.

Before going any further, I must state that parallel to our small meetings there, standing around and deciding who we were going to search for in their homes, like Grau, Portela, and de la Torre, the sergeants were contacting all the military districts situated in the interior of the country and informing them of the movement, all of which added to the action occurring in Columbia in the short period of an hour or hour and a half. It was already a fact that the entire National Army, with the sergeants at the forefront in every district, had incorporated itself into the revolutionary coup d'état, so that all concern had disappeared in regard to the possibility of a confrontation with military forces hostile to the revolution.

Once we had decided that Grau and José Miguel Irisarri, both coincidentally absent, would form part of the Executive Commission, it seemed to us most urgent that someone go to find them and Portela and de la Torre. I assumed that responsibility and left Columbia with you. We went first to Portela's home to inform him of what was going on; we required his presence at the Camp, and since he had the means of getting there, since he had an automobile which he drove or because he had a chauffeur, we went on to Grau's home on Seventeenth Street, which was dark. It cost us a great deal of work to wake him. At last, he came personally to open the garden gate that was closed and padlocked. We met with some resistance when we notified Grau and required his presence in Columbia, not only because Grau had ignored all that was occurring and it came as a complete surprise to him, but also because there was certain resistance from the family that Grau should intervene in events that had the aspect of adventure and risk, not to mention their strictly political character. It seemed to the family that the doctor of physiology should save himself for the duties of reorganizing the University.

Once Grau accepted, I went to fulfill my mission with the third individual already accepted by the rest of the DEU members in Columbia that night, that being Carlos de la Torre. This time the difficulties were greater because *don* Carlos and his family resisted longer and it was a hard task, a really laborious task, to convince *don* Carlos that he should go to Columbia to be one of the "pentarchs."

Upon my return to the camp, I found that already the group that I had left in the Sixth District headquarters had moved to the Officers Club and were ready to begin a meeting to staff *a new organism,* created artificially in that moment: *the "Agrupación Revolucionaria de Cuba,"* (Cuban Revolutionary Association, ARC) to be formed in its entirety by the members of the DEU, both present and absent. Then it was agreed that all present, by their own right, would form part of the ARC. Also included were several civilians intimately tied to the Directorio, like Grau, Gustavo Cuervo, Alejandro Vergara, Emilio Laurent, Sergio Carbó, Julio Gaunard, Oscar de la Torre, and Fulgencio Batista as the only representative of the armed forces.

To preside at this meeting and direct the debates, *Carlos Prío Socarrás* was selected.

The first point of debate was a brief declaration of principles whose drafting, I think I recall, was assigned to Carbó, and that was approved without discussion. Immediately we proceeded to the formal designation of those who would make up the Executive Commission. There were no disagreements regarding the first four names that we the members of the DEU had selected earlier: Grau, Irisarri, Portela, and Carbó.

To occupy the *fifth position,* in accordance with what was previously agreed, *I proposed Mr. Carlos de la Torre, but,* to my great surprise, *Rubén León proposed Porfirio Franca,* stating that his presence in the Executive Commission would be a conservative counterweight that would inspire confidence in certain social sectors to whom the imminently professorial group previously selected would seem too radical. By majority vote, Franca ended up being elected, which calmed *don* Carlos, who had accepted with reluctance.

In practice, the Executive Commission functioned for the five days it lasted with only four members, since for reasons that I have never been able to understand, Franca evaded the duties of the functions of the post for which he was designated, without making either statement or presence.

As soon as the election of the Commissioners was finalized, the meeting adjourned. We agreed to do so, considering that from that moment on the pentarchs were those who had to enter the action and face the multiple problems awaiting them.

Carrillo: We're going to recapitulate. In the first meeting, which was held in the Enlisted Club, the audience was comprised of *corporals and soldiers of the army,* and it was there *in the course of which you read the program of the DEU.* The *second meeting* occurred in the *Officers' Club and Sergeant Batista, who had already become a leader of the movement, representing the Armed Forces, attended that one, as well as the leaders of the Directorio and the other revolutionary elements allied with the DEU who signed the manifesto of the "Agrupación Revolucionaria de Cuba."* I want to say that, according to my interpretation, that at that moment there was only one military leader representing the corporals and enlisted men of the nation. But I would appreciate it if you would tell me if you remember *at what time the last agreements were reached.*

Rubio Padilla: The time of the final agreement was around *five o'clock in the morning.* Of course, in the course of the second meeting, civilian elements continued to arrive at Columbia, and I remember perfectly that among these *there appeared* in the camp outstanding *members of the Communist Party* and their related organizations, who arrived expecting us to admit them to the meeting in the Officers Club. The door was of wood and glass, and they requested entry, banging on the door, which was closed at the time. *Among the faces that I remember* there wanting to enter — I will never forget them — were those of *César Vilar, Joaquín Ordoqui, Gustavo Alderguía,* and some others, including some members of the Student Left Wing. At first, there was an instant in which the military elements wavered on whether to allow the unexpected visitors to enter or not, but *we decided to give instructions that they permit no one to enter,* so that the communists found themselves prevented from participating in the meeting.

Half an hour later, there appeared in Columbia *three or four* members of *the Célula Directriz of the ABC,* and some other figure representative of that organization. Justo, that is to say that there is a photograph that has been widely published, taken at that time in the camp, *in which appears,* among the outstanding members of the ABC, *Doctor Jorge Mañach who at the time was not a member of the Célula Directriz, but who always was a prominent member of the organization. Those Alphabetic gentlemen shut themselves up with Batista in a ground floor office of the Círculo Militar (Officers' Club)* and held a long interview with him. When the conversation ended, Batista told us absolutely nothing about what he had discussed with the leaders of the ABC, and because of basic decency neither did we ask what had been the object of that visit. A short time later, I would have to find out about the contents of that strange visit.

A few days later, I saw Jorge Mañach with the intention of breaking the oppositionist block against the new government, and Mañach flatly rejected my attempt at accord. *He told me that it was a matter of principles based on the question of subversion,* since the government that had assumed power owed it exclusively to a military subversion *that they could not accept because of the grave danger the precedent implied for Cuba and that, furthermore, for the ABC it was a matter of principle to reject its origins in the sergeants' barracks.* I rejected the argument, saying to him that we could not revise the Sergeants' Coup because we were tied to them in the September 4

Movement and that, by the same token, it was a matter of principle for us to defend the revolutionary pronouncement of the NCOs and enlisted ranks, and we were not disposed to change that attitude.

A few days later, in a conversation with Batista, I told him of my interview with Mañach and the matter of principle he had mentioned. *Then he told me,* with plenty of details, *that when the ABC visited him in Columbia in the early morning of September 5, between 5:30 and 6:00 a.m. — the reason for which the Alphabetics had never wanted to tell us — that they had suggested that if the sergeants rejected the Directorio's program, adopted the program of the ABC, and ceded power exclusively to the Alphabetics, they were disposed to accept and politically support the revolutionary coup.* That is to say, of course, that the statement Mañach made to me, that an accord with the government was impossible as a matter of principle, since military subversion was the origin of our power, was completely false. *The historic truth is that the military coup d'état was bad if it did not favor the ABC and good if it installed the ABC in power.*

The Events from September 5 to 10

The dialogue with Rubio Padilla, which permitted me to gather extremely valuable testimony from one of the most outstanding components of the Directorio, continued along these lines:

Carrillo: It is my impression that your narration of the events in Camp Columbia the night of the Fourth of September 1933, and of how a military mutiny for classist demands was transformed into a revolutionary movement, is completely illustrative and will permit the formation of a judgment over what really occurred on that historic night. But now I need for you to recount for me what occurred from the fifth until the ninth of that same month; that is to say, from the installation of the Executive Commission or Pentarchy in the Palace until the night it was decided to replace the collective regime with a presidential one and Doctor Ramón Grau San Martín was elected as Chief of State, and his inauguration the next day, the tenth. Of course, that day I, the youngest of the founders of the DEU, arrived at my legal age of majority. I had signed, nonetheless, the takeover of power, six days before, being a minor in age.

Rubio Padilla: Certainly, it is difficult to detail all that occurred in the course of those five days, when, with greatest reason, it was enough superficially to review the history of Cuba in order to state that there are no other five days, considered in isolation, in which there were recorded more important nor more relevant events for the future of the nation. Nevertheless, in the attempt to overcome the obstacles that surge around us in trying to evoke those days so heavy with historic transcendence, I am going to start by referring to what constituted one of our basic concerns at the time, starting exactly on the fifth. Who was going to command the army? We were conscious that there existed an extensive group of young officers graduated from the Military Academy, with a select group of which we had personal contact in the agitated period that fell between the twelfth of August and the fourth of September. For them, because of their technical preparation, their moral standing, and the prestige which they enjoyed, it would have been a crime if we had voluntarily or consciously excluded them from full participation in the future of Cuba.

From the first moment, or rather immediately after the fourth of September, we maintained personal contact with this group of young officers; and so we can say that a committee representative of all of them met with us several times in the Presidential Palace.

In the course of our conversations, there arose a formal disagreement on a matter of principle that the officers raised and from which we had to find an adequate way out. Who would call them back to service? They understood that an officer of the army could not receive orders from a sergeant. So, in the normal selection mechanism from which was derived the list of officers that would return to the army, the decisive factor in the formation of such a list could not be the sergeants. The actual recall to service had to be initiated, dictated, or ordered by a higher ranking officer, not by the sergeants. It had to come from an officer of high rank, superior, that is, to all the rest, who would order them to return to their command posts in the installations.

[Editor's note: as a result of the Sergeants' Coup, not only was the interim government overthrown, the military was also, in effect, deposed. Before the armed forces could again function, a new military hierarchy would have to be established, starting with the Army Chief of Staff. Once the Chief of Staff was appointed, he could order his personnel to return to their posts and the army would again be in a position to maintain order until other civilian agencies could be established to assume that function. Until the personnel were ordered back to duty, the army, in effect, did not exist.]

Immediately we devoted ourselves to the search for that individual. Naturally, he had to meet the approval of the young officers. That is to say, he must be a superior officer, to be named by the government as Chief of Staff, on the conditions that he recall to service the untainted officer corp of the army and that, in order to attain that objective, he could rely on the loyalty of the immense majority of the officers tied to his command. From the beginning, the revolutionary civilian government's authority to name that Chief of Staff to recall them to ranks was implicitly accepted.

The first individual, acceptable to them and to us because of his honest conduct during the entire Machado government and the respect he had gained both within and outside the Army, was Lieutenant Colonel José M. Perdomo y Martínez.[6] I personally tried to establish immediate contact with Lieutenant Colonel Perdomo, but all of the fifth passed without my being able to do so. At last, I spoke with him at five in the morning on the sixth. I explained to him with dazzling clarity the importance of the patriotic point of view of the measure that led me to bother him at that very inopportune hour. I must say that he received me pleasantly and seemed to consider the transcendence of the service that Cuba asked of him, but he asked me to allow him a few hours, until shortly after noon, to offer me his final answer, because he had to confer first with people without whose collaboration or approval he could not make a truly responsible decision.

When, a little after noon, I reestablished my contact with Perdomo, he answered me with an absolute negative. When I asked what circumstance caused him to adopt that decision, I found out that the people with whom he had wanted to consult, or those of whom he required previous approval, were lodged in the Hotel Nacional. He had gone to the hotel, but once there he was not permitted to speak with anyone at all without prior authorization from Colonel Sanguily who, obviously, maintained within the bounds of the hotel an absolute control over all the military personnel that had already gone in there.

Frustrated in his attempt to gain beforehand the cooperation of certain officers, whose names he never mentioned to me, the former chief of the National Police declined to accept the post of Chief of Staff of the Army.

Carrillo: Did Batista accept Perdomo or did you not need to depend on or consult with Batista?

Rubio Padilla: Batista accepted Perdomo because he already figured in the list of the officers that were perfectly acceptable to the committee of sergeants and students that had discussed the matter and, of course, Perdomo was one of those at the head of the list.

Carrillo: Of course, that was before Batista was promoted to colonel?

Rubio Padilla: Yes, naturally, before Batista's promotion. I would be lying if I said that there had been the least indication that Mr. Batista aspired to command or promotion. Mr. Batista was at that time simply terrified and as desirous as we to find a solution to the military problem, because what worried him most was not the future of Cuba, nor the revolution, nor even the personal well-being that he might have derived from advancing or capturing some position of command. I know for a fact that at that time Batista's preoccupation — I would say that ninety-nine percent of that preoccupation — was his own hide, since he was filled with terror and the fear that we would arrive at an agreement with the officers of the army that would permit them to judge the rebel sergeants as authors of the crime of military rebellion and shoot him. Simply put, he was a coward. That is my impression of that time.

Carrillo: After that with Perdomo, what was the new proposal?

Rubio Padilla: The possibility of a solution based on Perdomo having disappeared, I returned to contact the young officers, meeting with them again in the palace in order to see, of the high ranking officers that were not already in the Hotel Nacional under Sanguily's control, with whom we could consult over the possibility that one would accept the post of Chief of Staff. There arose the name of Lieutenant Colonel Miguel Guerra Pérez, whom I knew personally.

Guerra was a superior officer, hierarchically above all the other young officers, a person of honorable and irreproachable conduct in his relationship with the subalterns, and he had not participated in any of the political or pseudo-political activities in service to any regime.[7] Acceptable to the officers and acceptable to the sergeants, Miguel Guerra would have been a solution even though he would subsequently have to go into retirement, since he was quite advanced in age.

Once Miguel Guerra was accepted as a possibility, I proceeded immediately to try to contact him, but, well, because he may have found out why I wanted to talk to him, or because upon learning that I searched for him he had presumed the object of the pursuit, whatever the reason — the truth is that I never found out — he left his house and remained hidden for a day or a day and a half, avoiding me. Finally I found him in the early morning in the Hotel San Luis, on the Belascoaín highway. Miguel Guerra, after listening to me with the greatest attention, answered me in a completely frank manner without setting any conditions as Perdomo had done. Going directly to the problem and using strictly military language, Guerra refused from the first moment to assume the post of Chief of Staff, in such a way that the possibility of depending on him as a solution disappeared automatically with that interview. This was very close to dawn on the eighth.

Carrillo: And in the time intervening, did the North American warships arrive in Cuba?

Rubio Padilla: Well, I must tell you, in answer to your question, that I have chosen to isolate the themes and develop them at length over those five days, setting aside extremely important things that were occurring at the same time.

But from the strictly chronological point of view, I must clarify that when I interviewed Miguel Guerra, which represented the second failure to find a quick solution to the army officers problem, the boats had already arrived. They entered the port of Havana on September 7. If you would like to set aside for the moment the problem of the army so that I can answer the question concerning the ships with the required amplitude, I could tell you that this is the most dramatic episode of all those in which a large number of persons participated and that, probably, the massive presence of the people — it is my impression — was a decisive factor to stop the impulse of the United States government and its ambassador in Cuba. It was that which conclusively altered relations between the two countries.

Carrillo: I consider the event so important and so little known that I think it absolutely necessary that you cover the sequence of events from the initial command to send the naval units to Cuba until their departure on the return trip.

Rubio Padilla: On the morning of the seventh of September, the Havana newspapers and radios came out with the news that around noon the Secretary of the Navy of the United States, Admiral Swanson, would arrive in the Cuban capital aboard the *Indianapolis*. Apparently, at least, the United States was entering into a stage in their relations with the revolutionary movement that greatly resembled, for its outward characteristics, the old *gun-boat* politics, which was so abused in Latin America. Naturally, the secret origin of the order to send a fleet to Havana and the reasons that determined the threat to send in the marines would have to be found in the documents of the era stored in the files of the Department of State or in the National Archives that reflect the correspondence between the Embassy in Havana and the Department of State.[8] But the fact is that in those moments we did not have the time nor the abilities to verify the extent of the order nor its intent. With the speed and audacity characteristic of the Directorio, without which the history of Cuba could have been completely different, as soon as we knew of the imminent arrival of the Atlantic fleet, we drew up a short manifesto that was read on all the radio stations. In it we invited the public to receive the *Indianapolis* adequately and demonstrate our firm and unwaverable decision physically to resist any attempt to land. We invited the Cubans to repair to the Port Esplanade and make their presence known, and if unfortunately there was some attempt to land, to repel it energetically. It was very clear that we were inviting everyone who was willing to fight to come to the port, even though I don't believe that we suggested bringing firearms because that was implicit in the fact that we were disposed to resist forcefully the least attempt to disembark.

Not surprisingly, but still with far more support than we could have hoped to have, on the final stretch of the Malecón [Seawall, refers to the street and the seawall itself] near La Punta Castle, as well as the entire Avenida del Puerto [Port Avenue] and beyond the Port Customs building, there was an immense mass of humanity which could only be crossed with difficulty. I recall very well that we were concerned that, if there were any aggression or hostile act, that it not be our provocative aggression. That is to say, we had a plan to impede a landing of the Americans but not to attack the fleet if it limited its activities to those proper for a mere visit. So, the chief of the National Police, Emilio Laurent, in a car — a Lincoln that had belonged to or been in the service of General Alberto Herrera — Emilio, you yourself, Justo, and I spent the two or three hours that the episode lasted running up and down the avenue with great difficulty, even though being who he was, Emilio, the chief of police, was able to open a passage through the enormous crowd. I well remember that the sector where the attitude of the people was the most aggressive, where the enthusiasm was greatest, and where the nationalist fervor shone brightest with the cries of "*Viva la revolución,*" "Down with Yankee Imperialism," was around the building occupied by the Customs Authority and near the place where the boats that sailed to Casablanca, Regla, and Guanabacoa were anchored.

Around two or two thirty in the afternoon — in truth, I couldn't say exactly what time — at the height of revolutionary enthusiasm of all those people gathered there, the fleet appeared with the cruiser *Indianapolis*. It was a truly indescribable moment because our decision had been not only to invite the people but, furthermore, orders had been given to the Cabaña Fortress and the personnel of Morro Castle to position all their military resources in preparation for action, as is normally done when there exists the fear of a foreign invasion. Thus, all those cannons of Cabaña Fortress changed their angle to repel a possible landing, in case one was attempted.

In spite of our running around and the insistence with which we were imploring that the people not initiate the least act of aggression, at least until we knew if there really existed an attempt to land, there were "patriots" that were situated around La Punta Castle, where large vessels pass nearest to the coastline, who started firing .32-caliber revolvers when naval units entered.[9] I do not know if any North American sailor may have been grazed, but, in the end, it was something we could not prevent and the newspapers made much of it the next day.

When the *Indianapolis* had anchored in the middle of the bay, Ambassador Welles arrived in a car that, with difficulty, was able to open a passage among that multitude made up of thousands upon thousands of persons. Upon arriving at the San Francisco Wharf, the diplomat wasted no time in boarding a launch that had come for him. The ambassador stayed on board about half an hour, no more than forty-five minutes. The distance between the wharf and the *Indianapolis* was not very great and for that reason, from land, it could be clearly seen how the Ambassador descended by the ladder of the ship and boarded the launch that had carried him. Mr. Welles had gained a distance of 50 yards from the battleship when the ship began to raise pressure and spout impressive columns of black smoke. Before Welles's launch could arrive at the dock, the ship had already turned about to point its prow toward the exit of the port. The ship barely waited for the launch to return before heading out to sea. It all happened so rapidly that I believe that Welles had still not arrived at the Embassy on Las Misiones Avenue when the *Indianapolis* had already left Havana Bay, followed very closely by the remaining boats of the fleet.

I don't have to say that the crowd gathered on Avenida del Puerto and the docks raved with enthusiasm when the ship left. The patriotic exaltation was total. Looking back on the events of that afternoon, I must add that I don't know still if there was or was not any intention to land the marines, but I have no doubt that the massive demonstration by the people of Havana, the physical presence of hundreds of thousands of people on Avenida del Puerto and on the docks, had a huge impact on the North American policy in relation to the authentic revolution, and even Welles himself had to have shaken with worry. I must additionally clarify that I have always wondered if the marines would have landed if those avenues had remained empty through popular indifference.

And with this I have answered your question concerning the day the American ships arrived.

Carrillo: That occurred on the seventh of September, right?

Rubio Padilla: Yes, certainly, on the seventh.

Carrillo: I wish you would tell me your version of how and why the Executive Commission or Pentarchy, the collective governmental regime, was changed to a one-person regime, or rather, a presidency, and refresh my memory about the circumstances that determined Batista's promotion from sergeant to colonel.

Rubio Padilla: I shall try to develop that theme with a minimum of interruptions, and so I would tell you that when the possibility of designating Lieutenant Colonel Miguel Guerra as Chief of Staff, with authority fully accepted by the young officers to call them to ranks, evaporated, a grave problem arose. There was one reality: the army could not remain without a head. It was really impressive to go physically, as I went, because I wanted to see it myself, to the barracks of Columbia and contemplate with horror the little that remained of the classic discipline of an army. I must say that I could see with my own eyes that of that [discipline] there remained absolutely nothing. I entered some of those barracks and could see the ugly spectacle they offered. The majority of the soldiers that occupied them were lightly dressed, some only in underwear. I could observe with no fear of being wrong that from the fourth of September the area had not been swept and the floors were full of empty cigarette packs, old used newspapers, and all kinds of rubbish. In a word: rather than military barracks, they appeared to be the quarters of Bohemian bachelors. Also there was a truly intolerable cloud of smoke, since almost the whole world was smoking at the same time. The disorder and lack of discipline were evident, but not lack of discipline in the sense of disobedience of orders, since such orders did not exist. Perhaps, it would be preferable to say that, rather than giving a sense of a lack of discipline, it was more a sensation of anarchy, simply because the army, from the fourth of September, did not have anyone to command it. There were no duty officers, officers of the guard, officers of the day, or officers of the night. The sergeants were not receiving orders, and, because of that, since they were in the habit of relaying them when they received them, there was no one giving orders. That is to say, the physical sensation was that the interregnum of "no command" in the army had to end as soon as possible; the situation was simply intolerable. Meanwhile, the mechanism of sequestering the largest possible number of officers in the Hotel Nacional was working. Among those that never went to the Nacional, which permitted us to make contact with them, were Lieutenant Colonels Perdomo and Guerra; but each time a new name was mentioned it ended up that the person was already trapped within the rigid discipline of the Hotel. That is to say, within the discipline of maintaining the status quo [that existed] before the fourth of September, including the relations with the American Ambassador who resided in that same Hotel, the building and the gardens surrounding it had, if not juridically, at least in fact, a character of extraterritoriality, accented by the enormous North American flag displayed over the front entrance of the hotel.

After that, we were not disposed, nor did we think that it would have any effect, to make contact with any of the officers lodged there because Lieutenant Colonel Perdomo had told me already that when he tried to talk directly with some of the officers that were there, the military machinery functioned so rigidly that he could not speak with any officer without Sanguily's permission. Since that effort was useless, it placed us in a dilemma: was it better to allow the army to continue as it was at that moment, that is to say, a military institution in a state of absolute anarchy, or was it better to authorize someone to recall the officers to duty?

For me there was a misunderstanding, because I recall perfectly that we asked the young officers if they would obey orders coming from whatever officer or whatever person was given the authority of the civilian government to act with the rank of colonel and the answer was that if it appeared in the *Official Gazette* that the individual had been named by the Government, they would accept him.

Going from the basis that they were acting in good faith, I imagine that they thought that the government would promote an officer to colonel, so that he could issue the order permitting the return of the officers. But the real fact was that we did not have a single officer we could name to recall the young officers. This determined that we should discuss the possibility of the mechanism by which one of the sergeants would be promoted to colonel in order to recall the officers. Once done with this function and the officers returned to their commands, the colonel would resign and the situation of having a sergeant in command over the officers would be eliminated. That was the true origin of promoting Batista to colonel. Batista agreed that that would be the end of his military career, since once he had recalled the officers and they had returned to the army, he could not continue with any type of rank or grade. He accepted a transitional step in which he was going to fulfill a single function, and once he had fulfilled it, his presence in the Army was unnecessary.

I want to clarify that I was not among those present during the conversations in which Batista reacted in one way or the other. That is to say that I was only present during the earlier conversations that determined Batista's promotion to colonel. Thus, I can confirm categorically that in that moment we could not avail ourselves of any other solution, not even speculatively.

Carrillo: Do you believe that Batista acted in good faith when he said he accepted the rank of colonel in order to cede it later as soon as another person was selected to act as Chief of Staff, and do you believe that he was willing to leave the army because he could not return to the rank of sergeant?

Rubio Padilla: I believed so then, and today I continue to believe so. The impression that we received was that he acted in good faith and that explains why I do not think that the possibility of "stepping into" a position was in his plans for the future. I already said before that he was terrified and desirous above all to save his hide.

Carrillo: I have a cassette that records the testimony of Lincoln Rodón who names the people that were present when Carbó consulted with members of the Directorio concerning Batista's promotion to colonel, and all those present at that time reacted favorably. I would like to hear your version of that meeting.

Rubio Padilla: Well, I was present at the meeting in which we adopted that decision. Whether or not Mr. Carbó had consulted beforehand with other persons, I do not know. What I do want to emphasize is that those of us who participated in the meeting, including those of us who had maintained contact with the young officers that went to the Palace, could not find another solution to the problem other than promoting Batista and designating him Chief of Staff. The reality was, unfortunately, that we were at a dead end and what really worried everyone was the downward spiral of the entire Cuban army toward anarchy; in fact, it was deteriorating not by the day but by the hour. Columbia was in true chaos. No one gave orders, and no one obeyed. It was simply an accumulation of a thousand soldiers, each of whom did individually what he felt like doing, and that anarchy existed within a precinct that had been until then a military installation. That could not continue. On the other hand, the situation at the Hotel Nacional was true blackmail to which we could not yield the future of Cuba, because the people who had found refuge in the hotel were ratifying the old stance of many Creoles that "the Americans have come here to resolve the problem because they are the ones who have the historic authority and are going to continue to have it." That entirely Plattist position could not be accepted in any form. We were aware that we had to find an adequate solution to the conflict we were facing, but in no way could the solution be in the Hotel Nacional, under the protection of the Stars and Stripes. It was not at all important that later Welles would abandon the hotel. They knew well what they wanted, and what they wanted we could not accept. The blackmail functioned in the sense that it obligated us to do something that they were presuming, as military men, could not be done, but what they did not know was that we had the audacity for that and much more. I am aware that, upon analysis of the events in historic perspective, it is necessary to recognize that Batista's nomination, because of the nature of the person, was a true disgrace for Cuba. But it was because it was Fulgencio Batista, whose moral quality was not at the height the nation and the revolution demanded of him. As we all know, a very short time later he was already conspiring with the North American Ambassador and all the elements most representative of the counterrevolution in Cuba to stab those that had made him colonel in the back, precisely for the sake of his wretched personal interest. That is to say, he was trying to maintain command of the very army that he feared was suspect and in danger of not being accepted by the old semicolonial machinery of the traditional politicians of Cuba combined with the North American interests. That is all.

Carrillo: Well, Juan Antonio, now within the chronological development of the events, we must return to the purely civil question of the conversion of the Executive Commission or Pentarchy into a unipersonal presidential government. That is to say, I return the floor to you so you can tell us about that subject.

Rubio Padilla: Practically from the first days, that is, from the fifth or sixth of September, there were those who were eager to show that what we were doing was an exaggerated thing or out of place. There arose criticism to the idea of an Executive Commission in which the highest maximum authority of the country would be shared by five different persons. I recall the fierce attack on the Pentarchy made during our first contact at the Palace with representatives of those so-called political sectors, meaning all those that had participated in the Mediation plus Menocal's people who had not intervened in the Mediation, but who were represented at that meeting. They severely criticized the revolutionary movement, and they did not forget to mention, as one of the totally unacceptable things for them, the Executive Commission, that is to say, the dilution of the highest authority among five persons. Therefore, the Pentarchy encountered an atmosphere of great hostility or at least of nonacceptance on the part of many people.

That was aggravated by the fact that, from the first moment, even we realized that the division of functions among the Executive Commission was totally inoperable in practice. Each of the pentarchs had been placed in charge of two or three departments or cabinet secretaries, but what actually occurred was rather colorful because the dependencies that had been assigned to Mr. Franca did not function.

None of them had any authority because Mr. Franca never appeared. The others were operating very inefficiently because the rest of the pentarchs were so deeply affected by the events, so unfortunately influenced by "the other side," that neither did they go to the [cabinet] secretaries nor did they act like an executive authority dealing with one thing or another, so that in many aspects the administrative machinery of the nation, not just the military but also the civilian, lacked command. The question rebounded even more because there were no cabinet Secretaries, and without the cabinet, the sensation grew that the departments did not have any type of authority. It is not strange, therefore, that within our own forces an unfavorable climate would immediately grow that seemed to indicate that perhaps we had selected a bad time to introduce to Cuba the Executive Commission as a system of government. There were many basic motives we had to fight against simultaneously for a new idea like that, and it became apparent to us that perhaps it would have been better, more expeditious, more executive, more agile, to depend on a President and not on five pentarchs.

Of course, even though we were not in agreement with the statement that the functioning of the Executive Commission was wrong or inconvenient, some of the members of the DEU, including myself, took little time to realize that the idea of returning to a presidential system was perfectly negotiable if, at any given moment, we should reach an agreement with the political sectors. The question was undertaken in a meeting on the night of the eighth and ninth of September in the reception hall of the Presidential Palace, a meeting that began at approximately nine or nine-thirty at night and did not end until seven in the morning of the following day. It was probably the longest meeting the Directorio had held in its entire existence, and not only did the entire DEU attend, so did a series of people who worked closely with the Directorio. These were the people who had been so very closely tied to us and whom we esteemed so highly that we had found ourselves obliged to create the Agrupación Revolucionaria de Cuba on September 4.

Among them, of course, was Grau, who was at that time a member of the Executive Commission. But I recall perfectly that there were some new faces, among whom stood out someone who had not had this intimacy with the Directorio, but who after the fourth of September did show the most enthusiasm supporting the movement, at least apparently. I refer to Aurelio Alvarez. Do you remember Aurelio Alvarez?[10]

Carrillo: Yes, of course!

Rubio Padilla: Well, the meeting became an interminable dispute that lasted nearly all night, debating whether we should or shouldn't maintain the Executive Commission no matter what. The issue was not easy to resolve because the change, apart from implying a departure from the DEU program, implied a concession to "the other side" which had been shielded in the Hotel Nacional under the banner and asylum and protection of the North American flag without the least intention of cooperating nor of accepting any of what was happening. After many polemics and extensive discussions that lasted nearly all night, we arrived at a final agreement to abolish the Executive Commission and return to the presidential form so that the designated President could be provided a Cabinet with Secretaries who would immediately be put in charge of the different departments with the object of throwing the civil administrative machinery into gear without further delay.

Once this decision was adopted, we passed to the point of who would select the President of the Republic. Then, I don't know if it was because of weariness or some misunderstanding, or perhaps it was the product of a manipulation by someone that was interested in removing the discussion of the election of the President from the sphere of the meeting, but a new proposal was offered. We must believe that it was most likely a misunderstanding, but regardless of the motivation, a vote of confidence was proposed to authorize the pentarchs to select the President.

I recall quite well that "Lulú" Durán — Clara Luz Durán, one of the oldest members of the Directorio — tenaciously opposed that vote of confidence. The personal trait of "Lulú" was intransigence, and, be that as it may, it was one hundred percent honest and sincere even to her brutal frankness in saying what she thought, liked, or didn't like in other people. Since we had been companions in the Directorio and were completely aware of her manner, it did not seem strange that she would argue against such a proposal or that she would very emphatically insist that for such a grave and important thing as the selection of the Chief of State, a vote of confidence should not be given to anyone. And then Aurelio A. Alvarez stood up. He was a very impassioned man, a very vehement and good orator, or at least very loquacious. He fired off a somewhat bombastic discourse, but of such sincerity and vehemence that he was crying, with tears that reached his cheeks and, in the middle of the longest silence on the part of those who were listening, appealed to the members of the Directorio, insisting that it was not conceivable that we, with men like — and he named the men of the Executive Commission — who had been battered through so many years in the struggle against the tyranny, who had gone to jail and suffered persecutions, exile, for their loyalty and identification with the Directorio, how could we in that moment doubt the capacity of those individuals to the point that they did not merit our confidence.

I must confess that I felt the same way "Lulú" Durán did, that in a way I don't believe that certain public functions should be delegated, and that was the case with what was being discussed. It was a mission too important and responsible to entrust it to other people. Nevertheless, the real truth was that Aurelio Alvarez's language forced a final accord in the Directorio to issue a vote of confidence to the Executive Commission, that is, to the pentarchs, that now were not pentarchs but only tetrarchs, since Porfirio Franca had disappeared two or three days before, to elect whomever would be the new President of the Republic.

Since it was now daylight — around seven in the morning — and all the tetrarchs were present at the meeting, the four agreed to invest the entire day of the ninth of September conducting personal interviews and meet again at nine that evening in the Palace. That assumed that they would use the entire day to hold their interviews and with the information that they would accumulate in the course of such conversations, compare that information, weigh it, and, then in the meeting, decide who was the best political selection for the Presidency of the Republic.

So it was done the day of the meeting. I recall perfectly that I left Irisarri at his home in the La Sierra district. For me it was like a liberation since it was the first time, since the night of the fourth and fifth of September, that I had gone to bed in the course of those days. I arrived at my house after eight in the morning. I tried to sleep, but I was unable to. No matter how hard I tried, since I felt tremendously tired, I could not sleep, and I was unable to do so because it seemed to me that the election of a President of the Republic was a thing so very, very grave and so very serious that I feared greatly that a majority of the Executive

Commission would prevail in their judgment to utilize the transformation of the Executive Commission into a Presidency as an instrument of negotiation with the counterrevolutionary opposition that would determine that the balance would fall to one side or the other. In a word, the same thing occurred to me as to "Lulú" Durán, and now that the agreement on the vote of confidence had been adopted, I developed a great uneasiness, much pain, much anxiety, because I feared that the entire revolution would end in the election of a new President of the Republic. And effectively, without sleeping, I got up, shaved and bathed, got dressed and went out again into the street with the intent of stirring up, of verifying, of finding out in the places where, by the nature of the people designated for the election, I might find out what was going on.

Around quarter past one in the afternoon, I arrived at Grau's home on Seventeenth Street in Vedado, and there his sister-in-law Paulina told me that Grau had gotten up around eleven thirty in the morning, bathed, had brunch, and had just left to interview Doctor Presno. Paulina already understood what the tetrarchs were to do that day. That is to say, she understood that they were looking for a person to designate as the new President of the Republic in the meeting that evening. I had a brief conversation with Paulina in the course of which she anticipated me in her belief that Presno was Grau's candidate. She told me at the same time that she did not know if Grau was going to have other interviews after the one with Presno, but that at that time he was in the home of one of his friends from the University faculty.

Of course, I did not go to Presno's home, since there was not a single reason that would justify my presence there. But I did not want to remain sitting there in Grau's house waiting for his return, and I did want to find out what I could in certain places where I thought I might acquire additional information. I left Grau's residence directly for that of Gustavo Cuervo, on O Street and Twenty-first, and there I found out that around nine or ten in the morning Irisarri and Portela had been there to offer the Presidency of the Republic to Gustavo and that he had accepted. I also found out that at the meeting in the Palace at nine — which I had known nothing about — Gustavo's designation would be formalized.

I asked where he was at that moment so I could speak with him and find out more details of what was happening, and I learned that Gustavo had gone to see General Menocal at his home. I returned to

Grau's residence just after he returned from the interview with Presno and asked Grau if the tetrarchs had any meeting.

Grau told me no, that they had not had any meeting, that they had agreed to act individually in personal interviews and meet at the Palace at nine that night.

Then I informed Grau what had happened at Gustavo's house, that Irisarri and Portela had been there as early as nine that morning to offer the Presidency to Gustavo, and that he had accepted, and that, in accordance with what was agreed upon, that night at the meeting scheduled to start at nine, Gustavo's designation would be formalized. Grau told me that he had not spoken with him and that he did not know if Irisarri and Portela were expecting Carbó's vote to confirm Gustavo or if they had been able to find Franca to cast the third vote in the meeting of five in order to clinch Gustavo's election. They had neither consulted him personally nor informed him of this offer of the position of Chief of State made to Gustavo. Then Grau added:

> Be it one or the other, Carbó or Franca, I don't believe that Irisarri and Portela would have dared to make a serious offer of the Presidency to Cuervo Rubio if they were not absolutely sure already that tonight they are going to get the agreement of the Commission because the two votes seem to me a little daring to offer that high post. Whatever might be the explanation concerning the third vote of the five, either Carbó or Franca, one thing is certain, and that is that the President of the Republic is Gustavo because when they have already gone to offer the Presidency it is because they are sure that they can do it.

Then I told Grau:

> Well, Doctor, not I, because who authorized you a vote of confidence to elect the President? The Directorio! Therefore, if the Directorio makes a decision revoking that vote of confidence, automatically you would be relieved of that obligation.

Grau consulted his watch and told me:

> It's five in the afternoon. It seems to me very unlikely that the Directorio would have time to meet before nine this evening and to inform us of a new agreement. There is too

little time. Since that is a totally impossible point, we can say that the decision is practically already made.

I understood the logic behind Grau's reasoning, but youth's own audacity and the revolutionary urge carried me to say to him:

Well, I am going to try to repeal the vote of confidence. What I do want is that, when you arrive at nine this evening at the Palace, do all that is within your means to delay the final decision of that meeting and give us time to adopt the accord of revocation.

And with this arranged, we separated, Grau and myself, at quarter or half past five in the afternoon. From Grau's home I went directly to the home of Doctor Boza Masvidal, to the home of the family of the bishop of that last name.

Carrillo: You allude to Doctor Aurelio Boza Masvidal, who was professor of Italian Literature at the University and for some time occupied the post of Secretary General, and was the brother of the bishop.

Rubio Padilla: Aurelio had been one of the professors that had supported the Directorio very effectively in every way he could. I remember having been to many meetings that were possible because Boza had made them possible. I believe I recall that several Directorio meetings took place in the estate he owned in Wajay and some others were held in the large old Boza family house on Línea Street — of course, Justo, very close to your home, on the block of Paseo between Calzada and Línea.

Many DEU members used to drop by the old house of the Bozas, and so, whenever we needed to find a companion, the first thing we would do was go by there and see if any one was there. Since we were so scattered throughout Havana, many times acting, not only in groups of two or three but also individually, we felt impelled to find out what was happening. I was almost sure that I would find several members of the Directorio there. I went there with that object and in fact I found "Pepelín" Leyva, "Polo" Miranda, Raúl Ruiz, and "Cuchi" Escalona. I don't remember if there was anyone else, but the fact is that I found four or five members and right away I explained to them the drama of the situation, how urgent it was that we make a new decision, and how the possibility of doing something before nine that night, or at least at nine, depended on our splitting the Directorio membership list and bringing to the Palace that afternoon those four, five, or six assigned to each of us. Without delay, over a table, we created a list of the DEU and distributed the names of our companions to those who had to find them. I don't know if it was the dramatics or the urgency, but the fact is that among the members of the Directorio present, there was not a single doubt about the importance of the meeting so informally called. Thus, at nine on the dot that evening the entire Directorio was there, in the Reception Hall (or Hall of Mirrors) of the Palace, in the end closest to Zulueta Street and the La Carona tobacco plant. The pentarchs were already on the third floor, according to the reporters, when we arrived at the Palace. Of course, that night the press room on the ground floor was full, since in addition to the reporters who normally covered the palace news, there were many foreign correspondents, including, of course Mr. Phillips, the correspondent from the *New York Times*. All were waiting for the accord that the Executive Commission would adopt concerning who was going to assume the Presidency of the Republic.

It is not necessary to say that the Directorio meeting was extremely tense and conducted under the notion that something grave was happening and that something had to be done with the greatest urgency. But there were few who really knew what it was and I could say that the whole world was going crazy to know the truth.

When we had a meeting of this type, we normally selected one of our companions who was particularly adept at moderating debates to be the chairman. He had to be very strict on questions of order, interruptions, and what decisions the deliberation would pursue, because all those things led to a loss of time and made meetings interminable. "Mongo" Miyar had already demonstrated in previous meetings that he had the capacity for that work, and that he relied on innate abilities to cut short the long speeches and prevent false questions of order. So the first thing we did was to elect "Mongo" Miyar chairman of the meeting. Of course, the first problem that "Mongo" proposed was that we explain to him the origin of the citation and who had made it. I stood up and briefly explained what was happening, but quickly "Mongo" took me out to the passage and asked me to formulate a concrete proposal.

The concrete proposal that I presented was the following: a) to revoke the vote of confidence given to the pentarchs to elect the

President of the Republic; b) once the duty of selecting the president was returned to the Directorio, to designate Grau San Martín as such, and c) as soon as Grau or whoever was designated — I was planning to propose Grau — to appoint a committee to go upstairs immediately to the third floor and notify [them] of the decisions because I did not know how Grau would be able to delay things to give us time to act, since they were called to meet at the same time. By then, the four had been there since nine — Franca definitely did not attend — on the third floor. Grau knew that we were going to meet there in the Palace and knew also that I was trying to force the revocation of the vote of confidence. Naturally, Grau's capacity to delay the meeting was limited and that meant that what would be decided had to be decided as quickly as possible.

To my great surprise, Felipe Pazos immediately stood up and protested that the motivation to call the meeting with the intention of revoking the vote of confidence given to the Pentarchs originated in my assumption that Gustavo Cuervo was a Menocalist. Felipe very harshly assessed my opinion on that basis and insisted that my assertion that Gustavo was a Menocalist was a calumny against Gustavo, whom he praised to the heavens with a series of descriptions with which I was totally in agreement: a gentleman, a decent person, a doctor who was an honor to his profession, a competent professor. In all that I agreed but, according to Felipe, what was totally false was my assertion that he was tied to General Menocal, since Gustavo was above all a man unconditionally allied with the Directorio.

The question became more complicated as we tried to settle a very disagreeable dispute between Felipe and myself in which my position was extremely uncomfortable. I was the offspring of an old clan from Pinar, from the Rubio family, in which almost the entire world was Menocalist except my father, and lately, every one in the family knew who they were and who we were not. The latter, that is to say, those of us who were not partial to the former President, were very few, and furthermore, those that were had, like the rest of the Cubans of like mind, a very deep devotion to the general, an unlimited admiration, and followed him unconditionally. Therefore, I appeared to be a bad person from the clan who was using information I naturally had because of the family to damage a man that, in the opinion of Felipe Pazos, was entirely loyal to the Directorio. For me it was extremely difficult since I, on a personal level, had enjoyed the best of relations, and continued to have them after that, with Gustavo Cuervo, who was always a man so great of heart that, in spite of this episode — in which it was, in a practical sense, my question that kept him from becoming President of the Republic at that time — he continued to treat me with the utmost respect and affection. In the end, the argument ended disagreeably, but, for sure, the chairman of the meeting, "Mongo" Miyar, put an end to it because the personal problem between Felipe and me was of absolutely no interest compared with the national problem. And he forced Felipe to be specific and Felipe made specific his proposal not to deny that we had met, but at the same time, not to revoke the vote of confidence.

Nevertheless, the first point was taken to vote and the vote of confidence was revoked.

Carrillo: After all these years, Pazos, with his honesty as always, has sufficiently clarified all this in a letter that he sent to us and which says:

Dear Justo:

The narrative by Rubio is the truth, the whole truth, and nothing but the truth.

If I find the time in the next days I will write a few lines explaining my position which, apart from this, I would repeat now, of continuing to believe that a man of Cuervo Rubio's capabilities had to follow his own judgment — and not to be a mere follower of Menocal — given that because of intellectual prejudices and being historically anti-Menocalist (because of my family) I believed Cuervo Rubio superior to Menocal. I admit, nonetheless, that Rubio was probably right.

The other reason is that then I was much more conservative than now (conservative in the generic sense, not in affiliation): even though I doubt that the vote for Grau and against Cuervo would signify that the Directorio would think Grau was going to realize the social reform that [he] effectively realized — why was a doctor of the aristocracy, nearly a millionaire, going to be a radical president? What I believe carried the most weight was the absence of fear and concern — (irresponsibility) — of Grau in terms of the situation, demonstrated in the meeting with the factions (night of the sixth and seventh) and with the DEU (the following night), when Aurelio Alvarez cried.

Yours truly, with a strong hug,

Felipe.

Rubio Padilla: Right away we went on to the second point of my proposition, the one about designating Grau as President. Even though the previous events demonstrated that Grau had the confidence of the majority of those gathered there, nevertheless, since now the assembly held the image of the great electors, four nominations were presented for President. Of course, the first was Felipe's, once the vote of confidence for the Pentarchs to designate the Chief of State was revoked, and he proposed Gustavo Cuervo. Inés Segura Bustamante had the candid ingenuousness to propose for President of the Republic Enrique José Varona, who three months later would die not in an automobile accident but of senility. And Rubén León proposed José Antonio Presno.

Those were the four candidates of that night: Grau, proposed by myself, Gustavo Cuervo proposed by Felipe Pazos, Enrique José Varona proposed by Inés Segura Bustamante, and José Antonio Presno, proposed by Rubén León.

Since the situation was of extreme urgency, tension, and nervousness, no one was given the opportunity to sing the individuals merits of each candidate, but without loss of time the matter was put to a vote and by an overwhelming majority Grau was designated.

Carrillo: But, was there not before the vote an intervention by Chibás in favor of Grau?

Rubio Padilla: No, Chibás absolutely did not intervene there for anything of that. There is more; I understand that Chibás was not at the meeting, because years later he confessed to me that he had not been at that meeting. I specifically do not recall him participating in the debate, but in another later episode with Chibás — in the period in which he sang the glories of Grau on the eve of the "glorious journey of the First of June" — he went to find me so that I could tell him the story of how Grau had been elected, and at the time I in no way wanted it to reach Grau's ears. I stupidly believed that Gustavo did not know the truth of how the vote of confidence had been revoked, because he was at home waiting for them to call him to go to the Palace, since he had been formally offered the Presidency of the Republic. Whatever, I did not have the least interest in publicizing the truth of what the means had been by which the vote of confidence had been revoked. I was set on not divulging the mechanism of the revocation of the vote of confidence, since it hurt me to have injured Gustavo on a personal level, and when I told Chibás this story I told him repeatedly that I did not want him to tell it in any way on the radio. He always broadcast a half-hour radio program every Sunday, dedicated to political propaganda, and since it was the eve of the elections that would make Grau the constitutional president, part of Chibás's propaganda was directed at placing Grau in the clouds. Things being thus, Chibás went to see me because he wanted to know how Grau had been elected as Provisional President.

I told him the story on these same terms, but I advised him that I did not want the fact of my interview to appear in the story, nor of the information obtained in Gustavo's house, nor that I had obtained it. The next Sunday Chibás told his story on the radio, but since he knew or assumed that it would be impossible for me to clarify things because I did not want to tell the whole truth, he attributed to himself all that I had said concerning what happened the ninth of September, and thus he appeared to call the people, request the revocation of the vote of confidence, and propose the designation of Grau. Later, he did not dare to mention himself as one of the three who went up to the third floor to notify the Pentarchs of the decision.

The historic illustration of this episode on Chibás's part was so coarse (because Chibás himself told me that he had not attended that meeting and that if he had, absolutely nothing would have been agreed) that Grau himself called me at home to ask me to clarify it for him because Chibás's story was a pack of lies. That is to say, Grau himself, who was benefitting from the Chibás's propaganda at that point in his political life, was bothered by the broad adulteration of the matter. I answered Grau that I had no interest in clarifying anything, that if it bothered him so much that Chibás had adulterated what had occurred, that he clarify it, since he knew the truth of what had happened. Of course, Grau did not clear up anything because at that time it was not convenient for him to fight with Chibás and lose the radical support Chibás was giving him, and the thing was left like that. The matter was never clarified.

After Chibás rendered his false story to the public, which I did not rectify for the reasons I explained, many people refer to Grau's election based on Chibás' narration, which is no more than a coarse alteration of the true history, at least in terms of the players. But, in the end, that is not important.

The third proposal was to name the committee to notify the Pentarchs, who would go up right away to the third floor. Rubén León, Carlos Prío, and I were designated to fulfill that mission. The three of us hurried up to the third floor. I don't really know if you are interested in the details of what occurred there. To me they seem interesting, but I don't know how they fit into your project.

Carrillo: At least, tell me the most important.

Rubio Padilla: The fact was that after a series of dramatic incidents, the members of the Executive Commission were notified of the Directorio's decision. It is interesting to underline that the meeting was going to be held in the presidential study that then existed on the third floor and that had been Machado's private study until August 12, and it was that to which the political chroniclers referred when they spoke of the "Transcendent Floor," since it was thought that people received in the third floor study were people on a high political level. That study disappeared in 1934 or later, and then there was nothing more than an official study, on the second floor. Well then, when Grau arrived there, the first problem he posed was that he had not eaten all day, so he was practically faint with hunger, and that, as a prior requisite, sine qua non, indispensable, he had to eat or drink something. Then the Pentarchs went to the dining room and what they had there was, as the Americans say, a full dinner that took a long time as is natural. But it served perfectly for our discussion of the revocation of the vote of confidence and the designation of the President, which was not very long but naturally required some time. That is to say that when we arrived at the third floor the Pentarchs had not even formally met yet to discuss the pending problem. After a series of incidents that I'm not going to relate — one of them with Portela, very disagreeable — we notified them of what had been decided. Carlos Prío was the one who did it, after which Portela attempted to throw us out of there.

In a certain way Portela's attitude was explained since he did not know what had occurred in the meeting on the second floor and had made his decision to designate Gustavo Cuervo as President, and all that was left to do was to execute it. Portela believed he had achieved, with Irisarri's collaboration, a formal accord of the Executive Commission to that effect and it seemed to him that our presence there interrupted his plans, his tactics, or whatever it was. The fact is that he made a gesture through which he invited us to leave and it was then that Carlos Prío rapidly stood up and said,

> But it so happens that serious and transcendent meeting that you must have to designate the President of the Republic is no longer necessary because those that gave you the vote of confidence to designate the President, the members of the Directorio, have been meeting since nine this evening on the second floor and have come to a decision to revoke that vote of confidence and to directly elect the President. And the elected president of the Republic is Ramón Grau San Martín.

Thus it was that Grau was informed, from Carlos Prío's mouth, that the Directorio had designated him Chief of State. Then we turned our backs and returned to the second floor and notified the Directorio that our mission had been accomplished and that we had arrived in time to notify them before they could come to any decision. That was, in a few words, the mechanism that led to the elevation of Grau to the presidential seat.

Later Grau came down to the second floor and joined the Directorio's meeting. There he notified us that the inauguration would be the next day at noon and that he would meet with us in order to come to an agreement concerning the election of the rest of the members of the Cabinet, among whom he had already selected three. So you can see with what speed Grau selected three of his closest collaborators. When he came down to see the members of the Directorio, he had already decided on three persons to place in his Cabinet. The first was Doctor Carlos E. Finlay, who would be the Secretary of Health and Welfare, and who was a great selection over all from the point of view of international public opinion, since he was the son of an illustrious doctor, Carlos J. Finlay, discoverer of the mosquito vector of yellow fever. In his own right, doctor Finlay Shine, an oculist of great prestige, was an excellent person, professor at the University, and intimately allied with the Directorio, and now I must add that he carried out his duties well. The second member Grau had already selected was Antonio Guiteras to hold the position of Secretary of the Interior. Grau personally selected him at Irisarri's suggestion. And the third member of the cabinet selected by Grau was an old functionary of the Customs Service, José M. Barquín, who was known as a very honest and competent individual.[11] But for reasons that I don't know with certainty, Grau changed his mind and ended up naming Colonel Manuel Despaigne Treasurer, who was himself a magnificent selection. the Directorio intervened in that matter, the nomination of Despaigne.

The next morning, when we arrived at the Palace to attend Grau's inauguration, we found the judges of the Supreme Court there with their robes, since according to constitutional tradition in effect through the power of the Constitution of 1901 and the pseudo-constitution of 1928, it was before them that the President of the Republic had to take his oath. There were protests by the Directorio members based on the fact that we had bitter memories about the activities of the Supreme Court and, after a series of discussions, disputes, and caucuses, we put the problem to Grau and he accepted effectively that it was not proper that the president take an oath before the Supreme Court, since he was not going to occupy his high post by virtue of the Constitution of 1901 or anything else. He only had to take his oath before the people. That was what he did, and for the first time the oath of the President of the Republic was sworn, not in the parlors of the Palace, but on the North Terrace, before the great multitude that was there. That is the end of the story.

BATISTA FROM SEPTEMBER 5 TO 10

After having seen, through Rubio Padilla's narration, what occurred from the dawn of September 4 to the designation of Grau San Martín as president, we shall see now the conduct, during those same days, of the sergeant-colonel Batista, Ambassador Welles and the mediationist politicians, Sergio Carbó — as a pentarch in charge of the departments of Interior, Communications, and War and the Navy — and the Plattist military aristocracy, that would maneuver with such ability that it was able to seize not only the political direction of the old ousted officer corp but also to solidify under its command the immense majority of young captains and lieutenants that before the Fourth of September had been proposing the elimination of the high military commanders from major up and who responded in the end to the esprít de corps.

We shall begin with Batista. Before the Sergeants' Movement, Batista had managed with ease and with capacity to advance through the ranks. As a mere infantry soldier from the Fifth Squadron of the Rural Guard in Columbia, he had managed to become custodian of the estate of President Zayas. As a sergeant he had been a participant in the homage of his associates to Machado, but without distinguishing himself nor *calling attention to himself.* As a stenographer in the Sixth District, he had managed to place himself in a position to lend his services to the Courts-Martial that judged the revolutionaries. In this last position, he was not necessarily hated, since as a simple clerk he carried out a function that served to establish personal contacts with the most energetic opponents of the regime and that, at the same time, permitted him to appear as a supposed ally of the persecuted when he betrayed his loyalty to the Machado regime by selling copies of the trial transcripts to defense lawyers.[12]

After Machado's fall, he mixed with the rabble, changing sides immediately after eight years of playing both sides. In the well-attended burial of the three victims of Atarés — student Alpízar, labor leader Iglesias, and sergeant Hernández — upon finding out from the kinsmen of the last that no one had been sent by the High Command to give the eulogy, he had stood next to the grave to speak in the name of the armed forces.

Among others, Manuel F. Goudie and Gerardo Fernández Centurión, an officer and a civilian, had listened to him. The pleasant and serene Batista of the courts-martial had transformed into an agitator of the left, without embracing, of course, neither then nor later, a single political philosophy. It was enough for him to make his first debut with a well-applied opportunistic technique.

Within the syndical movement of the rank-and-file soldiers, little by little, with slowness but firmness, Batista assumed a certain authority through conduct that did not require the audacious participation of a bold and valiant fighter, as had been the case with sergeant Miguel Angel Hernández and the majority of those other sergeants who had been in prison on the Isle of Pines. A large number of those who finally made up the Junta of Eight had honored Machado; now he could stand out among them as their leader. Furthermore, the fact favored him that, as a stenographic sergeant, he was the highest ranking enlisted person among those in his regiment.

He failed to overcome one snag: Sergeant Pablo Rodríguez Silverio, president of the Enlisted Club for many years, had been making arrangements to get volunteers and create a favorable climate for the proposal of class demands. Rodríguez had a large following due to his achievements among the men of Columbia and because of his efforts to improve the living conditions of his enlisted compadres. He was, undoubtedly, the most well known and popular of the sergeants in the camp, not as a holder of military title nor as a great agitator, but as a useful servant to others.

Batista heard in the group that it was necessary to send someone to Matanzas to "prepare" the regiment there. It was indicated that the envoy would have to be capable and brave. Batista proposed, "Then it must be Pablo Rodríguez!" There was no malice in the nomination in spite of the fact that in order to fulfill the mission, Rodríguez would leave his military command vacant. During that absence — which lasted about ten hours, according to the statement Pablo Rodríguez himself made to me — Batista assumed command of the syndical movement and acted as chief in the course of various meetings that took place that Fourth of September, relying primarily on his ability for *cabildeo* (lobbying; intrigue, scheming) in every sense of the word, rather than on the most military style of Pablo Rodríguez, even though neither of the two ever displayed natural gifts of command.

During the night of September 4, Batista gave lavishly of his time and energy, with pats on the backs of sergeants of equal rank and the corporals and soldiers. Among these last, he treated Mario Alfonso Hernández in a special manner. Hernández would be promoted to lieutenant colonel and later would be assassinated by men under the command of Major Manuel Benítez Valdés, carrying out Batista's "orders."[13] Calling them by their first names, Batista engaged in courtesies with his companions, like one who is "receiving" at a cocktail party, even though trying to present himself as "first among equals."

The natural military leader Emilio Laurent said, "Batista is a representative of the masses (of enlisted men). He does not command, he only consults" (*Bohemia,* August 19, 1934, 14 and 65). This statement is not absolutely correct. It is certain that Batista commanded neither his companions in grade nor those supposed subalterns, corporals and soldiers, but utilized a special technique to "involve them." He would meet with the sergeants in his closest confidence in order to indoctrinate them on his position and inculcate in them what he proposed toward the integration of subordinate levels, with the aim of making them believe that they were making decisions. Those small groups ended up by agreeing to the self-same purpose that he had indirectly suggested to them.

Having achieved leadership over the sergeants, Batista, who was above all else an intuitive politician, had another flash of brilliance when, in the meeting of the *Agrupación Revolucionario de Cuba*, he was offered membership in the Pentarchy. He declined the honor. The wile culminated when he, signing last at the foot of the proclamation of power seizure, acting as an ordinary "*descuidero*" (so they called in Cuba those who committed petty thefts in moments of carelessness on the part of the owners) furtively put below his signature the title, *Sargento Jefe de las Fuerzas Armadas Revolucionarias* ("Sergeant and Revolutionary Chief of All the Armed Forces of the Republic," according to Welles Cable 192, September 5, 1933, 382).

In just a few hours, he had reached three objectives: to replace Pablo Rodríguez as natural chief of the movement; to avoid participation in the Pentarchy, in which his decisive role would not have been the equivalent of one-fifth; and to assume, from then on, the command of the armed forces.

To those who go through and battle in life with moral principles, Bismarck's thought applies: "A man of principles is like one who walks through the woods carrying a long rod" (Scheler 1961, 137).

Batista had been, in respect to Pablo Rodríguez, disloyal and efficiently opportunistic; in relation with those nominating the pentarchs, inhibited, reverential, and modest; before all the signatories, cunning and devious — all this in the moments in which the Republic lived its most dramatic destiny. We shall now see how he behaved immediately after signing the ARC proclamation that ended by saying that we were "confident that Cuba will be respected as a new sovereign nation which arises full of vigor to take part in international life" (translated in Welles Cable 192, September 5, 1933, 382).

Now entering into the morning of the fifth, the pentarchs, the members of the Directorio, and the other members of the newly created ARC set out for the Palace where Céspedes would arrive at eleven. In that encounter the well-known conversation occurred in which Céspedes resigned without renouncing office and left for his quarters in order to pack.

According to the chronology of the logbook, the Pentarchy or Executive Commission — its official title — came to order as the instrument of power at one in the afternoon on the fifth, according to the Extraordinary Official Gazette Number 26 of that date. The deposed president, Carlos Manuel de Céspedes, abandoned the Presidential Palace that same day at 2:10 p.m.

And what did Batista do in that interim? According to Ambassador Sumner Welles, in his cable on September 5, sent to Washington at precisely 11 in the morning — before President Céspedes himself knew of his expulsion and also before the Pentarchy was able to assume power:

> Sergeant Batista accompanied by Sergeant Santana called to see me at the Embassy. . . . Neither of them seems to have any clear conception of what the movement of the soldiers and noncommissioned officers is responsive to. The purpose of their visit was to ascertain what my attitude was toward the so-called revolutionary group and whether the installation of a government headed by this group would be favorably regarded by the Government of the United States. I replied that I had no comment to make (Welles Cable 193, September 5, 1933, 383).

Certainly, they were not inquiring into the acceptability of the Sergeants' Movement, but *whether or not the revolutionary group and the installation of its government would or would not be accepted favorably by the North American government. That was what was negotiable.*

He who had signed the document expressing confidence that "Cuba will be respected as a new sovereign nation which arises full of vigor to take part in international life" had gone to the Embassy of the United States, even before establishing the new government, in order to submit himself then to the foreign proconsul.

From all the above are derived two observations. First, Welles failed, in terms of his imperial will, for not having ordered Batista to restore Céspedes, which he could have done in good measure by returning to Columbia to try to reverse the course of the movement.[14] But Welles did not know then that the United States would end by throwing the officers overboard and come to an understanding with the sergeant-colonel. Second, Batista recognized no ethical standards of conduct; he travelled through life with no moral compass whatsoever.

WELLES FROM SEPTEMBER 5 TO 10

As for Sumner Welles, we shall see how he was going to try to develop a new technique so the United States could continue to manage Cuba as a colony. After describing what had occurred the night of the fourth, he went on to say,

> For the moment I recommend the immediate necessity of sending at least two warships to Havana and one to Santiago de Cuba at the earliest moment (Welles Cable 191, September 5, 1933, 379).

At ten in the morning, in telephone conversation with the Secretary of State, according to a memorandum by Hull himself, Welles said the following:

> He [Welles] stated that it was very important that a battle cruiser be sent to Havana at once; that the small destroyers we were sending would be of some help in the meantime, but not of sufficient use (Telephone Memo, September 5, 1933, 380).

Two hours later, in Cable 192, after having identified the three university professors he thought were members of the Pentarchy (he had confused Irisarri with some other professor) as open communists, he said,

> I repeat that it is urgently necessary in my judgment, however, that two destroyers arrive here at the earliest moment possible and that a battleship likewise be sent. As stated in my previous telegram, a warship should be sent to Santiago without delay. It is very likely on account of the serious labor agitation which had existed already that additional vessels should be sent to other ports to guarantee the safety of American lives (Welles Cable 192, September 5, 1933, 382).

And having further demonstrated his interventionist aims, he added,

> I wish to make emphatically plain that I shall do my utmost to prevent in every possible way the necessity of any armed intervention by the United States. *Since such a step, however, may later have to be taken by our Government* [emphasis added], I strongly urge the desirability now of explaining

the Cuban situation fully to the representatives of all the Latin American Republics (Welles Cable 192, September 5, 1933, 382-83).

That same day, the fifth, at 5:30 in the afternoon, in telephone conversation with Secretary Hull, Welles expressed the following:

I have had a conference with the political leaders of the Republic, and they are of the opinion that *it would be wise to land a certain number of troops from the American ship* [emphasis added]. It would be my idea that what we would do in that case would be to have a certain number come to the Embassy as a guard and a certain number to the National Hotel (Telephone Memo, September 5, 1933, 385).

This comment referred to the meeting held at 12:30 in the afternoon on September 5 with colonels Mendieta and Méndez Peñate, General Menocal, Doctor Miguel Mariano Gómez, and doctors Martínez Sáenz and Saladrigas of the ABC, to which Cable 194 also refers.

Three totally new factors now appeared. First, the old style politicians of the early republican tradition were taking advantage of the Platt Amendment, which they now invoked in order to return to power. Second, the new "revolutionaries" of the ABC, who before had accommodated themselves to the colonial regime by joining the Mediation, now solicited an armed intervention. Third, Welles requested permission to post troops at the Hotel Nacional, where he lived. But the request for military protection at the hotel prompts the question: Did there not exist some relation between the 12:30 meeting of the professional politicians of mediationism at the Embassy and the request to land troops, some of whom would go to the Hotel Nacional?

Perhaps it isn't strange that Sumner Welles would request the landing of troops in order to protect both the Embassy and the Hotel Nacional. In a strange coincidence, the next day, Julio Sanguily Echarte went to the Hotel Nacional. He had been replaced as Chief of Staff of the Army because of his acute illness and convalescence from an operation for a perforated ulcer, but he took up residence in a hotel instead of reentering the clinic where he had the operation. And he didn't register at a hidden and discreet hotel, but in the same hotel where the North American Ambassador had moved, into that same hotel that a short time later would be filled with hundreds of officers of the National Army, and which was, according to Welles, "the only place open to them [the officers] in Havana which can be readily defended" (Welles Cable 217, September 8, 1933, 407).

There is more: Welles did not report his move to the hotel until after 21 cables. On the eighth, three days after requesting a marine guard at the hotel, it was finally in this same cable that he stated,

> The Hotel Nacional in Havana, where many members of the American colony are living at the present moment and to which I myself have moved since the lease on my house expired . . . (Welles Cable 217, September 8, 1933, 407).

To which he immediately added:

> . . . has been decided upon today by the Cuban Army officers as headquarters.

And two days later, the tenth of September, he again said,

> I moved to the National Hotel because the lease on my own house had expired and I expected to sail on September 14th. I had been living there 2 days before any Army officers had taken refuge there (Welles Cable 228, September 10, 1933, 419).

Finally, he closed that dispatch by expressing that

> I have not changed my residence both because my doing so would have been at once misinterpreted and also because since the hotel is owned by an American company and many Americans have been residing there I believed my continued stay was helpful in view of the complications existing.[15]

Could it be that he forgot to mention his move the same day he relocated? We might even accept such forgetfulness if it were not for the fact that on the seventh of September, Ambassador Welles had discussed in detail a military plan presented to him by the former Secretary of War and the Navy of the deposed regime, Colonel Ferrer, a plan in which Welles was so deeply implicated — as we shall see shortly — that he was preparing the groundwork for proving the necessity of landing American troops. Then, after supporting and endorsing the Ferrer plan on the seventh, on the eighth he reported his move into the Hotel Nacional and stated, furthermore, that some five hundred fully armed Cuban Army officers had established their headquarters there (Welles Cable 217, September 8, 1933, 407).

At this historic moment, the intertwining of the Cuban political and military interest favoring military intervention, of which Welles was the standard-bearer, becomes evident, confirming what Ferrer said in his book *Con el rifle al hombro*:

> ... [Welles] was counting on all the officers gathered at the National Hotel, and that same afternoon he was going to visit the leaders of the political parties that had fought Machado to invite them to a common course of action (Ferrer 1950, 375).

This is how Welles said it on the evening of the fifth of September:

> It was the unanimous opinion, likewise, that the only way in which a government of the character proposed could be maintained in power, until a new Army could be organized under the Cuban Army officers, was for the maintenance of order in Havana and Santiago de Cuba and perhaps one or two other points in the island by American Marines (Welles Cable 199, September 5, 1933, 388).

To that proposal Secretary of State of the United States, Cordell Hull, replied immediately and flatly over the telephone:

> It seems to us that the whole thing down there revolves around the army, and *the question comes up with us as to whether the landing of men before we are absolutely compelled to do so— if we should land a thousand men there— it would in all probability mean intervention, and while we will not hesitate to go in if compelled to,* [emphasis added] we do not want to unless compelled. Because if we have to go in there again, we will never be able to come out and we will have on our hands the trouble of thirty years ago (Telephone Memo, September 6, 1933, 389).

In spite of this definitive position against the landing, Welles again insisted the next day, now ascribing the initiative to the political leaders, stating:

> There is not one political leader with whom I have talked who did not of his own initiative suggest the dispatch of American warships and for the Department's confidential information *the leaders of even so radical a group as the ABC urgently requested me yesterday afternoon to insist that the Department authorize the landing of American Marines*

both in Havana and in Santiago [emphasis added] (Welles
Cable 202, September 6, 1933, 392).

The next day, the eighth of September, the Undersecretary of State
who would later replace Welles, Jefferson Caffery, communicated the
following to the Ambassador himself:

> . . . we have no intention of landing marines except in the
> single case where they are needed for the protection of lives
> actually in danger (Caffery Memo, September 8, 1933, 408).

CARBÓ FROM SEPTEMBER 5 TO 10

Now against this backdrop, I shall analyze the case of Sergio Carbó.
In Rubio Padilla's testimony, we saw the fruitless attempts to find
a ranking officer who would accept command of the General Staff.
Neither Lieutenant Colonel Perdomo nor Lieutenant Colonel Guerra
accepted this elevated position, but it was evident that the Republic
could not continue with absolutely no leadership in the military sector,
without someone to take on the responsibility of maintaining order in
the whole country. Today I still do not understand why Colonel Julio
Aguado Andreu was not suggested. He had been the principal figure
in a military conspiracy against the Machado tyranny, an action that
cost him the command of the Seventh Military District (La Cabaña) and
a sentence of several years in prison. The omission is stranger still for
two notable facts. First, barely days after the Sergeants' Coup and, to
be exact, during Grau's presidency which began on the tenth of
September, Colonel Aguado acted as Secretary of War and the Navy.
The other observation is that, perhaps, the officers who did not suffer
persecutions or sentences also would have rejected his nomination to
the General Staff. At least, that is what can be deduced from the strictly
sectarian military historian Ricardo Adam Silva when, in his conference
on the Cuban National Army, he barely mentioned Colonel Aguado's
conspiracy of the fifth of October 1930. He limited himself to saying that
"several officers were discharged." He, thus, seemed to express
sympathy more for the expulsion rather than for those expelled, whom
he did not even mention by name in his general review of the history
of the army. He only referred — in a didactic manner — to the things
that conform to and accommodate his vigorous partiality.[16]

There existed a severe crisis in the Pentarchy. Porfirio Franca,
deeply rooted in the economic and financial classes of the country, had,
for all practical purposes, disappeared. He was not seen in the Palace

nor the treasury department nor anywhere else. José Miguel Irisarri, perhaps intuitively oriented by the fear of the loyalty of the sergeants, each morning got off the tram at the corner of the Presidential Palace and limited himself to repeating to those who were near him, "Any time, the soldiers will come and take us out and put another five in." Meanwhile, Guillermo Portela, university professor of penal law, who was in charge of foreign relations, did not hide his feelings of deep depression over the difficulties the newborn government was encountering in its affairs with the Department of State in Washington.

In fact, only two pentarchs remained firm and fully assumed their responsibilities. One was Ramón Grau San Martín, who without showing it, aspired to the Presidency by way of the Directorio Estudiantil, and the other was Sergio Carbó Morera, who likewise aspired to power, but in this case by way of the armed forces, by virtue of his control through the Secretary of War and the Navy.

Under these circumstances, Batista was promoted from sergeant to colonel through Decree 1538 on September 8, 1933, authorized exclusively by Carbó and inserted in an extraordinary edition of the *Official Gazette.*

It is possible that Sergio Carbó may have subconsciously received the direct message from a phrase contained in his own book about his journey to the Soviet Union, in which, referring to Lenin, he said:

> This great leader of men, who possessed the aggressiveness of a tiger, had likewise the cunning of the fox. . . . He was unorthodox, but not lunatic, because he discovered how to modify himself along the march, adapting himself to the accidents of the soil like a serpent, without ever losing his only and immediate objective, the conquest of Power (Carbó 1928, 152-53).

Should Carbó have consulted with the Pentarchy, as it is said that he failed to do? Shouldn't he have consulted with Franca, even though finding him might be extremely difficult? Wasn't it possible, likewise, to share the responsibility with Portela and Irisarri for this important decision, as well as all others? Still, Carbó did not act completely alone: we have seen in Rubio Padilla's story that he had participated, together with three other members of the DEU, in the decision concerning Batista, whom Carbó had consulted.

And now we shall see another opinion. I refer to that of Lincoln Rodón who, in fact, was another member of the Directorio since, unofficially, he represented the Directorio Estudiantil from Oriente, participated frequently in our meetings, and had been the student of Law who was selected to defend the traitor Soler in the drum-head court-martial in which he was tried.

Rodón declared the following:

> It was eleven in the evening on September 7, I think, when we saw Sergio Carbó coming out of the office which used to be the president's. He immediately approached our group and soon began to confide to us how worried he was. He had consulted Sanguily, Perdomo, Guerra, and other colonels. But they expected Batista to be made a prisoner. However, as it came up during the conversation, Batista did not want anything else beyond being included in a board constituted by the colonels, without himself expecting any promotion. So, in the face of the situation we all were confronting, Carbó's idea seemed the only plausible alternative. He wanted to hear the opinion of six or seven of us, and we all agreed with his point of view. Of those who were there, I remember Juan Antonio Rubio, Willy Barrientos, Carlos Prío, Rubén León, and I, and a few others. Perhaps, there was also someone else outside of the Directorio, but I am not sure.[17]

Even though I myself was not consulted on the matter because I was not in the Palace at that time, though I am not accustomed to eluding my responsibilities, now I must ask: Could the army continue without a commander? With the possibility of Colonel Aguado already explored and the rejected offers made to Lieutenant Colonels Perdomo and Guerra, who could be named? The overthrown Colonel Ferrer, the former Secretary of War, now a daily visitor at the Embassy? General Armando Montes, whose return to service had been the detonator of the rebellion? The old retired officers, whose return to service on August 22 had provoked the ire of the young officers? Some of the lieutenant colonels, majors, captains, or lieutenants, also living in the hotel, still totally subordinated to the hierarchy of General Sanguily?

Furthermore, as we shall see immediately, the officers sequestered in the Hotel Nacional were tied, apparently the immense majority of them, at least, to a great project to recover power. The passion generated by their displacement and their decision to return was such that Emilio Laurent — who, along with Feliciano Maderne, was the only officer that fought against Machado with arms in hand — stated in his book:

> A few hundred officers, gathered at the National Hotel, practically threw me out of the place upon hearing my proposals, which caused me, as I headed for the door, to say offensive words against my former colleagues (Laurent 1941, 140).

Sergio Carbó, with his long life of solidarity with the causes of progress and contributor, as no other, to the unpopularity of the Machado regime, had to pay the price of becoming a magnet for all the criticisms directed against Batista's promotion. Even though he later became a triumphant newspaper impresario, one could say of his official public life that he was in power barely five days and that all his activity is represented by a single act of singular importance: Batista's promotion from sergeant to colonel.

WELLES AND THE PLATTIST OFFICERS

Before considering Welles and the officers holed up in the Hotel Nacional, I must point out that the bulk of the Cuban military establishments — the Rural Guard in 1900, Artillery Corps in 1901, Permanent Army in 1908, Cavalry School in 1909, Cadet School in 1912, and so on — all these organisms were created under the First or Second American Intervention and all under the psychological influence of the Platt Amendment. It is not strange, therefore, that these organisms would have ingrained within them the concept of limited sovereignty, a dependent mentality, and overall a subconscious tendency to look to the United States before making decisions that could be vetoed by the powerful neighbor. After all, that neighbor had attached to the constitution of the Republic the right to intervene in determined circumstances and the requisite that Cuba consult with the U.S. government before arranging any negotiations that might affect the public treasury, such as loans.

The fact that the officers of the Liberation Army would occupy key positions in the Executive Power in the early days of the Republic, starting from the presidency on down, as well as the highest levels of the rank structure of the armed forces, simply extended the Plattist mentality. It ran so deeply that on many occasions the Amendment was invoked in secret by opposition leaders trying to use it against the government in power, while publicly denouncing the constitutional appendix as a self-negation of republican sovereignty.

Furthermore, the military instructors were North American and so were the members of the review boards; U.S. Navy warships were sent to Havana and Santiago de Cuba in times of disturbance or insurrection; and the Department of State in Washington, on more than one occasion, warned Cuban governments concerning the possible landing of troops should they become incapable of protecting North American lives and properties on the island. While all this went on in the political arena, in the economic and financial arena a bilateral agreement between Cuba and the United States was arranged in which, with the pretext of supposed reciprocity, our country authorized its counterpart preferentials for more than a thousand North American products while Cuba received preferentials for only four or five of her own products. Additionally, since public services such as telephone, electricity, transportation, banking and securities, as well as extensive portions of arable lands and the majority of the sugar processing centers were in the hands of U.S. corporations or citizens, it is understandable that the tired spirit of those who fought for independence and that of the Cuban people themselves, pretending that a better economic situation was emerging, would subconsciously accept the national Plattist mentality to survive until the revolutionary process of 1930-1933 offered an alternative.

It is precisely in that period when the vision of politicians and military men was obscured; they agreed not to recognize the true significance of the revolutionary attitude of the student body. They, therefore, were not attuned to the new wave implied by the demand for a "total and definitive change of regime," including relations between Cuba and North America and the implied abolition of the Platt Amendment, both from the juridical and the psychological point of view.

At this point, it seems opportune to transcribe precisely the clash between Plattism and anti-Plattism as it was expounded by a member of the DEU, Rafael García Bárcena.

> At the time when the Directorio Estudiantil Universitario represented the most advanced element of the Cuban revolution, its presence in power constituted a true national necessity. The other existing political forces were gathered around the Céspedes government, produced by the imposition of the Platt Amendment. A 180-degree turn in the nation's course was absolutely necessary. Those who were

still mentally trapped by the imperatives of the Constitutional Appendix could not make this turn. Only those who dared to rely on the abolition of the onerous Amendment could change the national destiny (García Bárcena, September 4, 1952, 61).

First, it is necessary to examine how far the entrapment, if you will, had gone. Before that, though, I must say that I would not believe it if I had not read it in the cable correspondence between Welles and the Department of State in Washington.

On the sixth of September 1933 the Associated Press transmitted from Annapolis, Maryland, the following cable:

> Warship *Indianapolis*, with U.S. Secretary of the Navy Claude Swanson on board, left port this afternoon at five with destination Cuba. Departure — the ship was anchored a few miles offshore — was delayed for some time due to unknown reasons. Previously, it had been set for four in the afternoon.[18]

Furthermore, in addition to the ships still in the Havana bay since the fall of President Machado, Ambassador Welles had requested the previous day (the fifth) that war vessels be sent and even the limited number of troops at his disposal be authorized to land. With the further knowledge that the *Indianapolis*, carrying naval units and the Secretary of the Navy, was weighing anchor outside Washington, one could logically assume that a decision for armed intervention by the United States had been made.

For the Plattists, the AP news cable concerning the voyage of the Secretary of the Navy meant — as we shall see — the development of a plan to recover power with the decisive support of the Yankee marines. The anti-Plattists developed a belligerent attitude that evolved into multitudinous demonstration of rejection, as related by Rubio Padilla in his testimony. Even the North American Secretary of State, Cordell Hull, in fact, favored us, as he demonstrated three months later when he told the Cuban delegate to the Seventh International Conference of American States in Montevideo, Portell Vilá, that

> I have given good evidence of my sincerity on recent occasions, such as the trip of the Secretary of the Navy, Mr. Swanson, who did not land in Havana (Portell Vilá 1934, 27).

It was at this time, with the *Indianapolis* carrying Secretary Swanson travelling full speed toward Havana, that the Secretary of War and the Navy of the deposed regime, Colonel Horacio Ferrer, returned to visit Ambassador Welles after the overthrow. His first visit had occurred on the morning of the fifth, when he nearly crossed paths with Batista leaving from an interview similar to that for which Ferrer was arriving. The cable regarding Batista's visit is marked eleven o'clock, and Ferrer arrived precisely at midday, that is to say, twelve noon (Welles Cables 193 and 194, September 5, 1933, 383-84).

What national humiliation and what Cuban misery! The Secretary of War of the deposed regime and the leader of the military regime that produced the coup d'état had both set out to consult with and submit themselves to the North American ambassador!

Why did Colonel Ferrer return to the embassy now? He went to propose a plan to the foreign proconsul. Since the sergeants stationed at Cabaña Fortress had been deceived into their participation in the mutiny, they were prepared to realize some reparation for their action; they were ready to prepare a written communication to that effect for President Céspedes. Doctor Ferrer stated that he had arranged with the sergeants that they would require the revolutionary group (in power), which was now trying to persuade the officers to resume their positions, to reappoint Major Patricio de Cárdenas, the last commander at La Cabaña, and return all his subordinate officers (in whom Ferrer claimed to have total confidence) to their previous posts. As soon as these preliminary measures could be carried out, he, Ferrer, accompanied by eighty officers, President Céspedes, and several members of his cabinet, would go to Cabaña on Friday, the eighth of September, to proclaim the support of the Seventh Military District for the *legitimate government of President Céspedes* the following day. According to Ferrer, the Fortress was impregnable and stocked with food, and if there were still sergeants hostile to the project in the fort, they would be expelled. According to the ambassador, Colonel Ferrer demonstrated that he had already been in contact with officers from Pinar del Río and Matanzas, as well as with others, and he assured the ambassador that immediately after the reassumption of command, the loyal troops and officers throughout the country would make a simultaneous proclamation and the Pentarchy would be overthrown (Welles Cable 206, September 7, 1933, 396-98).

Ferrer's consultation-request culminated with the request that, if the plan were carried out and the Céspedes government requested the landing of U.S. troops from the ships now arriving in Cojímar, immediately to the east of the Fortress, the United States lend help to the Cuban government to maintain order.

Now we see the whole scene of Batista's promotion in its full dimension: the understanding with the lower-ranking officers, that is to say, from major down, was irreconcilable with their submission to the commanders and superior officers; there were no officers in command positions in the Army when Colonel Ferrer requested the landing of North American troops in order to aid the *legitimate (?) Céspedes government* to maintain order; and Lieutenant Colonels Perdomo and Guerra had rejected the possibility of being nominated to serve as Army Chief of Staff.

At this point, Cuba saw itself facing a choice. Either a North American military intervention would reinstall the Mediation government to power and maintain Cuba's status as a dependent territory of the United States, or Batista would be promoted to colonel and the revolution could begin the promulgation of the laws proposed by the DEU in its August 22 document.

Colonel Ferrer told Ambassador Welles that, in the course of the last twenty-four hours, he had been in constant conference with the political leaders of all the groups that had backed the Céspedes government and that his plan relied on the approval and backing of them all. Menocal, Mendieta, Gómez, and the ABC were demanding, this time through Ferrer — as their leaders had done personally before — the armed intervention of the United States. In the consultative cable to the Department of State, dated exactly at noon of the seventh of September, Welles recommended the aid of a U.S. armed force as a police power, and he committed the monstrosity of saying that "such assistance would most decidedly be construed as well within the limits of the policy of the 'good neighbor' . . ." (Welles Cable 206, September 7, 1933, 298).

Unfortunately, President Roosevelt, at eight in the evening, after having received the consultation at four in the afternoon, communicated his final order to Welles through Secretary Hull:

> We feel very strongly that any promise, implied or otherwise, relating to what the United States will do under any circumstances is impossible; that it would be regarded as a

> breach of neutrality, as favoring one faction out of many, as attempting to set up a government which would be regarded by the whole world, and especially throughout Latin America, as a creation and creature of the American government" (Hull Cable 90, September 7, 1933, 402).

Welles did not retreat, and in spite of having received the final word from his president, the next day he informed his government that

> Under these circumstances, I feel it is a wise precaution to have the *Richmond* anchored in the harbor where men can be landed at short order rather than outside the harbor, which would involve considerably more time in landing men in the event of urgent need (Welles Cable 214, September 8, 1933, 404).

That same afternoon he tried to demonstrate why the Céspedes government was representative of "the enormous majority of the Cuban people" (Welles Cable 216, September 8, 1933, 405). He practically confronted President Roosevelt to object to the phrase, "favoring one faction out of many" (Hull Cable 90, September 7, 1933), because, he said, it was

> . . . lending friendly assistance at its request to a Cuban government presided over by an impartial President and supported by every element of importance in the Republic.
>
> . . . nothing, in my judgment, would create more disastrous effects in Latin America than a prolonged military intervention in Cuba. If, at the request of the Cuban Government, we temporarily afford them the moral assistance a small number of Marines would create in maintaining order after such Government had established itself and until a new Army could be organized, such assistance should be construed as just as much of a friendly act as the facilitating of a loan. In the one case we would lend the Cubans police and in the other, money, neither of which they possess (Welles Cable 216, September 8, 1933, 406-7).

In no uncertain terms he *informed* his government that to land marines would be the same as making a loan of money and, furthermore, would be considered consistent with the *good neighbor* policy.

HOW THINGS STOOD ON SEPTEMBER 10

And now we reach the tenth of September. Grau San Martín took possession of the Presidency of the Republic, and Colonel Ferrer came back to push his plan. That afternoon he again visited the Ambassador, who gave this account of the interview:

> This afternoon Dr. Ferrer called at the Embassy to advise me that the Army officers wished to petition me to agree to have a sufficient force of American Marines landed to disarm the soldiers and the innumerable civilians who are armed and that should I agree they would at once proclaim that President Céspedes was the sole legitimate President of Cuba and undertake the recruiting and training of a new Army. I replied that I would not even receive such a petition and that it was absurd to imagine that the Government of the United States would undertake it at the request of 200 deposed Army officers. In reply to a further inquiry whether my Government would definitely refrain from recognizing the new regime, I replied that I most decidedly refused to make any such commitment. . . .
>
> My replies to these inquiries, I was later advised by a civilian present, were accurately transmitted by Dr. Ferrer to the assembled officers (Welles Cable 228, September 10, 1933, 418).

So there was an assembly . . . Who and why? The officers of the Army met to vituperate again the most recent meetings of the enlisted personnel. The fundamental hierarchy and discipline were still in shards through all levels of the Cuban Army after six days; the character of the meeting was nondeliberative. On the fourth, sergeants and enlisted ranks had held a meeting and approved the governing program of the Directorio Estudiantil Universitario that Juan Antonio Rubio Padilla had read to them; now the officers were deliberating in an assembly to reconsider Welles's rejection of deposed former Secretary of Defense Colonel Horacio Ferrer's request for the landing of marines.

An author on the theme, Luis E. Aguilar León, blames the Directorio for having "stuck" the military into politics. True but false. Until the twelfth of August, the Army had upheld the "constitutionalist" policy by maintaining regimes that arbitrarily prolonged their terms or reelected themselves. Until the night of September 4, the Army had respected the designation of a president — Céspedes — by an ambassador. The Plattist mentality had been applied from the subconscious of the Cuban military commanders, as we have just seen. So, to produce an overthrow and establish for the first time in more than four hundred years a government produced by the national will for change, was this not, perhaps, in terms of their original aims, the most adequate "meddling" in politics for idealistic students and men in uniform?

Therefore, simultaneous with Grau San Martín's inauguration, Doctor Céspedes would be proclaimed the legitimate President of Cuba, so the landing of the marines could be requested for no other purpose than to disarm the soldiers and the armed civilians. Even Welles, impressed by President Roosevelt's message, and who up until that moment had been the standard-bearer for armed intervention, considered the petition absurd!

Thus ends the recapitulation of the dramatic days that Cuba survived between the dawn of the fifth and the evening of the tenth of September, 1933.

Rubio Padilla told of the disintegration of the Pentarchy and the designation of Grau San Martín as president, complete with details of the fruitless search for an Army Chief of Staff, Batista's promotion to colonel, the short stay of the Secretary of the U.S. Navy, Claude Swanson, in the bay of Havana, and the impassioned and aggressive popular rejection of the Indianapolis in which he had traveled.

I, for my part, have analyzed Batista's conduct during that time, the machinations of the mediationist politicians, the behavior of Sergio Carbó, and the maneuvers of the Plattist officers, whom Colonel Horacio Ferrer represented.

What is the balance of the situation?

It was now the tenth of September. Grau San Martín had just assumed the presidency of the Republic, as designated by the Directorio Estudiantil Universitario. But the Directorio once again stood alone. Even though all the people supported the group, there did not exist any organization among the masses; the DEU had no resources or techniques of popular mobilization, nor did it know how to use pressure groups. Furthermore, the DEU had no control over the media. Against the DEU and its government stood all the traditional forces, the professional politicians, reinforced by the active and militant reincorporation of the ABC, an organization that had been born originally as an ally of the DEU and that was now its most vigorous antagonist. Against the DEU also stood the Army officers who had overthrown Machado on August 12 and who now, according to Welles, had converted the Hotel Nacional into their headquarters, and, as the ambassador himself put it, were "fully armed" (Welles Cable 217, September 8 1933, 407). Against the DEU stood the communications media and against the DEU stood the now equally new colonel, Batista, who twelve hours after the historic coup had the audacity to go to negotiate the possible delivery of a civil government to the North American ambassador.

On the other hand, the Directorio had their adherence to their fundamental principle of the Cuban people's right to sovereignty and self-determination. And, greater still, and as a result of high-level international efforts to manage and resolve this grave situation, *the Directorio had as counterweight the backing of the two highest figures in United States foreign policy*: President Roosevelt, who had emphatically declared his opposition to

> . . . set up a government which would be regarded . . . as a creation and creature of the American government (Hull Cable 90, September 7, 1933, 402).

and Secretary of State, Cordell Hull, who in a telephone conversation with the U.S. ambassador in Mexico told him,

> I would rather walk from here to the South Pole than to have to intervene [in Cuba] (Daniels letter, September 9, 1933, 415).

Beyond these noninterventionist statements from the United States, the Cuban government, which at the time was the Directorio, could count only on the backing of Spain and Mexico, countries both traditionally hostile to North American interventions in Latin America.

The rest of America was divided. Cuba, as a nation, was considered dependent on the United States. Its delegation to the Sixth Pan-American Conference in Havana in 1928, during Machado's presidency, had heatedly defended the North American right to intervene. In economic terms, Cuba could then have easily qualified as actually forming part of the Yankee economy. It seemed unlikely that now, through the eruption of a student group into power, that psychological and economic colony could truly declare itself free, independent, and sovereign.

The Chief of the Latin American Affairs Division of the Department of State, Edwin C. Wilson, called a meeting with the diplomatic representatives of Guatemala, the Dominican Republic, Paraguay, Honduras, Haiti, Costa Rica, Nicaragua, Peru, Venezuela, and Panama. The functionary of the chancellery presented the Cuban case with great care, emphasizing that

> ... there was no thought of intervention or interference with Cuban political affairs, but that the ships were sent to Cuba for the purpose of protecting American lives (Wilson Memo, September 6, 1933, 393).

According to that same memorandum, the ministers of Guatemala, Paraguay, and Honduras seemed satisfied by the attitude of the North American government toward Cuba and recognized

> . . . that, of course, the United States had the right to intervene. . . .

even though Wilson added that,

> . . . our effort to avoid intervention and to let the Cubans work out their own problems was making a fine impression in Latin America (Wilson Memo, September 6, 1933, 393).

Two days later, the Minister of Foreign Relations of the Dominican Republic told the North American minister in that country, Schoenfeld, that

> . . . President Trujillo had given instructions that American military aircraft could utilize freely the territory of the Dominican Republic (Schoenfeld Cable 36, September 8, 1933, 404).

adding that

> . . . the aircraft of the Dominican Republic would be placed at the disposal of the American government if so desired (Schoenfeld Cable 36, September 8, 1933, 404).

And the United States Chargé d'Affaires in Guatemala communicated with the Secretary of State:

> Minister of Foreign Affairs requested me this afternoon to inform you that President Ubico feels the Cuban situation is exceedingly grave principally because of communistic tendencies. Consequently, he is of the opinion that American intervention is essential to preserve order and insure

establishment of constitutional government (Lawton Cable 23, September 6, 1933, 393-94).

In positive contrast, the Latin American superpower, Argentina, on learning from the president of the United States himself of the lofty principles under which he was considering the political disturbances in Cuba and of his fervent desire to avoid intervention, the Platt Amendment notwithstanding, responded in these terms:

> The statements made will do honor to American traditions and by their example history will know that no state arrives at the maturity of democracy and the fullness of destiny without experiencing, as a necessary accompaniment, the travail of difficult conflicts (Argentine Communique Translation, September 8, 1933, 409).

This document from the Chancellery of Buenos Aires additionally points out these vital concepts:

> The capacity to maintain order and to assure the reign of law emerges by itself as a fruit of this experience within the *exercise of sovereignty, which must be characterized by absolute internal autonomy and complete external independence*[emphasis added]. Such principles are developed by a formative process in all youthful nations and, especially in recent times, by the demonstration that the reestablishment of normality requires a natural flow in the spontaneous development of national tendencies (Argentine Communique Translation, September 8, 1933, 409).

In reviewing this scenario, I must ask myself: Why the very firm decision of President Roosevelt not to intervene militarily in Cuba?

I perceive three reasons:

First: In 1906, and at the request of President Estrada Palma, the government of the United States had intervened in Cuba, landing troops and assuming power. After a corrupt administration, the provisional North American governor, Magoon, was retired and General José Miguel Gómez was elected president. The experience had been so negative that now, in 1933, Secretary of State Cordell Hull said,

> . . . if we have to go in there again, we will never be able to come out and we will have on our hands the trouble of thirty years ago (Telephone Memo, September 6, 1933, 389).

Second: If in the previous intervention North American troops had landed at the request of President Estrada Palma; now they would have to "go in" to overcome the opposition of a revolutionary government and the people of Cuba, as proven by the multitudinous popular demonstration at the bay of Havana when the Secretary of the Navy of the United States, Admiral Swanson, arrived aboard the *Indianapolis*. This intervention, seen clearly, would have occasioned thousands of deaths.

Third, and perhaps the most important factor in President Roosevelt's decision not to intervene militarily in Cuba, in spite of the repeated requests by the professional politicians and the Plattist officers, backed by the North American ambassador, Sumner Welles: the Seventh International Conference of American States was due to begin in December 1933, just a few weeks away.

Another North American ambassador, then accredited to Mexico, Lorenzus Daniels, had advised the State Department on two separate occasions concerning the danger of intervention on the eve of the conference in Montevideo. On September 6, Daniels had stated that the Minister of Foreign Relations of Mexico

> believes, and I concur, that intervention would impair Pan American friendly relations and might in advance destroy the hopes in connection with the Montevideo Conference (Daniels Cable 178, September 6, 1933, 394).

Three days later, on the ninth, he communicated to Secretary Hull, in response to his question concerning what the ABC countries — Argentina, Brazil, and Chile — as well as México, would think, in regard to a possible American intervention. He replied that

> they feel that if we intervene it will destroy the Montevideo conference (Telephone Memo, September 9, 1933, 413).

Could the U.S. appear before the Seventh Pan-American Conference with its marines occupying Cuba, after a landing that would have caused hundreds of deaths and confronting an increasingly popular movement?

It is within this national and international panorama that the President designated by the Directorio, Ramón Grau San Martín, was going to execute the program of government presented on August 22, 18 days before.

NOTES

1. The demands solicited by the rank-and-file soldiers present at the assembly authorized by Lieutenant Colonel Perdomo, because of their classist nature, could not lead to a revolutionary coup d'état. The barracks insurrection developed into a coup exclusively because of the actions of the DEU.

2. The dialogue between Ravelo and Batista is related by Lieutenant Francisco Albear and transcribed in Ricardo Adam Silva's book, *La gran mentira: 4 de septiembre de 1933*. It went like this:

> Then the camp Officer of the Day, Captain Demetrio Ravelo, arrived, and the same scene, more or less, developed: "Batista, I've come to see what's going on! "Now you are seeing it, Captain!" went the response that continued thus: "We aren't going against anyone; for the time being we are going to take care of ourselves and later we will see!" (161)

Concerning this episode, one can also refer to *Cuba — El fin de la República* by the same author (1973).

3. The photo, made by a photographic reporter from United Press International, is reproduced in this book. Guillermo Cabrera Infante, the most notable Cuban writer, in his book *Vista del amanecer en el trópico* (Barcelona: Seix Barral, 1974, 113), comments thus on the photograph:

> The photo is a curious symbolism. It signals the end of a military tyranny while it exalts a soldier. All points of the photo converge on the soldier, who stands over the statue of a lion at the beginning of a lane in the capital. The soldier stands erect with his rifle held high in his right hand, while his left is extended toward one side, perhaps trying to keep his balance. He holds his head high and erect, celebrating the moment of triumph that is, apparently, collective.

> At the extreme left of the photo, one of the demonstrators has removed his straw hat to salute upward toward the soldier. To the right and center another more casual demonstrator (he is in shirtsleeves) removes his cap while praising the soldier. All are surrounded by a small crowd exalted by the triumph of their cause, it seems.

> Behind the soldier one sees balconies with iron railings and windows with French venetian blinds open in pairs. Further away, on the corner, there is an advertisement for an airline, in English. The photo has been reproduced in all parts as a testimony of its epoch — or better of its moment.

4. It should be noted that the historian Louis Pérez, Jr., commits an error in his book when he emphatically states that at the end of August the command structure of the Army abrogated the decree that permitted the sergeants to complete the programs of officer training in order to obtain nominations on equal standing with the graduates of military service institutions. Pérez's declaration that states "from there on the priority was assigned to the graduated cadets" is false.

5. August 22 is called the "Day of Confrontation." That is the date on which the Directorio made the Céspedes government, as we have seen, feel all the moral force that proceeded from its historic struggle against the Machado dictatorship and the weight that signified its unbreakable line of conduct. From then on, the traditional politicians grouped with the Mediation government were unable to ignore the DEU. In the days that followed until September 5, the Directorio achieved such authority that it can be said that it reached power in anticipation of actually gaining it through the "Sergeants' Coup."

6. José M. Perdomo y Martínez came from the Liberation Army and entered the National Army as a sergeant. He was commander of the Tactical Regiment in the Fourth, Sixth, and Eight Districts (Matanzas, Havana, and Pinar del Río, respectively). He served in Matanzas when Machado appointed him to command the National Police. His conduct in that position was discreet. He committed neither abuses nor outrages. He ended his military career with the rank of lieutenant colonel.

7. Miguel Guerra y Pérez, also lieutenant colonel in the National Army, was second in command of the Sixth Military District (Columbia). He did not use his position to commit abuses.

8. Concerning this matter, one can consult the following communications in *Foreign Relations of the United States*, 1933, Volume V, pages 385-407:

> Memorandum of the telephone conversation between the Secretary of State Hull and Ambassador Welles, and between Auxiliary Secretary Caffery and Welles, September 5, 1933
>
> Welles Cable 199, of the same date, to the Secretary of State
>
> Memorandum of the telephone conversation between Hull and Welles, September 6
>
> Welles Cable 202, same date, to the Secretary of State
>
> Welles Cables 206 and 209, September 7
>
> Welles Cable 214, September 8
>
> Cable 36, from the American minister in the Dominican Republic, Schoenfeld, to the Secretary of State, on the same date
>
> Welles Cable 216, also on September 8

Through all this documentation one can clearly see Welles's insistence on sending in the United States Marines, supported, according to his statements, by the Cuban political leaders that he cites: Menocal, Mendieta, Martínez Sáenz, M. M. Gómez, and Saladrigas, among others.

9. Adolfo F. Arenas was witness to the statement that Rubio Padilla makes. That day Arenas was in the Spanish Casino in Havana, talking with his future father-in-law, Alfonso Gómez Mena, and upon seeing the crowd headed toward the entrance of the bay, which was very near there, they both decided to go along and watch the entrance of the *Indianapolis*. Arenas relates that upon the arrival of the ship, one of the protestors near them took a revolver out of his belt and fired several shots toward the boat while shouting strong insults against the United States and its armed intrusion into Cuban affairs.

10. Aurelio Alvarez was a lieutenant in the Liberation Army and an active politician. He was militant in the Partido Conservador from its foundation and distinguished himself with his vehement oratory. He was a senator until 1925. He was president of the Conservative Party but resigned because of a disagreement with the policy the party followed in reference to Machado. Later, he was a member of the Executive Council of the Asociación Unión Nacionalista in opposition to Machado. Finally, he identified with the position of the Directorio. In 1949 he returned to the Senate, this time for the Partido Revolucionario Cubano (Autentico) (Authentic Cuban Revolutionary Party). He held the highest post until the dissolution of Congress by the Batista dictatorship.

11. Barquín was, on top of honest, an experienced General Director of Customs from 1933 to 1939.

12. One of his clients was Eduardo J. Chibás (father of Eddy Chibás) detained and accused in one of the many cases for sedition brought against the oppositionists. Chibás accepted his lawyer's recommendation to send Sergeant Batista the twenty pesos requested in exchange for the illicit sale of a copy of the judicial file.

13. Mario Alfonso Hernández, chief of the Eighth Military District (Pinar del Río), paid with his life for the assassination of Juan Blas Hernández during the battle at Atarés Castle, after its surrender on November 8, 1933. On August 22, 1934, Major Manuel Benítez Valdés, accompanied by enlisted personnel in whom he had absolute confidence, presented himself at the headquarters of the mentioned Regiment, and after taking command, ordered his subordinates to go to the residence of Hernández, a half-block away. They knocked on the door and feigned to be carriers of an urgent message from the High Command. Hernández, upon opening the door, was shot down by the visitors.

14. Even though the reversal of the course of action would not have been completely easy for Batista, he could have achieved it because he had already become Sergeant and Revolutionary Chief of All the Armed Forces, because

the reversal would have affected only the civilian part of the government, and because the syndical demands of the military movement were obtained.

15. The condition of being American property assumed during that period certain immunity to act outside the norms. Under that protection, Welles tried to create an impregnable focus of agitation.

16. Conference entitled "The Cuban National Army in History" at the Koubek Center of the University of Miami, May 19, 1979, 15. The conference has been published, but the folio that contains it lacks the publisher's imprint.

17. The words of Lincoln Rodón are recorded on magnetic audio tape that can be found in the author's collection.

18. Admiral Swanson carried powers to act as circumstances would dictate, but the sight of the agitated multitude alongside the harbor induced him not to attempt any landing, not even himself personally. It is very probable — as Cordell Hull said to Portell Vilá in Montevideo — that Swanson could have consulted him and that it was Hull that made the decision. The *Diario de la Marina* stated, the next day, that the ship stayed in the bay only hours.

Chapter 3

THE REVOLUTIONARY GOVERNMENT I: FROM SEPTEMBER 10 TO NOVEMBER 30, 1933

PRESIDENT GRAU

An equally critical period was about to begin. The revolutionary government, headed by Grau San Martín, ready now to enact legislation, would have to do so while plagued by the traditional political factors backed by Ambassador Welles; by the excitations of the press — dominated by commercial interests — that abused the freedom of expression without cease; by diplomatic negotiations that alternated with explosions of violence within Havana itself like those on the second of October (Hotel Nacional) and on the eighth of November (Atarés); by actions of the North American government, which, in each declaration concerning the recognition of Grau's regime, encouraged his removal (a policy that avoided armed intervention); and by the prevailing state of violence in which bombings and shootings occurred with such frequency that the abnormality of the collective life of a weary society became a daily routine.

Consequently, this legislation, of course, could not be measured, rhythmic, or totally coherent, since events would continue to impede it in some cases, draw it out in others, or at times precipitate it. The daily flow of events and commotion further agravated the difficult task of enacting revolutionary changes, occasionally developing into totally unforeseen situations requiring immediate and decisive attention.

Nevertheless, the legislation followed the general outline traced in the DEU program. The DEU had developed that program over the previous three years, starting from a limited socio-economic and revolutionary culture acquired in prisons and enhanced by contact and polemics with workers and *campesinos,* who perhaps influenced us more than the political texts.

Since the positions of each one of the factors in the process are already known, I can present the historic tape at greater speed, intermixing events with legislation, as if they were graphic curves on the electrocardiograms of the country.

Following a logical course, the first legislation promulgated was the Constitutional Statutes, decreed four days after Grau's inauguration, outlining the general guidelines by which the Provisional Government would govern.

The Statutes were preceded by the following events:

- On September 11 the U.S. Secretary of State, Cordell Hull, cabled to his missions in London, Paris, Rome, Berlin, Madrid, Tokyo, and Peiking, as well as to the American Consul at Geneva, and to all missions in Latin America except Cuba, informing them that

  . . . there is not the slightest intention of intervening or interfering in Cuba's domestic affairs. It is our earnest hope that the Cubans themselves will work out a solution of their own difficulties and that they will be able to form a government capable of maintaining order (Hull Telegram, September 11, 1933, 422).

Since the recently established Grau government was not capable of maintaining order, the United States implied that the Cubans, opposing the newly inaugurated regime, would depose the government and themselves put together a new one that was capable of maintaining order.

- That same day, the President of the United States authorized Secretary of State Cordell Hull to declare that

  . . . our Government is prepared to welcome any Government representing the will of the people of the Republic and capable of maintaining law and order throughout the island (Hull Cable 96, September 11, 1933, 424).

This declaration implied that Washington would opt for the overthrow of the government put together twenty-four hours earlier.

- In perfect synchronization, the *Unión Nacionalista* issued a declaration signed by Colonels Mendieta, Méndez Peñate, Hevia, and Torriente in which they stated that only a "government of concentration" would be able to govern the country until it was possible to install a permanent constitutional government.

- Also on the eleventh, and forming part of the orchestra, the ABC, described at this time by Welles as "in many ways the best organized and most energetic political organization in Cuba" (Welles Cable 231, September 11, 1933, 419), declared in an extensive program that it would, ". . .*without needless imprudent ostentations, maintain the same decidedly anti-interventionist position* [emphasis added] it had stated in its manifestto program . . ." (Soto 1977, Vol. III, 104). And this the ABC expounded after having fruitlessly solicited, just days before, the landing of American Marines. The Alphabetic declaration lashed the military coup, saying, ". . . there can be proved beyond doubt that the Government of Dr. Céspedes was essentially a Government of public opinion" (Welles Cable 231, September 11, 1933, 419).

- General Menocal very briefly declined all responsibility for the new government (Welles Cable 231, September 11, 1933, 420).

- By September 12, the United States had, in effect, *abandoned* the officers in the Hotel Nacional and, having achieved an understanding with Batista after his promotion to colonel on the eighth, encouraged him to return to power the same persons that had been overthrown. Welles cabled Washington that day:

  Owing to the fact that all of the servants in the National Hotel left the hotel last night, . . . I and the Americans still remaining there were forced to leave the hotel this morning (Welles Cable 238, September 12, 1933, 428).

This differed notably from his dispatch the day before when he had commented:

  It is my hope that . . . some arrangement will be made which will permit the officers to leave the hotel with guarantees (Welles Cable 231, September 11, 1933, 420).

Obviously, Welles's attitude toward the officers in the Hotel Nacional had taken a new direction. He told the Department of State on the twelfth that he had advised the electric company, if it should receive orders from some government authority to cut off the electricity ". . . it would be wiser on their part to comply with the demand made" (Welles Cable 238, September 12, 1933, 428). (Evidently, Welles operated quietly in favor of Batista and against the officers.)

The next day, the thirteenth, the government of Mexico informed the United States, through Assistant Secretary of State Caffery, that

> . . . *as it seemed that a stable government capable of maintaining order had been formed in Cuba,* [emphasis added] it did not seem necessary to go any further with efforts to induce other Latin American countries to make suggestions at Havana that a stable government capable of maintaining order be formed (Caffery Memo, September 13, 1933, 429).

The Mexican Chargé d'Affaires in Washington, who delivered this message, added:

> *This view was shared by the great majority of his colleagues . . . . [They] believed that [the United States] should remove [their] naval vessels from Cuban waters* [emphasis added] because they (he and his colleagues) feel that the opposition political leaders in Cuba will not cease their efforts to overthrow the *de facto* government as long as our naval vessels remain there (Caffery Memo, September 13, 1933, 429).

The Cuban Ambassador in Washington, Manual Márquez Sterling, had expressed to the Chargé d'Affairs of Mexico, Luis Padilla Nervo, that he "believed that none of the political leaders in opposition could now count on a large following in the Island. . ." (Caffery Memo, September 13, 1933, 430).

Meanwhile, Luis Padilla Nervo, trying to secure a pronouncement from the chancellery on the Potomac, inquired directly of Mr. Caffery,

> Could not you make some sort of public declaration to the press here that you hope that Dr. Grau San Martín's government will be able to establish itself solidly in the Island and be able to maintain law and order throughout the Republic? (Caffery Memo, September 13, 1933, 430).

Caffery replied that such a statement would be a partisan declaration, while they wished to remain neutral, and that

> . . . that declaration would be construed to mean that we have decided to support the *de facto* authorities and we would be attacked for it by all of the Cuban political leaders. We can not commit ourselves that far yet (Caffery Memo, September 13, 1933, 431).

North American neutrality, therefore, consisted in refusing to recognize the revolutionary government, declaring it incapable of maintaining law and order, and encouraging the establishment of another government that would meet Yankee specifications.

- On that same date, the thirteenth of September, Welles cabled that the officers remained in the Hotel Nacional and that a small group of officers from the interior of the island, who apparently could have brought in arms and munitions, had gained access to the hotel. He added that, even though water services had been cut, they — the officers — had water stored in tanks that apparently would last some ten days, and sufficient food was available for a much longer period. He indicated that General Sanguily had been placed in charge. He ended with a strange phrase: ". . . the officers now appear to desire an encounter if the soldiers are willing to provide it" (Welles Cable 246, September 13, 1933, 431-32). Of course, the encounter would be armed. Welles, after having indicated his abandonment of the officers in Cable 238 the previous day, now seemed to consider this shuffle useful. Could it be that he was playing with two decks simultaneously, contradictory within themselves — one with the officers in the Hotel, the other with Batista? Well . . . Yes.

THE GOVERNMENT LEGISLATES I

On the fourteenth of September, President Grau and his cabinet promulgated the juridical instrument that served as a basis for the actions of the new regime. It appeared in the extraordinary edition number 30 of the *Official Gazette*:

> Sixty-five years after the 1868 Cuban Revolution for independence erupted, the first fundamental declaration of the Provisional Government — with the faith of its honor pledged in its fulfillment, for it was then, it is now, and ever shall be, what will embody the national honor and prestige — is that, in response to the most vivid and fervent aspirations of the people, it will proclaim and sustain, over all other interests and ideas, the absolute and immaculate independence of the Country, for the preservation of which all present-day Cubans, like those of yesterday, are willing to sacrifice lives and homes, which mean nothing when such a glorious ideal is involved.

A necessary consequence of this fundamental declaration is that the Provisional Government shall observe as an invariable guideline of international policy regarding all the free nations on Earth, to whom it offers its good will and friendship, the pursuit and achievement of a better harmony and a more perfect accommodation of their reciprocal economic interests, but at the same time maintaining above all the principles of the free determination of its internal conflicts, the juridical equality of the Statess, and the national independence and sovereignty.

With full realization of its historic reponsibility, the Provisional Government declares its profound respect for the sanctity of those international treaties spontaneously entered into in the name of the Republic of Cuba and its firm and decided intention of complying with them to satisfy the revolutionary purposes which gave life to its organization.

Concurrently, in compliance with the principle of political science established by the philosophers of the eighteenth century and brought up from the deepest recesses of social order by those historic tempests called Revolutions to expose them to the light of the consciences of free men, it acknowledges and proclaims, as a basic postulate of its organization and conduct, that the national sovereignty resides in the People of Cuba, and, consequently, it will immediately call on the people freely to approve, rectify, or try and punish its performance; and, to that end, it shall in a very short time convoke a Constituent Assembly that will determine the Government that shall rule the country and to which this Government shall concede the powers which it now exercises.

Since the political crimes and common felonies committed during the Machado regime, repugnant to all sentiments of humanity and civilization, shocked the consciences and caused untold misery and ruin to the people, and at the same time created a difficult situation in the Public Treasury, the Provisional Government declares that, without vacillations or unjustifiable leniency, it will execute all sentences that shall be imposed upon those judged responsible by the Court of Punitive Sanctions, which shall be created specifically for this purpose in deference to popular expectations. It shall respect the arguments of the defense and administer impartial, serene, and orderly justice.

These statements duly express the ideology that motivated the revolutionary movement that culminated in this Provisional Government and its international policy. However, the Government takes special interest in further stating that, as long as it exercises the powers vested in it by the people of Cuba, it will ensure that life, property, and the full exercise of individual liberty are respected with absolute guarantee and with no other limitations than those required by their social function.

In accordance with the postulates expressed in this preamble, the Provisional Government, by its free and spontaneous will and with the consent of the people of Cuba, promulgates and obligates itself to fulfilling the following STATUTES:

First: The Provisional Government shall assert above all the absolute independence and sovereignty of the nation, the principle of free determination of the people in the resolution of its internal conflicts, and the juridical equality of the States.

Second: In regard to international policy, the Government shall endeavor to achieve the best possible harmony and the most perfect adjustment of the political and economic interests of Cuba, and reciprocally those of other countries, and will respect and abide by the Treaties signed in the name of the Republic of Cuba.

Third: Elections shall be called as soon as possible to elect Delegates to a Constituent Assembly that shall consider and rectify, or try and punish the actions of the Government, organize another upon which this Government shall confer the powers which it exercises, and formulate the Constitution of the State.

Fourth: The Government shall organize a Court of Punitive Sanctions that shall be empowered to judge those individuals accused of crimes, whether granted amnesty or not, committed for political motives or in defense of the deposed tyrannical regime and which, with due respect to their right of defense, shall impose corresponding punishments.

Fifth: Since the *Provisional Government* would incur grave responsibility should it abandon the responsibility of power to seditious interests, *it shall be within its authority to temporarily subject individual liberties to a regimen of government surveillance, in discharge of which it shall duly inform and be accountable to the Constituent Assembly* [emphasis added].

Sixth: No one shall be deprived of his legitimate property except by qualified authority and by justifiable reason of public concern, subject to corresponding indemnification. Should this requisite not be in order, the Judges of the Court shall protect and, as the case may be, shall compensate the affected individual.

Seventh, The Secretary of Justice is hereby authorized to propose to the Government the Regulations necessary to determine the number, organization, and functions of the Courts of Punitive Sanctions, as well as for the execution of the provisions of these statutes.

Given in the Palace of the President, in La Havana, this fourteenth of September of nineteen hundred thirty-three.

R. Grau San Martin
President of the Republic

J. Río Balmaseda	Antonio Guiteras
Secretary of Justice and	*Secretary of the Interior*
Interim Secretary of State	*and Interim of Public Works*
Manuel Despaigne	Manuel Costales Latatú
Secretary of Treasury	*Secretary of Public Education*
	and Fine Arts
Carlos E. Finlay	Gustavo Moreno
Secretary of Health	*Secretary of Communications*
and Welfare	

Julio Aguado
Secretary of War and the Navy

The statements in the preamble expressed the fundamental ideology of the revolutionary movement and the direction of its international policy. It emphasized, though, that while the provisional government exercised the powers conferred upon it in the name of the people of Cuba, it would do so with respect and would command respect for life, property, and individual liberties, absolutely guaranteeing those rights, and hold itself to the limits of its social function.

Obviously, the mere reproduction of the text of the statutes does not give a clear idea of the grave problem Cuba faced. Several specific points must be made to clarify statements in this pronouncement in relation to that problem. First, in the statement of motives, there is that declaration of "profound respect for the sanctity of those international treaties spontaneously entered into in the name of the Republic of Cuba."

The inclusion of the term *spontaneously* had to and did provoke the ire of Sumner Welles who in the cable to his superiors stated,

> In my judgment the use of the word "spontaneously" in this context clearly implies the intention of denouncing the permanent treaty with the United States (Welles Cable 258, September 15, 1933, 436).

From this statement, it can be deduced that even Welles himself admitted that the execution of that treaty had not been spontaneous.

Furthermore, the revolutionary government emphatically declared its decision to call a Constitutent Convention that would consider and rectify or try and punish its own activities and organize some other government body to which it would cede its powers and duties.

The preamble also reveals a subtle suggestion concerning the goal that drove it temporarily to submit individual rights to examination. It would be interesting to apply this examination of rights to the freedom of the press, since experience indicates that the privileged factors that, in a determined historic moment, oppose the process of change, will become the greatest enemies of the institution driving that change once the process begins. But now, having permitted myself this observation, I must say that even though this problem still has not found a solution, in the end, respect for free expression of thought must prevail; but it must be balanced with a similar respect for the greater good of the people.

Finally, to answer the charge of communistic tendenciees in the newly established government, the President and the Cabinet made a final declaration concerning the *right to private property*, even though Welles mentions this aspect in none of his cables. The curious thing is that this right to property clause did not stimulate the interest of the economic classes or the professional politicians. This fact, simply, emphasizes that the situation had gone beyond reason and into passion.

THE DEU-WELLES INTERVIEW ON SEPTEMBER 15, 1933

Ambassador Welles held marked odium for the Directorio for having destroyed his August 12 formula for colonial vassalage. He was not unfamiliar with the historic force of our battle organization and always cast the DEU in a negative light when communicating with Washington. In spite of all his efforts to discredit us with the Department of State, he wanted, nevertheless, to hold a conference with the DEU and, at his request, we agreed to receive him. In the few days of struggle for power in Cuba between the United States (as represented by Sumner Welles) and the restorationist forces of the past against the DEU and the people of Cuba, Welles had been losing. He was not able to gain the authorization he had repeatedly requested between the fifth and the tenth of September to land the marines; he was not able to reestablish the Céspedes government; he learned through the press about the conversion of the Pentarchy into the one-man presidency of Grau San Martín. But as always, he liked to shuffle and stack the cards; he wanted to sound out the possibility that the Directorio might fall into a grave error on which he might capitalize.

For that reason I have always believed that the interview between Welles and the DEU was a mere testing of the waters, a careful and direct examination of a group that had been consistently hostile toward him, a means of getting to know the human qualities, characteristics, and driving force behind this antagonistic organization. But the simple fact that no additional meetings were agreed on, nor would the Directorio designate any type of committee for possible later interviews, proves that both parties considered themselves incompatible in terms of the future.

During the interview I recall having passed a note to Rubio Padilla while he was speaking to Carlos Prío, advising him that, when it fell to him to speak, he should point out that certain topics being discussed were not appropriate for discussion between a foreign ambassador and the new Cuban political power. Of course, when this was called to the ambassador's attention, Welles immediately returned to topics of conciliation between the United States and Cuba. Of course, Welles reported his interview to the Department of State almost immediately after the meeting ended, that is, at two in the morning of the sixteenth of September 1933. In Cable 265, he said,

> I had an interview tonight with the full membership of the Directorio Estudiantil. I indicated the reasons for the recent features of our policy toward Cuba and expressed very emphatically our earnest desire to be of friendly assistance should the Cuban people desire it. I stated my belief that in these very grave moments all elements of Cuban public opinion should put all feelings of rivalry and ambition to one side and cooperate for the benefit of the Republic. The interview was extremely cordial and most of the lady members were not unreasonable (Welles Cable 265, September 16, 1933, 439).

Before ceding the historic narrative to another notable member of the DEU, Agustín Guitart, it is necessary to make two mere annotations to Sumner Welles's cable. First, in reference to setting aside rivalries and *ambition*, Welles had initiated that rivalry when he began his mediatory process with an imperial attitude toward the different political factions in dispute in the "colony." The Directorio was independent and sovereign and did not agree to the stage-managing of the work. What is inconceivable — and what Welles did not even mention in the interview — was that business of setting aside ambitions. The only faction that did not have a single ambition was the Directorio. After three years of struggle, the loss of several of its members, imprisonment and persecution, the overthrow of two governments, and the seizure of power, *none of them had assumed a public office nor collected a single centavo for the services the Directorio continued to give freely to the nation.*

Concerning the conduct of the female members of the DEU, it is safe to say that any of them could have mingled with ease with Welles's mother and the other members of his family because of the exemplary conduct they always maintained. Lulú Durán, Sarita del Llano, Silvia Martell, and Nena Segura Bustamante, the only four who had been with us from the beginning, had struggled with us and had assumed the greatest of risks. But they also know how to comport themselves in an exemplary manner in reception halls and parlors. In spite of the familiarity that necessarily develops in the daily struggle and the camaraderie that common combat generates, those four great ladies always displayed exemplary conduct and lovingly committed themselves to four other members of the Directorio, with whom they married immediately after the victory. Their husbands were Luis Barrera y López del Castillo, Guillermo Barrientos Schweyer, Ramón Miyar y Millán, and Manuel Antonio de Varona y Loredo, all brilliant fighters who had postponed their marriages until after the fall of the regime.

Well. What of the fact that the ambassador qualified "most of the lady members" as not having been "unreasonable?" Only a psychiatrist very experienced in human relations could explain this incomprehensible favorable description from a so-called ambassador.

Agustín Guitart described the conference to me in a personal letter. He wrote:

> I recall many details of that interview. Welles sent us a message saying that if we wished to talk with him he would be disposed to converse with us. Our reply was that if he was interested in speaking with us, it would not inconvenience us to receive him. He accepted, and the interview took place in the home of [Eddy] Chibás, at the corner of Seventeenth and H in Vedado. The first thing that surprised me was that he greeted each and every one of us there by name. Sumner Welles spoke to us in perfect Spanish. After he explained his reasons for talking to us, the members of the DEU responded, firing back with the motivations and reasons behind our movement. Among other things, I recall that Welles told us that the administration of the new president, Roosevelt, had implemented a series of measures that had prevented a revolution in the United States and that the "New Deal" represented a total change in the policy from previous administrations regarding the countries of Latin America. Finally he told us that, after having met with us and listened to us, he could assure us that *"if I were Cuban, I would be honored to be one more member of the Directorio Estudiantil Universitario."* In spite of this statement, the Directorio left with the feeling that Sumner Welles would continue to recommend that Roosevelt not recognize the provisional government of Grau San Martín.
>
> Many years later, I found out that, after Doctor Grau was elected president in 1944, he was invited to visit Washington.

During the dinner given in his honor at the White House, President Roosevelt told him that he could never adequately express his regret over the error he had committed in not recognizing the provisional government following the Pentarchy and that in this policy of nonrecognition, he had been very strongly influenced by the direct reports of Ambassador Sumner Welles.[1]

THE GOVERNMENT LEGISLATES II

- Five days after the promulgation of the Statute, the government of the revolution decreed the *maximum workday* to put an end to the abusive system of exploiting the working class (Decree 1703, *Official Gazette*, September 28, 1933). It declared:

Whereas: In every country free from historic class biases Labor in the broadest sense of the word constitutes the center of gravity of their existence;

Whereas: Once the traditional principles of respect for life and property, which are the irreplaceable essence of our social fabric, are recognized, immediate attention to the proletarian problem becomes by organic derivation a fundamental necessity;

Whereas: In all countries throughout the world the time of rendering services is limited by law;

Whereas: After exhaustive studies in the United States as well as in South America and in Europe, human effort in the common pursuits of life has been limited to eight hours a day and has been so established either as constitutional amendments or as organic laws;

Whereas: Progress and civilization, though different things, run parallel in this case, seeking social prophylaxis and creating the sound output of Labor with the human warmth that should affect us all;

RESOLVED:

That, at the end of thirty days from the date of the publication of this Decree in the Official Gazette, compliance with the maximum eight-hour workday is to be mandatory throughout the Republic for all types of occupations of its inhabitants, whatever their line of work may be.

Given in the Palace of the President on the nineteenth day
of the month of September of nineteen hundred thirty-three.

Antonio Guiteras   Ramon Grau San Martin
Secretary of the Interior   President

The decree was countersigned by Guiteras as Secretary of the
Interior because the post of Secretary of Labor had not been created.
It was established on October 13, 1933, by Decree 2142.

- On September 16, the *laws of amnesty promulgated by the
  dictatorship to preclude punishment for crimes and offenses of all
  natures committed by Machado's repressive corps and the functionaries of his government were revoked,* and on the twentieth,
  in accordance with Article IV of the Statutes, *the National Court
  of Punitive Sanctions and the six provincial tribunals* were
  created to examine the crimes and offenses that had been
  perpetrated in order to sustain and defend the tyranny.

- On September 18, official recognition was extended to the
  National Medical Association, which would replace the Medical
  Federation of Cuba as the legal organization governing the
  medical community and determining the requisites to practice
  medical and surgical professions (Decree 1703, *Official Gazette,*
  September 28, 1933).

Similar measures to organize and govern various professions
were dictated on the twenty-fifth, creating the *National Pharmaceu-
tical Association,* and in following weeks the *National Veterinary
Medical College,* the *Gastrointestinal College of Cuba, Cuban Association of Nurses,* the *Cuban Association of Midwives,* the *National
Association of Architects,* and the *College of Sugar Agro-Chemical
Technicians of Cuba,* all created by decree, and all with the force of
law (Soto 1977, Vol. III, 427).

This legislative cornucopia demonstrates a response to sentiments deeply rooted in the extensive groups of Cuban professionals,
and even though the Directorio had not incorporated their recognition
in the program, the DEU was always willing to recognize the social
organizations that created channels for the exercise of power.

- On September 19, the political parties registered with the
  electoral tribunals were officially dissolved, fulfilling a point that

did figure in the DEU program as part of the slogan, for a "total and definitive change of regime."

* On September 20, barely ten days after President Grau's inauguration, and only six days after the promulgation of the statutes by which the Provisional Government ruled, a single-house Constituent Assembly was called and scheduled to open on May 20, 1934, only eight months away.

With that legislation, the new governors, far from pretending to perpetuate themselves in power, established for themselves an extremely limited term. Rather than creating the problem of sovereignty of the Constituent Assembly, this body was expressly commissioned to disapprove and rectify, or approve and sanction, the activities of the government and organize another governmental entity to which the Provisional Government would relinquish its powers.

Of course, the creation of a Constituent Assembly appeared among the demands formulated by the leaders of the opposition in its ultimatum to the Provisional Government on September 18. They had demanded that the convention begin within six months, whereas the decree established an opening date eight months away, a difference of only two months between the government's decree and the opposition's requirement. The question remains now as before: didn't the convulsed Cuba of 1933 deserve, after eight years of oppression and through the supposed liberation of August 12 that had delayed the revolutionary process by installing a president and cabinet at the services of the United States, that a spirit of compromise and mutual understanding should prevail, guaranteeing the security of the Republic? Of course, the oppositionist sectors — the only ones that counted, after the dissolution of the traditional parties that had supported Machado — solidified their demands that a Constituent Assembly be established within six months, and the Provisional Government, though not precisely responding to that petition, published the decree not forty-eight hours later establishing the Assembly, differing from the demands only on the matter of the time frame.

I did not understand then and with great difficulty can I understand now, after fifty years, how the civic forces comprising the opposition against the Machadato could not immediately reach a Saxon compromise to achieve a peaceful solution. The only explanation possible is that they lacked good faith. In the opposition sectors there were unmeasured ambitions and an inordinate desire for revenge, and the North American ambassador himself continued to work against Cuban interests. On the other hand, in the very heart of the military forces, who had revolted on the Fourth of September, treason and disloyalty had come to power. The proof of this will be revealed immediately.

WELLES AND BATISTA CONSPIRE

Also on September 21, in the cable quoted below, Sumner Welles informed the Department of State,

> I have just concluded an interview with Batista. He expressed this morning the desire through an intermediary to have a conversation with me. His attitude throughout the conversation was extremely reasonable, and he repeatedly emphasized the fact that neither the stubbornness of the Student Council [DEU] nor that of Grau San Martín should be permitted to stand in the way of a solution of the immediate political problem. It was very obvious, from my talk with him, that the students and presumably Grau San Martín himself have misled Batista as to the attitude of the United States Government since September 4th. I made clear to him our policy, convinced him that we have no prejudice and no partiality, and emphasized the fact that we would welcome any government in Cuba no matter by what individuals it was composed which fulfilled the requirements made clear in the official declaration of the Secretary of State last week.
>
> *He expressed the belief that solution was imperative* [emphasis added] . . . (Welles Cable 289, September 21, 1933, 451).

Was this an effort to gain that Saxon compromise and agreement among all parties to the elections for delegates to the Constituent convention? No. The foreign ambassador said to the chief of the Cuban Army that his country

> . . . would welcome any government in Cuba no matter by what individuals it was composed which fulfilled the requirements made clear in the official declaration of the Secretary of State . . . .

The Secretary of State of which country? Well, of the United States, of course. Nor does Batista take offense; he responded that *a solution was imperative.* So, seventeen days after the coup, the military chief accepted that the only solution available was to return that very same government to power that he, as a sergeant, had helped the DEU to displace, in the name of the authentic revolution.

In continuation, Welles added his suggestions, including these statements:

> We favor no group nor party in Cuba in preference to any other. We sympathize deeply with those ideals of social reform and honesty in government which so many of the important factors in Cuba's public opinion of today are proclaiming. We hope they will be carried into effect. But the Government of the United States believes that what is imperative in this moment of grave crisis is not alone the determination of a far-reaching program but the immediate cooperation of all groups in Cuba in the formation and maintenance and support of a government responsive to the will of the people lest all government in Cuba be destroyed. No party advantage, no political strife is the issue at this time. On the program of the provisional government all groups are in accord. *The issue is, on the contrary, the urgent need for the support by the people of a provisional and temporary government which can prepare the way through the carrying out of this program for the installation of a constitutional government elected by the majority of the Cuban people* [emphasis added] (Welles Cable 289, September 21, 1933, 453).

This proves that, on the twenty-first of September, Batista and Welles were already in complete agreement in terms of reestablishing in power the same political team that Welles had installed with the cooperation of the armed forces on August 12, 1933.

Welles wanted to put an end to the revolutionary legislation and, if possible, reverse the process altogether. Furthermore, he hoped to return Cuba to the political status of a de facto colony.

The Batista-Welles conspiracy would continue for nearly four months and would end only with Grau's overthrow. Batista had visited Welles barely a few hours after the Sergeants' Coup and asked him

> . . . whether the installation of a government headed by this group would be favorably regarded by the Government of

the United States (Welles Cable 193, September 5, 1933, 383).

From that very same morning, when the insurrection began, before the installation of the new government (the Executive Commission or Pentarchy), Batista was negotiating the removal of that government. Three days later — September 8 — he was promoted to colonel, after Welles had informed Washington on the seventh of a plan by Colonel Ferrer, who, aided by officers already established in the Hotel Nacional, was ready to reverse the events, recuperate the commands, and reestablish Céspedes as the President of the Republic.

Several days of intense historic concentration passed, at the end of which Grau alone was made president. He began to govern on September 10 and on the fourteenth he dictated several Constitutional Statutes through which he announced the intention to respect the international treaties and conventions *spontaneously* celebrated, by which he augured a future repudiation of the Platt Amendment. Immediately afterward the maximum workday of eight hours was made law, and immediately thereafter, the Court of Punitive Sanctions was created and professional organizations, groups which modern sociologists call *intermediate bodies* of the politically organized society, were established. At the same time, the political parties that had constituted the basic structure of the deposed dictatorship were dissolved, and, furthermore, a Constituent Assembly was called which would confirm or replace the provisional government, once its political accounts were rendered.

Of course, those five decrees established the future trajectory of the revolutionary legislation, and this was precisely the moment in which Batista and Welles betrayed their earlier positions, with Batista abandoning the Cuban interests that had been rescued from North American interference.

So it went. Welles began by washing his hands of the old officer corps, whose countercoup he had predicted on the seventh, eighth, and ninth of September, considering it more practical to come to an understanding with the recently promoted colonel. And Batista, who owed his new rank to the revolutionary movement, placed himself humbly at the service of Ambassador Welles and the financial interests that he represented. But Welles was unable to achieve his ends, at least in terms of legislation in the course of the next four months, which Batista could not impede. What the new commander of the army did achieve was to deliver to the Ambassador all the resources of the new military power in exchange for the consolidation of his personal interests.

The pettiness of supposedly high-minded politics! Welles had been nothing more than an usher at the wedding of Franklin D. Roosevelt. He had been a foppish graduate of Harvard and now served as special envoy of the North American president. Now he stooped to the same moral level as the *guajirito* [peasant] of Banes, who, after climbing over the ranks and ascending suddenly to the highest level, was negotiating as an equal with the first power of the world in betrayal of the most elemental principles of public morality!

According to Welles, Batista had complained bitterly during the interview about the attempts made by opposition leaders to undermine the loyalty of the soldiers toward him. So, Welles suggested that President Roosevelt make a declaration that would strengthen Batista's arrangement with the political leaders and in which the U.S. government would object exclusively to the civil government of Cuba without a single attack on the new military order. It is interesting to note that *in none of the cables from Welles to Washington, nor in any of the responses— many, to be certain— from Washington to its embassy in Cuba and in none of the official declarations of the North American government does there appear the least condemnation of the Sergeants' Coup.* All the attacks are directed against the revolutionary civil government installed in power as a consequence of the coup.

Batista began his arrangements by meeting with Miguel Mariano Gómez first, then with the splinter group OCRR, and finally with Mendieta. As for Menocal, Welles had already said, just a few days before, "that it is only a question of a short time before General Menocal will attempt to lead a revolution" (Welles Cable 236, September 12, 1933, 426). Originally, these arrangements tended toward the designation of a consultative junta composed of twenty members, which would come equally from among the government and the political opposition, with the junta responsible for designating cabinet members and under-secretaries. Grau would remain as president.

Welles tried to attribute more importance than was deserved to an uprising led by Colonel Juan Blas Hernández in the military zone encompassing the provinces of Santa Clara and Camagüey. He was immediately taken aback by the appearance of the insurgent colonel at the Presidential Palace, which reduced his credibility as a predictor of the future, even though the uprising itself had occurred.

Since the Directorio opposed Grau's replacement by one of the opposition politicians, the cables sent by the Embassy continued to be critical of the Directorio, to the extreme that *Welles cast Batista as the good guy in the movie.* He had informed the Department of State that the students had opposed allowing a truckload of foodstuffs to enter the Hotel Nacional, upon Batista's approval, which, of course, was absolutely false. He told his superiors at the same time that "since officers in the hotel only have food for one day more, they will presumably try to fight their way out tonight or tomorrow" (Welles Cable 294, September 22, 1933, 456).

Three days later, the twenty-fifth, Welles did not hide his astonishment that the declaration he had suggested to President Roosevelt was not forthcoming. In a new dispatch he insisted on the urgency of *a new government capable of maintaining public order and carrying out the functions of any stable government* (Welles Cable 304, September 25, 1933, 457-58, in reference to Welles Cable 289, September 21, 1933, 453). Trying again to pressure Roosevelt, he indicated that there only remained two alternatives if the president refused to make the recommended pronouncement and decided to

> . . . refrain from making our position clear by urging a common accord. The first [alternative] will be *a desultory revolutionary movement* [that is to say, an armed insurrection] *which will probably take a considerable time before it proves successful and which will impoverish still further the interior provinces . . . ;* the second is *the displacement of the present regime by a more radical group in connivance with a portion or the whole of the Army and which will be headed by some professional agitator. . . or some one of the Army sergeants"* [emphasis added] (Welles Cable 304, September 25, 1933, 457).

He went on to indicate that such a government would, in all probability, assume complete dictatorial powers and abandon the program of reestablishing a constitutional government through national elections.

Welles's cable dispatches continued to chronicle the machinations that occurred through his understanding with Batista. On the twenty-second, he communicated that Batista had met with Carlos Mendieta and again with Miguel Mariano Gómez, "upon both of whom he made an extremely favorable impression" (Welles Cable 294, September 22, 1933, 455). The following day, he mentioned interviews with outstanding representatives of Menocal and of the ABC, who, along with the delegates of Mendieta and Gómez, agreed unanimously that Grau's replacement "should be considered the basis of a compromise" (Welles Cable 299, September 23, 1933, 457).

Welles's dispatches demonstrate that the negotiations fell through on the twenty-fifth because of the final position the DEU adopted. But that same day, the ambassador, urging again that President Roosevelt formulate a declaration that would ultimately undermine the stability of Grau's government, expressed a most acid opinion of Cuba and the other republics of the Caribbean. He began by saying,

> You know how sincerely I believe in the policy of non-intervention in Cuba (Welles Cable 304, September 25, 1933, 458).

This is the statement of the man who had requested not the generic intervention similar to that which had continued over the years but who had urged the immediate landing of United States Marines, on multiple occasions: 1) Cable 192 on September 5 (382); 2) the two telephone conversations at half-past five and quarter-past six that same evening with Secretary Hull (385-87); 3) Cable 199 of the same date (387-88); 4) a new conversation with Secretary Hull on the sixth (389-90); 5) Cable 202, also on the sixth (390-92); 6) Cable 206 the following day (396-98); 7) Cable 209, also on the seventh (400-1); 8) Cable 214 directed to President Roosevelt on the eighth (403-4); and 9) Cable 216 on the eighth (405-7). All this preceded his statement to President Roosevelt that he had been against intervention in Cuba, after having solicited that very intervention ten times in the course of only four days.

He continued the cable of the twenty-fifth, saying,

> I likewise am convinced that the Cubans can never govern themselves until they are forced to realize that they must assume their own responsibilities (Welles Cable 304, September 25, 1933, 458).

From the very birth of the Republic, the first opportunity Cubans had to assume their own responsibilities began precisely on that Fourth of September. Unfortunately, not all Cubans understood that. Among those who immediately converged on the American Embassy were the professional political leaders, seeking others who would assume their responsibilities.

The cable continued,

> But you also appreciate the psychology of the peoples of the Caribbean Republics. *We have been generous and we have shown the utmost patience* [emphasis added].

This seems to imply that the interventions in Santo Domingo and in Nicaragua, both military, were considered by Sumner Welles as generous and demonstrative of North America's extreme patience. And the cable continued by saying,

> The impression is fast growing that our attitude is due to fear of public opinion in Latin America and that we will countenance a complete disregard by the Cubans of any international or individual rights we may possess here.

Here was a direct response to President Roosevelt, who had himself made clear eighteen days earlier, on September 7, that any promise concerning U.S. actions would be seen *"as attempting to set up a government which would be regarded by the whole world, and especially throughout Latin America, as a creation and creature of the American Government"* (emphasis added) (Hull Cable 90, September 7, 1933, 402). On the other hand, the international rights the United States had held in regard to Cuba would be abrogated scarcely months later, as was implicitly predicted in the Constitutional Statutes.

Welles continued the cable, saying,

> Respect for us is diminishing and the belief is rising, sedulously fostered by the radicals, that the United States can be flouted with complete impunity.

It must be stated that neither the Directorio Estudiantil, nor the Executive Commission, nor the provisional Grau government ever uttered any insult or derogatory comment against the United States or its governing officials.

The same cable said in the next sentence,

> That attitude in my judgment is due to the mistaken impression that our continued abstention from announcing a more definite stand than we have is caused by a policy of

weakness rather than by the policy of generosity and noninterference which we have in reality pursued.

Therefore, the mobilization of thirty warships around Cuba and the continued declarations against the recognition of the revolutionary government were to be interpreted as a policy of generosity and noninterference.

Finally, the cable stated:

> I feel very strongly that a statement of the nature suggested in my telegram No. 289 would have a decisive effect. I do not think it is too late. But if some measure of that kind is not taken, I fear that the situation here will take a turn which can only be regarded as disastrous to the Cuban people themselves as well as to our national interests.

Welles's request for a declaration from President Roosevelt to help Batista's developing machinations to replace the Grau government had not been favorably received by Roosevelt, but still, as he had in fifteen cables over four days, Welles insisted on the imperative necessity of the declaration. Once again, however, Roosevelt refused to follow the advice of his personal representative, and the declaration was not formulated.

The aggressiveness of this message to the president indicates that the first conspiracy had fallen apart and that Batista, on the twenty-fifth, did not have sufficient backing for a compromise involving Grau's overthrow and replacement with a malleable figure.

If the lack of respect for Cuba and Latin America contained in that cable was incorporated in the published cable correspondence, one can imagine what was said in the cables numbered 292, 293, 295, 296, 298, 300, 301, 302, and 303, sent by Welles between September 22 and 25, none of which were included in the public record.

It is also interesting that cable 289, in which Welles directly solicited the declaration from Roosevelt against the Grau government in order to facilitate Batista's *labor* involving the opposition politicians, stated bluntly that "on the program of the provisional government all groups are in accord" (Welles Cable 289, September 21, 1933, 453). (Events would later contradict that statement. The one thing on which they were in complete agreement was that no program was required.)

Later, at the end of September, after describing his interview with Sergio Carbó, Welles said he had told Carbó,

> . . . my Government would not only not oppose but would in every proper manner actively support such a program provided it were carried out with the consent of a majority of the Cuban people through the medium of a constituted government (Welles Cable 329, October 1, 1933, 462).

Thus, the Constitutional Statutes that led to the elimination of the Platt Amendment, the Court of Punitive Sanctions, the establishment of professional organizations, the eight-hour workday, and the convocation of a Constituent Assembly could not be valid because they did not rely — in Welles's judgment — on the consent of the majority of the Cuban people, nor did they come from a constituted government. Nevertheless, the legislative activities continued uninterrupted.

THE GOVERNMENT LEGISLATES III:
CONFRONTATION WITH THE COMMUNISTS

The next seven days saw seven new revolutionary decrees from the government, but the week also saw the eruption of violence on two fronts.

The revolutionary government knew that the communists were planning serious disturbances during the burial of the ashes of Julio Antonio Mella. It, likewise, knew that a military conflict could explode at any time between the officers billeted in the Hotel Nacional and the new armed forces surrounding the building. These dramatic omens did not daunt the government.

On the twenty-seventh of September, the government dictated four outstanding decrees. The first decree eliminated the so-called martial law that permitted military courts to extend their jurisdiction and judge offenses committed by civilians. The second suspended the Civil Service Commission and, along with it, the restrictions on removing personnel from the service, most of whom had served the Machado dictatorship. The third decree annulled the accord dealing with the emission of gold bonds by the National Treasury in the amount of 20 million pesos to the Chase Bank. This action relieved Cuba of having to pay excessive installments of $500,116.60 required as a deposit and to be deducted later and demanded the refund of $1.4 million paid to the Bank of Boston in lien guarantees. Machado had signed this obligation on August 7, the day of the massacre and his pact with the Communist Party. The fourth decree dissolved the Superior Electoral Tribunal and the provincial and municipal electoral boards. This action complemented the earlier measure dissolving the old political parties. In the process, the National Census Board was dissolved, also, finishing the dismantling of the whole political scaffolding of the dictatorship. *In only one day the revolutionary government promulgated more legislation than the Mediation government had in twenty-three days.*

On the thirtieth, two other complementary decrees were issued. The first granted a forty-five-day extension for the execution of eviction procedures in cases pending resolution — of which there were more than thirty thousand; the second granted a waiver of 50 percent of the principal in overdue city taxes until June 30, when the fiscal 1932-1933 year ended, as well as all surcharges, fines, and other penalties derived from the taxes. Landlords benefited in much greater measure than the tenants, receiving a 50 percent reduction of principal and interests, while the tenants received no more than an extension of terms. And this was called *communism!*

As the historic tape rolls on, two transcendent events within Cuba's tumultuous political history require close examination.

One of these events was the confrontation between the repressive forces and the communists on September 29 and the other the attack on the Hotel Nacional by the new armed forces. These two events bracketed the brief, prolific period of revolutionary legislation like parentheses.

The communists had sustained a more or less nominal struggle against the Machado regime, but in the course of that struggle, they had invested a greater part of their time and energy not in combat against the hired assassins of the dictatorship but in merciless attacks against the remaining opposition forces and, very specifically, the Directorio Estudiantil Universitario. Of course, they had been with us in the prisons, but they had not accompanied us in any of the student *tánganas* in which had fallen many of our companions, nor in subversive activities — that we shall review at the end of this work — in which the Directorio was engaged and in which we depended always on the active and militant collaboration of the ABC. At the end of the process, when Machado had already fallen before the general strike, the Communist Party had made a pact with him to stop the strike and had stepped in to order the return to work, an order that was neither respected nor obeyed by the striking workers. Nearly immediately afterward, they had appeared as a revolutionary force in the funeral of the three leaders whose remains had been discovered in the hillsides at Atarés Castle. Even though the murdered labor leader had not been a Party member, the communists took advantage of the tragic procession on August 19 to create a demonstration of force and organization. On the Fourth of September, they had appeared at Camp Columbia but were rejected and relegated to the fringes of participation in the Pentarchy government first, and in the Grau San Martín administration, later.

Nevertheless, since they considered the anarchic situation favorable to their cause, they ordered the constitution of *soviets* not only in the sugar mills and industrial plants but also within the armed forces, creating a favorable atmosphere for the election of commanders by the soldiers themselves. They also demanded the right to spread their communist literature in the barracks.

In addition to the famous occupation of the Mabay center, they occupied another fourteen mills, even though these "takeovers" were purely symbolic. The *soviets* in those locations had only six or seven members and virtually no support from other workers. The communists, by creating cells of subversion, assisted Welles in his damaging activities. His reports to the Department of State added fuel to the fire, hastening the chaotic environment that would justify his proposals for intervention. To illustrate the intensity of Communist Party provocation, suffice it to say that the most radical of the functionaries of the government, Antonio Guiteras, then Secretary of the Interior, issued a declaration:

> It is essential that the worker become aware of the reality we are facing today. It is impossible for the masses to gain political control; thus, instead of opposing this revolutionary government, they should cooperate with it to obtain the satisfaction of the most immediate demands of the workers and to avoid being an instrument of imperialist companies. The National Confederation of Workers will be responsible before History for the setback that the masses will suffer if we give the Americans a pretext to intervene (translation by Aguilar [1972, 185] of article appearing in *El País*, September 16, 1933).

Thus, the same party that had ordered the return to work to break the general strike against Machado tried just six weeks later to create revolutionary chaos in the city of Havana on the pretext of a public ceremony for the internment of the ashes of the student leader Julio Antonio Mella in the exact center of the city, in the *Plaza de la Fraternidad*, where not even the remains of José Martí rested. This was not planned as another massive funeral procession but as a springboard for agitation that threatened to end in a revolutionary assault on businesses and commercial centers, planned to precipitate the landing of the North American Marines aboard naval units in the bay of Havana.

In view of that situation, Guiteras not only denied permission for the ceremony, he also ordered that the demonstrators be dispersed. That action resulted, naturally, in deaths and injuries — of course, a very tragic thing — but it also prevented, in that historic moment, intervention by the marines. The next day, the Communist Party ascribed the responsibility for the attack to "the fascist bands of the Directorio Estudiantil." Welles apparently did not specifically discuss this event with the Department of State. To be sure, there is not a single cable omitted from the public record between September 27 and October 2, when the assault on the Hotel Nacional occurred.

Up until this point in Cuban history, every activity involving communist participation had been documented in great detail to justify all activity, however brief and symbolic their participation.

This is not the case, however, with the events of September 29. Every detail had been carefully worked out, with the knowledge that the American fleet anchored in the port of Havana would disembark the marines or the repressive forces of the existing Cuban government would break up the unauthorized funeral procession. The true objective of this maneuver is still not fully understood, even after fifty years.

What is known is that the antagonists in the August strike, the National Labor Federation of Cuba — part of the communist apparatus — on one side and the Labor Federation of Havana, that had successfully maintained the strike against Machado, on the other, returned to their former antagonisms. That was when communist leader Rubén Martínez Villena asked himself, "How come the Yankee marines did not land?" (*Bandera Roja* No. 1, October 3, 1933; Soto 1977, Vol. III, 182 and 376, note 102). The question implied the frustration of an entire tactic.

The Drama at Hotel Nacional

At the beginning of the events generated by the Sergeants' Coup of the Fourth of September, Welles had asked Washington for authorization to send the United States Marines to protect the North American Embassy and the Hotel Nacional before reporting that he had moved into the Hotel. Infuriated by the crumbling of his mediationist formula that had established the Céspedes government, he reacted as a proconsul and immediately conceived the establishment of a seditious focus of power attraction. Even though the exact date of his move to the Hotel — coincidentally, because the contract on his residence had expired — cannot be determined, it seems that the ailing General Sanguily, coincidentally, moved to the Hotel at about the same time. On the eighth, he reported the concentration of officers there, after hearing Colonel Ferrer's plan to assault La Cabaña Fortress in connivance with officers who should have been restored to their posts, and on the tenth, he finished by requesting the landing of the marines to disarm the Cuban soldiers. Finally, he abandoned the Hotel on the eleventh — since all the servants had left — and returned to the same house on which — he said — his lease had expired, situated on Ramón Mendoza Avenue in the Miramar district, which belonged to General Rafael Montalvo.

This rapid review of Welles's activities shows more clearly than close analysis Ambassador Welles's open complicity with the high military commanders among the deposed officers. As a result of these actions, dozens of officers who had not participated — in full consciousness — in any type of North American-Cuban conspiracy would fall during the course of events.

Logically, the subversive center could not remain in the Hotel indefinitely. After all peaceful efforts had failed, combined with the disorder provoked by the communists, it became imperative that the government recover the authority that had been impaired by the latent center of insurrection in the very heart of Havana.

Thus, three weeks after the counterrevolutionary center was established, the newly recalled armed forces committed the assault on the Hotel. In the first phase of the operation, many soldiers outside the hotel were shot down by expert marksmen within the hotel. This may have led to the impression that the deposed officers might be able to win a battle which, from all technical points of view, was hopeless.

That is one possible reason for the truce offered at noon on October 2. According to Welles's report to Washington, "conditions have been proposed to the officers which I think should be acceptable to them." (Had the Ambassador made that opinion known to the officers?) "The conditions are that if they will agree to come out unarmed, five at a time, their lives will be guaranteed, and they will be given all possible respect but will be held as prisoners until some definite decision is reached" (Telephone Memo, October 2, 1933, 464).

At one in the afternoon, *shortly before the truce but with the battle already begun*, Welles had cabled to Cordell Hull,

> . . . I received a letter from General Sanguily, the command-ing officer of the officers, in which he stated that the attack had been made upon the hotel by the soldiers and that the officers were determined to resist it and to bring about the reinstallation of the "legitimate Government of Cuba pre-sided over by Dr. Carlos Manuel Céspedes" (Welles Cable 330, October 2, 1933, 463).

This document implied that some previous accord must have existed, since there is no other way to explain why a Cuban general would address a North American ambassador in the heat of battle. Welles ended that cable saying:

> So far there has been no counterrevolution attempted in this city which, except for the district around the National Hotel, appears to be fairly quiet. Consular reports from all points in the interior show no signs of serious disturbances (Welles Cable 330, October 2, 1933, 464).

Consequently, it becomes quite clear that there existed some agreement to land marines and back the reinstallation of the Céspedes government if, while the officers fought off the attacks on the hotel-turned-fort, a general counterrevolution developed in Havana with apparent support demonstrated as serious disturbances throughout the Republic.

Welles had begun this cable saying that, "According to reliable information, two trucks heavily loaded with arms and ammunition broke through the sentries stationed around the National Hotel just before dawn this morning" (Welles Cable 330, October 2, 1933, 463). That would seem to indicate that the officers were responsible for provoking the armed incident.

Apparently, considering the tone of the cable, Welles and Batista had developed a firm understanding. In every reference he tried to minimize the army's responsibility, especially in the unspeakable attack on the officers after their surrender as they lined up on the grounds of the Hotel Nacional.

At 3:30 in the afternoon, the time limit Batista had set for the acceptance of the conditions of the truce the officers refused, the fire recommenced immediately.

Only an hour and fifteen minutes later — that is, at 4:45 in the afternoon — the officers surrendered themselves and "the soldiers immediately entered the hotel and lined the officers up by twos outside of the hotel grounds" (Welles Cable 331, October 2, 1933, 466). At that time the officers were attacked by the soldiers, according to what Horacio Ferrer relates in this fashion: "There remained only some seventy officers standing in line in the esplanade, awaiting vehicles to transport them, when all of a sudden they were fired upon by a group of armed soldiers and peasants that were near the tennis courts, and the firing immediately became general" (Ferrer 1950, 402).

This abominable act, committed against the surrendered former officers, is related by Welles in a form very benevolent to Batista, relieving him of responsibility, as we see here: "A very large crowd had collected and radical agitators in the crowd endeavored to incite the mob to seize the officers and kill them." He further added, "In order to prevent the mob from getting closer, the soldiers first fired in the air and later, on the mob and dispersed it" (Welles Cable 331, October 2, 1933, 466).

At nine that night, Welles reported again that Batista had posted a guard around the hotel to prevent "looting by soldiers and especially distribution of contents of wine cellars. He [Batista] assures me that the lives of all the officers now in custody will be personally guaranteed by himself and that I may feel confident that order will be maintained in the city tonight" (Welles Cable 333, October 2, 1933, 467).

The next day, the third, he reported the rest of the battle: fourteen officers killed and seventeen injured; of the soldiers and civilians associated with them, eighty dead and approximately two hundred injured; but he added, "It seems to be equally clearly established that none of the officers was killed up to the time of their surrender" (Welles Cable 335, October 3, 1933, 467). He added furthermore that "there have been continued rumors last night and this morning that the Student Council [DEU] and a portion of the soldiers wish summarily to execute the officers who are now in prison" (Welles Cable 335, October 3, 1933, 468). Since *Batista was the one who guaranteed the lives of the imprisoned former officers, and no participation whatsoever in this event had been attributed to the DEU until this cable,* it had to be Batista who tried summarily to judge and execute the officers, according to those rumors that Welles said he had received. Furthermore, the DEU lacked the legal authority or the military or police power to carry out the intentions Welles maliciously attributed to the organization. The ambassador's treacherous concealment of Batista's culpability and his assignment of all responsibilities to the Directorio are additional proof that the bond born in the September 21 interview not only had led to the September 29 attack by the communists and the October 2 attack on the Hotel Nacional, but it also persisted across time and space. *Now it turned out that the officers and the Directorio, separated historically by the event of the Fourth of September, were expressly excluded from any type of Cuban solution: Welles eliminated the officers, and Batista eliminated the Directorio.*

And both Welles and Batista would continue to conspire to *confirm the new officer corps, on one hand, and overthrow Grau* and reinstall in power the same servants of the North American interests that were overthrown in the Sergeants Coup, on the other.

Now it is time to look more closely into the process of linking the "national" interests of Cuba and the United States and the continuation of the "understanding." Batista went to visit Welles on October 4, and the cable containing the report began by stating that the meeting was a private conversation between the two and lasted about an hour and a half. Batista had gone to "inform" him about the battle. He discussed the conditions he had offered the officers at noon and their lack of response and stated that after the renewal of the battle at three in the afternoon, he had been prepared to agree to an extension of the truce until the following morning at the least. Finally, Batista had assured Welles that "the deaths of officers and soldiers after the surrender of the former was due to firing by the officers and that in the excitement which ensued it was utterly impossible for him to control the soldiers" (Welles Cable 340, October 4, 1933, 469).

Thus, Welles endorsed — by transmitting Batista's report — the entirely false "fact" that soldiers also died after the surrender, when the truth is that only the group of surrendered officers was executed. Later in the report, Welles tried to demonstrate Batista's magnanimity, describing his concern for the physical security of the officers during their transportation to the Isle of Pines. He also endorsed Batista's proposal that, since he could not prevent their trials, at least he might postpone them for as long as possible, so that passions might cool and he could insure that the courts would be composed of lawyers and not of soldiers or sergeants.

But Welles had to take advantage of this interview for much greater pursuits. He immediately declared the Hotel Nacional incident ended and asked Batista if he was going to continue permitting what Welles considered intolerable conditions of the last five weeks in the sugar plantations. Batista agreed to

> seize all foreign agitators and arrange for their immediate expulsion from Cuba and at the same time imprison Cuban Communistic [sic] leaders and would also guarantee the rights of the legitimate managers of such properties (Welles Cable 340, October 4, 1933, 470).

With Batista's agreement on this point, Welles annulled his former agreement with General Julio Sanguily and the officers who accompanied him and coldly turned this page of history.

Nevertheless, only a few weeks later, on Tuesday, November 7, the periodical *Alma Mater* published on the entire front page under the title of "Sumner Welles, guilty," five revealing letters blaming the ambassador for everything that had occurred at the Hotel Nacional from the time the former Chief of Staff of the Army Colonel Sanguily entered the Hotel.

The most accusatory letter came from Colonel González del Real, former chief of the Naval High Command:

> I, along with a great number of the officers gathered there, accuse the Ambassador of the United States, the Honorable Sumner Welles, for the events that came to pass in the Hotel Nacional of this city.

> The Ambassador, guest of the Hotel Nacional, forced the Chief of Staff of the Army, Colonel Julio Sanguily and all the other officers to move there, led by the offers of protection and help that we received. We concentrated in said Hotel

only to see our hopes, born from the promises that he made us, defrauded. Havana, October 10, 1933.

Julio Ortiz Casanova, legal advisor to the navy, wrote,

> . . . we certify by this statement that we were encouraged in said attitude by the Ambassador of the United States, the Honorable Sumner Welles, through mediation of other officers that were in contact with him. Later the Ambassador moved from the Hotel Nacional and left us abandoned to our luck.

Lieutenant Virgilio Beltrán said,

> . . . I am sad to say that in the atmosphere that existed within the Hotel Nacional hopes were maintained that in our case the Ambassador of the United States would be able to act as mediator in the problem of the officers of the Army and Navy.

Colonel Heriberto Hernández criticized the ambassador's equivocal attitude about the coup d'état on the fourth of September, saying,

> He encouraged the majority of the officers that met in the Hotel Nacional to remain.

Efraín Callava, first lieutenant in the coastal artillery of the National Guard, suggested equally that

> the equivocal attitude of the Minister of the United States of North America in Cuba contributed to encourage a large number of officers to persist in their protest for having been dispossessed of command by the ranks and soldiers of the Army.[2]

Thus, it ended, with one page that Welles had not foreseen and that remains as the historic record, describing the participation of a North American Ambassador who was no longer officially an ambassador, a man who earned the title of foreign agitator, while he requested that the commander of the armed forces jail those foreign agitators who (according to Welles's words) were disturbing the peace in the sugar mills.

THE WELLES-BATISTA PACT IS STRENGTHENED

The October 4 conference between Welles and Batista occurred under very specific and unique circumstances. The old officer

corps was imprisoned as a result of the military defeat; the Grau San
Martín government was still not recognized by the United States; the
traditional political parties had aligned with Welles; the Directorio
Estudiantil Universitario continued to push the revolutionary legislation announced in its program — precisely what most perturbed the
North American financial interests in Cuba; and Welles, who was
supposedly the most defeated in the battle of the Hotel Nacional, was
conversing alone for an hour and a half with the winner of that same
battle, Fulgencio Batista.

When the two finished discussing the incident at the Hotel and
Batista had agreed to imprison and expel foreign agitators from Cuba
and guarantee the rights of the legitimate managers of the sugar-
producing properties, he asked Welles for advice. According to his
report, Welles answered him that "in my judgment he himself was the
only individual in Cuba today who represented authority" (Welles
Cable 340, October 4, 1933, 470). That statement ordained Batista as
dictator of Cuba backed by the United States. Welles further stated that
he went on to tell Batista that

> . . . this was due in part to the fact that he appeared to have
> the loyal support of a large part of his troops and in part to
> the very determined and effective action taken by the
> troops in Havana as well as in a lesser degree in other cities
> against the Communistic [sic] and extreme radical elements.
> This I told him had rallied to his own support the very great
> majority of the commercial and financial interests in Cuba
> who are looking for protection and who could only find
> such protection in himself; . . . that the leaders of the
> important political factions with the exception of Menocal,
> namely, Mendieta, Gómez, Martínez Saenz, and Silverio [in
> other words, the "*Union Nacionalista*"] were in accord that
> his control of the Army as Chief of Staff should be continued
> as the only possible solution and were willing to support
> him in that capacity [emphasis added]. In some manner it
> must be evident to him, I said, that the *present government
> of Cuba did not fill any of the conditions which the United
> States Government had announced as making possible
> recognition by us* [emphasis added] and that I felt sure that
> he would realize that the events of the National Hotel had
> diminished very materially that very small amount of

popular support which the Grau San Martín regime may previously have possessed. I told him further that from my conversations with the representatives of the Latin American Republic[s] here, the affair involving the officers had very definitely removed the probability of recognition on the part of those Republics.

Obviously, Welles spoke to Batista in name of the commercial and financial interests in Cuba; in the name of the political sectors; in the name of the United States and of Latin America. . . . What a phenomenon!

From these lines elemental conclusions can be extracted. First, Batista was the power, the only existing authority in Cuba, and was recognized as such by the Ambassador of the United States, which he expressed in those very terms. Second, the communist provocation against the Directorio government had raised Batista to a unique and predominant position within the national situation. Third, the Ambassador of the United States, speaking now in the name of the four political groups allied with him, suggested that Batista's continued leadership of the army was the only solution possible, since various individuals — specifically, the ambassador and the professional political leaders — were disposed to back such a condition. Fourth, Welles himself, acting as the extraordinary envoy of President Roosevelt, stated that the Government of Cuba was unable to fulfill the conditions for recognition his government had announced, since the events of the Hotel Nacional had diminished that small amount of popular support it had previously held. Fifth, the Latin American republics, as a consequence of the Hotel Nacional incident, had conclusively determined not to extend recognition to the Grau regime.

But Welles's encouragement of Batista to depose Grau did not end there: further along, he played it up even more when he said,

> . . . without recognition by foreign governments the financial situation of the government was so paralyzed that even if it repudiated every obligation it would not for long be able to pay the salaries or function as a government; and *that should the present government go down in disaster, that disaster would necessarily inextricably involve not only himself but the safety of the Republic, which he had publicly pledged himself to maintain* [emphasis added]. I concluded by saying that it appeared to me after my conversations with

Carbó and with himself that all that stood between an equitable agreement on the part of all important factors in the country (almost all of which supported an identic [sic] program for the provisional government) [what program?] was the unpatriotic and futile obstinacy of a small group of young men who should be studying in the university instead of playing politics and of a few individuals who had joined with them from selfish motives. *I urged him in the interest of the Republic of Cuba itself to act as intermediary between the groups now at variance and through the force of authority which he represented in his person to insist* [emphasis added] that an immediate fair and reasonable solution be found *so that Cuba might once more possess a government which had the confidence of all* [emphasis added] and which would have a fair opportunity to tide over the critical situation which now lay ahead (Welles Cable 340, October 4, 1933, 471).

From these additional comments, additional conclusions may also be extracted. First, what Welles called "the affair involving the officers" served two distinct positions: one, it would materially diminish the popular support that Grau previously had; two, it would remove the possibility that the Latin American republics would recognize Grau. Thus, Batista was distanced from all the negative aspects of the Hotel Nacional — in Welles's judgment — because Welles implied that the only one responsible for the events was Grau. Welles identified Batista with the self-same Republic to the extreme of telling him that should the present government go down in disaster, "that disaster would necessarily inextricably involve not only himself [Batista] but the safety of the Republic, which he had publicly pledged himself to maintain." Second, those groups of youths "who should be studying in the university" were the only hindrance for the solution of all the problems. Third, he urged Batista — "the only individual in Cuba today who represented authority," — to fulfill the promise to guard the security of the republic by acting as an intermediary between the groups to find an equitable solution, but one that would necessarily involve the establishment of another government, since the current one did not "fill any of the conditions which the United States Government had announced as making possible recognition by us."

Of course, "Batista most emphatically agreed," and upon analyzing the different political factors, Welles went on to say, "He . . . expressed the belief that should any *rapid* [emphasis added] change in the government be made it might be difficult to control his troops without further bloodshed which he desired at all hazards to avoid." Welles repeated that "he [Batista] necessarily was the sole judge of the attitude of his own troops." With this statement, Ambassador Welles gave Batista free reign and all the time he needed to replace the existing government by whatever means he felt were necessary and appropriate.

In summary, Batista was ordained by President Roosevelt's special envoy as the sole arbitrator of Cuban national policy. The former military officers were already in prison, and the Directorio Estudiantil was to be removed from the political arena. The professional politicians had already submitted to Welles's will, and *Welles completely authorized Batista to make decisions against the government during whatever period of time he might consider necessary.*

Welles Cable 340 containing the report of that fateful interview was received in Washington in the early morning on October 5. Surprisingly, Secretary Hull waited until seven that evening to reply:

> I have just discussed your telegram 340, October 4, with the *President,* who desires me to say that it appears to him that *public opinion as reflected in the press here seems to regard the capture of the officers as indicating a consolidation of the position of the present government* [emphasis added]. He also believes that Cuba now is going through a period of storm and stress and that given all the circumstances, there must be some latitude, on the part of ourselves and of other states, in the application of the customary principles of international practice (e.g., as regards recognition) in view of these conditions (Hull Cable 113, October 5, 1933, 472).

That cable directly rejected Welles's assessment of the situation, but *as it did not contain any type of counterorder,* Welles seized the opportunity, only four hours after receiving the cable, to send another extensive cable in which he tried to demonstrate that Grau San Martín and the Directorio *were grafted onto a mutiny within the military,* and that Grau, along with the student leaders, had been searched out to provide civilian support for the Sergeants' Movement (Welles Cable 341, October 5, 1933, 473-4), and Welles further elaborated that "as

Batista becomes more influential, the power of the students and Grau San Martín diminishes" (Welles Cable 341, October 5, 1933, 473).

In reference to Hull's suggestion that official recognition might be extended, Welles bluntly replied that the United States would "incur the antipathy of those classes in Cuba which in reality constitute the dominant portion of public opinion and which, once these abnormal conditions have passed, will govern the country" (Welles Cable 341, October 5, 1933, 474). He ended the cable with the historic monstrosity of declaring that "*if we recognize a government now which does not possess at least a considerable measure of popular support, we postpone a return by Cuba to normal and stable conditions, and we incur once more the same measure of animosity on the part of the mass of the Cuban people as that which we possessed during the last 4 years of the Machado Government*" [emphasis added]. In essence, Welles was saying that Machado and Grau were equals.

On the seventh, Welles and Batista conferred again, and Batista "was deeply impressed by the fact that delegates of all of the important business and financial groups in Cuba had visited him this afternoon before I saw him to insist upon the creation of a government in which the public could have confidence (Welles Cable 347, October 7, 1933, 477). On the tenth, Batista could already rely on the total support of the opposition, *now including Menocal*, if he should throw his support to Mendieta, whom they were urging to accept the provisional presidency (Welles Cable 350, October 10, 1933, 479-80). The previous day, the ninth, Welles had said that "there is a growing feeling of optimism among those who are close to the city authorities and the government that a representative government will replace the present regime *in the very near future*" [emphasis added] (Welles Cable 348, October 9, 1933, 478). Welles would fall short as a seer.

The struggle between Batista and the Directorio Estudiantil was a silent one, since the DEU had only a limited awareness of the Welles-Batista conspiracy. The Army Chief of Staff, on October 10, declared, "there was no divergence between the Army and the present regime" (Welles Cable 351, October 10, 1933, 480). Welles pointed out, "the obstacles to the realization of this end are the reluctance of the students to accept the blame for the situation into which the country has been plunged and the hesitancy on the part of Batista to press the formation of a new government until he is sure that his troops will support such a move" (Welles Cable 351, October 10, 1933, 481).

Is it possible to conceive a more intolerable situation? The personal envoy of the president of the powerful neighbor country was practically directing a conspiracy against the constituted Cuban government. He was acting, apparently, on his own initiative, and at variance with the position of his commander in chief, with the collaboration of outdated national politicians who "have absolutely no popular following," and who certainly had already ceased objecting to the Sergeants' Coup in hopes that the new leader would return them to "administrative" power, even though the true power would remain in Batista's hands.

In the second fortnight of October, the contradictions between Batista and the Directorio grew more and more apparent, forcing Welles to report, "Batista's position seems to have weakened materially during the past few days" (Welles Cable 372, October 18, 1933, 492). In their clandestine meetings, Batista had continued to support a compromise that would retain Grau as president, over the objections of the financial and commercial interests against any compromise that included Grau. Welles said, "The desire for a mapped-out accord is due to the open disagreement now existing between Batista and the students" (Welles Cable 378, October 18, 1933, 493). He went on to say, "They are already conspiring to overthrow Batista or to assassinate him." This contemptible diplomat, having shown himself to be a pernicious foreigner (a term previously applied by the repressive corps to communists), suggested, based on information from God knows who, that the most pure and clean of the existing organizations during the 1930-1933 epoch planned to assassinate Batista. What the Directorio really planned, while continuing to discover invisible aspects of the Welles-Batista arrangement, was to expel Batista from his post and execute him before a firing squad, not to assassinate him, as the supposed ambassador put it. The Directorio had discovered Batista's successive waves of consultation in the conduct of his command. Likewise, the Directorio had discovered that Batista planned, with the foreign ambassador's support, to replace the Cuban president and was, therefore, trying to articulate the military forces necessary to impede that action. On or around October 25, the Directorio discovered the secret interviews with Mendieta and Welles, arranged through the collaboration of Colonel Blas Hernández, whom Welles described as "the only revolutionist whom Machado was unable to capture" (Welles Cable 395, October 24, 1933, 499). The Directorio also found out that on October 27, Batista had let it be known that he would accept that "Mendieta as Provisional President with a Cabinet of outstanding men and a legislative assembly composed of representatives of all political factions, labor, commerce, finance, and the university is the only solution that promises success" (Welles Cable 406, October 27, 1933, 501). Mendieta refused to accept on the grounds that he "would merely be Batista's prisoner" (Welles Cable 410, October 29, 1933, 502).

Then on the twenty-ninth of October, Welles told the Department of State that Batista had sent word "that a change in government is imperative," adding that "he [Batista] will only ask that the Secretaries of the Interior and of War be appointees in whom he has confidence" (Welles Cable 413, October 29, 1933, 503). Welles went on to say that at the same time, Batista had stated that "he will tonight urge the Student Directorate of their own initiative to suggest the change but that if they refuse, he will force them to abandon politics and return to the university." Then, in that very unstable situation, Welles tried again to predict the future, telling the Department of State in that same cable, "the general public expects the fall of the government tonight or tomorrow, although the change will not in my opinion take place before the middle of the week."

In such circumstances, the Directorio Estudiantil, after repeated interviews with President Grau, decided to call a meeting, together with the members of the *Agrupación Revolucionaria de Cuba* — the former pentarchs, President Grau, Colonel Batista, and all the members of the Directorio, of course, who had been designated as official members of the ARC regardless of whether they had actually signed the declaration or been present in Columbia on the Fourth of September.

At this point, I pass the narrative back to Juan Antonio Rubio Padilla.

The Meeting at the Carbó Home
and the Dissolution of the DEU

It is very difficult to apply the adjective "historic" to what I am going to relate, just as it happened, but I believe that what the Directorio planned and what Grau refused to go along with, could have changed the history of Cuba.

How easy it would be to write history if events would follow predetermined rules! The difficulty of history — the reason it is difficult to be a good historian — is that history, like life itself, follows neither diagrams nor prearranged programs, nor does it go by the numbers. It is a simultaneous accumulation of events that influence one another in such a manner that, when from that snarl one wishes to extract the thread, the essence, it is very difficult to distinguish the important from the trivial, and it is difficult to appreciate the intensity or the force that determined such or which fact.

The 1930 Directorio Estudiantil Universitario developed not for emotional reasons but because of personal decorum, conscience, patriotic concern, but never, not at the beginning nor at the end, was it an ordered or formal thing. From the time it began until it ended, it passed through so many different stages, the factors were so many that intervened, that it was in the final analysis an incredibly complex process. It is, therefore, impossible to determine, from a philosophic or academic viewpoint, what truly drove the program.

Nevertheless, since we are not going to speak of philosophy nor of a cheap history of facts, I am going to relate as briefly as possible the essence of the incident. Even in my advanced years, I am not a materialist of history. If it were necessary to classify me academically, I would at best be a providentialist. Overall, I believe that individual factors determine the essential twists of history, making it impossible to find a theoretic or academic explanation that would cast a light and interpret social forces, periods of history, generations, none of that. One man, one fine day, makes a determination that twists the path of history. It is a matter of strictly individual determination, perhaps a passion for a woman, drunkenness, bad digestion; but, nonetheless, the footprint remains indelibly engraved on history, independent of all academic discernment concerning why the events did not occur in a different way, and it comes about that they originated in small things. In Cuban history a word is usually used that I don't much care for, *suerte*, which can mean luck or fate, and in everyday life it is normal to hear expressions like these: "What luck you had! You passed the test. What luck!" or perhaps, "You didn't pass! You were jinxed!" No; it should be, "I studied or did not study and that is what determined my success or failure on the test," is that not so? But in spite of this standard being used arbitrarily or inconsistently, it is indisputable that luck is the one factor that gets the most emphasis. Well then, in Cuban history there is a reality that I am embarrassed to acknowledge, which is the disgrace that would be determined by two such incredibly perverse and negative men as

Fulgencio Batista and Ramón Grau San Martín. Whether that was a matter of luck or a matter of our incapacity to choose our men will never be ultimately decided. But in the episodes I am going to relate, it shall be seen how these two men conducted themselves.

The first news that the Directorio heard about an imminent coup d'état directed by the North American ambassador arrived on the morning of the third of November 1933. The last meeting of the conspirators had been held on the second, and in it, final agreements concerning the technique and process of the coup d'état had been arranged. Scarcely having discovered what was going to occur, Carlos Prío called an urgent meeting in the Presidential Palace. Prío told us the news and informed us that apparently all was ready and the execution of the coup d'état would come within a matter of hours. Then the Directorio displayed one of its most important qualities, one which was probably owed to youth or perhaps to a series of individual character-istics of some of its members, that weighed decisively in the decisions of the group. (Rubio Padilla refers to the homogeneity of the group, which after three years of collective functionalism, facilitated the rapidity of reaching agreements.) I must point out that the Directorio relied on its ability to act rapidly and its audacity, both of which permitted them to confront the most difficult situations. It was natural, therefore, that right there we should decide that we could not stand idly by nor could we waste time investigating or philosophizing over the matter. So we reached an agreement: immediately to call a meeting of the Columbia Junta or the *Agrupación Revolucionaria de Cuba*—that was the organization that officially directed the Fourth of September movement in the hours following the military mutiny. This Junta proved that the Directorio was not what was politically empowered by the military movement, but that it was a mixed group formed by the distinguished revolutionaries and by all the Directorio, since by being a member of the Directorio one was automatically a member of the Columbia Junta.

Completing the Junta were outstanding figures who had always worked closely with us, as well as the professors of the University who were present the night of the Fourth of September, and some personalities like Sergio Carbó and Oscar de la Torre, who, although not with us, launched the manifesto to the country on the fifth of September with the first public notification of civilian support for the military coup of the Fourth.

Then, while we were awaiting the coup d'état against the Grau government, directed by Welles, it occurred to us immediately to call an urgent meeting of the Columbia Junta to be held outside of the Palace, to which Batista necessarily would have to go, since he was likewise a member of the Junta.

The fundamental objective of that meeting was to have Grau accuse Batista and present his renunciation of the Presidency of the Republic, thus provoking a crisis; that is to say, we were trying to get ahead of the events. It was like a form of aborting the inevitable.

We called Grau to the Directorio meeting — that is why it was held in the Palace — and we told him the news we had and the plan we had designed to confront the conspiracy. Grau indicated his understanding, recognized the gravity of the situation, and accepted our proposal to do something to precipitate the events. He agreed to go that night to the Junta meeting at the Carbó residence in Vedado, agreeing as well to present his resignation and see what would happen then. I know for certain, because I saw it, that the atmosphere in the Palace that day, including among the presidential family, was one of evacuation. I saw the presidential family in the process of removing all their things from the Palace even to the point of bundling clothing in sheets like one would to send them to the cleaners. And from the onset, Grau completely agreed that what had to be done was precipitate the events.

Guiteras, the Secretary of the Interior and War, who was supposed to have very close ties to the military and naval district commanders, did not participate. Guiteras was alone, alone, alone, seated on a bench in one of the interior hallways of the palace, hoping that the Directorio meeting would end so he could find out what grave thing was happening. Upon arriving at the presidential mansion, he had discovered that he could not see Grau because Grau was in a meeting with the Directorio, and so he "got wind" that something grave was happening. The way Guiteras, who knew nothing, found out about what was happening demonstrates how peculiar that situation was. Not even the Secretary of the Interior knew a word of what Carlos Prío had already discovered and had told the Directorio, and this group had already reached a decision. It was then, at that moment, that Guiteras was informed of the extreme gravity of the situation and about a probable coup d'état directed by Welles and Batista to remove the Grau government from power. Already the Directorio meeting had ended and we were leaving. Then he, Guiteras, along with a small group that had started talking with him, decided that in addition to the meeting scheduled for that evening, he had to do something else. Guiteras considered what Batista was doing extremely bold, since he had been talking in the name of the army in the meetings with them [the mediation professionals and Welles], when Batista himself knew he did not have control of the army. It must not be forgotten that when the Fourth of September coup developed, Mr. Batista was a nobody. The most important people in the Fourth of September movement were the sergeants who represented districts with real numerical forces of soldiers. In spite of that quantitative point of view, and here we return to break the academic molds, from the first moment the military leader of the Sergeants' Movement had been Batista. But Batista did not represent any military district in which he had command of forces. Batista was the most resolute, the most — I would say . . . it is very difficult to categorize him without appealing to words of an obscene and vulgar order — hated of all of them, he who with extraordinary audacity and with an eloquence that impressed many people, made himself leader of the movement, but throughout that night, beginning at sunset on the fourth of September and ending at dawn on the fifth, he overestimated his pull within the troops.

Guiteras knew that, and said that what had to be done was to go quickly to visit the district commanders, inform them of what was happening, and sound out if anyone knew if Batista was counting on the second line in the army at that moment, that being the district commanders. I did not participate in the dialogue with Guiteras because it so happened that, upon leaving the meeting of the group, Doctor Grau San Martín had invited me to lunch at the Palace and I had accepted, but the truth is that there formed a small group of Directorio members, no more than six or seven, who accepted Guiteras' suggestion to go quickly and visit the district commanders.

And, sure enough, not one of the district commanders failed us. They all agreed with the revolution, that their program was the Directorio's, that they supported Doctor Grau San Martín, and that Batista was not needed. Furthermore, they concurred that, his attitude being so offensive and his actions reflecting nothing less than military treason in connivance with a hostile foreign power to bring down his own government, there was not a Military Code of Conduct in the world that did not demand that he be shot.

And now we come here to the part that I would call dramatic because it showed the capacity, or if you will, the aggressiveness of a small number of men, of seven or eight members of the DEU who, with Guiteras, in a short number of hours, rallied the full support of the district commanders. (The district commanders feared that the conspiracy with the United States would endanger their promotions with the return of the ousted officer corps.) And I say in a short number of hours because that meeting of the Directorio must have ended between one and two in the afternoon and we all had to be at the Palace at nightfall since the meeting that night would not be in the Palace. We planned to leave from the Palace in separate cars so that when we arrived at Carbó's residence on Seventeenth Street between N and O, we would present the physical and visual sensation that we were in agreement with Grau and that we fully supported him. And when we arrived at the Palace a little after eight, approximately between eight thirty and nine that evening — we found ourselves with this accumulation of fantastic, incredible facts, having received the district commanders' testimonies supporting the revolutionary movement represented in that moment by Grau San Martín, accusing Batista of treason and stating that he should be shot as a traitor.

The group moved to the Palace, met with Grau, and decided to carry out the following decisions. First, we had to prepare an order of arrest against Batista as a traitor; a Summary Court-Martial had to be called and the actions of that Court recorded along with its sentence ordering the immediate execution of Batista; the presidential decree ordering the execution would have to be prepared; and finally, we must immediately send delegates to the newspapers to hold publication of the morning edition for the report of Batista's execution. All that was completed in the brief hours between two in the afternoon and eight thirty in the evening. Not only was the paperwork completed with all the accuracy and elegance that these things require of the Chief of the Executive Staff, such as the work of magnificent typists, they were all signed. Juridically speaking, at eight thirty on the evening of the third of November, Mr. Batista was in the next world. That is to say that the members of the Directorio, who with Guiteras had visited the district commanders and who arrived at the Palace to go from there to Carbó's home to arrest Batista and conduct him to La Cabaña Fortress for execution, did not have to worry about the paperwork because that bureaucratic labor was already complete. Thus, the only thing left to accomplish was the physical act of carrying Mr. Batista to and placing him in front of the execution walls that already existed in the Laurels Moat, where so many people that did not merit it would be shot one year later.

When we arrived at the Carbó home, the military district commanders, the most punctual of everyone, were already there. We arrived with Grau. Batista had not arrived. Carbó's home had a central hall with two salons, one on the right and the other on the left, separated only by columns. In other words, from the street door the entire ground floor could be seen perfectly. In the salon on the right, in the background, Grau began to converse with Guiteras. We, the members of the DEU, because of a series of psychological or tactical problems, felt deep down that we would diminish or compromise Grau's authority if, in a meeting of this nature, one of us entered his conversation or even joined the group, fearing it would appear as if we were trying to monitor what Grau did or decided, or perhaps by situating ourselves behind him, we might prevent him from speaking freely, or some such interpretation. So all the members of the Directorio refrained from joining the President of the Republic's conversation with the Secretary of the Interior. We did not believe it necessary, on the other hand, since we had complete confidence in both Grau and Guiteras. Also, since seven or eight military men of the different branches of service soon joined the conversation, we understood that Grau and Guiteras were explaining to the commanders and officers that everything was now ready and there was nothing left except to wait for Batista to arrive.

At last, Batista did arrive, accompanied by his personal body-guard, a short, husky negro, incidentally named Batista as well, who always appeared with a machine gun at his shoulder as if he were about to fire. That is to say, he tried to strike fear in people, as though he was not an individual who had to be told to do his job, but that he was always ready to fire. Batista arrived with the air of a bully and entered, but we did not allow the machine gunner to enter. We left him at the door. I say we allowed Batista to enter because those who were at the door that night controlling who did and did not enter were Willy Barrientos and I. Of course, we opened the door to Batista, which was, at that moment, like opening the door of the rat trap. We allowed Batista to enter and as he did so we closed the door. Later, after watching gangster movies, I suppose that our attitude that night did give a certain suspicious appearance because what we did was we both stood there with folded arms, unarmed, blocking the entrance of a two-panel door, which we firmly shut. You can see the importance of that gesture. Well then, Batista entered, and on seeing the group around the President, he moved toward them, and when he found himself about a meter away, Grau, with the authority of Peter the Great, told him, "Listen, Batista, no, don't come over here, go away, because I am in conference with the military commanders and you cannot participate. We'll let you know when we want to speak to you." Then Mr. Batista, like a rat, moved away, looked around himself, and felt defeated.

Years later, Doctor Guillermo Alonso Pujol related to me Batista's version of that night. According to what Batista told Alonso Pujol, after hearing with what authority and with what disdain President Grau treated him and ordered him to leave the group, refusing him, the Chief of the Army, the right to participate in a military meeting involving his subordinates, the impact of the President's attitude was so great that he felt shot down, and his first impulse was to flee, but to flee physically like a *ratero* [petty thief] caught stealing oranges, and he headed toward the door to the street. When he came up against Willy Barrientos and me, whose names he knew well, he said that he felt dead, that is to say that our blocking the door was for him the death sentence. Then he began to wander through the salon on the left, seeming very nervous and awaiting the end of the meeting among Grau, Guiteras, and the military commanders.

In the exchange with the military commanders, it was agreed that at the end of the meeting (which would be held on the upper floor) they would seize Batista, conduct him to La Cabaña, and execute him. The meeting upstairs was very dramatic because the entire Columbia Junta was there, including personages like Portela and Irisarri who were not in the government since the dissolution of the Pentarchy, but who were summoned and attended because they were still members of the Junta. Actually, there were quite a few people, as well as nearly the entire membership of the Directorio. I had the good fortune of being able to situate myself in a privileged position to witness the drama to be staged in Carbó's library, which was full. Many did not have seats and stood in the back, but Grau, who was going to preside and in order to channel the debate, seated himself at one end. Batista was seated in front of him. I took the first seat to the right, so I was quite close to the principal protagonists of the drama.

Grau opened the meeting, stating that he had convened the Revolutionary Junta of Columbia to present his resignation as President of the Republic because, despite having known for days that the commander of the Army was traitorously conspiring with the North American Ambassador to overthrow the revolutionary movement, he had done nothing and that, therefore, he recognized that he did not know how to fulfill his duties as President of the Republic. He pointed out that the situation was of extreme gravity because there was no justification for the Chief of Staff of the Army to conspire. Then Batista began to try to interrupt him, but Grau got around him by saying in an authoritative voice, "You shut your mouth until I finish. Then I will let you speak when I think it's time." Batista collapsed again in his seat like a scared rat.

When Grau finished voicing various arguments, speeches were made opposing the acceptance of the President's resignation. Batista was not allowed to speak. And there was a nearly unanimous agreement to support the President of the Republic in conducting this military crisis as he considered most appropriate. In general terms, so as not to enter into details of some discrepancies that were examined, I must say that Grau addressed Batista, asking him, "You wished to say something?" Batista stood himself up and let loose one of the most abject, most miserable, and most cowardly speeches that I have ever heard in my life. He exceeded himself in his praising Grau. I recall that he said to Grau, "You, Doctor, whom I have always admired so much, for your civic courage, for the risks that you have run, for giving ideological, philosophical, and patriotic orientation to all the student movements, because everything has come from you, ... " He was trying to say that the Directorio was nothing, that only Grau was important. Well! Martí alive again would not have been the person that Grau was according to Batista's praises. And he continued his flatteries saying, "But you, whom I have always admired so much, you were a man born to silken diapers and received a first-class education," among other things. There were no such diapers of silk. Well! "But I am a poor *guajirito* [little peasant] from Banes, from the most humble extraction possible in Cuba, that when I was born I was placed in a manger." Many years have passed since I heard that speech and still I don't quite understand the mental confusion that Batista had that night with Christmas cards and his personal origin, because he mentioned the word *manger*. He is the only person in Cuba that ever claimed to be of such humble origin that when he was born they put him in a manger, a reference that is exclusive and proper only to the Nativity. He presented himself as an unhappy peasant and declared that he, trying to resolve the problems of the revolution, did not see anything wrong with going wherever he was called in search of solutions. One of the meetings he had attended, with best intentions, he said, had been in the residence of don Antonio González de Mendoza and it so happened that none other than the presidents of the opposition parties and the Ambassador of the United States were also there. He added that in spite of his presence there, he had absolutely not compromised himself and only intended to speak with the President and tell him what had been said, for his information, and insisted that he had not entered any type of agreement, and this I know and let me tell you. And he asked pardon in the most groveling form possible. But after his discourse, since I was at Grau's side, I appreciated better how he was rising out of the armchair, upholstered so it seemed very low, and as he left his seat he was advancing, until finally the moment arrived when Batista's right knee hit the floor, that is to say, that Batista's physical position trying to deceive Grau and show his nonexistent contrition, his physical position, I repeat, was on his knees, at least on one knee, according to what I saw. A truly emetic thing, and, as everyone knows, emetic means provoking vomiting.

Grau San Martín said something to him very contemptuously after that and then adjourned the meeting. I do remember that I was one of the first to get downstairs because I was very interested in witnessing up close the physical capture of Batista. The stairway was very wide and the group was quite large. When I was able to get downstairs, I found to my surprise that the military personnel were not there, or rather, that they had left. There were, therefore, no captors and, thus, I had to witness how Mr. Batista went completely across that hall, from east to west. Willy and I were no longer situated at the door to the street, our role there having now passed. To Batista's satisfaction, he and his bodyguard left unchallenged.

Then, right there, in the very residence of Carbó, the members of the Directorio rebuked Grau and we told him, more or less, "Well, Doctor, what happened to the capture, to the execution, with all the plan?" Grau answered, "I believe that with this scare we have given him, Batista will turn out to be the best choice. Why, this one has at least been scared to death." We responded, "But, Doctor, all the agreements, all the discussions today, all that we have done, all the plan, how can you change all that by yourself? Did you consult with anyone? Did you talk to anyone?"

His response was stunning. "No, no, boy, if everyone is equal, the same applies to a sergeant as to any other; all it takes is to look them in the eyes to see what they all are; they are all just a rabble." I will never forget it. It would be necessary to study Grau's entire biography carefully to know how to interpret certain attitudes he assumed in the course of his life. Mr. Grau San Martín believed that the personal virtues, courtesy, chivalry, honor, all that sort of thing, were of little value. Here [in the United States] when one is said to be well educated, it is understood that the reference is to academic instruction; thus, it is said that he has a B.A. and an M.A. and that he is working toward his Ph.D. That is what in this country is understood by education. In Cuba we are used to having a peasant from the backwoods of Guane who, because of his personal aptitude, could become the Mayor of Zalamea — that is to say, we do not have this discrimination that the honor or honesty of a person is determined by his social level or by his academic qualifications. And that day Grau changed the perspective on things; ". . . everything is equal. All are rabble. This one at least has the advantage of being scared to death." And the response was quite categorical and quite expressive: "You are wrong. That gentleman is nothing more than a son of a bad mother [son of a bitch] and should be shot."

Well, our indignation about Grau's unilateral destruction of our so brilliantly and audaciously organized plan made many of us decide for ourselves to go to the Palace to continue discussing the matter with the President. At five in the morning, standing in the Cabinet chambers, we were still arguing with Grau until he said, "No, no, I have made the decision and it cannot be changed." Then, those of us at the Palace, since we were not all there, came to a decision: we decided to call an urgent meeting of the Directorio to take place that same morning, the fourth of November. There was no use in continuing. The drama that had begun at ten in the morning of the third ended at six on the afternoon of the fourth. Now I will explain what we went through.

We, the members of the Directorio who were in the Palace, we who understood the enormous gravity of the fact that Mr. Batista was already back at Columbia, free from all danger and with presidential support, decided to call a meeting of the DEU for ten in the morning at the Palace. It was then five in the morning, and we were barely going to have two or three hours to sleep.

Indeed, at ten in the morning, the meeting began. We were gathered in a room on the second floor of the Palace, situated over the corner of Misiones Avenue and Refugio, across the street from the La Carona tobacco factory. And from that meeting attended by all the members of the Directorio certain decisions were urgently required. It was necessary to force Grau to eliminate Batista and, what is more, it was necessary to convince him that it was absolutely necessary to convene a court-martial and execute him. Of course, it wouldn't be easy! Batista was now warned; he had already had the luck to escape from the rat trap. Obviously, it would be difficult, using the same cheese, to bring the same rat back to the same trap. It would be virtually impossible. Suffice it to say that even the rats themselves knew it. But there was an advantage, strategic or tactical, in that the military district commander who would be called to replace Batista was Major Pablo Rodríguez, commander of the Sixth District (Columbia). And if I didn't mention this before, you must pardon me for the omission, but it is true that among the documents signed at eight on the evening of the fourth was the appointment of Pablo Rodríguez as Chief of Staff of the Army and Pablo knew it. And so, at eleven in the morning on the fifth, the situation was thus: Batista was in Columbia, but Pablo was still commander of the camp. And since the residence and offices of the Army Chief of Staff were right there, it was obvious that he could easily be made prisoner by the district commander. That is to say, the location of the office of the Chief of Staff of the Army was a purely topographical coincidence; the military force that surrounded his physical person was under the orders of Pablo Rodríguez, and since human nature is what it is, it seemed to me that it was an important factor that Pablo would replace Batista in command of the armed force. A plan for capturing Batista would not be difficult to execute.

We called Grau to notify him of the Directorio's decisions. There was a long period of polemics, but our arguments were so, so, so decisive against Grau that he, who normally was controlled in debate, and rational, more or less reasonable, but at least controlled, *lost his head* and said something that I will never forget, since for me it turned a 180-degree corner in the history of Cuba:

> The Directorio forgets that I am the President of the Republic and I give the orders here and Batista will continue as Chief of the Army.

He did not flourish the phrase. He shut his mouth and left us in a sepulchral silence for I don't remember how long. It seemed to me that it lasted ten hours. We did not look each other in the face. We were totally crushed and we could not figure out how to react.

Mongo Miyar presided over that meeting. He had special qualities that enabled him to handle difficult meetings when time was short and a lot was happening. He was very energetic in terms of interrupting speakers who wanted to seize a few extra minutes for themselves and so capable of seeing through to the heart of matters that he could not allow anyone even one minute extra. Mongo was the first to react [to Grau's statement]. He presided, as I have said before and, therefore, it was his responsibility to make some decision over the course of the debate. Mongo had a clear idea of the altered situation and told Grau,

> Well, Doctor, in view of the fact that you have suggested an extremely grave situation between the Directorio and the President of the Republic, we request that you withdraw because we have to analyze and discuss the newly arisen situation.

Grau stood up and marched toward the exit of the room. No one else stood up; no one accompanied him to the door. He himself had to open it and turn to close it as if he were a mere attendant in the Palace and not the President of the Republic.

As soon as we recovered from our stupefaction, we renewed the debate. It was necessary to discuss it in all aspects because only an open discussion could cast the light we needed. Naturally, all or nearly all of us were extremely hot-headed. But I still believe, as I did then, that all the opinions we offered and decisions we made were done in good faith. Such was the case, I believe, in the attitude assumed by one individual who has since died. He was a good friend whom we held in high esteem, whom we respected for his intellect and moral integrity. I am convinced that he was incapable of doing wrong for personal gain, a truly disinterested and spontaneous individual. So I must believe that what he did that day must be attributed to error and revolutionary immaturity, or maybe an immaturity of his political development, an optical incapacity to appreciate the social and historic reality of Cuba, if you will, to anything but bad faith. I refer to Rafael García Bárcena.

García Bárcena was one of those that heatedly proposed that the only thing left to do was to let it go, to dissolve the Directorio, and that if Grau wanted to rule by himself, without all the assistance of the DEU, the best solution was to withdraw and leave the responsibility to him alone. As you will notice, the solution that he proposed was absurd, impolitic, antihistoric, and functioned, in fact, as a disaster for Cuba.

Along with some others that I may mention in the telling, I was one of the proponents for maintaining the Directorio and I am not embarrassed about it; and, since I think that these things definitely must some day have a place, at least in the books of historical curiosities, I must say that the penultimate accord of the Directorio was to prohibit me from speaking because, according to Mongo Miyar, I had spoken seventeen times that day.

That was another disgrace of the meeting, since that day the chairman of the meeting was not impartial; that day the chairman, Mongo Miyar, was rabidly in favor of dissolving the Directorio. It is not strange, then, that Mongo, in part for his opinion and in part because of the opposition to it, would insist that in the seventeen times I had spoken I had, in one form or another, said the same things over and over. According to him, I was trying to weary the Directorio since we had gone without sleep nearly the entire night before; so if I were able to extend the meeting until seven or eight in the evening, we would have to declare a permanent session and call a recess until the next morning. He was sure that within the Directorio there was a small group that wanted to keep the Directorio intact a little longer so that, that same night, we could go to Columbia to arrest Batista, execute him, and install Pablo Rodríguez as Chief of Staff of the Army. Then we would return to the Palace, give the news to Grau, and ask him directly, "What do you think, Doctor, do you like it or not?" "Uh, I don't like it." "Well, *I am sorry,* you have to go home now," and we would put someone else in the president's chair. Mongo went on, saying that we had the audacity, decision, and character to do that, that he knew about excess, and because of that the Directorio could not leave without making a decision one way or the other. But anyway, he refused to accept the continuance [until the next day] and the declaration of a permanent session and leave us to our own devices to do what we believed must be done because we would do it even if it weren't in specific agreement with the Directorio, *as we did on the Fourth of September when we failed to meet together academically with the members of the Directorio so that we could acquire authorization to go to Columbia.* Far from it — we had confronted that situation and done something.

Two proposals were discussed. One advocated the dissolution of the DEU so that we would leave Grau all responsibility for the government. The other, diametrically opposed, held that in view of the fact that the President wanted to leave Batista as commander of the Army, we had to go to Columbia, arrest Batista, carry him to La Cabaña, execute him, and name Pablo Rodríguez to replace him. What Grau did after that was *"up to Grau"* as it is said here, and we would act accordingly. That was, in short, my position. Unfortunately, after six or eight hours of extremely impassioned polemics, the moment arrived to vote, and *by majority vote, the Directorio was dissolved.* It was, probably, in all the history of the DEU, its most grave error, at least in my judgment.

I can't stop without narrating an anecdote that will give a clear idea of how far passions had gone that day and to what level the perseverance and the constancy of a point of view had run. Within the Directorio there was what we could call an unwritten law. Basically, when we agreed to make a declaration, instead of presenting proposals to the full membership for inclusion in it, those who had proposals would instead meet with the committee appointed to draw up the document. I understood that perfectly, and with that in mind, they could not exclude me from the committee. When the majority voted for the dissolution, they had also agreed to publish our decision to dissolve. In other words, in agreeing to dissolve at that point in time, we had also agreed to publish a document to that effect as soon as possible. Naturally, they appointed to the committee one of the most passionate defenders of the dissolution who, at the same time, was fervently in favor of publishing the demise of the Directorio without delay so that whatever might occur from that moment on would not be ascribed to the DEU. That is to say, definitively, "It's over!" That meant, of course, García Bárcena. One of the girls was also nominated, and then, in spite of the fact that I did not agree with the dissolution nor with the publication of the declaration nor with any of that, I commenced to try to nominate others to the declaration committee. They dealt with me in the customary manner: they stuck me on the committee.

It was at that point that this deviltry occurred to me: the Directorio was already officially dissolved, but there was no doubt that there could be a way to eliminate Batista if it were not publicized that the Directorio had dissolved. Basically, since the dissolution would not be made known to the public until the following morning, we could still go to Columbia in the name of the Directorio, and still things could be done. Well now, if at ten in the night, the entire world already knew that the Directorio had dissolved, then we could not go anywhere in the name of the DEU. Then I tried a desperate maneuver when I met with García Bárcena and "Nena" Segura and told them, "I am dead beat; I haven't been to bed in two days. I feel totally incapable of sitting down right now to draw up a document." Bárcena responded to me with the following question: "And what is it that you propose, Rubio?" to which I answered, "That we meet tomorrow, say, at ten or eleven in the morning?"

As you will understand, the thing was completely academic. I was not interested in meeting the following day — the only thing that interested me was that the dissolution of the Directorio continue being, from the political and public point of view, a nonexistent thing by virtue of being unknown. Hoping for the success of my effort, I told Rafael G. Bárcena and Nena: "We are going to meet at ten in the morning," but then Bárcenas, in a gesture very much his own, told me, "I know you, you little masquerader. What you need is for no one to know tonight that the Directorio has dissolved, because you are capable of going to Columbia in the next few hours, and tomorrow morning, when we get up, we will find out in the newspapers that we have another Army Chief of Staff and another President of the Republic. It won't work! Like the famous members of the Convention, we will not leave here without drawing up the declaration. If you want to participate in the meeting because you aren't too sleepy, fine. But if you are so sleepy that you cannot participate in the meeting, we are very sorry, but we will not leave here without creating the declaration that the Directorio has been dissolved."

As one would suppose, I was not interested in the text of the declaration. What interested me was to impede it. Therefore, I did not attend the meeting in which the ill-starred manifesto was drawn up. I went home convinced that, at least for that night, nothing could be done by those of us who wanted to "do something." This occurred, as I have said before, on the fourth of November and, a few hours later, Prío and I would have to start on a journey, since we had been designated to form part of the delegation from Cuba to the Seventh International Conference of American States that would take place in Montevideo.[3] We had to leave Havana no later than the sixth of November because back then it was very difficult to go by airplane to South America. We had to go to New York and there take a boat that would arrive in Montevideo eighteen days later. I don't have to tell you that I had one foot on the plane and the other on the boat, but I was prepared to stay behind if events were precipitated because what was happening in Cuba was much more important, and, furthermore, I knew that I could still get to Montevideo if I had to. But in view of the dissolution of the Directorio and the impossibility of changing the Grau-Batista association, I couldn't decide where my greatest obligation lay.

After all these years, I maintain the opinion that I formed then, that Grau thought that Pablo Rodríguez would not be as unconditional a commander of the Army as would Batista, whom he had practically pulled out of the moat already shot. He believed that Batista would exhibit some moral sense of gratitude and loyalty that, up to that moment, he had not shown at all. Of course, he was wrong, because he had no reason to believe that Mr. Batista would change into his *cachanchán* [lackey],[4] but he was mistaken and there was no way of convincing him to the contrary. The phrase he so often repeated simply illustrated his misguided conviction: "After the scare we gave him, he is the best choice."

That was the situation on the sixth of November when we had to leave, Prío and I, for Montevideo, and we decided to make the trip since it seemed that the measure at the conference was one of the few things left to be done, if that government tottering under the menace of the expected coup d'état gave us time. I really thought that we would not arrive in Uruguay because of what occurred between the sixteenth and eighteenth of January.[5] I suspected that the coup would have to happen on the first of December because leading the armed forces was a man who had been confirmed in his military power, who was already mature, and was committed to carrying out a military coup, and the idiot of a President of the Republic, instead of shooting him, had declared his confidence in the man. If anything contributed to the delay of the execution of the agreed-upon conspiracy, it had to be the November 8 Alphabetic insurrection, which in the end did not damage the coup plotters,[6] since the failure of the counterrevolutionary uprising improved Batista's military position within the Army.

But, well, the rest is history. I don't know if I have been able to clarify your curiosities over how the events occurred, but Mr. Batista survived one of the most perfect plans that I will ever know, entirely conceived by Antonio Guiteras and apparently accepted by Grau. At least, when we arrived at the Palace at eight thirty that evening, Grau had accepted the plan. Why this changed later, I have never been able to understand.[7]

THE NOVEMBER 8 INSURRECTION FIASCO

On November 5, Grau and Batista rivalled in vulnerability. A situation of civil political vacuum existed: Grau had confirmed Batista as Chief of Staff of the Army against the recommendation of the Directorio and the Directorio had dissolved. The Directorio, simply, as a student organization turned wielder of real power — exercised indirectly — had constituted the essential power supporting the revolutionary government. The Directorio had the tremendous historic failing of not having organized the popular political force implicit in its program. Consequently, upon dissolving itself, an immense vacuum of support for the Grau government remained while Batista, in turn, remained in a situation of disequilibrium when the regimental commanders themselves had supported his arrest; this fragile situation was not alleviated by the President's support of the Army Chief of Staff.

In the following days, there was little official activity. Welles continued to try to justify himself to Washington after the declarations of several officers (*Alma Mater*, November 7, 1933, 1) who indicted him as the greatest instigator of the events at the Hotel Nacional (Welles Cable 436, November 7, 1933, 516), published in those first days of November; and the press remained at the service of the commercial and financial interests opposing the revolutionary government. Public opinion vacillated before the obvious contradictions among the political spheres of power.

On November 5, the student journal *Alma Mater* published on its editorial page demands by a popular movement for the immediate expulsion of Ambassador Welles as the "'envoy of Wall Street'; . . . conspiring to establish a government in Cuba which would obey orders from Washington; . . . engaged in preventing 'a Cuban delegation from reaching Montevideo to unmask the shameful conduct of the Yankees'" (translated in Welles Cable 430, November 6, 1933, 513) before the Panamerican Conference. That same belligerent opinion had been advanced during a political rally at the University in which — according to Welles — "the members of the former Student Directorate joined forces with the Left of Communist wing," appropriating Eddy Chibás as leader of the movement. Reminding the Department of State that Chibás had been the author of the cables sent to Latin America on September 9 accusing him of having taken the Cuban Army officers to the Hotel Nacional, he stated that Chibás directed a demonstration in support of his expulsion from Cuba by claiming that Welles was "'working for the interests of my own Government'" (Welles Cable 430, November 6, 1933, 514).

In the cable traffic of that week, Welles was asked if Batista would have sufficient control of the troops of Havana successfully to bring about the replacement of Grau. His response was:

> Batista's own violent animosity to Grau San Martín which is now growing due to his knowledge of a plot favored by Grau Saturday to seize Batista and replace him with another sergeant makes it inevitable that Batista will move against Grau provided he can be reasonably confident of the loyalty of the soldiers in the various Havana barracks (Welles Cable 340, November 6, 1933, 514).

Welles had obviously learned at least part of Guiteras's and the DEU's plan to seize Batista.

So many reasons existed to cast doubt on Batista's power in the military arena that, exactly forty-eight hours after this cable, the apparently vigorous uprising of November 8 exploded.

At two in the morning, a rebellion exploded with the seizure of the air corps headquarters and the military airplanes rebel pilots would use, as well as the Havana police headquarters and four substations, the Dragones barracks, the San Ambrosio barracks, and Atarés Castle.

How and why did that occur? How did the events evolve, after such an initial impact? The story comes from a participant and investigator.

As a consequence of the successful conspiracy of the sergeants, corporals, and soldiers on the Fourth of September, the members of the armed forces from those same levels who did not benefit, together in some cases with former officers that had not been sequestered at the Hotel Nacional, began to develop conspiracies, not understanding that the circumstances of the successful coup would not repeat themselves. Also, the oppositionist civilians, individually and indistinctly, began to conspire with the men in uniform at all levels, though they preferred to do so from the bottom up. The group that did so with the most dedication was the ABC, frustrated by not being the beneficiary of the new power. Among their recruitments were cases as original as that of an enlisted man from the Navy, signed up by Fernando Miranda, B-4 of the Botet branch, who later was assigned to guard Guiteras in his apartment in the Hotel Palacio at Twenty-Fifth and G in Vedado. This enlisted man went so far as to offer to "sequester Guiteras" when it might be opportune, an offer which Miranda elegantly declined.

This other conspirative process, developing in a disorderly manner, never achieved more than nominal coordination. Carlos Saladrigas, number two man in the ABC, recognized the conspiracy, decided to avail himself of the project, and assumed the responsibility of command, supported by another two members of the Célula Directriz, Alfredo Botet and Juan P. Bombino. With that, the conspiracy, though not officially sanctified by the ABC, since Joaquín Martínez Sáenz was exiled in Miami and the remaining members of the leadership were not even participants, came to be an attempt at overthrow that only served — in the long run — to consolidate Batista's position.

Those minimally coordinated conspiratorial actions determined the strange association that would emerge, in which the Alphabetics and the former officers, some noncommissioned officers, and the enlisted men were bound together with one another, even to the point of including some of the sergeants promoted after the coup. The professional politicians — Menocal, Mendieta, and Miguel Mariano Gómez — were above this type of conspiratorial conglomeration.

Saladrigas enjoyed the highest esteem of Sumner Welles. The ambassador considered him the only statesman among the juvenile groups. It appears that Saladrigas was confident that he could work directly with the ambassador and believed he would be the go-between among the high-level conspirators consulting Welles. This inference is uncertain, but it can be deduced from the absence of several cables from the collection published by the Department of State; there are no personal references to Saladrigas in the course of communications immediately prior to, synchronous with, or following the event.

What is certain is that Saladrigas moved about with unaccustomed activity to the point that he personally recruited pilots like Arístides Agüero y Montoro, his cousin. Agüero joined, but he did not think the plan would work, in spite of the promised support for the insurrection, including plans that enlisted personnel would seize the air field for

Lieutenant José Barrientos Schweyer, who would act as commander of the Rebel Air Force.

Upon his arrival at the air field, Agüero encountered a multitude of civilians drinking beer. He quickly made arrangements with Barrientos, Captain Martull, and Lieutenant Collazo to take off as soon as possible after coordinating various objectives among themselves. It was agreed that Barrientos would bomb Camp Columbia, only two hundred yards away from the air field, and Martull would fly over the Matanzas regiment, bombing it. Agüero himself and Collazo would fly over the encampments of San Ambrosio, Dragones, and Atarés — which should already be in the hands of the counterrevolution — to show that the air corps was aligned with the revolt. Agüero and Collazo would fly over the Palace without bombing it, since Barrientos pleaded for the safety of his brother Willy — a DEU member — who would surely be there supporting Grau, which actually occurred.

Still, the spectacular display of support by the aviation corps fizzled in a few minutes. The rebellious barracks, commanders, and police stations, as well as the general public, failed to realize that the air corps lacked a supply base. In a matter of three or four minutes, Barrientos, Agüero, Martull, and Collazo had taken off. Barrientos dropped a bomb of limited power over Camp Columbia and returned to land but could not take off again since the attempt to retake the air field had already begun. Martull did not bomb the Matanzas regiment, and his aircraft later appeared upside down in a field in Cárdenas. The pilot, having escaped injury, was able to flee to the United States. Collazo, participating for appearances's sake only, since he was really a double agent, landed near Barabanó, and Agüero flew first over the Presidential Palace, then over the already occupied military centers. When he failed to see the expected signal — a gasoline tank in flames — at the air field upon his return to indicate that the field was still in rebel hands, he decided to fly to the United States. He was forced to jump out over the sea, lost and out of fuel. The cargo ship *Western Sword* picked him up, dropping him in Boca Grande, Florida. In a taped interview, Agüero told me it had been basically an "operetta insurrection."

So, the alliance of the air corps with the insurrectional attempt lasted between fifteen and twenty minutes, even though it left a spectacular impression of support. Their immediate take-off and prompt disappearance was observed by the commanders of the various rebel units; their failure to show continued support caused morale among the rebels to fall.

The maintenance personnel at the air field were pinned down by gun fire from Columbia, so Barrientos could not take off again. Major Herrera, former chief of transportation in the military regime before August 12, and Lieutenant Pedro Morfi Linares, who operated the anti-aircraft batteries, as well as First Lieutenant Alfredo Cruz Torres, acting chief of operations, all realized the futility of the effort and acknowledged that their offensive power against Camp Columbia was insignificant, which accelerated the drop in morale.

It was said, by the type of historian who obtains his information through old newspaper reports and the writings of others, that no less than two thousand persons had gathered at the air field. In fact, the number was between five hundred and a thousand. Personnel had gathered in the Hotel Almendares next to the air field. They had not been able to gain access to the air field itself because they were unarmed civilian personnel from the camp itself; they numbered between a hundred fifty and two hundred, all Alphabetics. They had among them only fifty antiquated Crack rifles with extremely limited offensive power. Consequently, when Captain Querejeta appeared to rescue the occupied center, he met with little resistance before the counterrevolutionaries surrendered. "In the air field a true battle never occurred," according to Alberto Segrera and Fernando Miranda, two great fighters who were captured there. The desertion of some of Camp Columbia's military contingent, the ineffectiveness of the announced bombardment by the rebel planes, and the occupation of the air field together initiated the disintegration of the entire counterrevolutionary attempt.

What were Batista and Grau doing during this counterrevolutionary fiasco? Batista, suspicious of the commanders who five days before were ready to arrest him, had decided to designate as Chief of Operations a negro, Captain Gregorio Querejeta, an old officer who had supported the movement of the Fourth of September and who was honored for his military aptitude. He had put Querejeta in contact with his best sources of information — Infantry Corporal Angel C. Fajardo, who infiltrated the conspiracy strictly as an informant; and the recently promoted Lieutenant Fausto Collazo, who, even though he initially led the conspiracy at the air field and actually took off in one of the four rebel aircraft, had already informed Barrientos of his separation from the movement. With information from Fajardo and Collazo, with the opportunity Batista afforded him, and with his capacity and courage, Querejeta fully assumed his responsibilities. Batista, furthermore, decided not to leave Camp Columbia, but he did remain in constant motion in case the rebels should return to bomb the camp.

Grau San Martín personally directed the deployment of the antiaircraft batteries atop the Palace against the attacking aircraft, which were illuminated by twenty searchlights from La Cabaña Fortress. Two blocks away, at La Punta Castle, the Naval commanders concentrated manpower and material resources still loyal to the Secretary of the Interior, Antonio Guiteras, who was physically present there.

Of course, Grau and Guiteras, in face of the ostentation of the uprising, signed a decree early on the morning of the eighth declaring a state of war within the entire national territory.

In the course of the morning of the eighth, the civilian commander of the uprising action, Alfredo Botet — who had a brilliant service record in the struggle against Machado — had met with a pair of sailors on Trocadero Street. The ABC leader took out his gun, shot one of the sailors, and fled. Even though the sailors had not recognized him, he was filled with guilt and considered himself a target for retaliation. He resorted to giving orders over the telephone from the National Feminists Alliance headquarters in Vedado, where he was hiding. The movement, which had started as a military uprising but developed into an Alphabetic operation, remained in practical terms leaderless, since Saladrigas, who had developed the scheme, was a statesman rather than a man of action. And the true statesman never is a man of action, since the subtlety that influences the future of the State in the middle and long term does not mesh well with the immediateness of the execution of violence.

The rebellious Chief of Police, in spite of his proximity to the Palace, with a single tank parked menacingly outside, received telephonic information concerning Querejeta's total victory at the air field. In spite of the historic reports about the grandiosity of a bloody battle while his forces were advancing on the Palace, the truth is that chief of operations, Captain Arturo Nespereira, having received a negative signal from Columbia after being attacked by the Palace antiaircraft batteries, decided that the Headquarters should be evacuated quietly after negotiations between his commander and Eddy Chibás, who had been extremely active since the early morning.

After noon that day, the Tenth Police Station, with its magnificent topographical location, also surrendered. This had been a strategic military unit located across from the Almendares bridge on Twenty-Third Street. The bridge had not been blocked on the Marianao side nor blown up to prevent troops from Columbia from crossing. Those troops arrived that afternoon under command of Lieutenant Belisario Hernández, who forced the station's surrender with minimal casualties on either side and with total respect for the lives of the conquered. Rubén León, who had been "detained" for several hours during the brief occupation, was not rescued, as has been said, by the revolutionary Guillermo Ara. Since there never existed any type of animosity between the men of action of the DEU and of the ABC, he was permitted to "take his leave" before the rescue of the rebellion center.

Nevertheless, at noon on the eighth, Atarés Castle, Dragones Barracks, home of the Fifth Military District, and the San Ambrosio Barracks[8] were still in the hands of the counterrevolution. So were the Fifth, Tenth, Eleventh, and Thirteenth police stations, as well as the various departments, such as Communications and Public Health, and other minor dependencies, such as the Provincial Government and the Judicial Police.

Logically, with the fall of the Police Headquarters, it was very easy to reoccupy the other police stations — the Fifth, Eleventh, and the Thirteenth, as well as the Judicial Police, which had only been occupied since that morning. A small armed caravan from *Pro Ley y Justicia* achieved these reoccupations. Mario Salabarría, René Moreno, Armando (Bebo) Leyva, and Manolo Arán traveled with this caravan, thus dissolving the rumor that *Pro Ley* was cooperating with the counterrevolution.

Many of the civilians that had been in the Police Headquarters were transported to Atarés Castle — additional proof of the reigning confusion — while the mutineers of the Dragones Barracks decided to avoid frontal combat and silently left for the Castle as well in the afternoon and evening of the eighth.

Since the counterrevolutionary conspirators did not have a precise objective, they fired incessantly from the flat rooftops. The city itself was inundated by military personnel and civilians from the opposing bands who were searching vehicles. Because of the small area and the number of opposing military units, Havana fell into such chaos that groups would find themselves detaining their own members.

Since the gunfire from the rooftops and the explosions of bombs in Havana intensified during the night of November 8-9, the Government issued a decree on the morning of the ninth — this time under the exclusive signature of Guiteras — declaring Havana in a state of siege. Citizens were advised to stay off the rooftops and balconies and not to congregate in the public streets or pass through the streets after seven at night.

The San Ambrosio barracks was situated in central Havana at the edge of Havana bay. Even though it was poorly manned, it had served the rebels as a supply depot since it was the military arsenal. Major Ciro Leonard, a former officer well liked by the rank and file of his unit, who had replaced former lieutenant José Ovares, also of the former officer corps, had been placed in charge of the headquarters of the rebel post. It was, therefore, considered necessary that the cruiser *Cuba*, anchored in nearby waters, bombard the San Ambrosio barracks with its cannons. With news that Captain Gregorio Querejeta, who had already triumphed in the operation at the air field, was advancing on the barracks, the occupants of San Ambrosio realized the impossibility of defending their position and began to sneak away. But their decision to fall back toward Atarés Castle insured that the Castle itself would be the final redoubt of the counterrevolution. At that point, the old eighteenth-century castle was the only remaining rebel position.

So, in reports of the last dramatic military event, troop numbers were greatly exaggerated. If it had been certain that all the rebels of different units being abandoned were falling back to the Atarés Castle, the new operative center, there could have been more than two thousand men. But the troops defeated at the air field did not even get as far as the Tenth Police Station while it was still under the counterrevolution's control; the insurgents from Police Headquarters, two blocks from the Presidential Palace, began to disband as well and head for home or for new battle fronts; the insurrectionists from San Ambrosio and Dragones barracks, who decided to retreat in the face of their untenable positions, did not want to repeat the circumstance. It is logical, therefore, to think that the concentration of troops at Atarés would have to be much less than that reported in the exaggerated newspaper reports.

"I would say that we never got to five hundred," Rafael Rivera Hermosillo, the ill-tempered Alphabetic who fell prisoner during that irrational operation, told me, while all the published reports until now cite figures that fluctuate between one thousand and fifteen hundred men.

It remains inexplicable why quality military men such as Major Ciro Leonard and the members of the contingent of a fortification that served as home of the Fifth Rural Guard Squadron, whose mission was to serve as the presidential escort, could conceive that from that redoubt they could have obtained a victory.

It has been said that Leonard went there after insistent calls from Lieutenant Gener, who led the troops; it has been said as well that Leonard received a radiogram signed by Colonel Amiel — former military commander of the Santa Clara province — in which he recommended the retreat to Atarés as he advanced toward Havana with five thousand men. It is difficult to understand the military rationale behind the operation, since Atarés was a defensive position for the city of Havana in coordination with the Cabaña Fortress and the coastal artillery in case of foreign invasion, but it was not at all suited to resist an attack from the entire national army completely surrounding it on land and attacking by land and sea.

Neither can we discover anything from Welles's cables, since those numbered 437, 438, and 439, which must have been transmitted between the seventh and ninth of November, are missing. In his report on the ninth, in Cable 440, he said, ". . . the total force now defending Atares amounts to approximately 3,000 men fully armed and with ample ammunition" (Welles Cable 440, November 9, 1933, 517). He added that "The major part of the province of Santa Clara outside of the capital city is reported to have joined the revolution and to be in arms under the command of Colonel Carrillo."[9] Furthermore, ". . . the entire province of Matanzas is in arms including the soldiers, all supporting the revolution." All the information was so totally false that Welles himself concluded the cable with a request that the State Department not release these reports to the press, since anything given out by the Department went directly to Havana and that "under present circumstances it is desirable that no reports coming from me be made public." Is it not clear that he was only trying to impress the Department?

Meanwhile, what was happening within the Castle? Attacked from various fronts, its occupants could only resist for six hours, from eight in the morning until two in the afternoon, when the commander-in-chief, Ciro Leonard, committed suicide. Captain Querejeta, already triumphant in operations the previous day, deployed infantry troops around the Castle while he ordered the installation of the artillery. Naval units from the bay itself, the cruisers *Cuba* and *Patria,* bombarded the Castle, while from the rooftops at the corners of Concha and Cristina Streets large caliber mortars were fired. Rapid fire cannons opened fire toward Atarés from the Loma del Burro [Burro Hill] in Luyanó. At 11:35 in the morning, with the defenders of the castle in a totally indefensible position but prior to its surrender, Ambassador Welles reported,

> . . . it is intended in the course of the day to hold summary courts-martial and execute immediately all soldiers or police who joined the opposition movement and who have been captured. I fear that the opportunity will be taken on some pretext to execute at the same time some of the officers who have been imprisoned since the National Hotel incident (Welles Cable 441, November 9, 1933, 517).

According to him, hundreds of executions were imminent.

What was Welles doing but insinuating the inevitable necessity of landing the Marines? In case that was not sufficient, three hours later, after the Atarés garrison had already surrendered, he reported that an ABC commander (according to my knowledge, it was Alfredo Botet) had been informed that, beginning at three in the afternoon, American and English properties would be destroyed and that foreigners would be attacked. In that same cable he reported that "an anarchic situation which may have very serious possibilities seems imminent for tonight . . ." (Welles Cable 443, November 9, 1933, 518). This was exactly the type of situation foreseen by the Platt Amendment as requiring armed North American intervention; thus, it is obvious that landing the marines in port was exactly what he was suggesting.

At four in the afternoon, Welles cabled that Atarés Castle had surrendered, but that press correspondents confirmed "reports earlier received from Cuban sources that the revolutionists are marching through the southern portion of Matanzas and Havana Provinces." Also, "The anticipated revolutionary movement in Oriente Province appears to have commenced with an outbreak in Palma Soriano to the north of Santiago" (Welles Cable 445, November 9, 1933, 519).

And now we see the real numbers of the combatants at Atarés: four hundred were taken prisoner upon their surrender, according to Welles (Welles Cable 446, November 9, 1933, 519). In the surrender, of course, one of the most unpardonable crimes occurred: Colonel Blas Hernández — his rank was self-bestowed during his struggles against Machado — was executed, after surrendering, by the Septembrist captain Mario Alfonso Hernández, who was himself later assassinated, on Batista's orders.

At this point, let me point out that, both in the assault on the Hotel Nacional and in the counterrevolutionary attempt on November 8, a small percentage of the population of Havana for their own reasons rose up in support of the revolutionary government, and only a few hundred civilians participated actively in collaboration with the revolutionary government's armed forces. Such participation, even though it added a popular context to the official action, served also as a detonator for indiscriminate reprisals, unjustifiable from any point of view. Of course, Sumner Welles took advantage of that cause-and-effect relationship to cable on the tenth that there existed

> an extremely violent reaction in every element in Havana against the present government because of the incidents of yesterday and because of the slaughters of some prisoners after they had surrendered. *There is an open demand for intervention by the United States* [emphasis added]. The foreign colonies are criticising [sic] the failure of the United States to land troops (Welles Cable 449, November 10, 1933, 520).

Welles, astutely, attributed to others what he himself had been plotting and insinuating.

But, at the same time, he continued his arrangement with Batista without officially breaking with the former officer corps. Since he feared the renewed possibility of U.S. recognition of the revolutionary government, as soon as the new rebel centers were suffocated and official authority confirmed, he arranged an interview with President Roosevelt.

Grau and Batista now postured to consolidate their respective positions, more internationally than internally. Grau had returned victorious, but because of Welles's diligence, Grau was unable to improve his standing with the United States but rather lost ground, while Batista recovered totally from his position of vulnerability before the military commanders and was confirmed as the only North

American avenue for toppling Grau, the self-same person who had "pardoned" him and confirmed him in his post barely one week before.

Welles finagled a presidential interview on the nineteenth, during Roosevelt's vacation trip to Warm Springs, Georgia; but before departing he sent a message to Batista, who had sent word through Captain Belisario Hernández that he was not involved in the criticisms circulating in government circles against Welles. In his message Welles reminded him that the only way to prevent future disturbances and regain the Cuban public's confidence was to establish a new government, one that would be capable of providing guarantees to all Cubans (Welles Cable 463, November 16, 1933, 522-23).

Because Welles had suggested armed intervention, of course, Batista could have been ignored. Instead, he renewed his conspiracy with Batista and reminded him of their compromise for the constitution of a new government. He then left for President Roosevelt's retreat with the purpose of articulating *a policy of nonrecognition* that would lead to President Grau's overthrow.

Before turning to that policy, it is necessary briefly to analyze the reasons behind the failure of the November 8 insurrection.

After Chibás woke me around one that morning, I observed the attempt from several different locations. From my personal observations, I can state eight reasons for the failure of the insurrection:

1. The coup was initially conceived by former officers who tried to "infiltrate" into the new commands formed by military personnel who were previously their subordinates. For me, the idea that the officer *does not* know how to conspire in conjunction with the lower-rank elements — sergeants, corporals, soldiers — becomes *classic*. His mind remains frozen in the mold of his personal authority, and he is incapable of adapting himself to sharing with his subordinates.

   Such mental rigidity does not occur among officers. It is relatively easy for the superior to become friends with his subordinates and draw them into conspiracies; an officer is less able to approach enlisted personnel on a personal basis of any sort — and vice versa — because of the rigidity of military training.

   This basic fault within the coup produced loyalty to the status quo among the troops of the military encampments of Columbia and the Cabaña Fortress.

2. There was no attempt at surprise attack of the style exemplified by Curzio Malaparte in his *Técnica del golpe de estado*, and such an attempt would have been impossible because the accessory nerve centers of power — electric energy, telephones, telegraphs, transportation, and the press — were all in the hands of sympathizers of the regime. Furthermore, the coup of November 8 lacked, as we shall see, the military impact that would subordinate those factors to a new source of power.

3. The barracks occupied by the counterrevolution — practically "ceded" by their nominal commanders to their former commanders — were of minor importance, small detachments with the most inferior defense capabilities.

4. Although the air field was delivered — between beers and uproar — to the counterrevolution, the delivery only served for the takeoff of airplanes that spent little time in the air, without causing any decisive damage.

5. The police corps of Havana did not possess military power. We knew that throughout September 1933, and the personnel changes that had occurred were neither more nor less than expected in any administrative or bureaucratic department of the State.

6. Batista, more sly than intelligent, more intuitive than wise, and as snakelike as always, from the beginning cultivated the infiltration, the espionage, the treachery so that he knew from the beginning the course of the conspiracy. Therefore, he was able to destroy it easily, using a loyal black captain, Gregorio Querejeta.

7. The counterrevolution had no civilian head. Carlos Saladrigas was not seen by anyone that day, and his operative aide, Alfredo Botet, was in hiding after killing a sailor.

8. The counterrevolution did not have any military commander-in-chief at all. Barrientos was only the fleeting and ephemeral commander of an air operation that lasted only fifteen minutes. At the air field, the ground personnel had a confused headquarters. In the Dragones, San Ambrosio, and Atarés barracks, the command passed for all practical purposes to Major Ciro Leonard, after being shunned by several others in succession. With his limited material and human resources, he could not, in any case, have defeated Colonel Querejeta, Leonard's coequal as an

academy officer, and who had all the reserves in equipment and manpower at his disposal.

The operation only lasted thirty-six hours — from two in the morning on the eighth until two in the afternoon on the ninth, when Major Leonard committed suicide. But for all its spectacularity and confusion, as well as its inefficiency, and given the numbers of military and civilians that participated — I would say, perhaps three thousand, with dozens dead and hundreds injured — the event simply produced a grave national turmoil.

WELLES AND THE NONRECOGNITION POLICY: THE GROWING ENMITY BETWEEN CORDELL HULL AND SUMNER WELLES

We have already seen the policy of armed intervention Welles was developing with the professional politicians and "Plattist" officers until Roosevelt and Cordell Hull decided to assume a position against that intervention. Now we shall rapidly examine the policy of replacement that Welles would have to utilize with similar aggressiveness thereafter.

On September 8, in a telephone conversation with President Roosevelt and Secretary Cordell Hull less than seventy-two hours after the revolutionary coup, Welles requested authorization to draw up a declaration which would, in effect, emphasize that the North American government had not given *nor would give* any consideration to the recognition of the revolutionary group in power. Roosevelt interrupted the conversation to state that he would only authorize a declaration that no question of *recognition or nonrecognition* of the group in power in Cuba had been considered, therefore *making it impossible to state in the future that the United States had decided not to recognize Cuba* (Telephone Memo, September 8, 1933, 410).

In the cable dated September 10, Welles had stated:

> The next two or three days will determine whether any strong revolutionary movement against it [the Grau government] will be made. There appears to be no indication now that any successful counterrevolt can be carried through in Havana *if after a reasonable period the government attracts popular support,* [emphasis added] appears to be able to maintain public order even nominally, appoints responsible provincial and municipal authorities, and is able to

function as a government in the sense that it complies with its obligations and collects and disburses revenues; I should strongly recommend consulting with the Latin American Republics with a view to reaching a determination upon recognition; no government here can survive for a protracted period without recognition by the United States and our failure to recognize for an indefinite period if the requisites above-indicated are complied with would merely bring about in Cuba a more thoroughly chaotic and anarchic condition than that which already obtains (Welles Cable 224, September 10, 1933, 417).

In the same cable he indicated that the embassy was being attacked for its failure immediately to recognize the revolutionary government and that the possibility of intervention was being violently criticized. Yet later that day he added that to Colonel Ferrer, *"I stated that in the matter of recognition we had as yet given no consideration to the question"* (Welles Cable 228, September 10, 1933, 418).

The refusal of the Latin American countries — Welles also stated on the tenth of September — to accord immediate recognition had irritated the students to the point that they were sending violent cables on the usual theme of American imperialism to universities and radical associations all over the continent (Welles Cable 224, September 10, 1933, 416-18).

On the eleventh Welles expressed in a dispatch to the Department of State:

> . . . I desire once more to emphasize that in my judgment it would be highly prejudicial to our interests to intimate in any manner that recognition of the existing regime was being considered by us (Welles Cable 233, September 11, 1933, 423).

and he added nearly immediately:

> In view of its deep and abiding interest in the welfare of the Cuban people and the security of the Republic of Cuba, it [the U.S. government] cannot and will not accord recognition to any government in Cuba other than a legitimate and constitutional government unless conclusive evidence is presented that such government effectively represents the will of a majority of the people of the Republic, that it is

capable of maintaining order and of guaranteeing the protection of 'life, property, and individual liberty' and finally that such government is competent to carry out the functions and obligations which are incumbent upon any stable government.

Secretary of State Cordell Hull, that same day, September 11, emitted a declaration that contained practically the same concepts Welles had suggested, although instead of emphatically refusing the possibility of doing so in the future, he expressed that the American government was "prepared to welcome any Government representing the will of the people of the Republic and capable of maintaining law and order throughout the island" (Hull Cable 96, September 11, 1933, 424). The next day, Welles advised Hull that his declaration from the previous day concerning recognition

> . . . makes our position perfectly plain to the Latin American world and is heartily approved by all those representatives of the Latin American Republics with whom I have been able to get in touch. It is unanimously approved by all of the important Cuban political groups (Welles Cable 238, September 12, 1933, 427).

Concerning the theme of recognition, and reporting on the meeting with the members of the DEU on September 15, Welles said:

> The surprisingly friendly attitude shown towards me [by the students] was in part due, in my belief, to their realization that recognition by the United States Government is essential to any government in Cuba . . . (Welles Cable 266, September 16, 1933, 442).

Later, referring to a conversation with Grau San Martín, Welles attributed to him the statement that "every one in the country would support the government if the United States would accord recognition" (Welles Cable 271, September 17, 1933, 444).

On the eighteenth of September, he returned with ". . . under these conditions recognition from the United States will not be forthcoming" (Welles Cable 275, September 18, 1933, 447).

Obviously, the repetition of nonrecognition through the confidential cables was not for the benefit of the Cuban people, to whom he had already made his position known. It was intended to pressure the Department of State and President Roosevelt himself, so that the policy of nonrecognition would not waver. To understand fully what was really going on, though, one must realize that Welles was not the Ambassador of the United States, since the Cuban government was not recognized; he was only a special envoy of the North American president, and as such he was meeting with all the enemies of the revolutionary government, and very especially with Batista, whom he had already converted to his cause. Furthermore, on one occasion with the Directorio and two or three times with Grau, he tried to compel them to change over to the political line he suggested, refusing to discuss modifications to his own line.

His behavior indicated that he was acting openly as a professional agitator, an expression usually applied to the communists. His conditions for recognition included the maintenance of law and order, while he himself encouraged and provoked the disruption of normalcy and even permitted himself to say to his superior, as he did on the tenth, that ". . . our failure to recognize for an indefinite period . . . would merely bring about in Cuba a more thoroughly chaotic and anarchic condition than that which already obtains" (Welles Cable 224, September 10, 1933, 417). He, therefore, insisted on the maintenance of law and order as a requisite for recognition, while insisting to the Department that failure to extend recognition for an indefinite period would automatically create chaos and anarchy. It is perfectly clear, therefore, that he himself, by opposing recognition, had already chosen the chaos and anarchy that, in turn, would impede recognition.

Then, Welles further consolidated his pro-Batista, anti-Grau position. On October 5, after the officers who had held the Hotel Nacional, whose insurgent position represented a diminishing of the triumphant sergeants' authority, had been taken prisoner, Roosevelt suggested to Welles through Secretary of State Hull that "the capture of the officers [indicates] a consolidation of the position of the present government" (Hull Cable 113, October 5, 1933, 472). Roosevelt also expressed his belief that Cuba was undergoing a period of storm and stress and that "there must be some latitude, on the part of ourselves and of other states, in the application of the customary principles of international practice (e.g., as regards recognition) in view of these conditions."

Welles responded angrily that the capture of the officers only had increased the prestige of the army and placed the government at a disadvantage. He said the divergence between the army and the civilian elements of the government was daily becoming more marked and that, inasmuch as Batista was becoming more influential, the power of the students and Grau San Martín was diminishing (Welles Cable 341, October 5, 1933, 473-74).

In summary, Welles opposed recognition, first because

> . . . such action would imply our lending official support to a regime which is opposed by all business and financial interests in Cuba; by all the powerful political groups and in general, . . . not only by all the elements that hold out any promise of being able to govern Cuba but by a very great majority of the people as well. Such action on our part would undoubtedly help to keep the present government in power for a while but popular reaction against it, while delayed, would continue and would increase, until after a series of exhausting efforts which the Republic cannot effect, the government would either be overthrown or else, which is more probable, the country would be plunged into utter anarchy (Welles Cable 341, October 5, 1933, 473-74).

On October 16, Welles sent an extensive dispatch to try to demonstrate that, among the positive and negative alternatives concerning recognition, in terms of permanent policy in Cuba, *the nonrecognition policy was that which should be adopted because it was a policy "based on justice to the Cuban people, [!] one which will hasten rather than retard the creation of a constitutional government in Cuba and one which will expedite eventual stability"* [emphasis added] (Welles Cable 367, October 16, 1933, 490).

And he added, in a very precise way, *"Our own commercial and export interests in Cuba cannot be revived under this government"* [emphasis added]. Did those interests help create justice for the Cuban people, or was the justice administered through revolutionary legislation, in fact, damaging North American interests?

Since through his ruses Welles had achieved satisfactory success in terms of Roosevelt's suggestion through Hull, he did not address the subject again for several weeks. But with a new attempt to overthrow the Grau government on November 8 and 9, on the tenth Welles was obliged to echo the reports published in the North American press which stated that "recognition of the Grau government would have prevented revolutionary outbreaks" (Welles Cable 449, November 10,

1933, 520). Welles commented to them in that dispatch to the Department of State:

> I do not believe that any competent observer present here during the past two months would confirm that assertion. Recognition would probably have delayed revolt, but it would not have prevented it. And recognition would have been construed by the bulk of the Cubans as evidence of our willingness to ignore their right to determine their own destinies by lending the support both moral and material which our recognition represents to a government which had come into power after [against] the desires of the great majority of the Cuban people.

Obviously, the following picture was taking shape: Welles persistently held that nonrecognition created the chaos and the anarchy that would lead to Grau's overthrow. Supporting this opinion, rebellions broke out in the military and police barracks on November 8 and 9. The North American press — agreeing with Welles's opinion, although for very different reasons — expressed that recognition of the Grau government would have prevented such anarchic and chaotic explosions and agreed that the insurrection, which had been costly in terms of Cuban blood, would not have occurred if recognition had been extended. But it bothered Welles to see himself caught in his own trap, so he chose to state that recognition would have convinced the Cubans of the U.S. desire to ignore their right to self-determination, representing support for a government that had attained power against the desires of the great majority of the Cuban people. Perhaps, that is why the Céspedes government, according to Welles, had needed him daily "for decisions on all matters affecting the Government of Cuba. These decisions range from questions of domestic policy and matters affecting the discipline of the Army to questions involving appointments in all branches of the Government" (Welles Cable 172, August 19, 1933, 368). Considering that self-same government, a few days later, Welles had said:

> None of the real leaders of public opinion have, however, as yet had courage enough to come out openly against the popular agitation for revolutionary government and a resultant clean sweep of all of the former officeholders no matter whether they were legitimately entitled to the offices

they were holding or not (Welles Cable 180, August 22, 1933, 370).

So, the situation he had described on August 22 had forced him to arrive at the conclusion that his "original hope that the present Government of Cuba could govern as a constitutional government for the remainder of the term for which General Machado had himself elected must be abandoned" (Welles Cable 184, August 24, 1933, 371). Now it turned out that the revolutionary government had come into power "after [against] the desires of the great majority of the people of Cuba" (Welles Cable 449, November 10, 1933, 520). Which of the two recorded versions from the same person was correct?

Nevertheless, Welles did not delay in obtaining a new victory on the diplomatic front with the ratification of his nonrecognition policy. After advising that the opinions poured out by the North American press had jolted him strongly, Welles considered it necessary to see President Roosevelt personally, so he requested an interview, which was scheduled for November 19 in Warm Springs, Georgia.

The circumstance would be perfect for Welles to lead Roosevelt to his own evaluation for two fundamental reasons. First, Roosevelt was deeply engrossed in the particulars of the decision to extend recognition to the Union of Soviet Socialist Republics, which had just occurred on the sixth anniversary of the Russian Revolution, a transcendental event that in every aspect exceeded the importance of the Cuban question. Second, Welles was favored by the physical and political absence of one of his detractors, Secretary of State Cordell Hull, who at the time was traveling aboard the *S.S. American Legion* en route to Montevideo and the Seventh International Conference of the American States.

Welles's ploy consisted in securing the interview for a date on which Hull could not be present and, furthermore, on a date prior to the conference in Montevideo during which the issue of nonrecognition of the Cuban government had to come up.

There is another aspect that cannot be avoided. As Welles agreed to go to Warm Springs, Georgia, a letter signed by Grau San Martín arrived for President Roosevelt at the same time. Grau asked that Roosevelt put an end "to the perturbing action of Ambassador Sumner Welles," who "repeatedly disclosed his partiality by communicating and dealing with the enemies of the Grau government" (Early Telegram, November 22, 1933, 524).[10]

The letter also announced that Grau would welcome any representative of the *Good Neighbor* policy the President might send. Evidently, Grau did not take advantage of the opportunity to define what would be a real *Good Neighbor* policy. He had gone so far as to ask for the removal of a special envoy of the President of the United States, but he would go no further. It would have to be Roosevelt who dictated what the policy meant, as we shall see right away.

Welles, in spite of everything, gained a great triumph in convincing President Roosevelt to formulate the Declaration of Warm Springs, Georgia, concerning the recognition of the government of Cuba, which, dated November 23, stated:

> During the months which have passed since the fall of the Government of President Machado, we have followed the course of events in Cuba with a most friendly concern and with a consistent desire to be of help to the Cuban people.
>
> Owing to the exceptionally close relationship which has existed between our two peoples since the founding of the Republic of Cuba and in particular because of the treaty relations which exist between our two countries, recognition by the United States of a government in Cuba affords in more than ordinary measure both material and moral support to that government.
>
> For this reason we have not believed that it would be a policy of friendship and of justice to the Cuban people as a whole to accord recognition to any provisional government in Cuba unless such government clearly possessed the support and the approval of the people of that Republic. We feel that no official action of the United States should at any time operate as an obstacle to the free and untrammeled determination by the Cuban people of their own destinies.
>
> We have been keenly desirous during all this period of showing by deed our intention of playing the part of a good neighbor to the Cuban people. We have wished to commence negotiations for a revision of the commercial convention between the two countries and for a modification the permanent treaty between the United States and Cuba. On the economic side, we have been hopeful of entering upon a discussion of such measures as might be

undertaken by common consent between the two Governments which would redound to the benefit of both the American and Cuban peoples. No progress along these lines can be made until there exists in Cuba a provisional government, which through the popular support which it obtains and which through the general cooperation which it enjoys, shows evidence of genuine stability.

As has already been officially stated, the Government of the United States has neither partiality for nor prejudice against any faction or individual in Cuba. It will welcome any provisional government in Cuba in which the Cuban people demonstrate their confidence . . . (Phillips Telegram, November 23, 1933, 525).

The last paragraph is nearly equivalent to saying that *they would accept whatever government did not include Grau San Martín.*

Less than four weeks passed before the United States saw it necessary to approve — to avoid being the only dissenting vote — the accords concerning the recognition between States agreed upon and written in Montevideo on December 19 by all the Latin American republics meeting in the Seventh Pan-American Conference.

Even though such accords would not arise until several weeks after the interview in Warm Springs, the effects of the declaration Roosevelt issued would continue and, as demonstrated in the subchapter dealing with the conspiracy between Welles and Colonel Batista, the muddy machinations between the Yankee diplomat and the disloyal Army Chief of Staff proceeded behind the back of the Grau government, with the DEU already dissolved and, of course, with the Embassy's abandonment of the old plan to reestablish the former officer corps in the military hierarchy.

Welles would return to Havana only for a brief stay. Roosevelt seemed to oblige Grau's request for his replacement in the personal letter from Chief of State to Chief of State. Later Jefferson Caffery, who had followed Welles in the post of Under-Secretary of State, would replace him in Havana. The two functionaries made up a duo of executors of policy that was the express responsibility of those on the highest level, that is to say, Roosevelt and Hull.

Welles had won the policy outlined in Warm Springs, Georgia, and now he had only to enlarge upon it.

When the Ambassador from Chile, don Manuel Trucco, asked for information concerning the North American attitude "if various Latin American countries decided to recognize the Grau San Martín Government before the Montevideo conference convenes" (Caffery Memo, November 25, 1933, 526), Acting Secretary of State, William Phillips, answered by sending a copy of Roosevelt's Declaration on November 23. To that the Secretary added these insidious phrases:

> I would say also that I hope the other interested governments will bear in mind that any action they take might have important consequences on the possibility of the Cubans themselves reaching an agreement for a Government, which represents and is backed by the will of the Cuban people (Phillips Memo, November 25, 1933, 526).

Naturally, that was as much as saying that there should be no recognition until the Grau government was replaced by another, arranged by the North American government and complying with the requisites demanded in the declaration of Warm Springs, Georgia.

Before determining the final balance concerning Welles's policy and his final dismissal from the North American administration under proof of his homosexuality (Gold and Gold 1986, 114), we shall review Ambassador Trucco's appeal in the name of several Latin American countries on the threshold of that self-same conference in Montevideo.

Cordell Hull, the Secretary of State, traveled to Uruguay as head of the United States mission, while Welles secured the private interview with Roosevelt and secured the Declaration of Warm Springs that did not carry Hull's approval. Hull was not even consulted.

Hull had conquered Welles on September 7, when Welles had insisted on landing the marines and the Secretary had convinced the President not to, sending him the uncompromising decision that there would be no armed intervention. Now Welles — seventy-six days later — led the President to the final position concerning recognition. It would not be extended until the current Cuban government was deposed, and the same people dislocated by the Fourth of September revolution were returned to power. What that meant, simply, was the return of "Plattism" to the commands — but without the return of the deposed officer corps, since the insurgent sergeants' corps had already turned "Plattist." Neither the former officers nor the Directorio Estudiantil were to be part of the government. This, in its simplicity, would be the new power equation.

Welles had been informed by the "democrat" Rafael Leónidas Trujillo's ambassador that several Latin American countries were planning to extend recognition before the Montevideo Conference.[11] The movement was dangerous for the United States, since it had taken on a regional character. But Welles knew that it was much easier and quicker to convince Roosevelt, of whom he was a favorite, in the privacy of his vacation weekend, without his detractor Hull present.

Hull was neither consulted nor informed of the Warm Springs Resolution on November 23, and it was rushed to the press. When, on November 25, Ambassador Trucco consulted about several simultaneous recognitions "led off" by Mexico and followed by several Central and South American countries, he was answered with the Warm Springs Declaration and the additional consideration that any differing decision could prevent the Cuban people from resolving their situation. That is, Batista would have to abandon his planned coup d'état.

The consultation occurred on the twenty-fifth, and two days later, November 27, still aboard the *S.S. American Legion*, Cordell Hull cabled to acting Secretary Phillips (the same who delivered to Trucco the copies of the document) requesting that he cable to Montevideo "the controlling facts and conditions to date against recognition of the Grau San Martín regime in Cuba" (Hull Cable 13, November 27, 1933, 527). Hull wanted to have room to maneuver at the Pan-American meeting. No reply is recorded. All of that is highly revealing since, even though it seems that Hull did not receive a copy of the Warm Springs declaration from the Department of State, he still learned of it through the international cables posted on the bulletin board of the ship.[12] All he could do to express his disagreement was to inquire into the reasons against the recognition that, evidently, he was supposed to "negotiate" in Montevideo. That did not, of course, prevent Hull from voting there in favor of the "Convention on Rights and Duties of States," which tacitly extinguished the Platt Amendment, even though Welles and Caffery "continued doing their own thing," as we shall also see.

Welles managed to prevent Hull from negotiating Cuba's recognition in Montevideo — "my hands are tied," he had said to Héctor David Castro, chief of the Salvadoran Mission at the meeting[13] — but the maneuver consolidated the enmity between the two, and Welles still continued to ascend the ladder, eventually becoming the number two man in the Department of State through direct promotions by Roosevelt, although his payback arrived several years later.

On an official train trip, accompanying President Roosevelt himself, the Secret Service reported to the FBI that Welles had "propositioned a number of the train crew to have immoral relations" (*U.S. News and World Report,* January 19, 1983, 46). Even though the report did not get to Roosevelt immediately, wives of senators, discovering the fact, made sure it did get to him. He requested information from J. Edgar Hoover, director of the FBI. The Federal Bureau of Investigations only reported the inquiry to Welles, who had said that "he 'had been drinking rather heavily' and remembered nothing of the trip, except that he had become sick."

Hoover denied Hull a copy of the report, telling him to ask the White House. However, when Senator Owen Brewster, Republican from Maine, informed him that he should ask the Senate to order an investigation and report the results to him, the rumor began to reach the ears of the press. Hoover told Roosevelt's aides that a Los Angeles police officer and three persons from the movie industry in Hollywood had been overheard talking about the incident. Welles was dismissed. He was allowed, for diplomatic reasons, to resign because of his wife's illness.[14] Thus ended the diplomatic career of the most influential man in Cuba in his — until then — most dramatic moments.

Later we will see similar affinities in another strong North American in Cuba, Jefferson Caffery. He and Welles together constructed the Cuban policy and reciprocally aided one another in their plots against Cuba.

REVOLUTIONARY LEGISLATION: OCTOBER AND NOVEMBER 1933

The two counterrevolutionary events, the Hotel Nacional and the failed November 8 coup attempt, had serious military and political impact. The assassinations of prisoners from the Hotel certainly caused public outrage. Ambassador Welles attributed the military victories exclusively to Batista, while denying what was obvious even to President Roosevelt, the consolidation of the revolutionary civilian government in power. Welles continued to enforce his personal policy of nonrecognition, even though his own president had been inclined to extend that critical recognition. In spite of the military and political dramas playing out, the revolutionary government continued promulgating its progressive legislation through October and November.

The section of Labor was elevated to the level of department. It had originally been included in the Department of Agriculture, Industry, and Commerce, which was later renamed Agriculture, Commerce, and Labor. Machado, in an opportunistic move on May 1, 1933, his last Labor Day in office, had elevated the section to "Labor Division" in the twilight days of his regime.

Doctor Angel Alberto Giraudy was designated to head the new Department. He, Antonio Guiteras, and Carlos Hevia were the trio from which flowed the revolutionary legislative cornucopia for one hundred twenty-six days.

Giraudy had been appointed earlier as a Supreme Court judge for his brilliant record as municipal judge in Cienfuegos for many years. After the dictatorship fell, he was selected by all the political forces opposing the Machado regime to serve as mayor of that same city. As Secretary of Labor for the revolutionary regime, he produced a large portion of the revolutionary government's legislation. As a postscript to his short but bountiful revolutionary efforts, he finished his term within the revolutionary regime by leading the Cuban delegation to the Seventh International Conference of American States in Montevideo, in which the practical application of the Platt Amendment was abolished.

A few days after the Department of Labor was established, the suppression of the provincial tax requiring a seal of guarantee on every bale of tobacco produced in the province of Pinar del Río was enacted by decree on October 27.

In the first days of November, on the fourth, to be exact, the Revolution ratified what had previously been known as the Arteaga Act, which prohibited payment of salaries and wages with tokens or vouchers. This measure represented a fundamental reformation, just before the cane-cutting season, since the North American sugar plants were accustomed to paying with vouchers valid only in the commercial establishments of their own operations. Of course, there had been no way to intervene in the customary price fixing to prevent the double extortion represented by payment in vouchers of arbitrarily fixed prices in the only shops where — I repeat — the vouchers could be used.

Three days later, on the seventh, the law regulating the closing hours of drugstores and pharmacies, in effect since 1921, was modified. But the most important legislation on this date was the law of obligatory syndication. Its first article stated:

All workers or employers of the same profession, trade, or specialty, or of similar or related professions, trades, or specialties, within the same or within various firms or companies, may freely associate for the defense of their common interests, *without any previous need of authorization whatsoever* [emphasis added].

The law also granted the unions thus formed automatic juridical status, also without requiring prior authorization. The rights and privileges granted by this law were extended to the nonunion workers too, for "it is prohibited to force independent workers to join a union."

The articles regulated procedures for strikes, including those in support of other legitimate strikes decreed by other unions, but it required that demands be submitted and that an attempt be made to obtain mediation from the office in the Department of Labor in which the unions were registered. This office was required to attempt an immediate reconciliation with the employers or their representatives, appointing for that purpose an arbitration panel that would include the labor delegate, a representative of the employers, and a delegate from the Department of Labor.

The communists objected that Spaniards, Haitians, and Jamaicans were excluded from invoking the law by its eighth article. In order to be a member of a union's board, the following requisites were unwaivable: a) Cuban citizenship, b) legal age, c) the ability to read and write, d) no previous convictions for crimes or offenses, and e) technical capacity in the union's specialty of work. Were these five conditions exceptionally restrictive? At least the most fair judge of Cienfuegos, former magistrate of the Supreme Court of Justice of the Revolution and the Secretary of Labor of the Republic, Doctor Angel Alberto Giraudy, did not think so.

Law of Nationalization of Labor: Absorbed by the immediate pressing demands of the revolutionary struggle, the Directorio Estudiantil had not had the opportunity to acquire all the technical information necessary to deal adequately with all the various alternatives it would have to face if it were indeed to assume power. So the DEU had not taken into account, neither had it detected along the revolutionary process, the undercurrent of national demand for greater opportunities in the labor field for the native Cuban, particularly in the face of an economic recession comparable to the one the country had experienced during the years 1896-1897.

It made sense, within the grand unifying policy the Liberation Army and the first presidents would establish, that workers and professionals not be persecuted or displaced, not even those Spaniards who had been "enemies" of Cuban independence. This policy allowing open immigration was maintained by both the military governors from the United States and by the first presidents of the Cuban Republic. Immigration from Spain to Cuba continued at the same pace as before under the colonial regime, eventually creating extreme economic hardships on the island. The situation finally erupted in a general labor strike in 1902, about which Portell Vilá wrote:

> Significantly the conflict broke out among the cigar makers, workers in an industry that by then was already in the hands of one of the best organized trusts in the United States, the tobacco trust, whose expansionistic designs had the support of the most conservative among the Spanish elements then. They had control of that industry before and now they preferred to bow to the North American capitalists. The cunning of the *agents provocateurs* showed in their picking a real conflict to carry out their disrupting objectives. For the Cuban cigar-makers had always been the most patriotic and the most enlightened of all workers on the Island, and they were protesting that their opportunities were being given to Spaniards just arriving on the island (Portell Vilá, 1969, 348).

Between June 1902 and June 1904 Cuba had received 33,392 immigrants of whom 26,000 were Spaniards, while from July to November 1905 the number of new immigrants added to the Cuban population had reached 22,324 persons. The great majority (20,468) were Spaniards. Nevertheless, the 20,468 Spaniards and the 2,939 North Americans that had been added to the Cuban population — that still had not reached two million in 1906 — had been incorporated forever into the Cuban people. They had also cooperated to increase the prosperity of the country, which in turn attracted new immigrants.

After the initial extraordinary economic progress in Cuba until 1925 came the subsequent decline in the national budget to forty million pesos. Consequently, with the explosion of the revolutionary process, there arose as well struggles by private employees, since public employees were in the domain of the political machinery supporting the regime. Immediately after the fall of the Céspedes government, distinct labor movements arose in Cuba demanding that labor be nationalized. These movements differed among themselves in terms of the percentages of nationalized labor they demanded to be reserved exclusively for Cuban citizens, ranging from 50 to 100 percent. Grau San Martín, of direct Spanish descent, felt no sympathy for any of the measures; he himself had directly experienced the pressure of the different groups that had mobilized toward the Palace in demand of labor nationalization. The November 8 counterrevolutionary insurrection finally prompted him to take action on this issue. When the two rebel aircraft flew over the Palace, Grau San Martín himself had been up on the rooftop of the presidential home, along with several members of the Directorio, including Eddy Chibás and myself, directing the operation and movement of the antiaircraft weapons and personally giving the order to fire as one of the planes approached, which of course had to detour at greatest velocity.

Later, back down on the second floor, he said as he went toward his own study, "And now, perhaps, I 'push' the laws of nationalization of labor. . ." And he signed the most benevolent of the prepared decrees: Number 2583, known as the Law of Nationalization of Labor or the Law of Fifty Percent, whose text, published in the *Official Gazette* that same day, is reproduced here from articles one through five:

I RESOLVE

To issue the following

PROVISIONAL LAW OF NATIONALIZATION OF LABOR

ARTICLE I: *All juridical or natural persons established with the character of Employers in the National Territory,* [emphasis added] in the exploitation of agricultural, industrial, or mercantile enterprises, *are compulsorily required to hire in their respective line of trade at least 50 percent of native Cuban workers or employees and dedicate to their salary compensation at least 50 percent of the total amount of their entire payroll* [emphasis added]. Both proportional estimates are to be in operation, if they not yet are, within one month after the publication of this Law in the *Official Gazette* of the Republic.

ARTICLE II: In accordance with this Law, exceptions shall only be made in the computation of the employees and workers of an employer, the representatives or agents of the same and the technical charges, when there may be a lack of native Cubans with academic ability to fill those positions.

ARTICLE III: *Positions of workers or employees that vacate or are created from now on,* [emphasis added] in all agricultural, industrial, or mercantile enterprises established in the Republic are to be compulsorily filled by the respective Employers with native Cuban personnel.

ARTICLE IV: *Layoffs or cutbacks* of personnel *decided from now on,* [emphasis added] for economic or other reasons, in all agricultural, industrial, or mercantile enterprises established in the Republic *are to be effected on foreign personnel while there are such* [emphasis added].

ARTICLE V: *Those Employers who at the promulgation of this Law are employing native Cuban personnel* in a proportion higher than that required by same *shall maintain such proportion and increase it in the future,* [emphasis added] according to what is prescribed in the two preceding articles.

It is obvious that, in the cases of layoffs or cutbacks, the spirit of the law went beyond the "50-percent" formula, which was only the required minimum. Even though the decree did not state it expressly, it implicitly established priority for native Cubans in each of these circumstances. Even though it was not specifically clarified, the law equally affected Spaniards, Haitians, Jamaicans, Chinese, Hebrews, and other foreigners, even though because of the existing proportions, the number of those affected because of the quotas ended up being quite small.

The law had the support of hundreds of thousands of workers and sympathizers who for one or another reason were unemployed, but it also provoked the active opposition of the Communist Party and the ABC. The latter group took advantage of the opportunity to increase its ranks with thousands of Spanish commercialists who had begun to drift away from the ABC during the Mediation process. With their return, the ABC's interior political composition was notably modified. Nevertheless, the measure produced such positive political effects that later, when Grau San Martín founded the Cuban Revolutionary Party, student leaders Prío, Varona, and de León used the campaign slogan

"Cuba for the Cubans," which helped them tremendously in the elections of 1944.

On the other hand, the belligerence that arose because of the law was diminishing and the admirable relation that existed between Cubans and Spaniards during the entire republican process still continued a quarter of a century later.

The decree in question was signed by President Grau and Secretary of Labor Giraudy. Its contents complemented, in terms of the enormous unemployment problem that Cuba faced at the time, Decree 2232 of October 18, 1933, published in the *Official Gazette* on the nineteenth, signed by Grau and Secretary of the Interior Guiteras, which "authorize[d] the forced repatriation of foreigners, resident in the republic, that find themselves without work, and deprived of any type of resources."

The two decrees, consequently, led to Decree 133 in 1934 creating the Aliens Registration Office, something that had never existed in thirty-nine years of the Republic. Signed by Grau and Guiteras, this decree permitted an elementary statistical census that could be used later for sociological study.

Another decree was dictated on November 12 declaring unattachable and not subject to judicial retention the wages and salaries of employees and workers of the public service companies; a few days later, on the fifteenth, Decree 2686 was issued, whereby first class postage was reduced to two centavos per ounce or fraction thereof. These decrees, even though of secondary importance, both demonstrated a totally new trend in the official policy.

On that same day, the fifteenth, Decree 2687 was emitted, concerning *work-related accidents*. The law prohibited that any worker, who until the maximum work-day decree used to work ten or twelve hours a day and earned an average of thirty or forty centavos daily, remain without protection in case of accidents occurring in the course of his duties. Only extremely weak protections had previously been provided under the law instated on June 12, 1916.

The new law stated, "the employer is responsible for the accidents which occur to their [sic] workers because of and during the course of the work they perform."

Under the protection of this legislation, compensations were to be provided during recuperation of the injured party, up to 50 percent of the worker's salary at the time of injury. The indemnification for incapacitation followed another scale that started at 66 percent for total incapacity down to other, lower levels for varying degrees of partial incapacity. Additionally, provisions were made for benefits to the widows of injured workers in case of death. This decree was also Secretary of Labor Angel Alberto Giraudy's product. Of course, the decree was opposed by the Joint Committee of Economic Corporations in a public protest on December 27, 1933.

Legislation against Usury: The years 1932-1933 were considered by the *Foreign Policy Association,* in its study in 1935, comparable in their economic drama only to those immediately after the general concentration (1896-1897) of the populace, during which the property owners had nothing with which to pay their taxes nor the renters to pay their rents. It is easy to understand why pawnbrokers — who accepted as collateral a token or jewel of value for a loan for a determined amount of interest and for a fixed period of time — could flourish. This system developed a multitude of different types of loans, originating more through necessity than through legislative regulations, and eventually lenders took advantage of the most difficult economic situation existent to charge the highest interests possible.

So, on November 16, also under the signature of President Grau San Martín and the Secretary of Labor, Angel Alberto Giraudy, a decree declared null and void all interests in excess of 12 percent per annum in monetary loan contracts already executed or that in the future might be agreed upon and all pacts in said contracts that imposed monetary penalties on the debtor for his tardiness or obligated him to pay judicial costs and expenses.

The decree demanded a different approach to payments in excess of the interest in an interesting text which said, "In all the cases in which the lender may have received the amount of the capital lent and the interests over the same up to a maximum of 12 percent per annum, he shall be obligated to grant a letter of payment to the borrower, freeing him of all obligations derived from the contract." Thousands of debtors who had already paid — who through monthly and annual payments had paid much more than the total of their loans — were freed.

Also declared null and void were all the taxes decreed and embargoes unjustly applied to salaries and pensions of workers in procedures set forth for the collection of loans wherein the embargoes or retentions exceeded 10 percent of the affected pension, salary, or remuneration. It was prohibited in the future to place embargoes on the pensions of workers or employees. Furthermore, "the salaries of workers or employees shall not be the object of embargoes or judicial retention except in a one-tenth part of their amount."

Considering the serious economic situation at the time, late 1933, it was this decree, no doubt, which benefited the greatest number of people in the middle and lower classes.

Among the legislative flow during the month of November, Decree 2788, issued on November 21, *prohibited the exportation of legal tender as well as gold in bars, ingots, or any other form,* and conditions were fixed by which other legal tender in the form of metals, coins, or paper money could be exported.

And to finish off the legislation of the month, on the twenty-second of November, Decree 2809 stated that *within the armed forces the services of orderly or assistant to officers was abolished.* These services were rendered by low-ranking soldiers who acted as messengers, valets, chauffeurs, or whatever else might be ordered by the officer. It appeared among the first list of demands drawn up in the meetings of the rank-and-file soldiers in the early morning of the Fourth of September.

NOTES

1. This account appears in a personal letter to the author.

2. The original front page of the *Alma Mater*, from November 7, 1933, containing these five letters, is in the author's possession. See the photocopy of said document in this chapter.

3. Juan Rubio Padilla and Carlos Prío Socarrás were designated by the DEU, since even though they lacked diplomatic experience, they carried the student and revolutionary message that would inspire the Cuban delegation. Their presence in Montevideo, furthermore, would stimulate support from student movements in Latin America. The Seventh Panamerican Conference was very important because it would have to reopen the debate initiated in the Conference of 1928 concerning the principle of nonintervention. It was hoped that a pronouncement against foreign interference would carry with it the abolition of the Platt Amendment, whose stipulations, in contractual form, were contained in the Permanent Treaty of 1903 between the United States and Cuba.

4. *Cachanchán* or *cachanchá* literally means auxiliary, aide, or assistant of inferior status, usually servile and fawning. The word is almost always used in a pejorative sense.

5. This alludes to the events that culminated in Mendieta taking over as president of the Republic, or rather, Grau's resignation, the designation of Hevia to replace him, and his resignation after thirty-six hours in office, and the meeting of the representatives of the political sectors that proclaimed Mendieta president in the Palace on January 18, 1934.

6. Batista consolidated his position as Army Chief of Staff, first, thanks to Grau's treason against the Directorio's agreed-upon plan to deal with Batista, and, second, for the failure of the November 8 counterrevolutionary coup. Grau's reconfirmation of Batista, as shall be seen, simply reinforced his thirst for power.

7. Perhaps, the reason for Grau's conduct was that he was not completely uninvolved in the plot to overthrow his own regime. Ambassador Welles's messages to Washington indicate that Grau had tried to cling to power by submitting to the opposition sectors and the American ambassador before the elimination of the Directorio.

8. The San Ambrosio barracks was constructed during the Spanish domination as a military hospital. After Cuba achieved independence from Spain, San Ambrosio became the logistics center of the army.

9. The reference is to former Colonel Francisco Carrillo Bujeda, a relative of the author. Colonel Carrillo never joined the rebellion and, therefore, could not have led it.

10. The letter was sent by Grau San Martín, but President Roosevelt's secretary (Early) and William Phillips, Interim Secretary of State in Hull's absence in Montevideo, tried to see that the president did not receive it. See the messages between Early and Phillips on November 22, 1933, *Foreign Relations*, Vol. V, 524.

11. This information was provided personally to the author by Héctor David Castro, chief of the Salvadoran delegation to the Conference of Montevideo.

12. Since Juan A. Rubio Padilla traveled to Montevideo in the same boat as Hull, he also found out on board.

13. This information was provided personally to the author by the chief of the Salvadoran delegation.

14. The information over the drunken incident on the train can be read in its entirety in "The Secret Files of J. Edgar Hoover," *U.S. News and World Report*, December 19, 1983, 46-7.

Chapter 4

THE REVOLUTIONARY GOVERNMENT II: DECEMBER 1933 AND JANUARY 1934

MONTEVIDEO: TRIUMPH OF THE REVOLUTION, END OF THE PLATT AMENDMENT

The Directorio Estudiantil Universitario had declared, in the June 1933 document repudiating the North American Mediation,

> The Student movement endeavors to strengthen all the positive forces of moral order that operate in our society and one of those positive forces — perhaps the principal one — is the consciousness of being a free and sovereign people. This is absolutely necessary in order for a free social group to be able to maintain its individuality in the concert of nations, nurturing and realizing its collective goal and thereby effectively fulfilling its mission among those other peoples of the earth. If we do not rise up today and rescue the maltreated consciousness of national identity, we will have neither the strength nor the dignity to give to our country economic and political independence, nor ever again will we have the right to feel ourselves and call ourselves a free people. When a people does not consider itself free, it does not consider itself responsible; and an irresponsible people is incapable of carrying out any historic role and is liable to forever fall into the sphere of action of more powerful peoples.

And in its Manifesto-Program published August 22, 1933, the *1930 DEU* listed among the most important functions of the revolution-

ary government (to be installed by the Directorio), the convening of
a Constituent Assembly. That Assembly would be required to

> declare null and void the Platt Amendment and charge the
> Executive Commission with the arrangement of a Treaty of
> Friendship and Cooperation based on respect for Cuban
> sovereignty.

On the economic front, the document added,

> the Provisional Government shall denounce the Commer-
> cial Treaty in effect with the United States, proposing in its
> place a convention based on equality.

In terms of international policy, the document further stated that
Cuba

> shall intensify economic relations with Canada and the
> other countries of the Americas and seek a greater identi-
> fication on moral and cultural grounds with the Hispanic-
> American countries[1] (Padrón Larrazábal 1975, 157-72).

Since these pronouncements, made between June and August
1933, the Directorio had traveled a considerable historic route. It had
challenged the Machado government and the American mediation; it
had confronted the factions that had accepted the American meddling
conducted by Ambassador Sumner Welles; it had, likewise, opposed
the resulting Céspedes government and had succeeded in overthrowing it; it had shared responsibility for the Sergeants' Movement and
converted it from a mere mutiny for class demands into a genuine
revolutionary enterprise; and since the 4th of September until its own
dissolution two months later, it had confronted the American power
trying to undermine the Grau San Martín government first with threats
of marine landings and then with the nonrecognition policy.

The Directorio Estudiantil Universitario had disbanded, but its
views and ideas continued to live. They began to materialize in the
Seventh International Conference of American States in Montevideo,
Uruguay, in December 1933.

During that international event, Cuba would have the opportunity
to redeem the whole historic process by leading the conference to
adopt significant accords based on three specific ideological points in
the 1930 DEU's program. Those three points were as follows:

1. The proclamation of the principles of nonintervention and free determination of the people.
2. The policy on recognition of governments.
3. The proclamation of equal rights for women, with the logical consequence of granting them the right to vote.

Yet, the question of nonrecognition as an international policy tool had not been considered a specific point because the Directorio at the time lacked the experience it acquired during the two months it coexisted with the government it had put in power. At the time of its dissolution, the Directorio had said,

> . . . vested interests that would be inevitably hurt by the revolution, the activities of Cuban traitors who put themselves at the service of the big interests of foreign powers and renounce their own judgment before their tutors — from whose influence they could not free themselves — have been determining factors in the fulfillment of the program as a whole (*Diario de la Marina,* November 5, 1933).

A foreign power that had reconciled itself in turn with the traditional politicians and with representatives of the nonrevolutionary anti-Machado movement, that had been able to foster a state of turmoil and create a propitious environment for conspiracies under its protection, that directed all its operations through a formerly accredited ambassador to Cuba, now a mere representative with no business there, since his country refused to recognize the revolutionary government had driven the Cuban delegation to raise the issue of recognition for consideration by the Pan-American Conference in Montevideo.

The Cuban delegation boasted several distinguished members. Doctor Angel Alberto Giraudy, secretary of labor, had already distinguished himself with his legislation on social justice. Doctor Herminio Portell Vilá, professor of history in the School of Humanities at the University of Havana specializing in Cuban relations with the United States and Spain, had authored a four-volume work on the United States policy to control Cuba. Alfredo E. Nogueira y Herrera, an engineer, had been an active member of the ABC and later the OCRR, from which he separated when this organization joined the Mediation. Nogueira had always maintained close ties with the Directorio, sharing in many of its subversive activities.

Completing the delegation were two members of the 1930 DEU, Juan Antonio Rubio Padilla and Carlos Prío Socarrás, who in addition to acting as secretaries of the delegation, were, in fact, representing the combative spirit of the already dissolved Directorio Estudiantil Universitario.

On the day it opened, Monday, December 4, 1933, the conference named the Committee of Initiatives and proceeded to hold its first session. The Argentine Minister of Foreign Affairs, Carlos Saavedra Lamas, asked the president of the Cuban delegation who, as previous host to the conference held in Havana, was to give the opening speech — to confine himself to speaking in customary terms in tune with the preliminary character of that meeting in which were represented *the main Latin American powers*. An indignant Giraudy reacted vigorously to this insinuation. He answered:

> Cuba does not bow to powers in this or in the other hemisphere. No countries exert more influence on us for being stronger; in this conference, all the states share equally in rights and obligations, and what Cuba wants to avoid is for the United States to do to other countries what would be just as intolerable if done or intended by any other American republic (Portell Vilá 1934, 9).

And in the course of his opening speech, Giraudy said, among other things:

> We represent a government formed by the free will of the people of Cuba, and through the initial efforts of the students, professors, and workers who waged a cruel and tragic strife against tyranny, and who, having beheaded the monster, aspire to reconstruct the national life upon the basis of its most complete sovereignty and such political, economic, and social organization as fits the present historic moment and the distinct characteristics of the Cuban people (Portell Vilá, 1934, 57-58).

Later, in reference to singularities of that historic moment, he said that it was a time

> . . . in which the hypocrisies, the two-facedness, and the trickeries miscalled diplomacy must disappear.

He paid respects to the governments of Uruguay, Peru, Panama, Mexico, and Spain, the only countries that had recognized the revolutionary government, and said,

> . . . recognition should be accorded a government whenever it fulfills the conditions of effective authority and probable stability, its dictates are obeyed by the people, and especially in what concerns its capacity to fulfill international obligations and to contract new ones, respecting the rights established by common law.

As an indication of the position Cuba would adopt within the Committee on Rights and Duties of States, Giraudy suggested as a basis for the declaration to proceed from that committee the plan drafted by Peruvian Professor Martúa and presented to the American Institute of International Law. In one section of his plan, he proposed:

> The political existence of the State is independent of recognition. Recognition of the State is simply declarative and it is irrevocable. *International relations are alien to political forms, to systems of economic and social organization, and to the transformations of the governments* [emphasis added]. All possible modification of international relations when changes of government occur can only be determined by the inability of representatives of the State to prove their capacity to sustain their juridical relations in the international community (Portell 1934, 59).

But Giraudy's most important statement was this:

> That people, the Cuban people, wants to be free, independent, and sovereign, and it expects and demands to be respected in that, its free determination. Even though it recognizes, as General Leonard Wood said in a memorable letter addressed to former President Theodore Roosevelt, dated in Havana October 28, 1901, that *"Cuba is a very desirable acquisition and is worth as much as two of our Southern States and probably as any three of them, if we exempt Texas,"* [emphasis added] the people of Cuba want to be left at peace in their own living space, listening to the singing birds in the forest, the murmur of their rivers, the sad songs of the peasants; contemplating their perpetually blue skies, beautiful as the smile of a woman, the nights clear and

warm, busy in the sweet endeavor of creating a new world
for a home to the future generations (Portell 1934, 60).

Giraudy closed his speech on the cordial and friendly note of inter-
American spirit, saying that he was speaking

> . . . as the representative of a people that in its pursuit of
> liberty had the cooperation of generous, heroic men from
> all corners of the Americas, men who shed their blood for
> the Cuban ideal. Máximo Gómez, the Generalísimo of our
> Independence Army, was a Dominican; a Colombian,
> Avelino Rosas, was one of our most gallant soldiers; José
> Miguel Barreto was born in the motherland of Bolívar;
> Leoncio Prado and his brothers were from Peru; and at the
> decisive juncture our liberators fought shoulder to shoulder
> in San Juan and El Caney with American soldiers against
> Spain (Portell 1934, 61-62).

With that spirit of aggressiveness, but at the same time of
understanding, the Cuban delegate on the Committee on Rights and
Duties of States, Herminio Portell Vilá, met with the other members,
delegates from Brazil, Colombia, Ecuador, El Salvador, Haiti, and Peru.
At the outset, it became clear that all the members were of one mind
in one respect: all were against intervention. That attitude was
maintained throughout all the sessions until the end, on December 14,
when the declaration was completed and signed. All along, Portell Vilá
had been cautious to avoid any possibility of controversy that might
impede unanimity in the final vote. In addition to the seven member
countries of the committee, he expected the votes of Argentina,
Mexico, Nicaragua, and Panama as well, providing the necessary
majority for approval of the motion.

A review of the articles of the Convention on Rights and Duties
of States,[2] signed in Montevideo on December 26, 1933, shows
resounding victories of the policies maintained by Cuba (Portell 1934,
73-75). The first article states,

> The state, as a person of international law should possess
> the following qualifications: a) a permanent population; b)
> a defined territory; c) government; and d) capacity to enter
> into relations with the other states.

The essence of this article was expanded in Article Three, which said,

> The political existence of the state is independent of recognition by the other states. Even before recognition, the state has the right to defend its integrity and independence, to provide for its conservation and prosperity, and consequently to organize itself as it sees fit, to legislate upon its interests, administer its services, and to define the jurisdiction and competence of its courts.

> The exercise of these rights has no other limitation than the exercise of the rights of other states according to international law.

In light of this doctrine, the first North American intervention and its subsequent actions imposing limitations to Cuban sovereignty for the benefit of the United States were illegitimate acts of force against a small and weak people. Cuba should have been party to the Treaty of Paris or special pacts with Spain and the United States. Instead, in the strange arrangement between Spain and the United States, Cuba was excluded from the negotiation table; Cuba was not even consulted extra-officially on the fundamental points of her historic destiny.

Article Two of the Montevideo convention contained only a declaration that "the federal state constitutes a sole person in the eyes of international law," but Articles Four and Five went a little deeper into the subject of sovereignty. Article Four stated:

> States are juridically equal, enjoy the same rights, and have equal capacity in their exercise. The rights of each one do not depend upon the power which it possesses to assure its exercise, but upon the simple fact of its existence as a person under international law.

Article Five stated:

> The fundamental rights of states are not susceptible of being affected in any manner whatsoever.

Articles Six and Seven discuss recognition. Article Six stated:

> The recognition of a state merely signifies that the state which recognizes it accepts the personality of the other with all the rights and duties determined by international law. Recognition is unconditional and irrevocable.

Article Seven declared:

> The recognition of a state may be express or tacit. The latter results from any act which implies the intention of recognizing the new state.

But of all the articles of the convention, the most transcendent regarding Cuban destiny was Article Eight, which stated:

> *No state has the right to intervene in the internal or external affairs of another* [emphasis added].

This is precisely the article that constituted the juridical basis for the destruction of the Platt Amendment imposed on Cuba; this article determined the later annulment of the Amendment, in 1934, under another Cuban government imposed by the United States. Nevertheless, that annulment originated directly from the events of the Montevideo conference.

Article Nine dealt with the jurisdiction of states within their territories upon their populations, both nationals and foreigners, providing equal protection to both classes, so that neither national authorities nor foreigners could demand different or more extensive rights than those of the nationals.

Article Ten addressed itself to the conservation of peace.

Article Eleven, the last, stated:

> The contracting states definitely establish as the rule of their conduct the precise obligation not to recognize territorial acquisitions or special advantages which have been obtained by force whether this consists in the employment of arms, in threatening diplomatic representations, or in any other effective coercive measure. The territory of a state is inviolable and may not be the object of military occupation nor of other measures of force imposed by another state directly or indirectly or for any motive whatever, even temporarily.

Conflicts over this article erupted between Colombia and Peru, specifically in the historic litigation over the territory of Leticia. This regional discord caused the Brazilian and Peruvian delegations to refuse to approve this article. The United States took advantage of this impasse to abstain from the vote as well.

Despite reservations by Colombia and Peru, however, the essence of the article was applicable to Cuba, especially in terms of her early period of independence when the Platt Amendment was imposed on the newborn republic. Part of that imposition was the permanent American naval occupation of Caimanera base in Guantánamo. The permanent presence of North American troops in that portion of Cuban territory was not the result of the free determination of the people and the government of Cuba. Rather, it resulted from effective diplomatic coercion exerted first on the Constituent Convention of 1901 and later on the government of Tomás Estrada Palma, Cuba's first president. The spirit and terms of Article Eleven were fully applicable to this concrete case, with international juridical validity imposed by its approval by eighteen of the twenty-one nations then comprising the Pan-American community.

Since the ten basic articles relevant to Cuba had been unanimously approved by the conference, the next step was to submit the principle of nonintervention for consideration by the plenary session of the Assembly. Secretary of State Cordell Hull had only been able to follow the developments in the subcommittee meetings in a partial and sporadic way; the United States was not included in that committee. Yet, from what he was able to discern, he concluded that Cuba would achieve an even more resounding success in the plenary session, and with that in mind, he decided to try to have a talk with the Cuban delegate to the subcommittee. Hull contacted Portell Vilá the day before the full accords were to be presented to the full assembly.

Ernest Gruening, a member of the American delegation, approached Portell Vilá on Hull's behalf to arrange the meeting. Gruening was a liberal-minded intellectual with a great sense of justice who, from the pages of his weekly *The Nation*, had bitterly attacked the disrupting policies of Welles in Cuba.

Hull opened his conversation with Portell Vilá by telling him of his participation in the Spanish-American War as captain of an infantry regiment from Tennessee. He had been detached in Trinidad and Sancti Spiritus, and he mentioned that in the latter he had met the old and prestigious Iznaga family. Hull also recalled the hardships and difficulties the Cuban people had suffered at the end of War of Independence. He would never forget, Hull said, the misery of the poor Cuban peasant population, the famine, the diseases, the nakedness of the children, all victims of the concentration policy ordered by Spanish Captain General Valeriano Weyler.

Portell Vilá said he was very pleased to hear Mr. Hull speak in such sympathetic terms about Cuba. He pointed out that what Mr. Hull had witnessed in 1899 bore striking resemblance to the current situation of the Cuban people in 1933. Now as then, Portell Vilá said, the Cuban people longed to live and prosper and govern themselves.

Hull then said that "within ten years Cuba will be again on her feet and enjoying prosperity," to which Portell Vilá replied that ten years was too long a term and that if the United States would deal with Cuba in a spirit of justice, two years would be enough for the country to recover. The Cuban delegate stressed the point: *"If the United States were just, our problems would be minimal and superable."*

Promptly, Portell Vilá went on to address the mediatory process prior to Machado's overthrow and pointed out how Ambassador Welles had utilized that process to impose upon the country a regime that, much like Céspedes himself, lacked popularity, was odious to the public, and was indebted only to privileged interests. Then he went on to analyze the intervention utilizing the nonrecognition of the Grau San Martín government as a weapon. Portell stated that behind the nonrecognition was, along with Mr. Welles's insulted pride, the alarm of the vested interests, probably foreign, in face of the possible loss of their advantageous conditions.

Hull preferred not to mention the past but to take advantage of the future that "has an opportunity in store for us now that Mr. Welles has left his post in Havana." He said he was hoping for the possibility of carrying forward President Roosevelt's plans "for the complete liberation and rehabilitation of Cuba."

In his opinion, premature criticisms could hinder those plans. He said that the new ambassador, Jefferson Caffery, would conduct a preliminary investigation, after which everything would be handily taken care of. Hull announced further that the Platt Amendment would no doubt be abrogated and the Reciprocity Treaty modified. There would also be resolutions even for the question of the coal stations (sites on Cuban shores where the American fleet anchored and refueled), and before long Cuba could be at ease, respected, free, and prosperous, without any need for scandals.

Portell Vilá replied that despite the very pleasing sketch Mr. Hull presented, he feared that Mr. Caffery's investigation would in itself amount to intervention and the imposition of further conditions for U.S. recognition of the Cuban government. He added:

> What the United States should really do is recognize and then deal, not investigate in order to recognize.

And then he made abundantly clear that

> The opportunity I have, according to my instructions, to state precisely on behalf of Cuba a stand against the legitimacy of the Platt Amendment and the Permanent Treaty, I will not mortgage for any kind of promises.

The meeting ended with Portell Vilá voicing his hope that the attitude of the United States would be no less than adherence to and respect for the resolution on *nonintervention* that was to be approved by the assembly, and Secretary Hull expressing his belief that the new ambassador to Cuba, Jefferson Caffery, would achieve great success in his mission (Portell 1934, 24-29).

The session of the Committee on International Law of the Seventh Pan-American Conference was held on December 19, 1933. The public galleries of the old Uruguayan Senate were packed full. The news that they were going to discuss the subject of intervention had attracted enormous public interest. Uruguayan university students, responding to DEU leaders Rubio Padilla and Prío Socarrás, were among the most excited spectators. U.S. Secretary of State Cordell Hull was presiding over his country's delegation for the first time during the conference. Alfonso López, Colombia's president-elect and head of the Colombian delegation, along with Saavedra Lamas, Puig Cassauranc, and Cuchaga Tocornal, ministers of foreign affairs respectively of Argentina, Mexico, and Chile, decided to take part personally in the debate instead of relying on secondary delegates.

Immediately after the session opened, Tulio Cesteros, head of the Dominican Republic delegation, read an opinion on behalf of his country condemning intervention. This precipitated debate on the latent theme of the meeting. Héctor David Castro, rector of the University of El Salvador and head of his country's delegation, assumed the defense of the motion against intervention. He had participated in drafting the opinion and was repeatedly interrupted by the applause of delegates, journalists, and spectators in the galleries.

Cuba spoke next. Portell Vilá, who had, in fact, inspired the motion, rose to speak. His speech was a vibrant denunciation of both the Platt Amendment and the Permanent Treaty with Cuba on grounds of their juridical illegitimacy. It was the first time in the history of international relations that Cuba manifested herself with such independence. The other delegates witnessed a totally new Cuba presenting her case

> against the imperialist powers of the United States that imposed on us an unfair system of relations through military coercion and the basest diplomatic pressures during those terrible five years of 1898-1903 (Portell 1934, 31).

In the course of his intervention speech, Portell Vilá hinted at the possibility of disclosing some examples of chicanery on the part of persons who had intervened in the approval of the famous Joint Resolution of April 1898 by the American Congress. If put in a pressing situation, he said, he would right there reveal names of those involved and the nature of their chicaneries.

Intervention, said Portell Vilá, was the congenital vice of the Platt Amendment. This appendix to the first Cuban Constitution bore the name of its author, Senator Orville Platt. Portell Vilá related that in doing research for a work of history he had written, he had come across some papers in which Senator Platt confessed that the amendment he had proposed to the Congress in Washington *was a substitute* for the annexation of Cuba to the United States (Portell 1934, 77).

> In his closing words, Portell Vilá said that the Platt Amendment exhibits the vice of coercion; it was imposed on Cuba by the bayonets of the United States, and for that reason Cuba is now, and forever will be, opposed to the Platt Amendment (Portell 1934, 79).

The Cuban delegate was followed by the delegates of Haiti and Nicaragua, who likewise spoke in vigorous terms against intervention. The international conference thus abandoned its diplomatic character to some degree to adopt that of a popular assembly. Excited by the ovations and shouts of the audience, the delegates had joined the prevailing inflamed mood of the whole crowd.

Finally, the Mexican minister of foreign affairs, Puig Cassauranc, took the floor. He simply reiterated his country's traditional position against all forms of intervention and *recommended the recognition of the government of Grau San Martín as a demonstration of good will toward Cuba.*

The delegate from Peru followed, also speaking in favor of the motion. Then came the delegate from Ecuador, who said:

> What meaning is there in proclaiming justice and solidarity except to proclaim, precisely, that no country has a right to intervene in the affairs of another? Is there, perchance, anything more contrary to justice, Mr. President, than imposing on a nation a will that is not her own (Portell 1934, 31)?

The Secretary of State of Argentina, Carlos Saavedra Lamas, also voiced his country's position against intervention. The Colombian delegate tried to sidetrack the discussion toward the frontier conflict over Leticia but was quickly succeeded by Doctors Arosemena of Panama and Cohen of Chile, who presented their votes in favor of the anti-interventionist motion.

To avoid having the question of Leticia, which fell under the terms of Article Eleven of the Convention on Rights and Duties of States, delay the approval of the motion, a countermotion was made to vote on the first ten articles of the convention and leave Article Eleven for a separate discussion. The countermotion passed. Then the assembly proceeded to vote on the motion· amid an atmosphere of dramatic expectation. When time came for the United States to vote, the president of the American delegation, Secretary of State Cordell Hull, simply said: "Mr. President, I vote in favor of the first ten articles" (Portell 1934, 32). He later explained that the policy of the United States under President Franklin Delano Roosevelt would be different from that pursued by his predecessors in the White House. The other countries voted in favor, too, and the next day Venezuela, which had been absent, added its affirmative vote.

The principle of nonintervention was thus ratified in the hemisphere, and with it, its corollary, that *the entity of the state begins even before it is recognized,* during which time it has the right to organize itself as it sees fit. And so, all American interventions in Cuba were implicitly declared illegal.

Cuba's historic triumph, achieved in the Committee of International Law and submitted by the Committee on Rights and Duties of States, was confirmed when the articles of the convention — including Article Eleven — were approved that same day, December 19, and ratified on the twenty-second by the plenary session of the conference (Portell 1934, 29-34).

The 1930 Directorio Estudiantil Universitario had its most solemn historic commitment fulfilled.

WOMEN AND THE DIRECTORIO

The Cuban woman, who has distinguished herself for her contributions to the efforts on the road to independence, had no direct participation during the first decades of the Republic.

Women's active participation in public affairs, nevertheless, reappeared in 1930, when a university women's group joined the civic activities of the Directorio almost from the beginning. Their first public appearance occurred in October of that year, when they signed, even before the men, the historic manifesto for a total and definitive change of regime. Their votes had been decisive, showing perhaps a profound historic intuition. All through the revolutionary process, university women would be present in all its phases, including the experiences in prison.

Although a number of student manifestos of those days included the signatures of ten women, their number gradually decreased until they were only four who, having achieved the leadership level, remained fully involved in the struggle. As of this writing [1982], they are still alive, and I take great satisfaction in paying them due homage of admiration and respect. They are Sarah del Llano y Clavijo, Inéz Segura Bustamante, Clara Luz Durán y Guerrero, and Silvia Martell y Bracho. Incidentally, as noted earlier in this book, they all married other members of the Directorio.

Still at the beginnings of the anti-Machado struggle, in its February 3, 1931, manifesto, the Directorio had stated the goal of civil, political, and economic equality for men and women, something that would be recognized by the future constitution.[3]

When the end of the struggle was in sight, after all the experiences and risks shared together by men and women alike, it was elementary for the Directorio to include in its manifesto program of August 22, 1933, that *women shall be given the right of suffrage.*

It was perfectly understandable, then, since the subject was part of the agenda of the Seventh Pan-American Conference in Montevideo, that specific instructions on the issue be given to the Cuban delegation. They were to advocate and defend equal rights for women.

So, in accordance with the position of the government in Havana, in his opening speech the president of the Cuban delegation, Angel Alberto Giraudy, made a plea for the recognition of the rights of women in the political as well as the social and international fields, because woman was

> ... man's sister when it came to suffering, yet still his servant when she should be on an equal level with him (Portell Vilá 1934, 38).

Cuba's efforts on behalf of women in the conference fell short, however, when only Paraguay and Ecuador went along with the demand for equality for women.

But just a few days after the conference ended, the revolutionary government of Cuba, through Presidential Decree 13 of January 2, 1934, granted women the right to vote, to elect, and to be elected. Havana thus stood ahead of Montevideo.

The historic impact of the Directorio Estudiantil was of such magnitude that even after having dissolved, its aspirations were being fulfilled.

Legislative Depth in December 1933

As if it were occurring in different worlds, the legislation of change had not been slowed by violence, and in the middle of the aerial threats to the Presidential Palace, President Grau sat down and signed the Labor Nationalization act.

But even after the November 8 insurgent attempt had been crushed, still the government was confronted with the nonrecognition policy that Welles had obtained from President Roosevelt in his Warm Springs Declaration on November 23. Cuba, however, directly confronted the United States in Montevideo and continued its revolutionary legislation through December.

On December 1, certain precepts of the law regulating the process of administrative contention were modified. Also modified that same day was Article 230 of the Law of Municipal Taxes, giving delinquent taxpayers who had lost their properties the opportunity to recover them.

The next day, the second, legal recognition was granted to the Cuban Association of Midwives and membership therein made obligatory. On the fifth, the same recognition and obligatory membership was extended to the National Association of Nurses, an organization which included both male and female nurses.

On the fourth, Carlos Hevia began to assume a task that would culminate in several other decrees. By the end of the month, a decree created an award designed to stimulate better housing in the countryside. New houses would be built following certain guidelines: low cost, ownership or lease by Cubans, location outside the sugar plantations, and construction by Cuban materials.

On the fifth, the one-centavo-per-pound tax on rice was lifted. This decree stated specifically that the government wanted to promote the cultivation of rice in Cuba and that in order to do so, the tax would be applied only to imported grain and collected at the customs house. This also was Hevia's proposal.

Then came the boldest, perhaps, of all revolutionary measures of the Grau San Martín government. Decree 2974 of December 6, proposed by Secretary of the Interior Antonio Guiteras, overturned Military Order Number 2 of the first American intervention on January 3, 1902. This measure drastically reduced consumer costs of gas and electricity — by 45 percent for the city of Havana — and set a one peso per month minimum charge for ten kilowatts of service. A residential as well as commercial rate of ten centavos per kilowatt was fixed for all cities, and the rate of 4 centavos per kilowatt set for radio stations, newspapers, entertainment businesses, and public service enterprises.

The Cuban Electric Company was obligated to extend its services wherever needed and assume all installation costs. No deposits higher than the estimate for two months of service were permitted.

The text of the decree further included a four-month moratorium for all private consumers in arrears, with payments due divided in four equal parts to be remitted during the first fifteen days of the month. Finally, those private enterprises providing these services to the public — as was the case in some localities of the interior — were forbidden to lay off personnel or to lower their salaries, dependent upon the future incomes of such businesses.

This decree — along with a later decree complementing it — was Antonio Guiteras's greatest and most valiant coup. He became not only a national figure and a champion of popular causes but also gained recognition as such in the rest of Latin America as well, where they could not understand why electricity and telephone service in Cuba were not yet under state control. But it was also the beginning of the end for him. As an outstanding revolutionary, he had begun to stand out as well as the presumed leader of the military. He had functioned as the unofficial chief of operations of the War Navy on November 8. He could not just rise up with impunity, demanding that the United States respect the rights of Cuban gas and electricity consumers. His great gesture, now history, placed him directly in the sights of the North American ambassador. Welles would begin to push Batista to "bring down Grau . . . and Guiteras with him" (Welles Cable 500, December 7, 1933, 533-36; Welles Cable 509, December 11, 1933, 539).

On December 6, the Labor Nationalization Law was established. Furthermore, certain prison terms were reduced and the policy for pardons reorganized. Additionally, penalties were established for spreading alarm or producing public disturbances.

On the eighth, a decree was issued for the minting of twenty million pesos (then equivalent to $20 million) in national silver, the benefits thereof being earmarked for "salary increases not to exceed seventy-five pesos per month and to pay a portion of the national debt, with preference to the back salaries of public employees."

On the ninth, the Property Recorder's office was overhauled and new registration procedures were established.

On the eleventh, a six-month moratorium was granted for loans from pawnbrokers, and on the thirteenth, Colonel Manuel Despaigne, the incorruptible secretary of finances, was authorized to regulate the guarantee of silver certificates to be issued.

On December 15, the employees and workers of the Cuban Electric Company, as well as those of all other public service and land transportation enterprises, were included in the benefits of the Retirement and Pensions Law that theretofore had covered only the railroad employees and workers.

And on the same day, on the excuse of "being necessary for best guarding the coasts in order to impede smuggling," the Marine Infantry Corps was created, with an initial force of three hundred men, including officers, noncommissioned officers, and enlisted men.

Although that newly created military force would be placed "under direct orders of the Chief of Staff of the Navy," everyone realized that Guiteras's increasing influence in the marine sector of the military had been what drove the creation of the new force. Guiteras had personally carried the decree, his own creation, to Grau, thereby creating a counterweight against Batista's military power.

Of course, in desperate situations, superhuman efforts of survival — physical, political, and military — are understandable and justifiable. But to carry out by decree on the sixth the drastic reduction of the cost of electricity (an American concern) and on the fifteenth create an armed instrument for the purpose of shielding oneself against the United States and Batista, was infinite audacity, deeply rooted in *Cubanía* and revolutionary public-spiritedness, but it also contained a certain ingenuousness and an absence of a true sense of "timing," that magic harmonization of the precise lapse that must occur between the imaginative conception and the natural realization of that concept.

If the failed November 8 attempt had confirmed Batista in power, he who had reached his lowest level in the meeting in Carbó's home, from which he was rescued by Grau himself to his own and Cuba's disgrace, if Roosevelt's declaration on November 23 concerning recognition placed in Batista's hands Grau's deposal and the confirmations of all the promoted sergeants who deified Batista, if the great decree reducing the charges for electricity was the final detonator for the Chancellory in Washington to encourage Batista further to get on with the overthrow, how is it possible that Guiteras could believe that a military force of three hundred men — who still had to be selected, assigned, and trained — might counteract the concentration of real power, now ready to act upon the simple issuance of an order? Still, the energy tariffs decision was admirable.

If at first it was Guiteras, now it was Carlos Hevia, Minister of Agriculture, who would drive the revolutionary legislation. On December 19, he offered for Grau's signature Decree 3278 regulating the sugar industry. It contained two fundamental propositions: first, the idea, in part already inherent in the sugar industry, of a "regime of mediated and controlled economy," moderated though, in that "this revolutionary government favors measures that will make the general interests of the Nation prevail over the conveniences of private interest," and second, the consequent aspect of "establishing two kinds of mills in regard to the distribution of production quotas."

By that classification, the small mills, those termed "free," whose production in 1933 did not exceed sixty thousand sacks (each weighing 325 pounds), could process up to that same quantity in the 1934 harvest season, but they had the right as well to exceed that quota with cane from their own properties.

Conversely, the "quota mills," those which in 1933 would have produced more than sixty thousand sacks, could in 1934 produce that same amount, but they would "be obligated to grind twenty percent more cane from *colonos* [independent planters] than from *administration* [the sugar mill's own canes] and from *colonos* whose canes that mill should have both the right and the obligation to grind."[4]

All the big "quota" mills happened to be owned by foreign concerns, mostly North American. The administration canes they processed, as well as their commercial departments (where the workers had to pay arbitrarily fixed prices with tokens received as salary in lieu of cash), constituted the iron ring that oppressed the sugar working sector.

On December 26, the College of Sugar Agro-Chemical Technicians of Cuba was created and membership made obligatory for all such professionals.

Also on that date, posthumous promotions of two ranks were decreed for all soldiers and marines who died in the Hotel Nacional incident or as a result of the counterrevolutionary attempt of November 8.

This decree, although commendable from a humane viewpoint, came to symbolize the various historic factors that contributed to the fall of the Grau government. The alert reader can easily understand that the civilian revolutionary process — filled with fertile realizations — did not carry with it the automatic administrative implementation of its fundamental goals. Grau's ratification of Batista as commander of the army on the third of November carried with it the absolute control of military power. After Batista's triumph over the insurrection on the eighth, he became, with the approval of the United States government, master of Cuba.

So, despite all its efforts and measures benefitting the nation and the people, the civilian structure of the government was rapidly disintegrating. A number of us agreed with what Chibás said in an article we wrote together: "The real revolution, that of the great popular masses of Cuba, began to crumble under the irresponsible arrogance of the Army, administrative disorganization, demagoguery, conspiracies, palace intrigues and snares, self-seeking, and vested interests. The revolution ceased to be in the revolutionary government" (Chibás et al., February 4, 1934, 24).

And we added furthermore that "We have a power-wielding army in which gradual decomposition, progressive disappearance of the principle of authority, and resulting lack of discipline, give its members a free hand for mischief and delinquency." Of course, the military excesses had already begun and finally culminated with the murder in Camp Columbia of young student Mario Cadenas, which caused the university students to take to the streets in protest chanting, "King Kong, down with Ramón!"

Meanwhile, Sumner Welles continued to conspire, no longer in the shadows, but openly. He was now closer to President Roosevelt after having left Havana to act as undersecretary in charge of the Latin American section of the State Department. Actually, he had simply traded positions with Jefferson Caffery, who had been the undersecretary since Roosevelt had taken office. Caffery, an open homosexual, had been in El Salvador in 1932, where he sanctioned the mass-killings ordered by President Maximiliano Hernández Martínez during a serious communist subversive effort in that country. One of the victims of that blood orgy was Farabundo Martí, whose name is now used by the Salvadoran guerrillas of the *Frente Farabundo Martí para la Liberación Nacional* (Farabundo Martí National Liberation Front, FMLN).

The revolutionary regime was deteriorating so rapidly that there was only one way left to avoid civil power returning to the same people who had been thrown out on September 4. That alternative was the designation of a provisional president, someone from the Judicial Power, someone recognized as completely honorable, and someone who would quickly call elections for a constituent assembly, in which the people would participate in an organized manner through newly constituted political parties. That was the healthy formula that would have prevented the automatic and instantaneous return of the country to the old colonial molds. [We proposed Doctor Mario Montero, most dignified president of the Havana Provincial Court. Montero was later named Secretary of Justice by President Mendieta.] But for different reasons — those of old colonialism being most evident — neither Grau nor those opposing him accepted this plan, so the possibilities of a military coup against Grau continued to develop.

Even Cuban society had become strangely fragmented. One Saturday in the second half of December, Batista, his aides, and their respective wives went to spend the evening at the elegant Sans Souci night club, a favorite spot of Cuban well-to-do families and American residents on the island. It was the same cabaret where only a few months before that same crowd had awarded the then American ambassador, Harry F. Guggenheim, "an intimate friend of the Cuban dictator and his partner in not too clean business ventures," according to Horacio Ferrer (1950, 300), a prize for his dexterity as a dancer of the Cuban *son*. Supposedly, no Cuban present could have done it better. Cuban high society, definitely against Grau and even more so against "the nigger" (Batista) who had managed to climb to the highest military position in the country, was not in the least aware that the U.S. president had already approved measures by which the former sergeant would be given American endorsement if he just threw "the professors and the students" overboard. It was that "high society," prodded that evening by Mrs. Mariana de la Torre Mendoza (Mendoza's widow), who had left the night club en masse when they saw Batista and his group enter the room, leaving the group practically alone in the club.[5]

Poor high-living people of those days, poorly informed and even less intuitive: little did they know that in just a few days that same Batista would have grown so important that they would accept him not only as their arbiter but as their leader as well, even their spiritual guide, and that his wife would become their social leader.

January 1934: Legislative Fervor and Genuine Revolution

Now Jefferson Caffery entered the conspiracy more directly. Why? President Grau had sent a personal letter to President Roosevelt requesting that Sumner Welles be replaced. Caffery and Welles, in effect, traded posts — the positions of Ambassador to Cuba and Undersecretary of State in charge of Latin American Affairs. Caffery, then, became Roosevelt's personal representative in Cuba, though he could not actually function as ambassador since formal relations did not exist. He actually came to put in operation previously drawn plans aimed at Grau's removal from the presidency. Those plans were already outlined in the Warm Springs Declaration of November 23. Caffery arrived in Havana on December 18.

With that in mind, it is interesting to see how the United States would honor the agreement signed by Caffery's ultimate superior, Secretary of State Cordell Hull, and all the other delegates to the Seventh International Conference of American States in Montevideo five days later, on the twenty-third. In Article Eight the agreement stipulated that "no state has the right to intervene in the internal or external affairs of another."

Caffery arrived in Cuba not as secret envoy of the CIA — of course, since that organization did not yet exist — but as the personal envoy of the president of the unchallenged, first country of the world, the country that finally chose, sixteen years after the triumph of the Bolshevik revolution, to extend recognition to the Soviet Union. We shall examine how, as the "man in the field" from the United States, Caffery soon demonstrated how his country intended to fulfill the Montevideo accord. First, however, it is necessary to examine the innovative legislation promulgated in this particular time period.

This period of fifteen days displays two interesting characteristics when viewed from a sociological standpoint. I say fifteen days because Mendieta took over on January 18, after Grau had left on the fifteenth — without so much as the company of any Directorio member as he left the Palace. He was followed by Carlos Hevia, who renounced the presidency on the eighteenth, thus bringing the legislative period to half a month. But, since the first day of the year is always a holiday, and in half a month there are always two weekends, it would be more precise to call the legislative period ten days.

The first interesting characteristic of this period relates to the traditional behavior of regimes in their final hours in office. Traditionally in Cuba, the last days of a lame-duck presidency were a period of decay in legislative quality and of fallen standards of conduct, characterized by immoral executive decrees, the granting of undeserved privileges, cronyism, and a generally low quality in public services, which served as a final farewell from public irresponsibility. The final days of the Grau government did not follow that traditional decay.

Granted, Grau extended a number of executive pardons lacking in moral justification. Nonetheless, ten highly positive decrees were issued in those last days. This legislative activity comprises the second unique characteristic of that fortnight. Those revolutionary decrees provide an example of how a somewhat heterogeneous group, committed to a specific Program and still receiving popular requests for regulations the program had not foreseen, was capable, despite eventual contradictory waves of public opinion, of producing copious legislation.

On January 2, 1934, over the signatures of Secretary of Agriculture Carlos Hevia and President Grau, the Cuban Planters Association was created through Legal Decree 16. This decree was one of the most transcendent acts of the revolutionary government in all its 132 days. The sugar-cane planters association reached a membership of sixty-five thousand, representing, if families are included, more than a quarter million out of a population of around five million. It was a class vital to the national economy, a functional intermediate link between the workers and the sugar-mill owners. Living on the land and exploiting it directly, though in thousands of cases on leased fields, the sugar-cane planters had a deep sense of the national cause.

It is worthy of note here that their association, even before it was officially recognized, was never part of the other financial corporations' usual servile dealings with Washington. Because of its internal solidarity and a precise sense of its objectives, the organization was entirely in tune with the national spirit.

Those characteristics easily explain why the Cuban Planters Association did not join the Industrial Association, the Havana Traders Association, the Commerce Exchange, and the Sugar Mill Owners Association in signing a vigorous denunciation of the revolutionary regime's legislation, with emphasis on the labor nationalization law, the obligatory syndication of workers, the work accidents insurance law, and the tenants protection law, during the last days of the Grau government.

Those pronouncements by the country's big financial interests were proof of the revolutionary nature of the Directorio Estudiantil's government. If, as sociologists sustain, the essential characteristic of a revolution in power is a change of ruling class, that Directorio-supported government had it. To begin with, it came to power without prior approval from the United States. On the contrary, its program of economic reforms provoked immediate hostility from Washington and its historic allies, the big vested interests. The genuineness of the revolution consisted primarily of becoming independent from the dominant country and divesting those economic corporations of their power, who in consortium with the hegemonic foreign power, had snatched from the Cuban people, from the very first days of the Republic, all possibility of recovery and progress.

That government based on university students' ideals, which benefited workers, peasants, professionals, and the students themselves, to whom it granted university autonomy and free tuition for students from low-income families, was overrun in turn by popular initiatives that at one point demanded renters' protection and at another authorized the greatest representation of the cane growers. Neither of those demands appeared in programs prior to Machado's overthrow. Their realization now was proof that in a genuinely democratic regime, one of ample public liberties, popular demands arise spontaneously and create revolutionary changes.

The historic impact of that kind of legislation had ample proof in its potential to generate further changes. Such is the case of the tremendously influential Planters Association, whose creation, originated by Carlos Hevia and signed by Grau San Martín, *was the historic antecedent of the Sugar Coordination Law of 1937,* which would become the backbone of its support and through which the organization of the sugar industry and the fair distribution of its profits were achieved. The planters' clout grew to the extent that, according to one of its presidents, Amado Aréchaga, "the right to remain on the lands they occupied with whatever title [land owner or lessee] as long as they were used for sugar-cane production in the amount sufficient to cover their harvest quotas was the most important aspect of the law."[6]

In addition, the first chapter of the text of the law contained provisions for the protection of small planters, such as exempting them from measures restricting the sugar production in a given season. This implied a reduction in the quotas allowed the administration canes of the large American mills and the big planters as well.

That type of sugar industry legislation has not been adopted by any Latin American country in the fifty years since. Neither have its directives concerning distribution been used by any of the fourteen coffee-producing countries in Latin America. And of course, the benefits of this law have been completely ignored by the Castro dictatorship in Cuba, where all rights and advancements of planters and workers in the sugar industry granted by the nationalist revolution of the 1930s simply disappeared.

Interestingly, this Sugar Coordination Law did not originate within the Directorio nor the elected administrations of Grau San Martín or Prío Socarrás in 1944 and 1948. It was conceived and proposed by Batista collaborators Amadeo López Castro and Tomás Felipe Camacho in 1937, during the period (1934-1939) when Batista governed Cuba from Camp Columbia during Federico Laredo Bru's presidency, barely months after the congressional coup d'état inspired by Batista against Miguel Mariano Gómez, the first president elected after Machado's fall.

On that same date, January 2, 1934, another decree, unforeseen during the struggle against Machado, appeared concerning free university enrollment. Decree 41 was signed by Grau and counter-signed by the new Secretary of Public Education, José González Rubiera, and appeared in the *Official Gazette* on the fifth. Under the heading of "Considered that," three main reasons for granting that privilege were listed: 1) the extended economic recession afflicting the country made it very difficult for many young people to get a college education; 2) the closing of the university by the deposed Machado regime had deprived a generation of the benefits of academic culture, making it necessary to compensate by extension what had been lost in time; and 3) the government considered it a duty to give the young people who had fought with so much gallantry for liberty the opportunity to obtain a university education.

As a result, a thousand free tuitions were immediately granted, to be allotted to poor students from all six provinces in proportion to the population of each province according to the most recent census, allowing them to choose their fields of study.

Also on the second, another decree was issued setting down the provisions for the election of delegates to a constituent assembly. The date of April 22, 1934, was fixed for the elections. One delegate would be elected for every fifty thousand or fraction above twenty-five thousand people according to the latest census. *This decree also recognized the equal right of women to vote and run for office.* Guidelines were established for the organization of the voters in groups, organizations, or parties, and the minimum requisites to which the programs of these entities must conform. The Superior Electoral Tribunal was reestablished, as well as the Municipal Electoral Boards. Additional provisions were aimed at making it possible for the assembly to convene by May 20, 1934.

This was not the opportunistic gesture of a revolutionary govern-ment losing ground with public opinion and lacking sufficient popular support. It was rather the orderly process of calling an election for delegates to a sovereign constituent assembly to which the president would be obliged to present his resignation. Those were the terms set down in the Directorio's program and which Grau himself had repeatedly and publicly supported. Furthermore, they had been formally established in the official convocation made public three months earlier, on September 20. It was indeed an opportunity presented on a "silver platter" to the professional politicians, old and young alike, who had been antagonizing the regime in supposedly democratic demagogic union with a hostile media and a certain revolutionary chaos in the administration itself. The old traditionalist political opposition could very well have won seats for their delegates in those elections since it was formed by four large, important factions: the followers of General Menocal, the followers of Colonel Mendieta (*Partido Unión Nacionalista*), the followers of Miguel Mariano Gómez (later called *Partido Acción Republicana*), and the ABC, which, although considerably weakened, still enjoyed a certain influence among middle-class elements. Their total victory was most probable, therefore, since the government lacked any electoral vehicle of its own with which to sponsor candidates in an election only a hundred and nine days away.

Yet, five days later, Caffery, already in place as special envoy, informed the acting Secretary of State:

> . . . the government has called for elections April 22 for a Constitutional Assembly to meet May 20 but the opposition groups declare they will not take part asserting that they do not believe the government in spite of its repeated declarations on fair elections. However, they declare that they will participate in the elections if means can be found to provide for fair ones (Caffery Cable 5, January 10, 1934, 96).

Evidently, they were awaiting the coup fostered by Caffery and Batista and expected to begin just a few days later.

On the fifth, three decrees were issued, the most important of which, as we shall see, was the third. The first one granted complete amnesty to all persons convicted of slander or insult against President Machado; the second exempted the University of Havana from paying taxes, duties, or contributions, no matter their nature, to the state, the province, or the city for acts realized, contracts entered into, or documents released.

But the really transcendent decree, in regard to the national interest, was the third one issued on that date. It dealt in essence with the so-called "right of *tanteo*," granting the state the right to buy real estate at prices established by common bidding and without making a deposit in the corresponding municipal clerk office. In the terms of the decree,

> The territorial lands of Cuba, particularly those being exploited by the sugar industry, on which our economy is based, are not equitably distributed, benefitting in unequal proportion enterprises and private individuals, thus leading to inevitable and unjust huge estates in consequent detriment to the national interest.

The point was further elaborated in the third "whereas" of the text:

> The Mortgage Moratorium Law created an incomprehensible and irritating privilege in favor of those foreign mortgage creditors resulting from the practice of granting *mortgages outside the national territory.* This excludes from its benefits the Cuban debtors, who, equally affected by the [economic] crisis, have been left totally defenseless. This condition affects not only the debtors themselves but reaches out to the social order as well, as it touches all of those who in some way have entered into juridical relations with such debtors on the real estate subject to mortgage, *most of all the sugar-cane planters* [emphasis added]. Therefore, the State's lack of action in the face of a problem of such transcendent importance for the national economy would inevitably worsen the crisis and contribute to plunging the nation into an even more acute stage of latifundia.[7]

The decree also introduced modifications to several articles of the Law of Civil Legal Proceedings, especially Article 1508, which would appear this way:

> In matters of real estate, before the highest bid is approved, the judge will notify the State through the Secretary of Justice within the following fifteen days of the outcome of the auction. The State within those fifteen days following the highest bid will have the right of *tanteo* to adjudicate to itself the auction on the terms offered by the highest bidder, assuming his place and level. After that term is past without the State having exercised its right of *tanteo*, the judge will approve the highest bid.

What were the real motivations behind this decree? First of all, it represented a direct judgment against the large landed estates, quite explicit in the Directorio Program, which they had until then been unable to develop. It was emphatically repeated in the decree when it articulated the nationalist policy permitting the state to recover properties of foreign firms that had gone to auction. The measure also sought to thwart secret understandings in the auctions of large real estate properties in which the bidding prices were ridiculously and arbitrarily reduced in order to defraud second mortgagers and other bona fide creditors, nonprivileged stockholders, and the public treasury in the matter of inheritance taxes. But even more specifically, there was a case in litigation with the American company Cuban Cane, owner of the large sugar mills (*centrales*) of Alava, Conchita, Mercedes, Soledad, Perseverancia, Jagueyal, Lugareño, Morón, and Stewart. These processing centers had a combined daily output of 37,550 sacks, and Cuban Cane owned 342,210 acres of arable lands and rented an additional 321,420 acres. In other words, it controlled 663,630 acres of Cuban lands.

In the 1930 harvest those nine sugar mills produced 2,841,389 sacks, so *those properties represented ten percent of the Cuban sugar industry, while four thousand planters and over a hundred thousand workers and peasants lived there.* The company had been reorganized several times, and through an auction held in late January 1934, one bank had fixed the highest bid at a little above $5 million, while the sugar market's appraisal of the industrial equipments and lands ran to approximately $50 million.

According to Carlos Hevia, in an article published in *Bohemia* on July 9, 1934, the benefits would have been greater had the State exercised its right of *tanteo*. It would have been possible to put mortgaged lands in the hands of *colonos*, who, free from the burden of rents, would have been able to retire the debts pending on those lands. It would have been possible to distribute the nonexploited lands among peasant families living in the areas of those *centrales*. And if the State declined to administer those industrial centers itself, it could have rented them at a price per sack — as was customary — with the profits earmarked in part to cover the initial investment and the rest to maintenance of the industrial equipment.

I personally believe that it would have been possible to go much further. Had the state been able to exercise the right of *tanteo*— which was the express purpose of this decree — it would have been possible to assign the general management of the lands and the mills to the Cuban Planters Association, where there were many adept enterprisers with a thorough knowledge of the sugar industry. The nationalization of private enterprises has yielded negative results in countries of various ideological make-ups. But if the properties of Cuban Cane had been leased to so serious and responsible an entity as the Planters Association, which would have managed the whole agro-industrial complex with a private-enterprise mentality, free from political interference and under rigorous auditing scrutiny, the results would have been exceptionally positive.

But the U.S.-supported government, that captured power as a result of Welles/Caffery/Batista intrigues thirteen days after the publication of the corrected version of the decree in the *Official Gazette* (the decree was originally published on the eighth), chose not to exercise the right of *tanteo*. This government, formed by the same elements displaced by the Sergeants' Coup of September 4, was saluted by the big business corporations waving little Cuban flags. It distressed the heart to hear the most fashionable society reporter of those days labelling those who had failed to exercise the newly decreed right of *tanteo* as "illustrious Cubans." It signalled the country's loss of the best opportunity since the advent of the Republic for the nationalization of a part of the sugar industry, the liberation of thousands of planters, and the distribution of land among thousands of others.[8]

But let's continue with the January last-minute legislation. In the big American *centrales*, Chaparra and Delicias in Oriente Province, serious labor and supply problems had developed. The government ordered the temporary occupation of the processing centers. Hospitals, meat markets, livestock herds, bakeries, and other commercial interests in the two sugar-mill areas were placed under military control to keep them open to the public, ready to institute rationing of basic foodstuffs and other essential products should that become necessary.

On the eighth the government took action that would provide benefits to the State from one of the institutions that had not provided any important service within the State apparatus itself. This measure was aimed at correcting a long-established situation common to all Latin American countries: the enormous disproportion between the high cost of maintaining the armed forces of the country and the scant services they rendered to the people. Decree number 108 assigned to the Cuban Navy the following functions: familiarization with and application of the laws concerning navigation and fishing; pilotage service at the national ports; watch and semaphore maritime service; conduct of examinations and issuance of titles for the exercise of technical functions on board Cuban merchant ships; police patrol of maritime zones, coastal waters, and navigable rivers; the gauging of ships and designation of gauging experts; administration of proceedings in cases of shipwrecks, boardings, or damages, and determination of responsibility in such cases; registration of national ships; administration of concessions for salt marshes, fishing grounds, and seafood breeding areas; administration of concessions for dredging sand; construction and upkeep of lighthouses and all aids to navigation; and in general, oversight of all personnel and equipment pertaining to the merchant marine, the lighting and buoying of coastal waters, fishing, and maritime jurisdiction. The merchant marine, fishing, and coastal lighting section was specifically created to handle those latter aspects and other lesser responsibilities assigned in the decree.

That same day, the eighth, the school breakfast program was instituted in all public schools. As Secretary of Education and Fine Arts, José A. González Rubiera, explained, that measure was taken in response to hundreds of public school teachers who were concerned that their students often complained of being hungry. Cuba was then going through an economic crisis such as the country had not experienced since the war years of 1896 and 1897, when Spanish Captain General Valeriano Weyler dictated the forced concentration of the rural population in towns as a means of combatting the Liberation Army. The school breakfast program had not been included in any of the plans of any of the anti-Machado political factions. The only groups who had developed programmatic objectives were the Directorio and the ABC. In fact, with these two exceptions, none of the other groups had presented any post-dictatorship program at all, not even when they recovered on January 18, 1934, the power they had lost on September 4, 1933.

On January 11, a decree was issued that illustrated the revolutionary government's concern for the integrity of the national sovereignty. The Sugar Export Corporation, an entity designed to represent the interests of the Cuban sugar industry both internationally and domestically, had been ruled by a North American in connivance with the Cuban members of the board of the corporation. This American had conceived a plan for the sugar industry which, in some ways, compromised the interests of the Cuban nation. This caused all the Cuban members of the board to resign. Mr. Chadbourne, however, remained in his position as president of the company. It was then that the government intervened, issuing a decree that began:

> WHEREAS: the National Sugar Export Corporation is an entity of national and official character by virtue of the Law of 15 November 1930, as it can be appreciated, in its origin as well as in the purpose of its creation, with the exemptions and privileges it enjoys, *which gives its president opportunity to realize functions of sovereignty that involve the citizens, it is hereby resolved to dismiss Mr. Thomas L. Chadbourne for reason of occupying the presidency of the Corporation without being a Cuban citizen* [emphasis added].

The text of the decree — inspired again by Secretary of Agriculture Carlos Hevia, a sugar-cane planter himself, recommended in Article Six that the statutes of the National Sugar Export Corporation be modified to provide wider representation in its governing board to sugar-cane planters.

By decree number 116 of January 9, the Secretary of Agriculture and Commerce — Carlos Hevia, who the previous week had created the already described planters association — was authorized to give permission to resourceless peasant families to settle temporarily in lands abandoned by their owners because of criminal acts committed during the dictatorship, *or to dedicate such lands, totally or partially, to build schools of farming on them or use them as fields for farming experimentation*. This flexible authorization made it possible to combine the donation of lands with the technical farming preparation of their new owners.

The Secretary of Agriculture was further authorized to distribute among Cuban peasants arable lands belonging to the State with the exception of the forest reserves. This particular point was contemplated by the Directorio program and extended to apply also to private lands exceeding a determined limit. The measure represented the initiation of an agrarian reform policy which the overthrow of the revolutionary government aborted and which was not continued by any of the successive provisional governments. It was recognized and included seventeen years later in the 1940 Constitution but, in fact, was never fully implemented.

Carlos Hevia's fertile contribution during the brief period of the revolutionary government has best been expressed by José Antonio Guerra, one of the most brilliant figures of the 1930 Generation, whose excessive modesty always kept him out of the public glare. Guerra was an expert in the sugar industry and possessed a complete mastery of statistics. He worked closely with Felipe Pazos, another outstanding economist in theory as well as in executive capacity. It could be said of the two — as is said of Eisenhower and Walter Bedell Smith — that it was impossible to tell where the personality of Pazos ended and that of Guerra began. Guerra wrote to me concerning Carlos Hevia:

> Engineer Carlos Hevia exerted a profound influence, both direct and indirect, in the formulation and promulgation of laws regulating the sugar industry after the fall of Machado. That affected the life of the industry not only in reference to planters and sugar mill owners, but to the living standards of field workers as well.
>
> In regard to the relations between planters and owners, Hevia played a significant part as the author, as Secretary of Agriculture and Commerce, of a number of decrees issued in that respect by the Grau San Martín government of September 1933 to January 1934, such as:
>
>> *Decree number 214 of 1934, which established the tacit revision of the planters' contracts every two years* and recognized the *"right of permanence,"* [emphasis added] which became the basis of all subsequent sugar legislation since it granted the planters the right to remain on the lands they tilled. It also made it possible for the planters to later share in the profits and the management of the industry.
>
> But Hevia's most significant contribution, which only indirectly favored the sugar industry in its multiple and lasting consequences, was the creation of the Sugar Planters Association of Cuba through presidential Decree number 16 of 2 January 1934. The foundation of this association as an official juridical entity, for the purposes listed in the text of the decree, *produced the instrument that made it possible for the planters to propose and obtain all the benefits formulated* in subsequent legislation. Among those laws were the Law of

Free Planters, the Law of Coordination of the Sugar Industry, which allowed planters to rise to *a level of equality* in dealings with owners, and the Statutes of the Cuban Institute of Sugar Stabilization, which gave the planters the *veto right* and required the attendance of at least one representative of the Planters Association in every meeting of the Institute.

As for the field workers of the industry, by decree of 9 January 1934, their wages could not fall below 50 cents per 2,500 pounds of sugar cane cut and gathered up. Cutting would be paid at the rate of 31.25 pounds of sugar for each 2,500 pounds of cane, and carrying at 18.75 pounds of sugar per each 2,500 pounds of cane, which would be paid according to the average price of sugar figured biweekly by the Department of Agriculture.

On January 12, a decree signed by Grau and Secretary of Treasury Colonel Manuel Despaigne ordered the suspension of payments to the Chase National Bank of installments proceeding from 90 percent of the taxes created by the Law of Public Works of July 15, 1925, until a study was made of the amounts delivered up to the date of the investment.

President Machado's public works plan had established a special fund to be built by taxes especially designed for that purpose. The fund, which was to guarantee payments on the Chase National Bank loan, was administered through the Department of Treasury by persons loyal to the American Embassy. This went to such an extreme that, during the fiscal years of 1931-1933, the Chase National Bank was paid an approximate amount of three million pesos ($3 million) *in excess of the 90 percent of the revenues obtained by the taxes established by the Law of July 15, 1925.* That meant that President Machado's subservience, continued after August 31, 1933, by Carlos Manuel de Céspedes, was such that payments were made out of the special fund not only in the proportion determined by law, but in extreme excess over what it demanded — a zeal that could hardly be termed patriotic.

Finally, the crisis that had been brewing in the Cuban Electric Company finally erupted on January 14. The utilities company was a subsidiary of American Foreign & Power. Although "power" in this case was to mean energy, it also figuratively meant power in the political sense — American Foreign Power.

As was seen earlier, Secretary of the Interior Antonio Guiteras had decreed that the electric tariffs for the general public be reduced by 45 percent effective on December 6, 1933. From that time on until January 14 — thirty-eight days, to be exact — the Syndical Federation of Electricity, Gas, & Water Plants, established on August 20, eight days after Machado's fall, had been engaged in negotiations with the company regarding a list of forty-one demands, among them official recognition of their syndicate, maximum workdays for both day and night workers and for office employees as well, and minimum salary. One other demand was, of course, the right to strike.

By December 15, the company had accepted thirty-one of the demands and requested an extension of thirty days to decide upon the rest. When that time lapsed, on January 14, the company not only refused to grant any of the pending demands but even reneged on some it had previously accepted. Thus, the partial agreement previously reached was voided.

Consequently, the Syndical Federation of Electricity Plants declared a strike. Electric production in the city of Havana was totally paralyzed, and the workers announced that the strike would be extended nation-wide the following day. In view of these circumstances, the ever-ready Antonio Guiteras succeeded, much against Batista's energetic opposition, in having President Grau sign a decree ordering official intervention in the company. This intervention was to include all the company's dependencies — plants, shops, offices — and it would be carried out by specially named government inspectors "with the assistance of public force and in whatever form the Secretary of the Interior should deem necessary in accordance with the circumstances demanded by each case."

It was determined, however, that all plants, shops, and offices throughout the national territory would continue to operate, "the intervening inspectors being authorized to take whatever actions they consider necessary or convenient for the purpose of avoiding service interruption in any form or pretext in any of the said dependencies." Intervention was to be indefinite, for as long as it should appear indispensable or necessary.

CAFFERY ACCELERATES THE CONSPIRACY AGAINST GRAU

Naturally, Jefferson Caffery, who at the time represented the entire North American power, sure that the Soviet Union, recently recognized by Roosevelt, would not even make a symbolic protest over what would occur in Cuba, and humiliated by the January legislation culminating in the decree authorizing intervention in the power company's strike, decided to trigger, as quickly as possible, Grau's overthrow. "If I hadn't done so, I would have appeared a fool for the rest of my life," Caffery told Rafael Maceo, one of his consorts. (The personal envoy of President Roosevelt was an old homosexual who practiced his sexual deviancy without racial discrimination.)

A good deal of information about what occurred during that time is recorded in the cables between the Department of State in Washington and Caffery in Havana. The first cable arrived on January 6, 1934, drafted for Welles by Phillips, to Caffery, informing him that the "illustrious" Manuel Márquez Sterling, Caffery's counterpart in Washington as personal envoy of President Grau, "has been in to see me repeatedly during the past ten days" (Phillips Cable 5, January 6, 1934, 93). According to Welles, Márquez had been planning to leave for Havana "where he intended to take up his duties as Secretary of State," a position he held simultaneously with his post in Washington. But at the end of this cable, Welles said, "The impression he gave me [this morning] was that he had reached the conclusion that no peaceful adjustment of the problem was now possible." So it would appear that Márquez Sterling had joined the Batista-American band of conspirators. What a loyal personal representative Grau had in Washington!

On the eighth, Acting Secretary of State Phillips informed Caffery that the Foreign Office — as the department of foreign relations of the British Empire was still known — had stated to the American Chargé d'Affaires in London that "they recognized that special considerations were involved in the Cuban situation due to the Platt Amendment, but that had a similar situation existed in some other Latin American country, Great Britain would be on the brink of recognizing a regime similar to the Grau San Martín Government" (Phillips Cable 6, January 8, 1934, 94). Phillips further informed Caffery that "the British Ambassador called at the State Department on January 4 and in the course of a conversation with the Acting Secretary on the Cuban situation admitted that the pressure being brought to bear on the British Government to recognize the Grau San Martín regime came from the property owners in Cuba and especially the British-owned railway interests." Of course, the British ambassador "was told that in the opinion of this Government recognition of the present regime in Cuba would be a great mistake, that the sentiment of the Latin American Governments in the great majority was against such recognition." Obviously, the United States not only persisted in its own negative position, as reaffirmed in the Warm Springs declaration, but went on to assume that the great majority of the Latin American governments shared it — the same countries that just twenty days earlier in Montevideo had unanimously voted against the intervention of one country "in the internal or external affairs of another," as was seen earlier in this chapter.

On the tenth, Phillips, in another cable drafted for Welles, informed Caffery of yet one more visit from Márquez Sterling. He had told Welles that, because Grau had not heeded his recommendations during the last four months, he would encourage him to modify his policy in pursuit of recognition from the United States and the other republics of the Western Hemisphere. Márquez Sterling also informed Welles that, "unless Grau and his Government agree to follow his recommendations, he would resign his office and return immediately to the United States" (Phillips Cable 9, January 10, 1934, 94-95). Phillips noted, "it is obvious that he is hopeful of his own selection as a compromise candidate for the presidency."

That same day, the tenth, Caffery stated, "I agree with former Ambassador Welles as to *the inefficiency, ineptitude, and unpopularity with all the better classes in the country of the* de facto *government. It is supported only by the army and ignorant masses* [emphasis added] who have been misled by utopian promises" (Caffery Cable 5, January 10, 1934, 95). This further confirms my long-held opinion. The big corporations had gone publicly against the revolutionary legislation just a few days earlier. The high-society classes that a few days earlier had left the Sans Souci cabaret upon the arrival of Batista and his retinue were called the "better classes," and the rest were the "ignorant masses," deceived by "utopian promises." Thus, nearly one hundred decrees, most of which were already in effect, reducing workdays, raising wages, providing social security, and generally improving the quality of life, represented "utopia."

Caffery went on to say, "unless Dr. Grau decides voluntarily to give up power, it is my opinion that he can be forced to do so only by the armed intervention of the United States unless there is a break in the army which is now standing strongly behind the government" (Caffery Cable 5, January 10, 1934, 96).

Caffery's pronouncement about U.S. armed intervention is all the more strange since by this time he was already secretly dealing with Batista. "I find in the opposition," he added in the same cable, "little tendency to compromise and an insistence that the only way to clear up this situation is for us to intervene. They refuse to believe our insistent declarations against intervention."

Caffery also cited the economic situation. His description was quite eloquent: "In the background there is constantly the distressing economic situation in the interior; much actual hunger, misery, and want — all due manifestly to the sugar situation which is so bad at present that some American-owned mills do not seem interested in grinding. The recent difficulties at Chaparra and Delicias . . . arise from the fact that the company can pay average field wages of only about 15 cents a day." This testimony by the American ambassador provides sufficient explanation for Grau's January 6 decree ordering the temporary occupation of the dependencies of those two big sugar mills, including hospitals, meat markets, livestock herds, bakeries, and other commercial concerns, as well as the parallel decree on the ninth establishing minimum wages of 50 cents per hundred *arrobas* (2,500 pounds) of cane cut and transported from the field.

The cable added that the government had called elections for a constituent assembly that was to meet on May 20, without mentioning that elections for assembly delegates were scheduled for April 22, that the opposition had refused to participate, claiming that it did not believe the government in spite of its repeated declarations for impartial elections, and that it would only participate in an election if there could be found means to prove impartiality.

This is a cable that, in our slang, we would call *siniestro* (sinister, left-handed, ill-omened) in every sense. Caffery ended his dispatch stating, "I am meeting Grau and Batista again on invitation tonight. I have been told that they will make offer of 'changes in the government'." But Caffery was involved in the conspiracy and knew that Batista was ready to accomplish the coup, in loyal "reciprocity" to the same president who had confirmed him as commander of the army that evening of November 3, much against the judgment and wishes of the Directorio. This cable was a subtly manipulative communication, trying to establish that the "better classes" of the country considered the government inefficient, inept, and unpopular. (Were the "better classes" of the country more numerous than the "ignorant masses" of

Cuba?) He suggested the possibility of intervention, lied that the Army solidly backed the government, and said, furthermore, that "the *de facto* authorities . . . are relying more and more on radical and communistic [sic] elements, and we may soon be faced with the [*a*] very grave situation in connection with the protection of our manifold interests on the island," adding afterward that "some American-owned mills do not seem interested in grinding," and that the opposition would not participate in the elections.

In the meeting of the three that night, according to Caffery's statements, Grau said, "I believe that I can guarantee fair elections if I remain in the Presidency, but if the opposition are convinced that I cannot do so, I will be willing to give place to a non-political successor to be chosen by me from a panel of three names to be selected by the opposition on condition that one of the names, at least, must be acceptable to me" (Caffery Cable 7, January 11, 1934, 97). Clearly, Grau was already positioning himself to abdicate.

Caffery's cables 6 and 8 are missing from the *Foreign Relations* record. In Cable 9 (97-98), source of the above quoted material, he dwelt on the contents of cables 5 and 7. As Caffery put it, the opposition groups could not agree on a program. He was not, of course, referring to an ideological program but, rather, to what one might call a pragmatic set of objectives. He stated, ". . . for instance, the Mendieta group is interested in elections, while some of the other groups would rather pin their faith in a revolution or the hope that we will intervene *and put them into power; in fact, they are very indignant that we have not done so*" [emphasis added]. He continued, reporting that "the night before last, Batista had an interview with Mendieta in which they discussed in great secrecy the possibility of Grau's leaving the Presidency and either Dr. Presno or Dr. Costales Latatu assuming that office provisionally. They agreed either of these two men would be acceptable." And Caffery added (thus proving that he was in on the whole conspiracy), "Last night Batista decided that things were going so badly that he would force Grau's resignation at once, but he was persuaded not to take precipitous action by some of his friends."

Still, Caffery added a touch of caution to his reporting. "I do not mean the state of any of this is a certainty especially as the attitude of Guiteras and his naval and military adherents is unknown; also in view of what may eventuate out of the troubles of the Electric Light Company this evening or the troubles of the Havana Electric Railway (my telegrams No. 10 and 11, January 13, 6 p.m.) . . ." These cables, which necessarily must have been even more *siniestro*, are also missing from the published records.

Apparently bent on further impressing the Department of State — and especially President Roosevelt, who, of course, was kept fully informed — Caffery telegraphed on January 14:

> Situation is very grave. However, Mendieta tells me he is willing to assume the Presidency (provisionally, of course) at once, but only if he knows in advance that the United States will recognize him. Situation is such that some steps must be taken tonight, Sunday, to secure change in the government very soon thereafter. Batista tells me he will support Mendieta.
>
> I respectfully request at once authority to recognize Mendieta in the Presidency. If this is not done, Batista will probably turn definitely to the left with definite disaster for all our interests here (or declare himself military dictator) (Caffery Cable 12, January 14, 1934, 98).

That dispatch was written at three in the morning of January 14. That same day at noon, Caffery again reported:

> I think it is safe to say that a government headed by Mendieta and supported by Batista will represent a majority of the Cuban people: both of them without question are extremely popular in very different sectors of the public.
>
> I again respectfully urge immediate action in order to avert a catastrophe: the only other section of the public which has any chance of reaching power at this time is the extreme left (Caffery Cable 14, January 14, 1934, 99).

This last assertion was totally false. Caffery may have had in mind Guiteras because of his actions regarding the Electric Company. But Guiteras *had been attacked by the communists as a fascist*. Like Nicaragua's Sandino, he was, *if not necessarily anticommunist, at least and without doubt a noncommunist*. The communists in Cuba then represented only the extreme left and did not have the remotest chance of ascending to power, not to mention that they were under total control of the Russians, who were at the time unwilling to antagonize the Americans who had just recognized them.

Finally, at one o'clock in the afternoon on the fourteenth, the eve of Grau's resignation, Caffery again cabled the acting Secretary of State (Cordell Hull had not yet returned from Montevideo) demanding urgent reply to his previous telegrams, numbers 12 and 14, both of the fourteenth, seeking permission to recognize Mendieta as president before the fact. "The situation is very dangerous," he said, and added,

> *Grau as yet knows nothing of what is planned* [emphasis added]. He will be asked this evening to appoint Mendieta Secretary of State and transmit power to him (Caffery Cable 15, January 14, 1934, 99).

In yet another follow-up cable that same afternoon, Caffery simply said, "It is hoped, of course, to include representation of some if not all opposition groups in the Mendieta Cabinet" (Caffery Cable 16, January 14, 1934, 99).

He sent another almost immediately thereafter, adding, "[In reference to] My telegram No. 16, January 14, 1:00 p.m. Felix Granados says he believes that all the opposition sectors will accept Mendieta as President" (Caffery Cable 17, January 14, 1934, 99).

With all this as background, it is time to turn to the meetings at "Lillian," Enrique Pedro's country estate in Wajay near Havana, next to General Menocal's estate, "El Chico."[9]

HOW MENDIETA CAME TO BE PRESIDENT

What follows is an abridged version of my taped conversations with Carlos Manuel Alvarez Tabío, a man in whom Mendieta had total confidence. After taping our conversations, I summarized his story and sent him the document for his approval and signature, which he kindly gave. The document, of course, remains in my collection.

Tabío, born in Cuba on June 17, 1894, was an official of the Canadian Army during World War I. He opposed Machado actively almost from the beginning of his administration and was with Mendieta at the ill-fated Río Verde uprising. Named by Mendieta in January 1934 as director of the Havana Tobacco Commission, Tabío eventually became totally disillusioned with his former friend and resigned his position. He was so deeply disillusioned that, in the summary of his taped statements to me, he insisted that I end his narrative with this simple statement: "I did not attend his funeral."

The following is the text based on our recorded conversations.

The meetings were attended by Jefferson Caffery, ambassador of the United States, Fulgencio Batista, commander of the Army, and Carlos Mendieta, leader of the *Unión Nacionalista* Party, which had participated in the Welles mediation process and had supported the Céspedes government. Mendieta had become the outstanding figure in the opposition movement against Grau San Martín and was considered his most probable replacement as president. Those meetings were also attended by Major Jaime Mariné, a close aide of Batista.

Others attending were Carlos Manuel Alvarez Tabío, as friend and confidant of Mendieta, and an official of consular level at the American embassy by the name of Vixon, at the time Caffery's inseparable companion.

Three meetings were held during the days immediately preceding Grau San Martín's resignation, the last one during Carlos Hevia's brief presidency.

None of the other sectors opposing the Grau San Martín government were represented at those encounters: General Menocal's *Conjunto Nacional Democrático*; Miguel Mariano Gómez's party, later to be called *Acción Republicana*; the ABC, under the leadership of Carlos Saladrigas and Joaquín Martínez Sáenz; nor the OCRR (*Organización Celular Radical Revolucionaria*), led by Nicasio Silverio. Also considering themselves in the opposition were members of a group formed by former congressmen under Machado, whose leader was Carlos Manuel de la Cruz. They called themselves "*Ortodoxos*" (the Orthodox). None of these groups was invited to the meetings because Caffery and Batista considered all the opposition to be personified in the leadership of Mendieta, who evidently was the most popular among the opposition figures and accepted by all as the man to replace Grau San Martín.

While these conversations were taking place, there was a meeting of the *Agrupación Revolucionaria de Cuba* (ARC), that organization created in Columbia the night of September 4, 1933. The purpose was to discuss the popular and political crisis the Grau San Martín government was facing. The ARC decided to replace Grau with Carlos Hevia, who had been acting as Secretary of Agriculture. Hevia remained president for just a few hours. He had assumed the presidency on the belief that Mendieta — the most powerful factor in the opposition — would support him. When he learned that such would not be the case, Hevia resigned irrevocably. It was Alvarez Tabío who told him about Mendieta's attitude during a conversation at Enrique Pedro's house in Vedado. It appeared that Mendieta and his political group, *Unión Nacionalista*, refused to support Hevia on the assumption that a member of the Grau San Martín cabinet was bound to follow the same policies as the man whom he had served.

So Mendieta became the man of the hour, a figure of hope, both politically and popularly. His popularity had increased as Grau's diminished. Even the students had begun to demand that Grau leave power, backing, instead, the national discord that had continued to grow, and assumed that Mendieta was a man of character, capable of confronting the already powerful commander of the Army, Batista. He therefore became a man of circumstance and could attend the three meetings referred to earlier without the presence of the opponents to Grau San Martín, assuming that they would agree with his opposition in the scant hours that Carlos Hevia replaced Grau.

Therefore, Mendieta participated in the conversations as actual representative not only of his own group but also of Menocal, Miguel Mariano Gómez, the ABC, and the OCRR. That is to say, he could count on the support of the others. So, at that moment, only three men determined the destiny of Cuba.

The meetings took place on January 15, 16, and 17, 1934, and culminated with Mendieta assuming the presidency on the eighteenth.

Interestingly enough, in those meetings no political program was considered nor thought given to a possible date for elections. Measures to curb or prevent potential intrusions of military power in the civilian sphere of government were not mentioned, either. Supposedly, a man who represented public opinion and had the support of the United States would naturally see to it that the soldiers went back to their barracks and that, of course, Batista's continuous interference in public affairs would come to an end.

A marginal yet most significant incident occurred during one of the meetings at Enrique Pedro's country estate. The host invited those present, among them Ambassador Caffery, to go to the dairy barn nearby to have a drink of raw milk. But some of those who did not care for raw milk preferred to stay in the house. It was then that Vixon, Caffery's constant companion, made homosexual advances toward the host's son, a young man by the name of José Enrique Pedro. The young Pedro reacted violently, insulting Vixon and telling him that the offense was all the more repugnant for having been committed in the presence of his wife. In such bizarre circumstances that astonished everyone present, Batista's aide Jaime Mariné was not in the least surprised at Vixon's behavior. "It doesn't surprise me, since there is a constant scandal at the [American] embassy because of this same type of thing, and we frequently have to replace the soldiers assigned to guard the [American Ambassador's] residence." The American embassy was then located in the former residence of General Montalvo, on the Marianao side of the Almendares River on Ramón Mendoza Avenue in Miramar.

In those meetings it was decided to give no political support whatsoever to Carlos Hevia, who had first been nominated by the ARC. When the last of the meetings was held, Hevia had already resigned and left the Executive Mansion. It was also agreed that Mendieta would accept the provisional presidency and proceed to form a concentration government, following his best judgment, relying on the full support of the armed forces and the immediate recognition of the United States. Ambassador Caffery offered assurances, furthermore, that a new commercial reciprocity treaty would be signed that would greatly "benefit" Cuba.[10]

The next day a meeting was held at the Presidential Palace, with representatives of all the opposition sectors in attendance. It was presided by Miguel Coyula, an old-time politician with a legendary reputation for honesty, attending on behalf of Menocal. Coyula asked that a basic program be drafted for the Mendieta administration to follow.[11] But the idea was rejected by Carlos Manuel de la Cruz, who was an enemy of all ideological programs and wanted to ingratiate himself with Mendieta. Coyula's proposal was discarded when at noon Mendieta took the oath of office before the justices of the Supreme Court. There was no program, minimal or otherwise, for the government. Shortly thereafter, Carlos Manuel de la Cruz was named president of the Council of State.

Thus ends Alvarez Tabío's eyewitness version of those events, to which I can only add, "How awful!"

Some important activities were skipped in this narration in order to make room for Tabío's significant account, especially within the revolutionary orbit. Therefore, I shall go back a few days and take those other events into account.

When on January 14 Guiteras, with Grau's authorization, ordered state intervention in the electric company, it was no coincidence that on that same day Roosevelt's personal envoy in Havana should cable the State Department saying: "I respectfully request at once authority to recognize Mendieta . . ." (Caffery Cable 12, January 14, 1934, 98). But Mendieta was not yet in the Presidential Palace; he would not be there until four days later. Grau San Martín was still the president, and he had signed the intervention decree. Jefferson Caffery, however, in blatant disregard for the accord prohibiting any State from interfering in the internal or external affairs of another, requested the recognition of Mendieta as president. After recognition of the existing Cuban government had been withheld for four months, Caffery was asking immediate presidential recognition for someone who still wandered through the streets with a group of friends, confused and vacillating, going from one meeting to another.

As the events developed with incredible speed, Batista called a meeting of the ARC, that transitory and largely imaginary creation which assumed official responsibility for the September 4 Sergeants' Coup. That group had met only once after its creation, at Carbó's house on November 3, when Grau confirmed Batista (instead of letting him be tried and executed for high treason) as Chief of Staff of the Army, four days exactly before the November 8 rebellion, which resulted in the consolidation of his power.

The country was in a serious state of public unrest. The Directorio had dissolved and had ceased to exist; the press and the radio were furiously attacking the government; even the students were out in the streets clamoring for Grau's resignation, and resentful leftist Raúl Roa had published an article with the bitterly derogatory, slang title of *Mongonato, efebocracia, y mangoneo* [referring to Grau, the rule by teenagers (the students), and "ruling the roost," respectively]. Even the democratic and revolutionary labor movement, which had most benefitted from the revolutionary government's legislation, was reluctant to give its support to the government; they bowed to the influence of the Communist Party, which had been militantly opposing the government, not as a matter of principle, certainly, (do they have them?) but because the revolutionary legislation resulted in a reduction in their membership and also because the Soviet Union was being recognized by the United States.

The situation grew so desperate that at one meeting among Grau, Batista, and Mendieta, the president found himself under such pressure to renounce power in favor of Mendieta that he blurted out: "Right at this moment I can declare that I feel outside of the events, and my resignation is final." With that, the road to succession was expedited.

It was on this basis — that is, having heard directly from Grau himself of his definitive decision to abandon power — that Batista called an ARC meeting on the evening of January 14.

Owing to the suddenness of his call, however — only two hours' notice — the meeting had to be postponed for lack of a quorum until two in the morning on the fifteenth.

At the meeting Batista stressed the gravity of the situation, ascribed exaggerated importance to the opposition groups, and vehemently exalted Mendieta. Rubén León, the only leader of the no-longer-existing DEU present (Prío and Rubio Padilla had not yet returned from Montevideo and Varona was in Camagüey), immediately responded to Batista's statements. León delivered a passionate and courageous speech in which he accused Batista of having "gone over to the enemy" and earnestly begged him to help keep Grau in power. (León had not yet learned that Grau had verbally resigned just a few hours before.)

A minority of those present — headed, of course, by Batista — backed Mendieta; another minority group suggested Carlos Hevia; and a third group (of which I was a member) led by Eddy Chibás opted for a formula of succession that would assign the presidency to one of three men: the Chief Justice of the Supreme Court, Dr. Juan F. Edelman; the rector of the University of Havana, Dr. José A. Presno; or the chief magistrate of the Provincial Court of Havana, Dr. Mario Montero.

Edelman was rejected because he happened to be Carlos Hevia's father-in-law. Dr. Presno then seemed to be the ideal candidate — he was a prestigious professor in the School of Medicine; he had stood beside the DEU throughout the anti-Machado struggle and had served as Secretary of Health and Social Services in the Céspedes cabinet at the suggestion of all opposition groups. But Presno gently begged us "not to impose such a burden" on him. Consequently, our group opted finally for Judge Mario Montero, who had also comported himself in an exemplary manner during the Machado era, for which he had been elevated to head the Provincial Court of Havana. (Montero later was named Secretary of Justice in the Mendieta government.)

My group held the opinion that Hevia should not be president, "for the candidate should not proceed from the revolutionary junta nor the existing government, since the idea is to name a president in a position to promote peace and put a stop to the political discords today dividing the country," and Hevia at the time was Secretary of Agriculture.

This group of ours could boast a high level of moral authority. Among its members were José Miguel Irisarri, Guillermo Portela, Alejandro Vergara, Emilio Laurent, Rafael García Bárcena, Eduardo Chibás, Augusto Valdés Miranda, Orlando Alonso Velasco, Guillermo M. Cancio, Felipe Pazos Roque, Fernando González, and myself. In other words, there were two former Pentarchy members, the mayor of Havana until December 23, the former chief of police of Havana, and eight members of the dissolved Directorio Estudiantil.

Our position was clearly expressed in a joint article co-authored by Chibás, García Bárcena, Valdés Miranda, and myself. We said,

> To save the Republic and the revolution from the fall, there are only two alternatives: one, extend a bridge backwards in order to save the Republic by sacrificing the revolution as power is delivered to the opposition politicians; the other, extend a bridge forward that will save the Republic and the revolution by delivering the power to a new revolutionary government that can count on the support of the people. This is the solution we propose, for the members of this junta are the only true revolutionaries in Cuba (Chibás et al., February 4, 1934, 24).

Our intent, based as always on our cursed nonpolitical stance, was to prevent power from passing directly to the American Embassy through Batista and the counterrevolution. It was functional only in theory, though, for had any of the candidates we recommended actually been designated, he would not have been able to conduct the country to a peaceful new beginning of democratic reconstruction against the opposition of the political groups who wanted no other solution than one with the blessings of the American embassy. That revolutionary president, furthermore, could hardly have succeeded in calling a constituent assembly — which would have put everyone on the same level at the starting line. Even had we been able to get that far, we still lacked the political vehicle necessary for a major victory at the polls, even relying on majority support from the people. Their support was still — inevitably — not for the Directorio itself, but for the caudillo the Directorio Estudiantil had unintentionally created, Ramón Grau San Martín, the man who had signed all the decrees based on the demands of the people.

Hevia's name, however, kept coming up repeatedly in all the ARC meetings as well as in conversations before and afterward. That caught the attention of Sergio Carbó and others, and Carbó, along with Lucilo de la Peña and Raimundo Ferrer, one of Batista's aides, met with Mendieta and obtained from him a declaration of support for Hevia. Aware of this and at the urging of Secretary of Justice Luis F. de Almagro (the author of the right of *tanteo* decree) and, of course, assured of the backing of the sugar-mill owners and the planters, Hevia accepted the offered presidency.

This maneuver, by which Batista betrayed what he had been simultaneously agreeing to at Enrique Pedro's country estate in Wajay, was possible because the high command of the Navy, under the indirect influence of Guiteras, who himself entertained hopes of replacing Grau,[12] opposed the designation of Mendieta.

But then three things happened that allowed Batista to fulfill his Wajay commitments after all. To begin with, Mendieta's support for Hevia disintegrated. He had agreed to issue a public declaration stating,

> With no other guide than my conscience, and my duty as a Cuban who never eschewed any juncture, no matter how difficult, if it was a question of saving the nation, I hereby publicly declare before the Country that without the slightest reservation I give my support to the provisional government led by the honorable citizen Carlos Hevia, as I would likewise support any other willing to accept my cooperation as long as he should commit himself, as this man does, to the strict and peremptory obligation of calling a Constituent Assembly with total respect for and absolute guarantees of universal suffrage.

This declaration, however, was immediately disapproved by the leading committee of Mendieta's own party, *Unión Nacionalista*. In total dissent with their leader's solemn public pledge, the committee declared,

> We feel that Dr. Carlos Hevia, an aspirant to the provisional presidency of the Republic, does not represent the sentiment or the aspirations of the Cuban people, and that the person indicated in this case for his moral solvency, his political and patriotic history, and who would rely on the support of the opposition sectors, is Colonel Carlos Mendieta, to whom the *Nacionalistas* give unconditional support.

Understandably, the Nationalists' declaration provoked Hevia's immediate resignation. He sent the Revolutionary Junta a brief statement, saying:

> I accepted the office of president on the belief that I would be able to restore peace in Cuba and after being given assurances that I could rely on the support of Colonel Carlos Mendieta. I thought that on this basis I could also achieve the cooperation of the other parties too. But in view of the fact that the Nationalists have refused their support and the situation will remain the same, I have decided to irrevocably renounce the office I now occupy.

In addition — and this was the third factor — Hevia's statement was taken to the junta and delivered to Batista by none other than the commander-in-chief of the navy himself, Commander Menéndez Villoch, finally eliminating the supposed obstacles for Mendieta's designation. So the story goes back to the point where we left it: Mendieta was president. Little remains to be added to what Alvarez Tabío narrated about the meeting that took place at the Presidential Palace the 18th of January. A few thousand people, not many more, gathered in front of the executive mansion when Grau San Martín abandoned it. There were no crowds, however, when Hevia entered the palace nor when he left.

On January 18, 1934, thousands upon thousands, many more than those who went to bid Grau good-bye, filled the streets of Havana. The city took on the air of a joyous carnival. All levels of society — upper, middle, and lower classes alike — celebrated Mendieta's ascent to power. The crowds waved flags, while caravans of automobiles went by in a ceaseless din of horn-blowing. Thousands of miniature Cuban flags waved. Even the stage manager of this dramatic event, Jefferson Caffery, had the temerity to accept this miniature symbol of the Cuban nation — and smile.

While Mendieta took the oath of office before the chief justice of the Supreme Court, the guns of La Cabaña Fortress across the bay fired the traditional twenty-one gun salute.

Later that evening, search-lights from the Capitol pierced the sky, while those from La Cabaña illuminated the Presidential Palace.

The revolutionary legislation of the September 4 movement had only scratched the surface of the rooted colonial structure of the Cuban republic. Breaking that colonial mold would ultimately require a serious change in attitudes, not just in the governors of the "colony," but more importantly, in the attitudes of the leaders of the colonizing country. A general attitude of insubordination within the "colony" would never suffice. The breaking away would require a homogeneous leadership capable of conceiving and implementing *a gradual program of national reconstruction* and of organizing and commanding *a massive base of popular support*. Furthermore, it would be absolutely necessary to have the understanding and tolerance of the colonizing country, encouraging the rhythmic development of economic recovery programs to fill the gaps created by the loss of the colony. Thus, the United States, lacking leaders of great historic stature, men capable of strengthening the internal forces of public opinion to support the concession of complete sovereignty to Cuba, was incapable of allowing a *peaceful decolonization* process to develop.

Here lay Cuba's chances of reaching full nationhood at that particular historic moment. The United States, just entering the New Deal era, was a superpower in crisis that could have tolerated the upgrading of the international status of Cuba, since the influence of international public opinion in those days was far above normal levels.

Failing to take advantage of this unique opportunity was Mendieta's great historic crime. He inherited a process of national improvement and growth and all he had to do was keep it going. But then again, he had accepted the office consciously bound to submit tacitly to Washington.

No wonder the economic corporations were rejoicing on January 18, 1934. Roosevelt's Warm Springs conditions had been satisfied, and the new armed forces that had originated from the September Sergeants' Coup had received the benediction of Washington while the former cadre of officers, those who were overthrown on September 4 and who, with Welles, had asked for intervention, now languished in prison, totally forgotten even by those who previously had demanded their reinstatement to their former posts.

And, irony of ironies, not to be outdone in the general orchestration, the same "high-society" elements, those who haughtily had abandoned the Sans Souci scarcely four weeks before because Batista and his party had walked in, now shamelessly came forward to salute the consolidated "strong man" and congratulate him "for having liberated us from communism."

"Oh, I'm so happy!" exclaimed a superbly attired lady on approaching the tray — with the Cuban coat of arms engraved in gold — to raise a champagne glass and toast Batista. "To your health, Colonel; you, who are our liberator!"

The following Saturday, at the customary tea party at the Country Club, another lady friend of mine described to me the Batista toast. One had said, "You really acted the opportunist the other day with your toast to the 'Nigger'!" To which the other replied, attempting to play at semantics, "Better to be the opportunist than the inopportune!"

THE NEW YORK TIMES SERVES UNITED STATES COLONIALISM

The jubilation and the praises for Mendieta's rise to power — the twenty-one gun salute, the Capitol's searchlights, the multitudes in the streets, the high-society parties, and the champagne — were not limited to the Havana social circuit.

In the United States, the morning after the inauguration, January 19, 1934, the *New York Times*, supposedly the premier periodical in the world, now danced to the tune of Wall Street — as at other times it would dance to the music of Moscow — also celebrated Mendieta's inauguration in the entire January 19 edition. Certain statements which appeared on the editorial pages of that edition are presented here out of context better to emphasize their import.

Editorial Title: *Better Cuban Prospects*

Mendieta, according to the *Times*, "was the only man capable of reestablishing and maintaining order, causing the wheels of industry to move, and obtaining U.S. recognition. The President [Roosevelt] was just waiting for the establishment in Havana of a government that would be satisfactory for the Cuban people."

Yes, Roosevelt had been waiting since November 23, when Welles, behind Secretary Hull's back, secured his signature on the

Warm Springs Declaration that gave Batista the green light to over-throw Grau.

And as for being "satisfactory for the Cuban people," was the *Times* speaking of the six individuals meeting at the Wajay country estate, as related by eyewitness Alvarez Tabío?

From the *Times*: "He [Roosevelt] did not adopt the policy seriously propounded by the *New Republic* when it said that the only sensible course for the United States was to recognize any government in Cuba that can survive more than a few hours."

The *New Republic* was only honoring the spirit of Montevideo, where the policy of nonrecognition had been denounced as meddling in the internal affairs of other states. So right was this position that even Secretary Cordell Hull himself, still on board the ship bound for Montevideo, had demanded an explanation of the reasons for with-holding recognition (Hull Telegram, November 27, 1933, 527).

From the *Times*: "Cuba has been rapidly sinking in chronic disorders and bankruptcy. The whole process, alarmingly, has seemed like a slow suicide."

The "chronic disorders," such as the Hotel Nacional episode and the November 8 rebellion, were foreseen and even encouraged by the North American Embassy in Cuba. Did the New York newspaper simply ignore that?

From the *Times*: President Roosevelt "has made it patently clear that we will never intervene, even though, according to existing treaties, we have every right to do so."

And why? Because the *Times* is obviously Plattist. According to the Convention on Rights and Duties of States, adopted one month earlier, "no state has the right to intervene in the internal or external affairs of another."

From the *Times*: "It would be a great relief for him [Roosevelt] if the now brighter sky over Havana would mean the dawn of a new day for Cuba, keeping in check the insensate chronic revolutionaries, subduing with an iron hand the anarchists, and helping Cuban industry and commerce to function freely again."

What "anarchists?" Not even Welles, in his most perverse and hidden wickedness, ever spoke of them.

"Chronic revolutionaries?" Which ones? Those who passed a hundred decrees for the benefit of the people? "Iron hand?" Whose? That of José Eleuterio Pedraza, Batista's lieutenant and Chief of Police of Havana, assassinating democratic revolutionaries left and right?

"Industry and commerce to function freely" — oh yes, the economic corporations opposed to reformative legislation would be free to function, with open support from the occasional Wall Street mouthpiece.

Did the *New York Times* declare in similar terms the collapse of the entire Cuban economy under Castro? But, to return to the point, what were the "better prospects" that were assured in the title of the *Times* editorial from which all these quotations were taken?

Mendieta, who had the golden opportunity of reaffirming and continuing the work of redeeming Cuba from the old colonial shackles, missed it miserably when, a few days after assuming power, he forfeited the state's "right of *tanteo*" on the properties of the Cuban Cane Company, which would have turned over to Cuba 10 percent of the national sugar industry. Better Cuban prospects? No, *New York Times*.

But Mendieta further surrendered the Cuban economy to the United States with his signature on the 1934 Reciprocity Treaty, which even Machado severely criticized. In his book *Ocho años de lucha* (Eight Years of Struggle), the deposed dictator wrote from exile:

> He [Welles] was bringing a plan, a treaty almost finished, in which all the long-range objectives of his country were contemplated, with concern for nothing else, that is, without taking the Cuban reality into consideration, or worse yet, against it. The idea was to make us go back to 1925 and the old colonial system. And, in the face of such an intent, my government stopped the negotiations. Mr. Welles expected us to sign the Reciprocity Treaty, which was signed by Caffery and Torriente after I left Cuba (Machado 1982, 74).

Perhaps Machado's opinion can be challenged as being the result of his resentment at being overthrown. Perhaps sober evaluation by a true expert in international commerce and customs policy, and designer in 1958 of the entire Cuban tariff system, Juan F. Vizcaíno, might shed some light. He said,

The reciprocity of the Treaty signed by Cuba with the United States in 1934 consisted in the consolidation of almost the whole of the Cuban tariff system — at the expense of its industrial potential — in exchange for the sugar, which in the end was not consolidated since it was subjected to quotas — which kept being reduced in every Congressional redistribution. Such a situation generated obstacles to later negotiations through the General Agreement on Tariffs and Trade (GATT), which began to regulate the Cuban/American trade relations.[13]

Consolidation meant freezing trade tariffs in the industrial development of Cuba, since every new production needed tariff protection at least until it could reach a competitive level with the same import items from the highly developed countries. Would that be what the *New York Times* was advocating in order "to make the wheels of industry move?"

Concluded Vizcaíno: "The process of industrialization begins in earnest by what we might term the stubborn insistence of the Cuban negotiators at the encounters of Annecy and Torquay, already within the agreement."

Then Mendieta's successors — Barnet, Miguel Mariano Gómez, Laredo Bru, and Batista himself — until 1944 did nothing to remedy the situation, except perhaps to initiate the reforms emanating from the Sugar Coordination Law.

Those who were supposed to resume the liberation process initiated in 1933 during their respective constitutional terms, Grau San Martín (1944-1948) and Prío Socarrás (1948-1952), simply accommodated themselves to the existing socioeconomic status.[14] With the exception of Grau's so-called "sugar differential" and the institutionalization and new tariff policies promoted by Prío, no long-range follow-up policy was implemented during the eight years of their respective administrations. Neither did either of the two attempt to alter the internal military structure of the armed forces. On the contrary, Grau San Martín had discharged most of Batista's military cronies at the same time he handed out meteoric promotions of his own similar to those of the 1933 sergeants. A former aide of his, for instance, Genovevo Pérez Dámera, was suddenly promoted from lieutenant to general and appointed Chief of Staff of the Army. Many similar promotions were, likewise, extended via palace contacts or personal favoritism. Despite all that, however, the interest of the true military professionals in technical and class advancement led to the addition of academic courses to the curriculum of the *Escuela Superior de Guerra* (Senior War College) and the hiring of distinguished university professors to teach them, such as Herminio Portell Vilá, Roberto Agramonte, and Rafael García Bárcena. The influence of these men contributed greatly to the formation of a strictly professional, nonpartisan military mentality with due and profound respect for the civilian institutions of government.

That was the origin of the elite officers that came to be known as "the pure ones." They forced the discharge of Pérez Dámera and his general staff in 1949. But by then President Prío, unduly worried about a potential upsurge of military clout, failed to see the opportunity for encouraging a movement that would have brought dignity, efficiency, and discipline to the armed forces. Instead, Prío named as his Army Chief of Staff a nonentity, Ruperto Cabrera, a former carpenter of the September 4 sergeants' clan, a man incapable of promoting a military coup but just as incapable of warding one off. Batista took advantage of that in order to return on March 10, 1952, and to carry the military matrix to a state of total disintegration.

THE BATISTA-CASTRO PARALLEL: WHY DID CUBA FAIL TO ACHIEVE GENUINE AND PERMANENT INTERNATIONAL INDIVIDUALITY?

Exactly a quarter of a century after that "gay" inauguration of January 18, 1934 — with a margin of only eighteen days lacking for an exact coincidence — on January 1, 1959, Fidel Castro arrived to break the colonial mold and was given the reins of power by an overconfident Cuban people. This time the old colonial structures, which Batista had reaffirmed, would, indeed, finally be broken — but only to be replaced by far more sinister ones. All appearances to the contrary, Castro was not precisely moved by ideological or honest revolutionary motivations, right or wrong as they might have been, but rather by an insane voracity for power that arose out of a twisted personality nurtured by an abnormal family environment.

So, in the course of another quarter-century (1959-1984), Cuba, as a result of the radical Castro revolution, found herself in the shackles of a new international master. But here I will let three undisputed authorities on the subject substantiate the point.

The prestigious British historian Lord Hugh Thomas cited three basic points in his pamphlet *Revolution on Balance*.

On Batista and Castro, Thomas says:

> Batista prepared the way for Castro in a two-fold manner: first, he set down the standard . . . that if a band of armed men have a common cause, they very easily can proclaim themselves to be the State once they have taken hold of the government installations. Secondly, Castro continued (or completed) the destruction of the existing institutions in the country (Thomas 1983, 10).

"In place of the old regime," says Thomas, "Castro set up a State with himself as 'maximum leader,' presumably for life" (Thomas 1983, 10).

As for the subordination of Cuba to the Soviet Union, Thomas says:

> Carlos Rafael Rodríguez, vice-prime minister of Cuba, said, as quoted by *Pravda* March 11, 1972, that there was not one single sector of the economy in which Russian cooperation was not planned, and it certainly appears as if that cooperation is part of the entire society (Thomas 1983, 13-14).

Regarding the Soviet objectives in Cuba, Thomas adds:

> The purpose of the Soviet assistance to Cuba has been the establishment of a state as powerful as any other of the Soviet bloc, probably even more loyal than the rest. The Cuban Constitution is now a mirror copy of the Soviet one.
>
> This powerful State has been used to convert the nation into a great military camp. The military element in the regime propaganda, probably believed by the leaders, is far more noticeable than in other Communist states.
>
> As years pass, this military aspect of the regime has increased instead of diminishing (Thomas 1983, 14).

Further emphasizing the tendency toward military primacy over the civilian aspect of the regime, Thomas continues:

> In recent years, for instance, the historical significance of "apostle of liberty" José Martí (a civilian hero) has been downgraded in favor of Antonio Maceo, the "bronze titan" (a neat military figure), a rebel general veteran of the two Cuban independence wars, "whose life was a perpetual dialogue with duty," a man who, because of his Negro

blood, we are supposed to assume would have sympathized with "the anti-imperialist struggle in Angola, Ethiopia, or Zaire." "To honor him today is a war cry," Castro told me (Thomas 1983, 15).

Thomas concluded that "the first and most notable achievement of the Castro State has been the creation of a nation in arms," adding that "basically the Cuban military forces (as well as the police) are provided arms, uniforms, and training by Russia." The whole thing suggests, according to Thomas, "the morale of a nation whose leaders have been capable of simulating a permanent war through the aspiration to the permanent revolution" (Thomas 1983, 16).

His third point, very interesting and original, most energetically opposed the false interpretation of Castro's military regime as the representation of Marxist socialism in America:

> More and more, as one considers Cuba, parallels with fascism come to mind: the attention given to propaganda, the cult of the leader, the doctrine of the unending struggle, the exaltation of nationalism and violence, the emphasis on carefully orchestrated oratory, the deliberate exacerbation of the tension in the multitude before the leader speaks, the rhythmic reaction of the masses, the placards with ferocious slogans that the populace carry by intimidation, the mass rallies, and the atrocious prisons that constitute the salient characteristics of Castroism, all that without question reminds one of the fascism reached by Perón.

> So, this political system certainly seems to have been, above all, the first leftist fascist regime. What I mean is that this is a regime with totalitarian leftist goals, sustained and imposed by fascist methods (Thomas 1983, 18-19).

Let us now look at the Castro system from the economic viewpoint. In a personal interview, Professor Antonio Jorge, a highly qualified authority on the Cuban economy, spoke extensively on the subject. A summary of what he told me follows:

At present [early 1980s], — Dr. Jorge began — the bulk of international commerce between Cuba and the Soviet Union and the Eastern Bloc surpasses the level between Cuba and the United States. It is, furthermore, expected that the commerce between Cuba and the

Soviet Union will increase considerably during the second Five Year Plan (1981-1985), now in effect.

Cuba receives from the Soviet Union practically all it needs to survive. It receives, for instance, part of its military equipment, most of its food products, most of its raw materials, all the oil it consumes, and the great majority of its capital and investment stocks.

At the same time, Cuba exports to the Soviet Union more than 50 percent of its sugar, in addition to what it exports to the other countries of the Eastern Bloc. And Cuba still exports to the world market 30 percent of its sugar production, this being its source of much-needed hard currency.

As everyone knows, Cuba gets all its oil at much less than half the international market price, which is another form of Russian subsidy. However, in the latest meeting of the COMECON in June 1984, that subsidy seems to have been canceled, meaning that Cuba will have to start paying the world market price for its oil.

Nevertheless, it also seems that the price Russia has been paying for Cuban sugar is still maintained at levels far higher than those in the world market, and that, added to other forms of subsidy, results in the Soviet Union providing Cuba with aid in the amount of more than $4 billion annually.

I asked Professor Jorge if Russia absorbed the deficits in the Cuban trade balance. He answered that they have a compensation organ, implemented in 1975, through which the two countries adjust the deficits, which they manipulate by means of accounting devices.

I also inquired if that accounting might include military services, officially recognized, rendered by Cuba to the Soviet Union in the international field, as well as subversive operations not officially recognized. His answer was that it is impossible to know the cost of those services or where the payment comes from, since that constitutes top secret information. Besides, the accounting of such services is also virtually impossible as it cannot be determined what Cuba would have done with those resources in personnel and equipment had they not been sent abroad.

Cuba was never so dependent on a foreign power as it is today. The Castro regime failed to achieve the product diversification it had so much promised, something that had been a Cuban aspiration since the times of the Economic Society of Friends of the Country in the nineteenth century. On the contrary, Cuba's economy is exclusively dependent on one single product, sugar, which makes up more than 80 percent of the country's exports. Cuba, therefore, has even less capacity for self-support today than at any previous period in its history. In other words, the system has failed miserably in its capacity to provide for even the barest necessities of the population. It is an economy in retrogression — even less healthy, less balanced, less diversified. It has actually become a colonial economy, a plantation economy.

In the final analysis, we can point out — Professor Jorge continued — that in Cuba, during the decade of the 1950s, despite all the political instability, the conspiracies, the student protests, the social unrest, and the economic uncertainty itself, the gross national product rose at an annual rate of between 3 and 4 percent, an index so healthy that even the American economy has not been able to achieve this average. Today, if we consider the postrevolutionary period in Cuba from 1959 to the present with the most generous calculations possible, it could perhaps be said that, on average, there has been a 1 percent annual increase in their GNP.

It must be noticed, moreover, that the basic nutritional quota assigned to the Cuban population in the rationing books is even more strict today — twenty-two years later — than it was in 1962, when it was already scant.

If we look at international credit, the situation is just as dramatic. Right now [mid-1980s] Cuba owes the Soviet Union $6 billion and between $3 billion and $3.5 billion to the western banks. Payments on this debt to the Soviet Union were supposed to start in 1986 and the whole debt to be retired between 1986 and 2011. Just recently Cuba had to borrow over a million dollars to acquire a renewal that was being denied by one of the banks participating in the loaning consortium. It does not appear rational, therefore, to think that Cuba can start repaying the Soviet Union within two years, so that country will have to absorb the debt. With the western bankers, the situation is one of permanent refinancing — in some cases, with short-term loans to pay interests — and as these failures become chronic no positive forecast is at all possible for the Cuban economy.

Finally, let us turn to the assessment of one of the most lucid and respected representatives of the Latin American intelligentsia, Mexican Octavio Paz. In his book *Tiempo nublado* (Cloudy Weather), he includes this view of the Cuban experience after the Castro revolution:

The problems are real — where are the solutions? The most radical, after twenty-five years of application, has produced these results: Cubans today are just as poor or even poorer than before and much less free; inequality has not disappeared; the hierarchies are different but no less rigid and harsh; repression, like the hot weather, continues, intense and general. The island remains dependent, economically, on sugar, and politically, on Russia. The Cuban revolution has petrified: it's a heavy stone slab that fell on the people (Paz 1983, 187-88).

These views are presented here as a challenge to historians, sociologists, political scientists, or even philosophers who may wish to reflect on them and draw their own conclusions. From the restoration of the old colonial mold in January 1934 through two quarters of a century, each of a distinct character, Cuba has experienced two historic cataclysms, respectively, under two characters that, though essentially different, nonetheless exhibit striking similarities: Fulgencio Batista and Fidel Castro.

Here are some of the similarities or, if you'd prefer, coincidences: a) both bastard sons; b) both born in Oriente Province; c) both ascended to power at exactly the same age, 32; d) both of civilian origin, the one a stenographer and the other a nonpracticing lawyer — who became military for different reasons; but both politically backed by the armed forces; e) when Batista seized power for the second time on March 10, 1952, he assumed the office of prime minister; Castro did the same after consolidating his power in 1959; f) both Batista, a colonel, and Castro, a major, promoted themselves to general and eventually to president; g) both betrayed the civilian movements that had been their respective early bases: the 1930 Directorio Estudiantil Universitario and the Twenty-Sixth of July Movement; h) both reversed their respective social class extraction: Batista, originally a railroad worker, became a capitalist; Castro, the son of a *señorito* ("upper class parasite") educated in the exclusive Catholic school, Colegio de Belén, chose totalitarian communism; i) in order to rivet their dubiously acquired power, both Batista and Castro resorted to ruthless measures in dealing with political opponents and adversaries (in this aspect, however, with his methodical persecution, imprisonment, torture, and execution of all dissenters and potential enemies, Castro has astronomically surpassed Batista); and finally, j) in sharp contrast with legendary Independence general Antonio Maceo, who died in battle with twenty-three combat scars on his body, Batista and Castro, who used violence in their quest for power, always managed to come through unscathed. Batista, after the attacks on the Hotel Nacional and Atarés Castle, and two coups d'état, died without a single scar. Castro, after Cayo Confites, Bogotá, Moncada, and Sierra Maestra, has never been scratched.

In addition, their records show a diagonal coincidence in covert international matters. During long stretches of his tenure in power, Batista maintained silent understandings with Moscow, while Castro has maintained constant public or secret conversations with Washington.

Batista was born in 1901 and Castro in 1926. They are separated by a quarter-century in a huge historic relay in which the violence of March 10, 1952, was succeeded by the violence of 1959, when a *de facto* nondemocratic regime simply gave way to an ideologically nondemocratic one. These two characters, therefore, each in his own unscrupulous way, dramatically twisted and frustrated the natural historic destiny of the Cuban people, called by its early founders — philosophers, poets, writers, patriots, and martyrs — to live in a free, prosperous, and happy society. Instead, because of their respective actions, since the nominal foundation of the republic in 1901, that is, for seventy-nine years as of this writing, Cuba existed as an independent democracy — no matter how imperfect — for only about half that time. It is as if the twenty-five years that separated the birth dates of these two individuals were doomed to be the only democratic era for the island that, before these men were born, had seemed destined to enjoy — through its independence process, the character and hard-working nature of its inhabitants, and its privileged position in the hemisphere — a future filled with well-being, liberty, and happiness. Then, as if tragic predestination had hovered with macabre intentions for the island spot, Generals Batista and Castro seized and held Cuban power for a total (until the date of this writing) of forty-three years, more than half Cuba's seventy-nine year existence as a Republic, excluding three years of the second American intervention.

How is it that such a historic monstrosity has been possible? Some say that Cubans have lived fatalistically under the dictum that "people get the government they deserve." Others claim that these two peculiar leaders knew by instinct wherein lay the innate weaknesses of the Cuban people by which they could be bridled and put under the yoke.

Still there are those who see the root of the problem in the insufficient cultural development of the Cuban people, their lack of a well-cemented national tradition, something that, as is the case of the Polish people, comes only after centuries of struggle and varied historical experience. It could even be — another would point out — that the violations of the democratic rules during the respective reelections of presidents Estrada Palma and Menocal, and later the contrived term extension granted Machado, exhausted the Cuban people and destroyed their ability to exercise their democratic electoral options.

It has also been mentioned that the very privileged geographical position of the island of Cuba at the entrance of the Gulf of Mexico, at the pivotal point between the United States and Latin America, and possible supplier, in turn, of the premier consumer market of the world, has constituted its own disgrace through the contradictions of world power that its domination indicates.

A friend of mine, a seasoned participant in all the battles for liberty in Cuba in the last few decades, is convinced that the revolutions generated by the student movement of the 1930s and the Twenty-Sixth of July Movement in the 1950s tired the fighting spirit of the Cuban people to the point of tolerating first Batista and then Castro. And finally, the Cuban renegades, like many critics of the independence effort of the nineteenth century, offered the opinion that "Cuba was not prepared to govern itself."

Those interested in going to the bottom of the present Cuban reality will have, therefore, enough theories to choose from.

Notes

1. The document in question is in the archives of the author.

2. Articles appear in *Foreign Relations of the United States* 1933, Vol. IV, 215-217.

3. This manifesto can be found in the collection of Alberto Segrera, as well as in Soto 1977, Volume II, pages 55 and 84. The manifesto was signed in the home of Rafael Suárez Solís by the members of the DEU who were not in prison, and not as Soto states in his version of the signing, since the so-called Second or Surrogate Directorio never signed manifestos, a policy adopted deliberately with the goal of maintaining its anonymity.

4. The disposition formed part of a policy of protection of the small mills as well as the *colonos* at the expense of the *cañas de administración* [administration canes] of the North American centers.

5. This occurred December 19, 1933. Mrs. Mariana de la Torre, widow of Ramón González de Mendoza, was one of the most outstanding person-alities in Havana social circles. She participated in the revolutionary process and her son, José Ignacio, took part, along with Francisco Corróns Canalejos and Luis Pérez Hernández, in the frustrated attempt against Machado known as the *bomba sorbetera* (ice cream maker bomb).

6. From a letter by Amado Aréchaga to the author, dated September 28, 1982.

7. A *latifundium*, according to *Webster's New Twentieth Century Dictionary* (Unabridged), is "a large landed estate, as in ancient Rome." Therefore, the reference here is to the steady acquisition of larger plantations by the already bloated cane-processing companies, especially those owned by North Americans.

8. Before the end of the month of January, 1934, the First Instance Municipal Court of Colón notified the Cuban Government of the auction of the properties of the Cuban Cane Products Company, consisting of the sugar-processing centers that are mentioned in the text, plus some ten thousand *caballerías* (330 thousand acres) of land, should the government wish to exercise its right of *tanteo*. The auction had been held in accordance with a mortgage proceeding followed by the Central Hannover and Trust Company for a price of a little more than $5 million in principal and accumulated interest, on a loan that the North American bank had granted to the sugar-processing center in 1931. When the mortgage was taken out, the properties had a book value of some $64 million dollars and, on presentation of the demand, they had appreciated some $20 million. The Mendieta government did not deem it convenient to use the right of *tanteo*, which would have permitted the

government to acquire, for a little more than $5 million, goods and properties with a real value of at least $20 million. In face of the scandal that arose because of this decision, itself a result of pressure by the North American Embassy, the government called on the attorney general of Matanzas, instructing him to appear before the Municipal Court and demand the annulment of the judicial process for failure to notify the Cuban government in proper form, which the representative of the Public Ministry did precisely. There was, then, a new auction, and in June 1934 a committee designated by the government, presided by the Secretary of Justice, determined that it was still not convenient for the Cuban government to exercise the right of *tanteo*. The Mendieta government thus reaffirmed its position against the interests of the Cuban people and bowed again to the interests of the Yankee Chancellory.

9. Enrique Pedro was a close friend of Mendieta, who named him Chief of Police of Havana after assuming the presidency.

10. Never before had anyone tried what Caffery now did: to anticipate the decision of recognition. The Department of State refused him repeatedly. Concerning the reciprocity treaty, there is ample evidence that the benefits Caffery also anticipated would be refused.

11. It was the minimal program to which Welles and Caffery had referred and that on which all were supposed to have agreed. That agreement now consisted in that there would be no program.

12. At times Guiteras had a certain ingenuousness — perhaps an excess of audacity — since the recently promoted officers feared his ideological position. The War Navy, on the other hand, including the recently created Infantry of the Navy, was not a monolithic block nor a decisive factor against the army.

13. Juan F. Vizcaíno's opinion is stated in a report in the author's possession.

14. That accommodation implied the continuation of the corrupt practices of the previous administrations, the most ostensible being the Lottery Revenues, that continued to be a fountain of illicit resources for the most illicit ends. Neither did there exist in either of the two administrations a coordination between the legislative and executive branches that would permit legislation concerning the joint programs of government. When, during the Grau administration, a crisis of confidence was raised by the Congress, under the protection of the semi-parliamentary system of the regime, the president had recourse, in order to dodge the congressional appeal, to the maneuver of sending the entire cabinet on vacation and elevating the undersecretaries to the level of ministers, which caused them to be called, humorously, the under cabinet.

Chapter 5

A REVIEW OF
THE 1930s MOVEMENT

THE 1930 DIRECTORIO: FINAL SYNTHESIS

There could be little doubt that the students, particularly the Directorio Estudiantil Universitario (DEU), constituted the leading faction in the revolutionary commotion of the 1930s in Cuba. So, a look at their socioeconomic background, the prevailing ideas and sentiments that inspired them, what they did, and what they failed to do, will throw abundant light on the understanding of that period.

They were a group of well-meaning young men from the various schools of the university, with the limited cultural level of high school graduates. Most were freshmen or sophomores. As many as five came from the pre-law school. None of them was a poor student, and several finished their courses cum laude.

With the exception of five who had belonged to the *Juventud Universitaria Nacionalista* (Nationalist University Youth), none had been involved in political activities of any kind. And those five were quickly absorbed into the collective nonpartisan atmosphere of the group.

They came from all six provinces of the island, so when their influence spread with representative student groups throughout the island, they became an authentic national voice of concern and aspiration.

Through the extensive and constant discussion of ideas in connection with current events, they matured in their political conscience to the point of always being ahead of traditional leaders in the interpretation and assessment of what was occurring on the national level and were able to anticipate popular reactions. They, therefore, developed such a sense of self-reliance that their public statements and manifestos generally started with the phrase, "In the name of the Cuban people whom we represent . . . ."

The first spontaneous impulse of the group was to start a campaign for the liberation and full sovereignty of the Cuban people. With an open spirit of cooperation, they allowed members of other groups, such as the 1927 Directorio, and student leaders from the provinces to attend and participate in their deliberations. This fluid and permeable system of communication resulted in a practice by which the group became aware of the needs and concerns of the people, thus equipping them to elaborate lines of action that, with characteristic speed in execution, were immediately followed.

Being in the midst of the realities of the national frustration made the Directorio — originally based more in emotion than thought — progressively conscious of their historic role. With an acute thirst for a just and orderly state of affairs in the country, they continued to evolve toward the need for a change deeper than the simple return of the political liberties that had been snatched from the Cuban people.

In this coalescing process of sentiments and ideas, the rejection of the Platt Amendment, that constitutional appendix that had been imposed on the independence leaders, became one of their primary objectives.

This attitude, which actually meant a break with the historic past, led the Directorio to formulate their cardinal political thesis: the necessity of a "total and definitive change of regime." At the same time, within the still limited reach of their political immaturity, the essential components of a structural change in the search for a better state of economic justice and social welfare for the Cuban nation were taking shape in their minds.

The incursion of the students into the public arena during the national crisis of the 1930s was met by an avalanche of popular sympathy. But it was there that the Directorio committed one of its first historic failures. Instead of taking the opportunity to organize the thousands upon thousands of Cubans who enthusiastically embraced their leadership and finding a way to include that mass of nonstudent citizens in their struggle to achieve their goals, the Directorio patriots never even stopped to think about that possibility. They simply left that reservoir of popular support to waste away untapped and leaderless.

All the DEU managed to do in this respect was lead the university students and a few secondary students in civic activities. Their active and often heroic presence in the public eye helped to launch and exemplify in Cuba the respected concept of the "1930 Generation."

But, regrettably, they had neither the vision nor the will to create a militant revolutionary — or political — force around their program. On the contrary, they chose at all times to remain identified as "students" and thought it a virtue to remain active but uncommitted watchers of the national conflict and exert their influence from the defined enclave of the university walls.

Soon, however, reality confronted them. When the secret cellular revolutionary organization ABC appeared a year later and asked the Directorio to designate two of its members to their leading committee, the Directorio acceded. But in the process, it also relinquished leadership of the popular protest to the ABC, and those two designated members, likewise, shifted alliances and even became anti-DEU.

As for its socioeconomic composition, most of the Directorio members ranged from low- to upper-middle class. Five or six of them came from well-to-do families, sons of urban or rural landowners or well-known professionals of some wealth. But the families of the majority had barely the means to afford their college education in the capital; those from the interior had the added expense of having to live in boardinghouses (which, by the way, in time became revolutionary centers).

There, the sons of independence patriots mingled with those of Spanish immigrants; boys of refined upbringing fraternized with others of not-so-distinguished backgrounds. Very few owned automobiles, which they generally shared kindly, but most had to use public transportation. With rare exceptions, they were all white. However, there were absolutely no racial nor social demarcations among them: all were integrated in a common cause.

One who worked actively in the initial efforts to found the Directorio was Rafael Trejo, vice president of the Association of Law Students. Many of the meetings were held in the basement of the Law School, others in the country estate El Cotorro, near Havana, a property of the father of one of the members, Augusto "Polo" Miranda (who, incidentally, was responsible for my own recruitment).

Trejo became so involved in the ideals and the objectives of the newly born DEU that he considered it his duty to lead the march in a certain street demonstration that ended in violence. He was killed by a policeman in a hand-to-hand scuffle on September 30, 1933.

Trejo was the first student martyr of that era. Then came Félix Ernesto Alpízar, December 21, 1931; Angel "Pío" Alvarez, January 4, 1933; and Carlos Manuel Fuertes Blandino, April 7, 1933.

With the exception of three who were never identified by the police, all the DEU members suffered persecution and spent time in jail. For three years they were deprived of a normal home life.

During the struggle, the DEU issued five different statements delineating political or ideological positions. It also published eight manifestos, all printed clandestinely, denouncing crimes, tortures, and other excesses of the government and calling the people to resist. In the fleeting intervals when freedom of the press was allowed, they published three other manifestos addressed to public opinion.

From the outset, the DEU also embarked on a campaign of agitation that included street demonstrations involving clashes with the police, appeals to the public at movie houses and theaters, disruptions of social events, and interruptions of sports events. The harsh reactions of the authorities led them to the use of explosives. In order to obtain dynamite they had to use violence, carrying out assaults in search of the expensive materials, sometimes against stores where it was sold, and at times against mines where appreciable quantities were kept for extraction operations.

At first, the dynamite was used as simple firecrackers to punctuate explosive protests. There were times in which hundreds of sticks exploded throughout the city in a single night. Then followed the terror bombs placed in commercial establishments — preferably American, since the United States backed the regime until 1933 — and also in government buildings or homes of leading figures of the dictatorship. The Directorio, however, prided itself on not having caused personal injury.

This attitude was somewhat modified along the way, however, when the DEU resolved to participate in attempts against outstanding repressive elements in joint operations with the ABC. The Alphabetic organization had by then an extraordinary team of men of action, among whom Mariano González Gutiérrez and Alfredo Botet stood out. It must be admitted also that, moved by political passion, the DEU participated in the assassination of Clemente Vázquez Bello, who was shot leaving the Yacht Club. The ABC's aim had been to kill someone important so that the government would attend the funeral, the Havana cemetery having been previously mined with high explosives. Vázquez Bello, however, was buried in the family vault in Santa Clara, his home town. A gardener at the Colón Cemetery in Havana accidentally discovered the wires.

The government's reaction to Vázquez Bello's death was equally macabre. Four prestigious members of the opposition, the three Freyre de Andrade brothers and Miguel Angel Aguiar, totally innocent of the act, were shot by the police. Such were the sad products of the fratricidal conflict in which the government responded with terror to a corralled opposition forced to resort to terror.

The uncontrolled police repression reached incredible extremes. Two members of the Valdés Daussá family were killed simply for being brothers of Ramiro, a member of the Directorio and a cum laude student of the School of Engineering and Architecture.

Floro Pérez, a member of the Oriente Directorio, was arrested in Havana while accompanied by British descendant Wycliffe D. Grafton, known as "*El inglesito*" (the little Englishman), who was born and had always lived in the town of Gibara, Oriente Province. The police took them to different places. Floro and a brother of his were assassinated, but Grafton was released a few days later. "The fact that you are English saved you," a police thug told him. Later Grafton commented that, "If they'd only known that I don't even speak English . . . !"

Another tremendous family tragedy indirectly related to the Directorio was the case of the brothers Alvarez. Three of them were assassinated in Agüica, Matanzas Province, for simply being brothers of university activist Santiago Alvarez, a student of medicine.

These examples are only a few cited at random to illustrate the atmosphere in which the 1930 Generation was forged. For the Directorio the call to action ran parallel to their political and revolutionary preoccupations.

In May 1933, the United States initiated the mediation process conducted then by Ambassador Sumner Welles. The "Second" or surrogate Directorio acting then in Havana was caught unawares and for a moment had a mind to listen to Welles. Though also seasoned in the hardships of the daily struggle, they lacked the maturity and the vision acquired by the exiled founders through readings and discussions in prison. There were consultations, and the group in exile, at least eight of whom happened to be key decision makers in all crucial matters, said no to the mediation idea. In the explanation of their anti-interventionist stance, they put together the most beautiful and eloquent concepts that can be expressed in defense of a truly democratic position. Their statement against the Platt Amendment, even though somewhat romantic in style, constitutes a stellar document among all the political literature of the Directorio. It also signaled the irreversible point of departure from the ABC, which chose to desert its originally proclaimed revolutionary line and to accommodate the old colonial status quo. This led the Directorio to widen its own political horizons and to start thinking about the possibility of seizing power in order to implement the ideals of national advancement of which it considered itself the depository.

As explained in Chapter 1, the statement against the mediation was issued in June 1933 and was followed in July by another document — not made public, however, until August 22 — in which the problem of American interventionism in Cuba was analyzed in depth and a number of programmatic objectives were proposed in detail. Among them was the goal to establish an "Executive Commission" — later known as the Pentarchy — to carry out the program.

In this declaration the DEU also announced the creation of the ARPE, acronym for *Agrupación Revolucionaria Programa Estudiantil* (Student Program Revolutionary Association). This was a belated attempt to make up for their failure to organize the massive popular support back in 1930, which had reverted to the ABC with the help of the two deserting DEU members who joined the Alphabetic leadership.

And now the Directorio committed its second and even graver historic blunder. While announcing its decision to assume power, it paradoxically declared in the same breath that it would not exercise that power directly, but instead would entrust it to persons whom they would select. What immature and naive detachment! Born out of an idealistic revulsion against corrupted politics, the DEU became so antipolitical that it designed the ARPE for no other purpose than to assume the power it would seize but would not wield.

That document was penned by José Miguel Irisarri, an exemplary citizen, but a man of a very inhibited nature who passed on to the members of the Directorio his personal innate shyness for the public spotlight. And the Directorio, believing in the virtue of its idealism, did indeed hand over the reins of power to a group of select individuals, hoping that they would follow the guidelines of their program.

Yet, it was not exactly that Irisarri exerted some sort of irresistible influence upon the Directorio members. Actually, it was just the opposite. Having shared prison and ideas with the founders of the student organization, Irisarri had been impressed by their ethical attitude of shunning the direct responsibility of power. In fact, the ideologue and the organization influenced each other reciprocally to produce what were, in the end, negative consequences. Thus, the Directorio, never the follower and iconoclastic by nature, developed a kind of political altruism that ended up being its political grave.

If the Directorio had, instead, had the vision and the resoluteness personally to exercise the power that fell in its hands in 1933, or had exerted greater influence on the same individuals they had entrusted with that power, the subsequent history of Cuba would have been quite different.

Among other things, they lacked a strong leader. Their innate anti-caudillismo prevented one from arising, as would probably have occurred naturally had they chosen to exercise power. Then, after the Directorio dissolved, Guiteras, who had only come in contact with the group after the Fourth of September, emerged. But Guiteras was, as developments proved, a bit ahead of the historic moment, and was soon overcome by an arrangement of forces of the past.

The ARPE, the combat-oriented instrument belatedly conceived by the students for the purpose of channeling popular action and support, did not have the opportunity to develop fully because of Machado's precipitous fall and the ensuing clash with their earlier political allies who only wanted to turn back the clock of history. Those contrary forces had positioned themselves under the interested umbrella of the United States. Yet, the twenty-three days between the fall of Machado and the collapse of the provisional regime constructed through American manipulation turned out to be the most dynamic in the life of the Directorio. It was a period that demanded the greatest capacity to do right in the shortest amount of time, and the Directorio saw evident signs of popular support once it could act freely without risk of persecution and had open access to the press and other means of communication. For a time the students, indeed, held the historic destiny of the Cuban nation in their hands.

How and why they let that leadership and that opportunity escape them can only be analyzed today in retrospection. The weaknesses that account for their failure were basically a lack of a) a clear definition of their ideology, which, although essentially and unquestionably democratic, skipped the precise delimitations for the exercise of power; b) a better ideological articulation of the institutional patterns to be followed in the building of the new republic (only the prisons system reform, the fruit of their own personal experience, was specifically addressed); c) a technical or scientific approach to the utilization of human and material resources in the implementation of a government program; d) a sound industrialization plan (there had been one initiated by Machado that its author, Irisarri himself, had called "agrarian, antilatifundium, anti-interventionist, and nationalist"); e) a list of demands concerning the Negro, underrated in general and discriminated against in terms of participation and full integration into public and private life; and above all, f) the organized vehicle that would provide both the platform and the support throughout the whole process from beginning to end, what the political "scientists" call "transmission belts" in effecting changes.

Of course, it must be kept in mind that techniques of planning were unknown then in the democratic societies. (Even the Soviet "five-year plans" were carried out coercively and with difficulty.) The modern concepts of economic development had not yet been conceived; neither did there exist the international institutions that currently finance such projects.

The Directorio had its most dramatic confrontation at the end of those twenty-three days. On September 4, 1933, it faced the two most difficult junctures of its existence: the case of the traitor José Soler and the rebellion of the sergeants that toppled the Céspedes government. Both events, the capture of Soler and the Columbia military revolt, took place in the early hours of that day.

Soler was tried by a court formed by members of the 1930 and 1927 Directorios. Julio Gaunard, a journalist and a veteran of the 1931 Gibara expedition, acted as secretary. Soler was found guilty and sentenced to death. He was executed by firing squad that same afternoon.

While those who had attended the trial slept, exhausted after a day of intense emotional stress, other members who had been absent went to Camp Columbia to try to inject revolutionary content into a military revolt that originally was nothing but an opportunistic break of discipline demanding class benefits for the lower-rank elements of the Army. And the students succeeded in causing the conversion that immediately led to the formation of the first Cuban government to appear in the international community without the approval of the United States.

All authoritative witnesses of those events, especially Enrique Fernández, Emilio Laurent, and Luis Aguilar León, agree that without the DEU's intervention, the soldiers' revolt would have simply fizzled. The leaders of the movement would have been arrested and later released. Some might have been shuffled to administrative positions and most of their demands granted. A precarious discipline would have been restored, and that would have been all. But the speed with which the Directorio moved at the critical moment, as the only existing faction with public credibility, squelched all potential attempts to paralyze the movement, which proceeded now with a brand new revolutionary orientation.

Although dozens of officers of academic extraction joined the Sergeants' Movement after years awaiting merited promotions that never occurred, they were not immediately incorporated into the commanding cadres. The net result was, instead, to increase the percentage of officers coming from the sergeants' ranks, which prior to September 4 already accounted for 56 percent of all promotions.

When Batista gained total control of power thanks to the encouragement and support of the United States — Ambassador Caffery used to accompany him on horseback rides at Camp Columbia in public display of support — all the political elements that had opposed the revolutionary government were reinstalled in the administrative machinery. Batista "enjoyed rather than exercised power." In time, academic aspirations sprouted again within the military ranks, and the War College was created, with eminent professors of the University on its staff during the administrations of Grau San Martín and Prío Socarrás (1944-1952).

Although these two *auténtico* administrations proceeded to weed out from the commands most of the improvised officers placed there by Batista, they never had a true military policy based on a professionally qualified chain of command. The military schools produced new rounds of graduates, many of whom went on to perfect their technical preparation in international military academies, such as the Superior School of War in Mexico and senior military schools in the United States. From among these officers rose the conspiracy led by Ramón Barquín, who planned a simple *coup de main* that would have reestablished democracy in Cuba. The attempt was frustrated by an informer, and the result was that the army, navy, and air force were emptied of their best officers. The Cuban armed forces thus fell into the hands of the most inept. The five positions of general went to Batista's cronies.

To crown this succinct summary of the historic role of the 1930 Directorio Estudiantil Universitario, let me just mention five interesting facts.

1. The DEU never had a president. It had a secretary in charge of proceedings and correspondence. Silvia Martel served as such in the beginning, and Raúl Oms Narbona followed.

2. The DEU existed for 1,130 days, from September 30, 1930, till November 4, 1933. During that time it was the decisive factor in the overthrow of Machado and twenty-three days later the exclusive determining factor in the overthrow of the Céspedes government.

3. The amount of money it spent during the whole period was seventeen thousand pesos, which came from various sources — individual donations, benefits in theaters or arenas, and the sale of bonds to sympathizers. In the records of the permanent treasurer, Guillermo M. Cancio y Sánchez, oldest member of the Directorio, items such as this can be found: "Delivered to Rubén León to stamp a letter to the local Directorio in Manzanillo, 2 cents . . . ."

4. With the sole exception of Mario Labourdette, who during an emergency served for a few weeks as chief of police of Havana, *no member of the DEU occupied any position nor received any emolument whatsoever from the administration they installed in power.* Juan Antonio Rubio Padilla and Carlos Prío Socarrás were paid travel expenses and ten dollars per day living expenses for the duration of their mission as secretaries of the Cuban delegation to the Pan-American Conference at Montevideo. But *neither they nor any other member of the DEU permanently received viaticums, honoraria, emoluments, or salaries for their public services to the country.*

5. *The 1930 Directorio Estudiantil Universitario (DEU) was the only student body in the history of the world to have ever held power in their country.*

THE DEU, THE 1930 GENERATION, AND POLITICAL *AUTENTICISMO*

D o these three different terms — Directorio Estudiantil Universitario, the 1930 Generation, and *autenticismo* — define the same entity?

It would certainly appear that they do to the distant or superficial observer. However, some of us who lived through the genesis and developments of that period can show significant, if at times subtle, differences. In other words, those designations may overlap to a certain degree, but they are not by any means equivalent. The ambiguity arises from several coincidences in time and in persons. The political movement that came to be known as *autenticismo* (supposedly to embody the ideals of the "authentic revolution") created the *Partido Revolucionario Cubano* (Cuban Revolutionary Party, PRC) in 1934. Its main figure was Ramón Grau San Martín, whom the Directorio had elevated to the provisional presidency in 1933 (which he was able to exercise for 132 days). The *auténtico* party later carried Grau San Martín to the constitutional presidency in 1944. Then Prío Socarrás, a child of the 1930 Generation and perhaps the best-known of the Directorio leaders, succeeded Grau to the constitutional presidency in 1948.

Those coincidences have led to another unfair historical generalization. Since both the constitutional *auténtico* administrations of Grau San Martín and Prío Socarrás were tainted by unprecedented scandals and corruption, many have concluded that the salient characteristic of the 1930 Generation was "dishonesty." Carlos Prío himself has been known to accept this interpretation as correct.[1] But those of us of the same generation, who never practiced the vices that those two leaders practiced and promoted, object to our generation as a whole being branded with the worst moral qualifications or to its being exclusively represented by its least virtuous exponents — which is the case when "*autenticismo*" and the "1930 Generation" are assumed to be the same thing.

It is not a question of embellishing the past, only of clarifying its true profile.

Nevertheless, it is necessary to review from a historic perspective the trajectory of the DEU, then to place three of its members into what they became: a new party that, in spite of calling itself *revolutionary*, became a traditional party. True, it had granted to the people minor demands, but it was incapable of adapting the Cuban State "to its true ends and leave established an authentic democracy." Assimilated first into the corrupt political arena and later devoured by it, that "traditionalized" and "professionalized" party was so incapable of enacting basic solutions that soon its leaders were absorbed by the vested interests of the historic Cuban republic. *Autenticismo* — to which some erroneously assign the entire "1930 Generation" — was in the end incapable of carrying out, even with the power it enjoyed for eight years, the historic mission with which it had been entrusted.

The Directorio Estudiantil Universitario debuted in Cuba's political arena on September 30, 1930, with a bold street demonstration prohibited by the government. This marked the first turning point in the political history of Cuba, which had been a republic only twenty-eight years. The fact that one of the leaders of the demonstration, Rafael Trejo, was fatally wounded when the police charged to disperse them touched off an awakening of the national conscience. The public immediately rallied in spontaneous support of the students. Soon practically everyone was wearing black arm bands as a sign of mourning and protest. Encouraged by the popular response, the student leadership followed up with their November 18 manifesto in which the Directorio launched the slogan of the new struggle, "for a total and definitive change of regime," meaning that the national aspiration went beyond the simple demand for Machado's resignation.

In five years the Machado government had slid from the pinnacle of public admiration. Machado had enjoyed the support of all social classes, and even the University of Havana had bestowed on him an honorary doctorate. His vertical plunge began in 1927 when a group of university students were expelled for opposing Machado's reelection and the extension of his constitutional term in office. Parallel to that, one general, four colonels, and two other prestigious figures of the War of Independence founded the *Asociación Unión Nacionalista*, a political organization to combat the regime.

The "Nationalists," at first alone, were later joined by other groups in the antigovernment campaign, namely, the followers of former president Major General Mario García Menocal (1913-1921), those of former Havana Mayor Miguel Mariano Gómez, the son of a caudillo, and former president José Miguel Gómez (1909-1913). Together they formed a political opposition front whose aims went no farther than to revitalize the old colonial molds of the past that Machado had readjusted to suit his own personal ambitions. Their uppermost demand was the restoration of the 1901 Constitution, under the protection of which they had always managed to reap lush electoral and political gains since the birth of the republic. And while their incorporations contributed to inflate the opposition in a quantitative sense, they rather detracted qualitatively from it in terms of hopes for essential changes in the discredited political setup of Cuba.

The prohibition against organizing new parties or reorganizing the existing ones prevented the natural renewal of their leadership and the enlistment of the younger generations. Consequently, the flood-gates were opened to youthful activities beginning with civil disobedience and evolving into revolutionary activities. The public discontent, which had been gathering steam with Machado's scheming extension of office and made-to-order constituent assembly, soon emerged as moral and often active support of the young protesters.

The juridical violations of constitutional order were followed by the progressive elimination of civil rights and a brutal police repression that included persecution, illegal imprisonment, tortures, and assassinations. The process increased the negative balance of what a Cuban novelist, Carlos Loveira, had called a republic of "generals and doctors."

Along the way, the loss of faith in electoral proceedings had given rise to a nonpartisan detachment from the political processes as a form of direct protest against the traditional politicians. The substance of this detachment, *apoliticismo* (apoliticism), according to philosophy professor Jorge Mañach, "was but an irritation against the fruitless and corrupted professional politics; that political detachment also carried with it a certain liberation wish in the face of vested interests both from within and without" (Mañach 1942, 4).

That collective sense of frustration was further heightened by the uninterrupted disappointments of five successive republican administrations and aggravated by the limited sovereignty created by the Platt Amendment. It was a crushing feeling of defenselessness and bitterness that overcame the people every time an American ambassador rose to make public pronouncements in favor of this or that domestic government, no matter how corrupt or unpopular. Furthermore, the economic dependence on one single product, one single market to sell to, and only one market from which to buy one thousand products aggravated the stress of national limitation.

But it was not that the politicians of the early days of the Republic were so wicked as always to choose the worst of all options. It was rather that the suffocating status as a semi-autonomous political and economic protectorate, upon which the republic was originally established, went unchallenged by any counterforce of domestic virtue that might have caused the country to advance, even if only step by little step, toward an ideal of full national integrity and realization. Instead, according to Mañach, a vicious circle developed in which the existing political machineries simply avoided the problem of transforming the precarious colonial structures into a self-sufficient and self-respecting republic.

Mañach concluded his assessment that the old political parties were too inept for any task of national advancement, adding,

> . . . they have been formed, directed, and inspired in such a way that even if they wanted they wouldn't be able, whether in power or in the opposition, to carry on a genuine policy of national salvation. *They cannot go against vested interests* because those vested interests are represented within their own structures. *They cannot crusade against corruption in government* because they need that corruption in order to maintain their electoral weight, which comes from the bureaucracy, from "services" and privileges more or less oblique, and from the ever-increasing investment of funds that by no means can derive from licit sources. *They cannot go to the bottom* of the big economic problems on the international level because, on the one hand, they lack the unity and strength of thought forcefully to lay on the table the Cuban claims, and on the other hand, they lack the moral authority and even the administrative and technical know-how that are indispensable to prevail outside of Cuba over those interests they haven't been able to control within their own nation (Mañach 1942, 4).

That was the atmosphere of frustration, skepticism, and yet of hope too, in which the Directorio appeared on the national scene. It received its baptism of blood in the events of September 30, but when in November the DEU voiced its aspiration toward a total and definitive change of regime, the entire country rose in complete and unprecedented support.

Cuban society — never totally integrated since vanquished Spaniards and conquering Americans joined in unsuccessfully advocating the annexation of the island to the United States — was for the most part in favor of the change. That mass of young students — gallant, proud, and moved only by noble, disinterested aspirations, represented by beardless youths "without any complicity with the past," and willing to sacrifice themselves in the name of an idealized nation in their challenge of a dreaded dictatorship — received a public following such as had never before been witnessed in Cuba. September 30 saw the historic explosion that resulted from the popular weariness at the whole republican frustration, the public apathy resulting from the abuse of power and the illegitimate extension of terms in office both in the executive and legislative branches, the anguish generated by repressive official violence, and the emergence of a young generation ready to alter the course of history in a patriotic attempt to rescue and give new life to the nation.

That is the only explanation for how the tiny nucleus that originally formed the Directorio and signed Trejo's death notice — mere political debutantes theretofore unknown to public opinion, much less to most of their fellow students, immature and still without the intellectual base that must accompany the responsibility of leadership — could raise such waves of enthusiasm and expectations in the masses, reaching even to the other universities of the hemisphere and the most outstanding figures of the Spanish intellectual world.

But the Directorio was not emotionally conditioned for such a high calling. The result was a crisis of sensitivity that by a sort of sublimation developed into revolutionary mysticism. From then on the Directorio would stop at nothing, whatever the risks or the price.

Soon an implacable police persecution was unleashed against them. Some would land in prison; others, like Félix Ernesto Alpízar, Pío Alvarez, and Carlos Manuel Fuertes Blandino, would pay with their lives for daring to defy tyranny.

Later the Directorio confronted the American mediation, welcomed by all the rest of the opposition, including the ABC, which, until that moment, was a seemingly innovative force. The old and new leaders chose to hold on to the traditional role of the "colonial establishment," an attitude that came to be known as the "Plattist mentality" — a resigned acceptance of Platt Amendment status while taking advantage of its derived benefits. But within the Directorio itself there was, as Ortega y Gasset would observe, "a small minority of spiritual scouts, vigilant souls, who had a glimmering of distant tracts of territory still to be invaded." He added, "this minority is doomed never to be properly understood; gestures which the vision of new dominions calls forth from it cannot be rightly interpreted by the main body advancing behind and not yet in possession of the height from which the 'terra incognita' is being examined" (Ortega y Gasset [1931] 1961, 12). The Directorio had seen the "new dominions" down the road, still hidden from the mass of its followers. The Directorio saw the prematurely old young politicians rubbing elbows around the negotiations table with the white-haired solons of the old school. They did not exactly perceive yet the silhouette of President Céspedes and his submissive cabinet, but sketched them politically when they denounced the motives of the great intervening power and flatly refused to take part in the negotiations.

The spectacle of the old and the new leaders complacently going along with the American mediation left the majority of the public in confusion. But since the Directorio's example had injected a new faith in the hearts of the Cuban people, the prospect of a generation directing the true historic destiny of the country became a distinct possibility. For, to quote Ortega again, "a generation is not a handful of outstanding men, nor simply a mass of men; it resembles a new integration of the social body, with its select minority and its gross multitude, launched upon the orbit of existence with a pre-established vital trajectory" (Ortega y Gasset [1931] 1961, 14-5). From that dynamic interrelationship between mass and individual, the concept of generation emerges.

It was precisely in that Orteguian context that the DEU made its impact on the history of Cuba. It became the select minority, the leading cell of the 1930 Generation.

Its vision of a new Cuba made the Directorio a "center of social gravity" that, like a giant magnet, attracted to itself vast waves of people, young and not-so-young alike, who, moved by the age factor, inclined naturally toward one side or the other of the "date zone" that encompasses a generation. The Directorio, therefore, had become the *elect* that would direct the changing process.

Another distinguished contemporary observer and active participant, Enrique Fernández, perhaps the best chronicler of that period, expressed the DEU's role this way: "The University marched *en masse* into the battle and, already consecrated with the blood of a martyr, joined the opposition hoisting the principle that would transform its sense and its objectives" Fernández 1950, 18).

Then he went on to complement the slogan of "total and definitive change of regime" with a detailed rejection of specific vices of the Cuban political life:

> The Directorio is just that: a categorical NO! NO to dubious accommodations and compromises; NO to political opportunism; NO to conventional forgery; NO to the tolerance of crime, embezzlement, and bribery; NO to the immoral chronic disregard of punishable deeds committed by high figures in public office; NO to all the shameful realities that challenge its public appearance; NO to the sickening tendency to submit our domestic conflicts to foreign arbitration (Fernández 1950, 19).

The policy of total change expounded in the specific rejections detailed by Fernández indeed made the Directorio the political "elect" of the emerging generation. As Ortega put it, they were "conscious of the immediate past as something in urgent need of radical reform," through a "militant philosophy, the aspiration of which is to destroy and completely supersede the past" (Ortega y Gasset [1931] 1961, 12).

Later, when Machado was finally forced out of office only to be succeeded by the Céspedes regime, it was a direct result of the mediatory activities of the American ambassador.

The Directorio repudiated that succession in the name of the Revolution, Cuba, and Ibero-America. The sensation of generational relay was so vivid that the provisional president himself and even foreign observers perceived it.

Céspedes, first antagonized and then forced to resign by the DEU, interpreting the necessity of that relay, would say:

> I am one of the Cubans advanced in years, *one of those who fought in the 1890s. We, the men of that generation, failed in not giving Cuba what she ought to have. We must make way to younger men. It's their turn to prove what they can do* [emphasis added] (Krogh 1966, 272).

And another follower of the Cuban process, the American Peter Frederick Krogh, said that "a great portion of the Cuban people wanted not only to get rid of Machado but wished also a general sweeping of his regime and of the entire established order" (Krogh 1966, 258). And that exactly was the DEU formula: for a total and definitive change of regime.

Furthermore, Krogh went on, "the crisis Cuba was experiencing in August 1933 was a fundamental conflict of generations, in which the candor and the frustration of the young people confronted the craftiness and the moderation of the elders" (Krogh 1966, 269). In other words, in Krogh's mind, the 1930 Generation and the Directorio were one and the same thing.

After only twenty-three days, the DEU and the masses confronted that same Mediation government, forced it out of power, and, for the first time in the Cuban history, installed a government that did not depend on North American approval for its establishment. Afterward, the Directorio continued to act as the driving political force within the 1930 Generation. Even though it invited criticism for its repeated vow to eschew public office, with or without pay, its influence on the actual government resulted in the initiation and implementation of legislations supporting the proposals published in its August 1933 program.

Of those decrees emitted in the course of one hundred thirty-two days of government — five of the Pentarchy and one hundred twenty-seven of Grau — there is not a single decision that was not previously outlined or implied by the DEU Program, except those measures which responded directly to popular needs and demands.

Somewhere, the idealism of guiding the government rather than running it had to run head on against the actual wielders of power. The showdown, of course, carried tremendous historical consequences. At that crucial meeting on November 3 in Carbó's home, to carry out the carefully drawn plans to arrest and execute Batista for treason, Grau San Martín suddenly and unilaterally reversed himself and instead confirmed Batista as Army Chief of Staff. His decision marked the functional termination of the 1930 Generation in politics and left the brief but powerful revolution unfinished.

After accomplishing Batista's elimination with full support of the military commanders, who all agreed with the DEU that Batista's treason would terminate their careers, the Directorio would have gone on to complete its historic program. A constituent assembly would be called, into which would be incorporated all the factions plotting Grau's overthrow, who had been denied power by Batista, who would no longer exist.

This forced incorporation of government supporters and opposition factions into a constituent assembly would have forced the DEU to transform from a student organization into a true political force involved directly in government. The entire 1930 Generation would have become a real force in changing the political, social, and international destiny of the country.

Instead, Grau betrayed the DEU, the military commanders, and indeed, the very destiny of the Cuban people and allowed Batista to continue his sleazy machinations. His frustration of the simple plan to arrest Batista — and with it the concomitant frustration of the plan to renew Cuba — *forced the dissolution of the betrayed student organization directing the government, and their abandonment of responsibility for consequences that would ultimately be borne by the people of Cuba.*

True, the DEU's revolutionary momentum lingered for a while and culminated in the abrogation of the Platt Amendment in Montevideo in December 1933 and the concession of the right of suffrage to women in Havana in January 1934. But it is no less certain that "generations are manifest only at times, in certain types of societies, during especially critical periods, or when significant innovations occur" (Julián María 1967, 162). Nor do generations necessarily occupy a precise chronological span.

The 1930 Generation had exploded onto the political scene without having passed the normal preparatory stage of "social preparation." It combined two other phases, those of "operating in power" and "retreat."

But realistically, what really occurred in the series of mutations from DEU to 1930 Generation and ultimately to the *auténtico* movement? Simply stated, the DEU united valiant but noncharismatic leaders and just average dedicated individuals, all moved by the same patriotic zeal and lofty ideals. Riding on the unexpected wave of public support, the group as a whole exuded a charisma that reflected a common unity that Ortega called *vigencia colectiva* (vital sensibility).

All, leaders and average members alike, followed a code of ethics by which they measured their conduct and which compelled their actions. This moral code passed from individual to individual, emanating from the inner sense of sacred mission, nurtured by popular support. In living by that code, the members discovered a euphoria, a spiritual satisfaction that minimized concern for personal risk and produced exceptional personal valor that in normal times might never have emerged in their individual characters.

The ultimate result, then, was that these average individuals, caught in the same sphere and moved by the same incentives and aspirations, drew on the collective energy, that vital sensibility, to act in harmony with the elite. But the great majority, inspired though they had been with the high spirit of the heroic struggle and dedication to the idealistic cause, found it extremely hard later to transfer their dedication to the uninspiring arena of political professionalism. In fact, only three of them, precisely those who had shown discernible signs of a political aptitude before, Carlos Prío Socarrás, Rubén León, and Manuel Antonio de Varona, decided to enter traditional politics. They were the co-founders of the *Partido Revolucionario Cubano (Auténtico)* and reaped successes in electoral politics, though no longer with that same sense of self-sacrifice or spiritual commitment.

Why did only three of the DEU members choose to remain in public life, and why did the 1930 Generation, of which the DEU was supposed to have been the political elite, dissolve silently with it like the ancient Mayan race in southern México and Central America shortly before the Spanish conquest?

Simply stated, the generation possessed, due to its exaggerated idealism, only a transitory desire to govern, but no true vocation for power. It began the struggle romantically with the rescue of public liberties, and, without meaning to, deepened the struggle. When it received national support, it felt consecrated to a mission and therefore to the undertaking. Later, when they saw how all of those that had accompanied them in the struggle ran toward the historic fountain of Power, the United States, the DEU developed the ARPE (*Agrupación Revolucionaria Programa Estudiantil*) idea and defined its government program. Upon seizing power, the DEU promptly delegated it. When the individual designated to hold that delegated power chose to betray them, they had no alternative but to dissolve the organization. It disappeared like the old Mayans. They had only seemed to retain some vestige of their previous influence because of the three politically inclined members arising from the organization. Because of those three, it appeared that the 1930 Generation was still in charge.

Having already taken power and given it away, and having savored the bitterness of disloyalty, it lost its transitory desire for power which was just that — transitory.

Then came the "political" stage ten years later. Grau San Martín, as leader and main figure of the *Partido Revolucionario Cubano* (PRC), was elected president in 1944. Significantly, the DEU did not accompany Grau San Martín; only the three, Prío, León, and Varona, accompanied him into the political arena. Only those three possessed any political vocation, having begun with the AUN before the founding of the DEU.

And how did those three products of the DEU fare?

The one who reached highest was Prío, succeeding Grau in the presidency in 1948. Incredibly enough, Prío was the most apathetic regarding power. But he was favored by seniority in the *Auténtico* movement and, since the times of demonstrations and manifestos, his name had been constantly in the public ear. As customers do in certain stores, Prío had taken his number and just waited for his turn. Grau had held number one; Prío, number two. It was a long but rewarding wait. He, "the disciple," succeeded "the professor" in the presidency.

Rubén León was, of the three, the least. He was a member of the *Juventud Universitaria Nacionalista* (Nationalist University Youth) before becoming a member of the DEU. In the interior he had been a man of action, but in the capital just an orator. His political trajectory was tortuous. Betraying the *Auténtico* movement, he followed Carbó in the adventure of the *Partido Nacional Revolucionario* (National Revolutionary Party). Its basic purpose was to accommodate the Batista reality in the early 1940s, and it became cynically known as the "realist" party. Pepelín Leyva, also from the DEU and of the same class in the School of Veterinary Medicine, used to say of León that "since he never graduated, he secretly practiced curing himself."

Manuel Antonio ("Tony") Varona surpassed the other two in human quality. Although a notch below Carlos Prío intellectually, Varona nevertheless subordinated himself to Prío in disproportion to their respective political statures. Prío was more of a national figure, but Varona held more political sway as party leader in the larger Camagüey Province than Prío did in the smaller Pinar del Río. Varona was the most determined and brave, and personally had more character than the other two. Yet, an innate intolerance bordering on rudeness shut many doors to him and prevented him from reaching a greater historical role.

One might wonder if the masses of the 1930 Generation, those who had followed the leadership of the DEU on an active basis, simply went home after the demise of the organization and the resignation of its leaders. The answer is no; Grau and the few DEU representatives who accompanied him were followed by a silent majority of second-line activists, the anonymous heroes of the whole process, the restless figures of the barrio, the township, and the province who transported everything, who accomplished everything. They were the direct link with the masses, "the transmission belts of the instruments of the struggle," as the political "scientists" would say. But they constituted only a second-level tier that did not lead, much less give orders. Meanwhile, the higher echelons of the party were gradually infiltrated by elements of the vested interests — great landowners, sugar mill tycoons, big cattle ranchers, high executives of the public utilities companies. The contradictory reality became exactly what Mañach had clearly described — the traditional parties could not fight the vested interests that had become an integral part of their organizations. This reality also explains how the two consecutive *Auténtico* administrations, during their eight years in power, produced less legislation than the provisional government of the 1930 Generation in its mere 132 days (September 1933 to January 1934) in power.

Grau San Martín, the beneficiary of the entire revolutionary legacy of the idealistic young generation, sole heir of the historic effort of thousands of persecuted, imprisoned, and murdered revolutionaries, inheritor of the political wealth gained by scores of popular laws, took advantage again of the superior position *caudillismo* offered him. He consolidated his power with a political machinery of his own and the support of a credulous populace, disregarded the commitments of the original *auténtico* movement, threw the Directorio overboard, and embarked on an orgy of scandal and corruption that by far surpassed the worst precedents of Cuba's political history.

Those are the main reasons the 1930 Generation concept cannot accurately be applied to the *auténtico* political movement later headed by Grau San Martín. The generation idea emanated from the historic role of the 1930 Directorio Estudiantil Universitario that suddenly ended following Grau San Martín's unexpected about-face in the famous November 3 meeting at Carbó's house. From then on, naturally, the generation, as a defined movement, could not be reborn under the aegis of the same man that had betrayed it and dug its grave.

The Cuban people, on the other hand, sealed their own fate when they conferred on Grau San Martín the political legacy of the 1930 Generation. Popular perception was blurred by the fact that it had been during his provisional presidency (appointed by the Directorio) that the epoch-making legislation had been enacted. There coincided also a certain void of national leadership. Guiteras, for instance, had founded a radical organization named *Joven Cuba*, but he was hunted down by Batista and killed by soldiers on May 8, 1935, after an informer told them where he and a few followers were waiting for a ship to México. That made Grau for the time being the only national figure of the *auténtico* movement.

Certainly, outside the DEU there were other high-caliber figures in the generation. People like Alejandro Vergara, Carlos Hevia, Eddy Chibás, and even Sergio Carbó himself enjoyed wide public prestige if not necessarily national leadership. If men like these could have competed in open political contest with Directorio leaders such as Rubio Padilla, Valdés Daussá, Felipe Pazos, Mongo Miyar, and others like Rafael García Bárcena and even myself, perhaps the moral force of the revolution could have been preserved. Sheer moral force might have achieved results far greater than the sum of all individual efforts.

Grau San Martín decided on November 3, 1933, to remain with Batista and rid himself of the Directorio. Although some loose creative forces remained active for a while, the combative vanguard of the 1930 Generation, the Directorio, had its obituary written. Two and a half months later, Batista would, in turn, throw Grau overboard, replacing him with the more pliable Mendieta. In the press photos of Grau leaving the executive mansion, no member of the Directorio that had appointed him president in September 1933 appears.

A few months later, however, Grau returned from México to assume the leadership of the newly organized *Partido Revolucionario Cubano*, popularly know as the *Auténtico* Party. His past glories as provisional president made him the caudillo of the masses, who idolized him beyond measure. He would thenceforth be the last depository of all the accomplishments of the generation. As such, perhaps Grau San Martín himself was the "1930 Generation."

This brings up the question of whether Grau San Martín could actually be considered as belonging to that Generation.

According to sociologists, the concept of generation must be defined in the chronological light of both "contemporaneity" and "contemporaneousness." This being so, it can definitely be asserted that Grau San Martín was not a representative of the 1930 Generation.

I concur with what Julián Marías said regarding Ortega Y Gasset's concept of contemporaneity: "It includes individuals who not only live in the same time span but who also share a common childhood and a common youth, that is to say, who are of the same age" (Marías 1967, 162). Thus, he defines the concept more in sociological than grammatical terms. If we go by the age yardstick, it is elementary that Grau is automatically excluded from the 1930 Generation. He was precisely ten years older than the oldest of the Directorio members, Guillermo M. Cancio, who in turn was several years ahead of the next eldest in the group, Carlos Prío Socarrás. So, even if the age factor alone may not function as a determinant, the respective environmental circumstances do. While the students shared in common all the typical aspects of campus life — classroom fellowship, chatting in the unforgettable Patio de los Laureles, the innate rebelliousness of young people — Professor Grau's world was quite different: his chair in the School of Medicine, his private practice with a select clientele, his upper-class social level. It is true that Grau seemed to identify with the ardor and the audacity of *los muchachos* — but only until November 3, 1933. What in the young students became a nearly mystic battle, in the prestigious professor was merely the cool ambition for power. This contrast ought to be sufficient to exclude Grau San Martín as a member of the 1930 Generation.

But what about Prío? Could he not be measured by the same standards? When Prío joined the DEU in 1930 he came with an early record of participation and interest in politics. He began as a follower of Rafael Guas Inclán in the Chávez district of Havana, who had already gained prominence in the Liberal Party. Then as a university student, Prío began to vacillate, declining to join the 1927 Directorio when it initiated the struggle against Machado's schemes to perpetuate himself in power. Yet in 1930, Prío joined the anti-Machado *Asociación Unión Nacionalista* party, rising to the post of secretary general in its student wing, the *Juventud Universitaria*. But despite the apparent contradictions, Prío historically and chronologically belonged to the 1930

Generation as well as the Directorio Estudiantil Universitario, a member of the DEU from its conception until its dissolution on 4 November 1933. Later, after the frustrated insurrectional attempts against Batista's shadowy power in which he, de Léon, and Varona maintained the somewhat flagging generational spirit that was not really their own, he began to drift away. They became but the remnants or vestiges of the Generation to which they had "belonged." When Prío served as a delegate to the Constituent Assembly, and later as a Senator, Prime Minister, and Minister of Labor — in a period of only eight years — did he demonstrate any exceptional abilities? It is proven neither in the fact of his governing nor in his overthrow; his abilities were substantiated, however in that he capably navigated the waters of professional politics.

But, paradoxically enough, Prío actually lacked the desire for power. He was nominated for the presidency by the *Auténtico* Party more or less by elimination. Varona was not interested in running, and the other possible candidates were less qualified within the party and ranked less in Grau's favor. Massive financial support from public sources helped him win the election, and his opening cabinet was not exactly first-rate. His administration was rather mediocre, characterized by an alternating succession of high and low points in which positive achievements were mixed with shameful scandals. For instance, he "saved" old paper money from incineration after it had been pulled from circulation and replaced by new bills. On the other hand, he did promote decidedly positive legislation as well. And he was president on March 10, 1952, the target and victim of Batista's coup d'état. The man with no great desire for power sought asylum in the Mexican Embassy, giving up without a fight.

Ultimately, Prío alone possessed no great personal virtues or outstanding accomplishments. Under the emotional and moral influence of the DEU he functioned as a capable leader and dedicated fighter; without the moral yoke of the Directorio to guide and influence his efforts, he exhibited none of the exemplary traits that distinguished the 1930 Generation.

It should be stated for the record, however, that, notwithstanding their respective flaws and minuses, all four men — Grau, Prío, Varona, and León — shared common genuine democratic ideals, passionately advocated for public liberties and civil rights, and execrated political crime. And, of course, all four of them were outright anticommunists.

Now let us take a look at one of the most colorful and singular figures of that period: Eddy Chibás. A fighter by nature, he entered the political arena as a member of the 1927 Directorio Estudiantil Universitario, opposing Machado's crafty attempt to extend his constitutional term in office. Later, he founded the *Partido del Pueblo Cubano (Ortodoxos)* (Cuban People's [Orthodox] Party). Was he or was he not one of the 1930 Generation?

Yes, without a doubt, although no historian or political critic classifies him as such, since he never actually held the reigns of "power." How could he be a part of that generation exemplified by the corrupt Grau and Prío administrations, he who was their prime historic antagonist?

But Chibás is indeed a pure child of the 1930 Generation, both through his contemporaneousness and through his participation. On behalf of the 1927 Directorio, his signature appeared next to those of Prío, Varona, León, and the others in manifestos of the 1930 Directorio, including the one issued on September 5, 1933. He thus shared in the "militant philosophy" of destroying the past by "radically reforming" it (Ortega y Gasset [1931] 1961, 12). ("Why not also the present?" he told me once.) Yet, his loyalty to Grau San Martín caused him on occasion to lower his moral standards. At one point, he publicly defended a dubious administration policy of international "bartering." In the case of the Cienfuegos mayoralty, in order to follow the government line, he used all kinds of dirty electoral tricks against candidate Rodrigo Bustamente, an honest and respected citizen.

Concerning this sort of contradiction among the representatives of a given generation, the comments of Ortega y Gasset in that regard come to mind:

> Beneath this general sign of identity, individuals of so diverse a temper can exist that, being compelled to live in close contact with one another, inasmuch as they are contemporaries, they often find themselves mutually antipathetic. But under the most violent opposition of "pros" and "antis" it is easy to perceive a real union of interests. Both parties consist of men of their own time; and great as their differences may be their mutual resemblances are still greater (Ortega y Gasset [1931] 1961, 15).

Obviously, however, one can only speculate as to how Chibás's party — whose composition was the same that Mañach ascribes to the traditional parties — would have done had it achieved power. It is my feeling, having known Chibás personally and having been privy to his ideas, that despite a certain "irrationality" (that, not without grounds, was attributed to him), Chibás would have turned out to be a man of very positive accomplishments in government — contrary to the Cuban popular wisdom that says "good in revolution, bad in power." His well-known irrationality was deliberately used in the opposition. He carried considerable responsibility, for instance, for undermining the corrupt Prío regime, so easily toppled by Batista on March 10, 1952.

I am personally convinced that Chibás would have been a far better man in government than either Grau or Prío. In a way power frightened him; he was afraid of his image being tarnished in the process, of not being able to live up to his own high standards and expectations. He aspired to be a great achiever and set an example for Cuba and Latin America. Because he was aware of his personal limitations, he endeavored the more to learn the mechanics of making decisions when faced with different alternatives — which is one of the basic requirements of the science of government. Those who lived in those days can attest to what extent Chibás made me his confidant. I cite them as witnesses today to assert that Chibás understood the fundamental importance of selecting an executive apparatus of sufficient homogeneity and solidarity in thinking to eschew untimely ambitions while carrying out its duties. He also knew that the ability to reconcile opposing views and interests was essential for getting a Congress to pass legislation that would transform theory into pragmatic measures. Chibás likewise understood the role of public opinion in the realization of a government program and how important it was to be able to change the skepticism and disbelief of a public used to being chronically disappointed into enthusiasm and cooperation.

Only a man with a natural disposition for government, needing only experience to mature his innate capabilities, or one who, knowing his own weaknesses and handicaps, vehemently desires to overcome them, can become a great head of state. In my opinion, Chibás was very close to being such a man, despite his characteristic tendency toward the high-sounding and the strident, which perhaps he would have overcome had he assumed power. It is my judgment that Chibás would have been a great chief of state *in a constitutional framework with the three branches of government properly counterbalanced.*

Chibas's political impact on the public subconscious reached such depth that in power it would have become — in contrast with Grau and Prío — the operating spirit of the 1930 Generation. His strong vocation to service could find satisfaction only in the opposition, for he longed for glory rather than material gain.

According to Jaime Suchlicki, "Chibás monopolized the rhetoric of revolution, becoming the exponent of the frustrated old generation and the leader of a new generation bent on bringing morality and honesty to Cuban public life" (Suchlicki 1969, 55).

What of the rest of the thirty-six Directorio members? What became of them? What did they accomplish? Where did they go?

Well, the DEU, the genuine revolutionary elect of the 1930 Generation, had ended its mission inconclusively, in failure, deficiently, if you will, in the sense that their accomplishments were only partial and were never completed. As a generation whose historic political role had ended, exhausted and resigned, it simply disappeared like the ancient Mayans. And where else did those students go, but back to where they had come from — to the classrooms, to continue their abandoned studies, rejecting — without even needing to consider — all possibility of getting involved as active participants, much less as provocateurs in professional electoral politics.

Typically iconoclastic in their youth, not believing in gods of flesh and bone, the DEU group had scorned political "saints" and unrelentingly fought against *caudillismo,* to the point of introducing in Cuba the formula of the collegiate executive to avoid creating another caudillo. When that collegiate executive branch — the Pentarchy — failed, the DEU was defrauded almost immediately by the very man they had elevated to the presidency. And that man, ironically, later became the idol of the masses, the new, improbable caudillo, the patron saint of the people, but also the individual who would defraud them miserably.

So, what could the Directorio have done? The young student leaders suddenly found themselves confronted with a dilemma. Iconoclastic by nature and by the lessons of history, they could not go along with the crowd and kneel before the new false idol of the masses, the very same one who had so devastatingly failed them. No; better to retire from the struggle that now would not be heroic. It had been, in and of itself, rewarding, before it became a part of the new public contention, one with less moral satisfaction, supporting a new *caudillo* that now they would never be able to respect. To continue with those frustrating efforts would interrupt their academic careers. They had finished their journey through the halls of Power, so they had to revert: from power to the Halls.

What, then, was the final balance left by the Grau and Prío administrations? And was there any other participation from members of the 1930 Directorio Estudiantil Universitario?

During his administration (1944-1948), Grau can be credited with having instituted the "sugar differential," a device by which the price of Cuban sugar bought by the United States was automatically adjusted to the cost-of-living index in that country, so that the "difference" would result in higher salaries for the Cuban sugar workers. Grau also instituted pension funds for professionals as well as for the labor force. On the other hand, there existed a pervading sense of corruption, supported by inflated payrolls and corroborated by pejorative comments like *"come candela"* (fire eaters) and *"gatillo alegre"* (trigger-happy), both epithets alluding to official protection and impunity that many armed delinquents who passed for revolutionaries enjoyed. Grau even made such frivolous public statements as "the women rule" while commenting in private, "God help us if that ever happens!"

Grau was succeeded in the presidency by Prío, a former DEU leader and chronologically a man of the 1930 Generation. Prío was nominated by the *Auténtico* Party with Grau's blessing and won the 1948 election. (The press called him "the disciple," an allusion to his submissive loyalty to Grau, who had been a university professor.) Prío, a veteran of the heroic days of the Directorio, had the golden opportunity to start a moral reconversion of the *Auténtico* movement in government and restore it to the ideals and the canons of the 1930 Generation. But Prío lacked the moral stamina, the strength of character, the unbending will, and above all the vision that an endeavor of such nature required. Instead Prío broke entirely with his revolutionary past; it did not even occur to him to hold a meeting with his former fellow members of the 1930 Directorio. Occasionally, he did represent the aspirations and dreams of the generation, but normally he simply oversaw a continuation of Grau's version of Authenticism, characterized by vice, pleasure, *"pachanga"* [frivolous, shameless exercise of government], and *"dulce para todos,"* "sweets for all." (These were cynical attempts to justify corruption on the grounds that "everyone" benefitted.)

True, his administration left for the record a few positive highlights, such as the creation of the National Bank, the Bank of Agricultural and Industrial Development, and the Court of Punitive Sanctions.

Ramón Grau San Martín and Carlos Prío Socarrás in their consecutive administrations were constitutionally granted eight years of practically unrestricted power with a tremendous reservoir of popular support. They actually had carte blanche to fully implement the Directorio program. But they missed the historic opportunity. Before that the *Auténtico* Party had already shifted from an insurrectional policy — when strong-man Batista ruled uncontested through puppet presidents (Mendieta, Barnet, Laredo Bru) — to the electoral path after the 1939-40 Constituent Assembly and the subsequent "constitutional" Batista administration of 1940-1944. In view of its revolutionary background, it was to be expected that the *Auténtico* movement, once in power, would have embarked on what Mañach used to define as the task of transforming Cuba from a virtual colony to a fully sovereign and self-sufficient republic — the old dream of the Cubans. But, as history sadly shows, that expectation turned into sour disappointment.

The *Auténtico* record in government is perhaps unique in the annals of political developments throughout the world. Here was a ruling party that observed total respect for public liberties and absolute freedom of the press, while at the same time exhibiting a sorry disregard for its promises and commitments in the immediate past. Enrique Fernández (1950, 19) called it the fight against the conventional fraud, the dubious compromises, the tolerance of crime, embezzlement, bribery, the disregard of punishable deeds committed by public figures, and an unprecedented laxity in morals that became fertile ground for all kinds of vices and excesses. That was the critical point where the 1930 Generation and the old Directorio parted ways with the debased *Auténtico* movement.

Did Grau and Prío strengthen, with their public conduct, all the positive forces of moral order of our society, as the DEU promised in June of 1933?

Do the Directorio Estudiantil and the 1930 Generation merit, after promising in 1933 "a purge of the system, adjusting the political machinery to the true ends within an authentic democracy," to be considered even indirectly guilty because their promises were mocked by the two greatest beneficiaries of the Generation?

Of official *autenticismo* (the September movement politicized), it can be said that it turned out to be a huge sham of the ideals of national advancement and furtherance that the people had entrusted to the DEU and which they proclaimed during the 1930-33 revolutionary period.

This summary historical review ought to be sufficient to underscore the abysmal gap that separated the Directorio and the 1930 Generation from the *Auténtico* political movement. Grau San Martín and Prío Socarrás defrauded the Cuban people of their destiny and paved the way for even greater depredations on their national trust. They set the scene for Batista's return on March 10, 1952, and ultimately for the darkness from which Cuba still has not emerged, thirty years later. Should the Directorio Estudiantil and the 1930 Generation bear the great guilt and the historic responsibility that belongs to the Authenticism embodied in Grau and Prío?

Felipe Pazos, a former member of the Directorio, a true man of the 1930 Generation and with a distinguished career as an economist, has observed at close range the Venezuelan experience. In a discerning opinion confided to me, Pazos said that if, instead of Grau and Prío, Cuba would have had as presidents at that particular time men of the caliber of Rómulo Betancourt and Rafael Caldera [Venezuelan presidents, 1959-1963, and 1969-1973, respectively], the destiny of our country would have been quite different.

Some small measure of credit is due, however, to Prío, who upon occasion, and in the company of former Directorio members, was capable of joining forces and attaining some positive common goal. In those instances, he would again resonate the goals and ideals of the 1930 spirit and generation — but only in a transitory manner. His temporary returns to the idealism he had felt with us never penetrated to the depths of his spirit, nor did they have any lasting impact upon his presidential administration.

Authenticism itself did not equate to the 1930 Generation nor reflect the true beliefs and goals of the vanguard of that generation, the Directorio Estudiantil Universitario. Illustrious Spanish thinker, writer, journalist, and professor Julián Marías, in his poignant essay on the historic method of generations, said,

The distinction between minority and the masses is perfectly real; it is a functional structure of the collective body. So much is this so that one cannot be a man of the mass or belong to a select minority *a nativitate* [by birth], but one or the other happens according to the role or function one plays. No man can rest assured that he is a select individual, for as soon as he gives up tension and strain he behaves as a man of the mass. Nobody is doomed to be but just the latter, for as soon as he begins to make demands upon himself and to follow an authentic living, he detaches himself from the mass and comes to join the leading minority (Marías 1967, 108-9).

How does this concept apply to the 1930 Generation during the Prío presidency?

The Directorio came to be the select minority, the political elite of the 1930 Generation. But when its members found themselves in the position of having to decide whether to follow the political profession or other professions, they almost unanimously opted for the latter. They returned to the classrooms and to private life. They neglected the public "role or function." They gave up "tension and strain," and, in the words of Professor Marías, they began to "behave as men of the mass" and disappeared from the scene, just as the ancient Mayans disappeared from history — after creating the most exact calendar known up to that time.

The greatest beneficiary of the endeavors and sacrifices of that generation was Grau San Martín, who, significantly enough, called to service in his own government only one other DEU member: Carlos Prío Socarrás. The affinity between the two, the former professor of medicine and the former student of law, was thus cemented, so much so that Prío naturally became Grau's presidential heir.

Under Grau, no other member of the old Directorio was asked to serve in the administration, not even Chibás, representative of both the 1927 and 1930 Directorios, the grand master of propaganda. Chibás was elected senator in the 1944 general election, called *la jornada gloriosa de junio* ("the Glorious Journey of June"), only to become so disenchanted two years later that he decided to abandon the party and found his own, the *Partido del Pueblo Cubano (Ortodoxos)* [Cuban People's (Orthodox) Party]. With the same vigor and passion he had previously expressed in support of the duo, Chibás now pointed his verbal guns at Grau San Martín and Prío.

Is it not strange that those thirty-six men and women of the 1930 DEU should be totally ignored by the very same man whom they had picked and literally carried to the executive mansion, not on a sightseeing tour or as a simple visitor, but as the president of the Republic in 1933? Did Grau perhaps feel that, except for Prío, who was his prime minister and then succeeded him has president, the student leaders were not up to the high ethical standards with which he meant to conduct his government? The record shows quite the opposite to be true: Grau was the great champion of immorality who betrayed Cuba, the revolution, and the 1930 Generation.

And Carlos Prío — how did he act regarding his former companions from the Directorio? In truth, he, too, ignored the group as a whole, but he remained in close contact with some individuals, calling them to assume important technical positions in his administration. He entrusted Felipe Pazos, for instance, with the task of organizing the National Bank of Cuba and named him its president. To me, President Prío assigned the mission of reorganizing Cuba's international economic affairs as an ambassador (1948-1950). He later appointed me president of the Agricultural & Industrial Development Bank (BANFAIC) (1951-1952).

In our cases, we were two members of the 1930 DEU, who, for fifteen years, had been just mass-men according to Julián Marías, who now, "as soon as he begins to make demands upon himself and to follow an authentic living, he detaches himself from the mass and comes to join the leading minority." We were going to play "a role" and to exercise "a function." We were going to recover a given up tension. Once again, if only transitorily, we became a part of the late elite of the 1930 Generation.

Felipe Pazos, first president of the National Bank of Cuba, says of his experience in the Prío administration:

> For seven years — because of vested interests and fears of a *peso* devaluation — a law creating the Central Bank of Cuba had "rested" shelved in Congress until Carlos Prío took office as president of the Republic. Prío acted with incredible ability, overcoming fears and resistance and succeeding in having a new project formulated and unanimously approved by a senatorial committee after exhaus-

tive discussion. That made possible the miracle of its passage by both the Senate and the House without a single dissenting vote. The unanimity with which the law was passed, and how the public welcomed the directors nominated by the Executive (José Antonio Guerra, José Miguel Irisarri, and myself), permitted the institution to start getting organized without *public distrust*, as there were no grounds yet to expect confidence given the atmosphere of profound skepticism that pervaded the country at the time. Good management caused the bank to gain the full confidence of the country quickly, thus proving that Carlos Prío had wisely selected the men he named to be its directors.

Neither during the organizational period nor during its subsequent operation did Carlos Prío recommend or name any personnel to the bank, nor did his government take advantage of the young institution to obtain loans.

In my dealings with Carlos Prío during the discussion of the law, the organization of the bank, and its operation as well, I had before me a head of state of absolute integrity and elevated patriotism, who conducted his presidential function admirably, in an intelligent, careful, disinterested manner, both personally and as a politician, on the whole achieving results beyond all praise.[2]

And I, myself, can likewise attest:

I had two experiences with fellow DEU member and later President of the Republic Carlos Prío, and the two were favorable.

As Cuban ambassador in charge of economic affairs (1938-1950), I enjoyed his total support in our delicate negotiations with the United States. He vested me with plenipotentiary authority with words I will never forget: "Consult if you have to, but rest assured that the national sovereignty goes with you and act in harmony with what you have been, a member of the DEU."

Later, as I functioned as president of the Agricultural & Industrial Development Bank (BANFAIC) from January 1951 to March 1952, positions in the bank were filled according to record and competitive examination, without

any favoritism and without the president ever recommend-
ing anyone. Neither did he try to obtain loans, despite
political pressures in that respect that I learned were being
exerted on him.

During my tenure at the BANFAIC — that began and ended
with his administration — Carlos Prío conducted the
foreign economic policy of Cuba and that of the bank as an
exemplary president.

Our testimonies should bear witness to one fact: former DEU
members who in fifteen years had not engaged in any public activity
whatever — none had been minister, undersecretary, department
director, or even a candidate to elective office — upon joining the
administrative staff of a president who was a former DEU member
himself, recaptured the emotional historic waves of the eve, and the
three, "recovering a given up tension," acted like what they had been
in the past.

And here the story leads up to a number of conclusions:

1. Looking at the existential reality of the Directorio from a sociological viewpoint, ample grounds exist to affirm that the Directorio
   Estudiantil Universitario (DEU) constituted literally the revolutionary vanguard of their generation. This assertion is substantiated by the following facts:

   a. The Directorio was a "youthful community" in which, as
      Edward Wechssler has pointed out, "what is really important
      is the moment of its emergence in history" (Marías 1967, 129).
      Concerning the university itself, the Directorio eased the
      institution's stigma for having conferred an honorary degree on
      President Machado while expelling over a hundred disgruntled
      students. Externally, the DEU stood heroically against the
      dictatorship — its contrived extension of the constitutional
      term, its administrative corruption. It reaffirmed the national
      sovereignty and, synchronizing with similar movements in
      Latin America, launched its call to arms, "for a total and
      definitive change of regime."

   b. The age range among the DEU members was almost identical
      to the optimum Zamora established (Marías, 140-1). There was
      a difference of only fourteen years between the two extremes.
      Cancio, the oldest, was born in 1898; Pazos and Carrillo, the

youngest, in 1912. In addition, all of them, men and women, were single.

c. The Directorio fulfilled the requisite advanced by Ortega y Gasset, Pedro Laín Entralgo, and all those who make generation the fundamental concept of a historic event: a radical vitality (Marías 1967, 146).

d. The definition given by Mentré was likewise fulfilled in the Directorio: "a generation is a group of men coming from different families, whose unity is the result of a given mentality and whose duration encompasses a specified period" (Marías 1967, 113).

Considering their families, the DEU members covered all the social levels. There were representatives from all six Cuban provinces, and the Directorio extended its presence through a number of provincial and local groups.

As Mentré would also say, all of the DEU members "felt united by their similarity in origin, beliefs, and aspirations. The sway of the facts led them to formulate and carry out a collective program."

e. They had developed Dilthey's "sense of togetherness" (Marías 1967, 65) in the classrooms. That sense of unity continued to gain strength in the risks of their protests, in the common struggle, in prison and in exile, until it developed into a more profound relationship in which "it is not the individuals but the collective will that determines the ultimate decisions."

f. That sense of unity generated a kind of equality that, as Petersen observes, was not determined by birth. It was instead a unity of existence, a vital similarity that was the result of a common destiny which, in turn, implied an equality of experience and objectives (Marías 1967, 126).

g. It was also a "decisive generation." The DEU erupted into the Cuban political arena at a moment in which the younger generation "for the first time think new thoughts in total clarity and in full possession of their sense." It was neither a precursory nor a continuing generation, but a decisive one (Ortega y Gasset 1965, 70).

2. When initially it catapulted itself into the Cuban public arena, the Directorio was nothing but "a group of guys." From that point on, however, it began to gain in relevance and in historic stature, accelerating its generational momentum until it overflowed the strictly student and academic boundaries. When, as a result of the dynamic interrelation between minority and the masses, it evolved into the "national conscience," the Directorio blended with the people as a whole and thus became the people's representative entity. From then on the Directorio was a historic gravitational force. *It was the moment in which the generation took on a national character.*

During this phase the Directorio became outpost, popular vanguard, select minority, leading class, elite. *From "auto-designated," the DEU members came to be "the elect."* Paradoxically, they constituted the "aristocracy of their generation," and this historic dimension was consecrated when, in just 132 days, "their government" fulfilled an incredible proportion of their program. *It was the moment when the human task force took possession of society.*

The "biological projectile" (as Ortega y Gasset [1961, 16] described it) completed its trajectory even after its dramatic dissolution in the final stages of the process. That explains how the phases of "gestation" and "operation" fused into one, and how their creative work — which hit zenith with the elimination of the Platt Amendment, thus making Cuba a full nationality — proceeded immediately, with hardly any pause, from the destructive to the constructive tasks.

3. The DEU's sudden decision to dissolve itself when its historic mission was still unfinished was the direct — and hasty — reaction to the frustration of being betrayed by the man they had made president. It was like a generational suicide that left its leaders and followers without a banner. Communist commentator Leonel Soto and military historian Adam Silva erred in attributing the DEU's dissolution to bitter criticism from the university student body. All that was needed was to substitute the title "Directorio Revolucionario" for "Directorio Estudiantil Universitario;" the DEU, because of its assumed function of "power," had virtually ceased to be a student organization. During the dissolution meeting the student question did not even incidentally come up.

With the demise of the DEU, the mystic spirit of the struggle vanished as well. The moral dome that used to cover all its members, the scale of values of sacrifice, idealism, and self immolation that had grown throughout the whole process also perished.

4. Since individual generations do not leave a permanent impact, the set of moral values the 1930 Generation had projected soon began to disappear. Some of the former DEU members went into professional politics, further eroding the remaining moral influence and the capacity for revolutionary struggle. In time, one of them, Carlos Prío, was elected president, and another, Rubén León, (first in the school of Medicine and Veterinary Medicine) was named Minister of Defense. In such positions, as heads of the armed forces, they had the maximum responsibility as custodians of the national heritage — constitution, tradition, democratic system.

How did these two react when confronted with a crisis of the gravest proportions?

Fulgencio Batista had been allowed to return from a golden exile in Florida when he was elected senator for Las Villas Province. He was also assigned a personal security escort. When Batista expressed distrust about this particular escort, President Prío authorized him to select his own escort from among his former followers in the Army. Batista thus gained the advantage of being surrounded and protected by men in whom he had absolute confidence, who of course would be discreet about his activities, whatever these might be.

In 1952 Batista became a candidate for the presidency for his own minuscule party, *Partido Acción Unitaria* (Unitarian Action Party, PAU), which never carried more than seven percent in any public opinion polls. Consequently, yielding to his own ambitions for power and encouraged by the nearly chaotic state of the Prío administration, Batista began to conspire with both active and retired officers of the armed forces.

With the coup already in motion, Batista offered the nominal presidency to Vice President Guillermo Alonso Pujol, who had a reputation as a very smart politician. Alonso Pujol declined Batista's offer but promised him absolute discretion. He offered a bit of advice as well. "You need your Calvo Sotelo," he told Batista, alluding to the noted Spanish parliamentarian whose assassination in 1936 prompted the uprising of a large portion of the army, soon under the command of General Francisco Franco.

Sure enough, on February 12, 1952, Alejo Cossío del Pino, a popular *Auténtico* leader who had served as Minister of the Interior, was assassinated. The motives and the perpetrators of the crime were unidentified at the time, but the public was profoundly disturbed.

Fearful that Batista had taken his "Calvo Sotelo" suggestion literally, Alonso Pujol went directly to President Prío and, without exactly revealing his secret, begged him to "declare a state of emergency, surround Kuquine [Batista's country estate near Havana], change the military commands!" Prío did call an emergency meeting of the Cabinet but excluded the vice-president from it.[3] Tony Varona favored drastic solutions such as having Batista arrested and spirited out of the country. But Prío preferred to listen to his prime minister, former Machado follower Oscar Gans, who advised him to do nothing. Batista meanwhile continued widening his contacts, aware all along of the dangers should his activity become known. And just that happened. The *Grupo Represivo de las Actividades Subversivos*, known commonly as GRAS (Repressive Group of Subversive Activities), headed by Major Gómez Sicre, got wind of the conspiracy — its members, meeting places, and aims — and promptly sent a confidential memo to the president.

Moreover, Lincoln Rodón, president of the House of Representatives, while riding with Minister of Defense Rubén León, told him about the dangerous situation. León's reaction was a confident, "I have the Army in my hands," underlining his words by clinching his right hand into a fist.

The days passed with no action and March came. Senator Rubén Mendiola, from Matanzas, was informed by an officer stationed in his province, Captain Manzano, of signs of conspiratorial meetings in the district under his command. Mendiola took the information to the president, who then satisfied himself with passing it to the Army Chief of Staff, General Ruperto Cabrera.

Cabrera was arrested by the conspirators at his residence within Camp Columbia at 2:40 in the morning on the tenth, as the initial step of their coup.

Cabrera's wife advised President Prío by telephone, at his country estate "La Chata," and Prío left immediately for the Presidential Palace, where the leaders of the *Federación Estudiantil Universitaria* (FEU) — the new version of the old Directorio — having heard the news, arrived almost simultaneously. The students had come to offer their support and urge the president to take action. On the presidential desk rested the GRAS report with details of the conspiracy, unopened. At that extremely critical moment there was only one thing for Prío to do: go with the students in a motorcade and head to Camp Columbia, just as he had done as a student on that early morning of September 4, 1933. After all, he was the president, the commander in chief, and therefore possessed a huge psychological advantage; he could reasonably expect to assert his authority and take control of the situation. But Prío lacked the courage and the will to play that card. He vacillated and precious hours were lost. He made a number of telephone calls and learned that various regiments in the interior were still loyal to the legitimate government. But Prío still waited a while longer before leaving for Matanzas, where district commander Colonel Martín Elena had been waiting for orders to fight. Finally Prío decided to get on the road, *incognito*. But by then it was too late. As he approached the city of Matanzas, sixty miles east of Havana, news reached him that the garrison there had given up to the spreading military turnabout, whereupon Prío, losing heart, made a U-turn right there and headed back to Havana. The useless round trip meant three more hours lost.

And what was going on at Camp Columbia meanwhile? Despite the total control over all the command centers in the interior, which had fallen like dominoes under Batista's control, Batista sensed that he was no longer regarded by the troop as the charismatic barracks caudillo of eight years before. The composition of the army had changed in the interim; it was quite different from what it had been in the years 1933-1944. So Batista did the only thing he felt might help raise the spirit of those men: raise their salaries. That he did by decree in the afternoon, ten hours after having entered the camp.

Thus the last constitutionally elected president of Cuba was ingloriously put out of office. Back in Havana, Prío quickly sought asylum at the Mexican embassy. For the moment his only worry was that he had left four hundred old one-thousand-peso bills in a drawer of his presidential desk at the palace. He called historian Emeterio

Santovenia, a friend of Batista, to intercede with him for the recovery of the money. Batista granted his request.

The other former Directorio member in the government, Minister of Defense Rubén León, the same man that a few weeks before had told Varona that he had the army in his fist, scurried into hiding when he learned that Batista was in Columbia, and sought asylum in an embassy, too.

As university students, one from the School of Law, the other from Veterinary Medicine, both Prío and León had figured prominently in the 1930 Directorio endeavors. In addition to public manifestos, street demonstrations, and many other related activities, both took part in the revolutionary transformation of the September 4 Sergeants' Coup and were likewise present in the dramatic November 3 meeting at Carbó's residence in Vedado to carry out a plan to have Batista arrested for treason and summarily tried and executed.

But now, years later, after their youthful revolutionary fervor of the 1930s had faded away and they had adopted the parochial ways of political professionalism in the *Auténtico* movement, Prío and León exhibited an entirely different personality and, at the critical moment, displayed a pitiful lack of character.

That is the final and definitive proof that the 1930 Generation concept cannot in fact be equated with the political deviation of its spurious outgrowth, the *Auténtico* Party.

As for Batista, the erstwhile enlisted man, corporal, sergeant, and colonel, when he trespassed through guard post number six that early morning, he could not have known that, in disrupting the constitutional democratic process, there entered with him through that same post, like a ghost, someone who would outdo him in the use of violence. As was well said many years ago by Luis Aguilar León, along with Batista there entered the camp as well the most sinister shadow of Fidel Castro . . . (Aguilar León 1962, 4).

Notes

1. Luis E. Aguilar, in his book *Cuba 1933: Prologue to Revolution*, says,

> During an interview with former president Carlos Prío, I asked him, rather bluntly, for the causes of the Auténticos' public dishonesty. "It was basically a matter of generation training," he answered. "As Machado was despotic and pro-American, we learned to fight for democratic freedom and nationalism. But as Machado was honest, we failed to incorporate honesty as one of the objectives of our program; we didn't learn to associate dishonesty with a basic evil." (Footnote, 241)

Prío's statements about Machado's honesty and that of the 1930 Generation are absolutely false — it ignored the extent of dishonesty as a capital public vice.

2. The document containing Pazos's statements, written especially for this book, is in the author's collection.

3. Information given to author by Doctor Alonso himself.

THE PLATT AMENDMENT

During the military occupation of Cuba by the United States, following the withdrawal of the Spanish authorities in 1899, Military Governor Leonard Wood ordered that a general election be held on the island to elect delegates to a constituent assembly to draft and adopt a constitution as a first step toward the establishment of an independent Cuban government. But the American government preoccupation with the apparent trend of events in Cuba, caused by justified fears among the Cuban people of American interventionism and limited sovereignty, led Senator Orville Platt to present to the Committee of Island Affairs an amendment that would be attached to the U.S. Army Budget Law. The amendment, which was to be annexed to the Cuban constitution, was approved by the Senate on February 15, 1901, and by the House on March 2. It established that in the constitution the Cubans would adopt, as part of its text or as an attachment to it, the following should be included:

I.   That the Government of Cuba shall never enter into any treaty or other compact with any foreign power or powers which will impair or tend to impair the independence of Cuba, nor in any manner authorize or permit any foreign power or powers to obtain, by colonization or for military or naval purposes or otherwise, lodgment or control over any portion of said island.

II. That said Government shall not assume or contract any public debt to pay the interest upon which, and to make reasonable sinking fund provision for the ultimate discharge of which, the ordinary revenues of the island, after defraying the current expenses of government, shall be inadequate.

III. That the Government of Cuba consents that the United States may exercise the right to intervene for the preservation of Cuban independence, the maintenance of a government adequate for the protection of life, property, and individual liberty, and for discharging the obligations with respect to Cuba imposed by the Treaty of Paris on the United States, now to be assumed and undertaken by the Government of Cuba.

IV.   That all acts of the United States in Cuba during its military occupancy thereof are ratified and validated, and all lawful rights acquired thereunder shall be maintained and protected.

V.   That the Government of Cuba will execute, and as far as necessary extend, the plans already devised, or other plans to be mutually agreed upon, for the sanitation of the cities of the island, to the end that a recurrence of epidemic and infectious diseases may be prevented, thereby assuring protection to the people and commerce of Cuba, as well as to the commerce of the southern ports of the United States and the people residing therein.

VI.   That the Isle of Pines shall be omitted from the proposed constitutional boundaries of Cuba, the title thereto being left to future adjustment by treaty.

VII.   That to enable the United States to maintain the independence of Cuba, and to protect the people thereof, as well as for its own defense, the Government of Cuba will sell or lease to the United States lands necessary for coaling or naval stations at certain specified points, to be agreed upon with the President of the United States.

VIII.   That by way of further assurance the Government of Cuba will embody the foregoing provisions in a permanent treaty with the United States (*Foreign Relations of the United States* 1902, 321).

Once this imposition on Cuba became known, modifications and suggestions were proposed, but to no avail. The United States remained inflexible. There was no other alternative: either Platt Amendment or military occupation.

In its session of June 11, 1901, the Constituent Assembly under duress officially approved — 16 to 11 — the Platt Amendment as an Appendix to the Constitution (Grupo Cubano de Investigaciones Económicas 1963).

Appendix II

Microbiography of Carlos Manuel de Céspedes

Carlos Manuel de Céspedes was conceived in the Cuban country side and born during the Ten-Year War on August 12, 1871, in New York, sixty-two years exactly before the date of the three major resolutions passed during his mediated regime. His childhood and infancy were closely linked to the independence process. He never knew his father, who was called the Father of the Country after the uprising of "La Demajagua" in 1868. Carlos's father died at the hands of Spanish troops just a few years after the birth of Carlos Manuel and his twin sister Gloria. After the war in Cuba ended, eight-year-old Carlos and Gloria moved with their mother to Paris, where Carlos eventually obtained his Bachelor's Degree. During their residence in Europe, he travelled to Germany, Italy, and England. He translated the diary of Christopher Columbus into French. In 1892, at the age of twenty-one, he moved to Venezuela, where he became involved in agriculture. In 1895 he returned to Paris to publish a biography of his father. Upon learning of the outbreak of the Revolution of Baire, he went to the United States and soon joined the Liberation Army. He arrived in Cuba on October 28, 1895, landing near Baracoa, Oriente, as one of the members of the "Laurada" expedition. He was Civil Governor of Oriente within the organization of the Republic in Arms; delegate to the Constituent Assembly of Yaya; as a colonel, served as Chief of the High Command of the Inspector General of the Liberation Army, and at the end of the war, once again a delegate in the Assembly of Representatives of the Cuban Revolution (Santa Cruz del Sur, El Cano, y El Cerro, 1898-1899). In this Assembly Céspedes gained stature when he vigorously opposed the removal of Generalísimo Máximo Gómez as Commander-in-Chief of the Liberation Army.

In summary, up until 1899, he led a life of service to the cause of Cuban Independence.

Céspedes was elected and then reelected to the House of Representatives for Oriente province in early 1901 and 1904. During the administration of Liberation Army General José Miguel Gómez (1909-1913), he served as Minister Plenipotentiary first in Italy, then Argentina. In 1914 President Menocal designated him Plenipotentiary Minister from Cuba to Washington, where he served in those official spheres for eight years — he served in Washington longer than any other Cuban diplomat — and it was there that, in my opinion, he developed his psychological and political understanding with the Chancellery on the Potomac. In that period an unusual international situation developed. In 1916 presidential elections were held in Cuba and President Menocal won. According to opinions from that era, this reelection was the product of electoral fraud, since the electorate had really favored the Alfredo Zayas-Carlos Mendieta ticket.

Zayas and Mendieta only won in Havana and Camagüey provinces, but the *Partido Liberal* challenged electoral results in two other key provinces, Santa Clara and Oriente. The Liberals' belief that the elections were manipulated was not entirely groundless. The results from the six electoral colleges from Santa Clara province, which included Guadalupe and Pedro Barba, registered some twenty-four hundred votes, some fifty-nine more than the total number of electors. From those twenty-four hundred votes, only thirteen were liberals, guaranteeing the President's fraudulent victory in Santa Clara. Because of the apparent electoral fraud, the Liberals decided on February 4, 1917, to rebel. The Liberal caudillo, former president and general José Miguel Gómez, rose up in arms; nearly immediately the North American Chancellery declared that "the government of the United States extends its confidence and support only to governments established through constitutional and legal means." Thus, Minister Céspedes chalked up a "success" in his diplomatic career. In diplomatic circles of that epoch, it was considered a "success" if the Cuban Ambassador to the United States obtained praise, approval, or tacit backing for the President whom he represented as personal envoy.

A few weeks later, Gómez was imprisoned in Caicaje in Santa Clara Province and war had been declared between the United States and the Central Empires of Germany and Austria-Hungary. At that time in Cuba, according to the then-British Minister in Havana, "Only in the province of Oriente did there remain between five thousand and fifteen thousand insurrectionists." The North American government declared,

" . . . the government of Cuba is now collaborating in the war against Germany, and, because of that, if the insurrectionists do not return to legality, the United States may declare them enemies and treat them as such . . ." thus producing a "new diplomatic triumph" for Carlos Manuel Céspedes.

Four years later, in the last days of February 1921, Alfredo Zayas, as the candidate for the *Liga Nacional (Conservadores y Populares)* [National (Conservative and Populist) League], lacked sufficient votes to force Congress to proclaim him President-elect. It had been suggested that the nominee of the Assembly of Presidential Electors be selected from a slate of three individuals, Antonio Sánchez de Bustamante, Pablo Desvernine (Céspedes' predecessor in Washington), and Carlos Manuel de Céspedes himself. (At the time there was not a system of direct presidential election by citizens, but rather an indirect method through a group called presidential electors.) From among these three men — rivals among themselves only in terms of their reverence of the Platt Amendment — the Head of the Department of State Latin American Division in Washington, Benjamin Sumner Welles himself, had picked Céspedes. This selection would permit the question: did Céspedes beat his companions in the triad, while still the Minister in Washington, for his greater fervor for national independence, or because he held a more severe and solemn interpretation of Cuban sovereignty? According to Welles, his preference for Céspedes was a result of his "complete understanding of the desires of our government." Is this statement not perhaps sufficient to understand both his preference in 1921 and his later designation in 1933?

Céspedes returned to Cuba in 1922 to be named Secretary of State in the Honor Cabinet, as it was then called, and became the equivalent of Minister of Foreign Relations.

When Machado gained power in May 1925, Céspedes continued in that post until he stepped down in November 1926. He then went on to represent Cuba as the Plenipotentiary Minister in Paris. He was transferred to London in 1930 and the following year returned to Paris, then on to Mexico as ambassador in 1932. He represented Cuba there until May 1933; that is to say, until ninety days before the overthrow of the regime of which he was a part.

To sum up his services until 1933, then, except for the first six years of the Republic, when he served as a member of the Congress, he became a *top-hat-and-tails Cuban* who paraded with the high and mighty of Cuban society among the diplomatic dress suits in the glittering salons of the foreign chancelleries.

This list of official services clearly shows that Céspedes had been at the service of the regime until barely three months before his elevation to the Presidency of the country, then embroiled in one of the most agitated political and social struggles of the Continent. Even though there had been changes of government in Latin America, they were more accurately described as exchanges of heads of state, not necessarily preceded by the type of popularly supported tumultuous movement that was occurring in Cuba.

This brief personal review of Doctor Céspedes's background should make it unnecessary to go more deeply into extended explanations of his designation as interim president by the Mediation.

Within all Céspedes's public activity, it must be recognized that there was a singular instance of self-denial in which, in order to prevent bloodshed and out of a deep feeling of national service, he refused to allow any effort to return him to the Presidency. This was, in his entire personal history, perhaps his most dignified gesture.

In analyzing the only important Mediation Government decree, it is apparent that Céspedes did not have a single moment of nationalistic brilliance in that time period when the Cuban people clamored for their own historic demands — unlike Machado, who had a marked Cuban inspiration when, in 1927, he tried to initiate a process of industrialization with a moderately protectionist tariff; and unlike even Fulgencio Batista, who, on September 2, 1937, produced the Law of Sugar Industry Coordination, a highly distributive legislation within the sugar agroindustrial conglomerate. Céspedes — of course, within the few days of his government, but amid the most serious national desires — did not enact a single decision reflecting the aspirations of the Cubans, after their prolonged sufferings through a period of antiquated ideas and collective frustration. The only decree of any importance was issued under pressure of the manifesto "To the People of Cuba" by the Directorio Estudiantil, forty-eight hours after the manifesto's publication. The Céspedes government, already staggering, had to embrace the principles outlined by the DEU. History reveals that he did so with a deck of cards provided by Sumner Welles up his sleeve.

I myself am from a family of eight children — five brothers and three sisters — all involved throughout the entire cause of indepen-

dence. My extended family lost three members to the three independence conflicts. I have therefore been a fervent devotee of the heroic
effort the legions of the Liberation Army unleashed against the
powerful armies of Spain. My veneration for the process as a whole
enters crisis with the events derived from the war between the United
States and Spain. Cuba was arbitrarily refused legitimate participation
in the peace negotiations between Spain and the United States that
culminated in the Treaty of Paris. This treaty was discussed behind
Cuba's back in spite of the fact that our country, with its contribution
of fifty thousand men of several generations across thirty years of war
for independence, made possible the final conclusion of the conflict.
I disagree fundamentally, of course, with the imposition of the Platt
Amendment on Cuba, and equally I disagree with the international
booty that the United States gained through the appropriation of Puerto
Rico, Guam, and the Philippines. I believe that there is a close
interdependence between such antecedents and the ill-fated course of
the republican governments, inasmuch as it created a dependency that
changed many of the figures of the Liberation Army into solicitous
servants — at the expense of the Nation itself — who, being much
weaker, or loving power more, betrayed their own history.

I believe that Carlos Manuel de Céspedes y de Quesada, son of
the Father of the Country, is one of those cases. It is lamentable that
he should have confused his public obligations — to term them
benevolently — and that, interpreting his duties backward, would
accept responsibilities opposite of those which he had been called to
fulfill. If Céspedes believed sincerely that it was his obligation to
identify himself with the United States and serve that country loyally
from the time that Cuba became a Republic; if Céspedes understood
that he was fulfilling an official function at the service of Machado in
the successive posts while in all of Cuba students and workers died,
and in battles against the regime to which he was rendering services,
men of the Liberation Army such as the outstanding general Francisco
Peraza, were falling victim to assassination; if Céspedes believed that
this duty constituted his "moral" obligation with the United States, then
he would have had to reject the least involvement in a denouement that
was the direct result of provocation by all of Cuba's popular protest
against the Machado regime and his servants. To serve as an instrument
of the North American government in direct connivance with the
mediator could not have been, in any way, an act of good faith.

But although this involvement is highly criticizable in Céspedes, it was equally execrable in Liberators like Colonels Mendieta and Torriente, as well as more recent officers, and the leaders of the ABC. All these leaders had come to accept an individual gravely sympathetic to the past as they collaborated together and in singular subjugation to the United States.

This light analysis demonstrates that the Mediation was one of the most terrible episodes in Cuban history. It both indirectly and directly provoked a revolutionary movement that was rooted in the very development of that process. Upon Carlos Manuel de Céspedes and those representatives of national groups who accepted the Mediation lies the responsibility for the events that followed. Ultimately, I must end this simplistic analysis by relieving from guilt and responsibility those who opposed the North American power that, in a secret meeting with those national leaders, tried to reduce to nothing, in a transcendental moment in Cuban history, all the efforts of a people utterly worn out by grave political, economic, and social afflictions. The Platt Amendment fostered the Cuban sense of subordination to the United States, and the politicians both old and new inherited it from the historic subconscious. Only the Directorio confronted the change in destiny. The Cuban responsibility and guilt must be attributed, in the verdict of justice and the history of Cuba, to those who actually created the "Colony of Cuba" and, therefore, to those who provoked the national reactions.

MICROBIOGRAPHY OF
SERGIO CARBÓ

B oth journalist and politician, Sergio Carbó y Morera, son of Luis Carbó Carmenatti, also an outstanding journalist at the end of the last century and early in this one, was born in Havana on June 20, 1891. Shortly after Carbó passed adolescence, his father died, and Sergio was forced to abandon his studies to make a living first as a public teacher and later as a journalist. In the world of newspaper journalism, he began as a theater reporter, working initially with *El Fígaro* and later with *La Prensa*. In the latter publication he worked as a reporter while advancing into political interview editing for *El Día*. He wrote editorials for *El Día* as well, and ultimately became editor-in-chief in 1915. In 1921 he founded the Zayas-supporting daily *La Libertad*, which barely lasted a few weeks. He was always considered a fervent defender of President Menocal, whom he characterized as *el timbalero* (kettle drummer). This was not a musical reference, but alluded instead to personal courage, symbolized in the popular dialect by the kettle drums. President Alfredo Zayas later said, "The kettle drums are like furniture in the Palace."

He suffered serious political reverses during Gerardo Machado's regime. First, he was a candidate for Representative for the *Partido Conservador Nacional* (National Conservative Party) in the elections of November 1926. He was carried as number nine in the column of that Party on the electoral ticket and used an elephant on his placards, since that number corresponded to the elephant in Chinese Charades.[1] It was a partial election in which the province of Havana was to elect seventeen representatives. Carbó came in tenth in his Party, failing to earn one of the conservatives' six allotted Congressional seats. But the strange thing was not his lack of popular support, since he was the director of a weekly that, founded in 1925, had not yet reached the circulation and popularity that it would achieve after 1930. The strange thing was that Carbó should participate in the electoral process when

Machado had more than shown his hand as a tyrant. Already, Armando André Alavarado, director of *El Día*, for which Carbó had been a major columnist, had been assassinated, as well as the railroad leader Enrique Varona, anarchic activist José Cuxart Falgons, labor leaders Thomas Grant, Esteban Brooks, Felipe Luaces, and Baldomero Duménigo, Captain José Aguilar, director of the periodical *La Campaña*, and many others. Furthermore, many other leaders had simply disappeared, including labor leaders Alfredo López Arencibia, Secretary General of the Labor Federation of Havana, and Margarito Iglesias of the Manufacturing Syndicate, amid rumors that they had been assassinated. As well, dozens of Canary Islanders had been hanged in Ciego de Avila, accused of participating in the kidnapping of Colonel Pina.

And if that were not enough, the program of *cooperativismo* had begun, that ill-fated policy conceived by Senator Wifredo Fernández, so that the opposition party would assist the government, delivering their votes in Congress to approve laws such as that prohibiting the reorganization of current political parties or the organization of new ones, assuring thereby the indefinite maintenance of the Machado regime in power.

The small percentage of votes Sergio Carbó received seems to have carried him to the conclusion that the electoral route was not his best avenue to success. The following year, he went to the Soviet Union, and in 1928, he published his book *Un viaje a Rusia Roja* (A Trip to Red Russia). Even though there was in this swinging move some element of novelty-seeking, his anxiety and search for new experiences demonstrates the disquietude of someone who craves successes that would permit him to attain public power, independent of ideological grounds.

After Trejo's death, *La Semana* became a powerful organ of public opinion. One could say that it was a powerful orientator of the citizenry, who once a week devoured its pages with the hope of encountering therein, within its characteristic satire and irony, biting criticism of the men who remained in power. The weekly gained greater prominence and became the most active champion of the struggle against the tyranny. But the moment arrived when Carbó feared for his life and resolved to go into exile; a little later he joined the expedition project that in the end would be known by the name of the city in which it would arrive: Gibara. In this adventure, the audacity he had demonstrated as a journalist was dimmed in the combatant. Once the tiny town had been occupied, and because of the lamentable loss of twenty-four hours on the part of the seasoned commander, Emilio Laurent, upon hijacking a train to take the expeditionaries to Holguín, the mobilization of land, sea, and air forces of the Machado regime began to produce effects. Laurent had thought that calling in reinforcements and taking the city of Holguín would produce the vital sensation of triumph and create a revolutionary wave that would carry him into Havana and into power. Furthermore, since Machado's military forces would have to converge exactly halfway between Gibara and Holguín, Emilio Laurent and his army would have continued toward the capital with great probability of success, since the invasion would have already bypassed the bulk of the forces of the army, and the multiplicatory power of the victory would permit him a triumphal march into the capital. Nearly all the expeditionaries and many of the newly incorporated combatants marched toward Holguín, and others that feared the risks the route implied decided to march toward the hills, including Colonel "Lico" Balán and Carbó.

When the hijacked train derailed and Laurent's forces found themselves under attack by forces ten times superior, Carbó — who was quite far away, on another route — sought the protection of the Provincial Governor of Oriente, José Rafael Barceló, who sent him off to Jamaica, while his former companions in the expedition were led off to prison.

We met that exceptionally valiant individual, Emilio Laurent, in the Príncipe Castle, and he lived in our midst for a year. He told me a confidential version of the battle. Of course the version did not differ much from what was incorporated in his book *De oficial a revolucionario* (From Officer to Revolutionary), but it contained details that did not appear in the published work.

In balance: in spite of the errors that any public personage commits, Carbó was a fighter by temperament and character. Even though he did not gain the successes he sought on his road to power, he was nevertheless an extraordinary businessman in the journalistic world as a combatant for popular causes.

Notes

1. The game was publicly illegal but tolerated by the bribed venal authority. It was played by winning with different quantities of various numbers out of a series of thirty-six. The numbers were symbolic: one was the horse, two the butterfly, five the monkey, thirty-six the smoking pipe. With the words symbolized by the numbers, riddles (charades) were made that were rewarded when deciphered.

REFERENCES

Adam Silva, Ricardo. 1979. "El Ejército Nacional de Cuba ante la Historia." Lecture at the Koubek Center at University of Miami, May 19.

Adam Silva, Ricardo. 1973. *Cuba. El fin de la república*. Miami: AIP Publications Center, Inc.

Adam Silva, Ricardo. 1947. *La gran mentira: 4 de septiembre de 1933*. Havana: Editorial Lex.

Aguilar León, Luis E. 1972. *Cuba 1933. Prologue to Revolution*. Ithaca, New York: Cornell University Press.

Aguilar León, Luis. 1962. "Fidel entró por la Posta 4 (En Torno a un Aniversario del 10 de Marzo)." *Diario Las Américas*. March.

Alma Mater. 1933. November 7.

Bandera Roja. 1933. October.

Bohemia. 1934. July 9.

Borges, Jorge Luis. 1984. *Seven Nights*. Trans. Eliot Weinberger. New York: New Directions Publishing Corporation.

Carbó, Sergio. 1928. *Un viaje a la Rusia Roja*. Havana: Editorial Hermes.

Chibás, Eduardo R., Justo Carrillo, Augusto Valdés Miranda, and Rafael García Bárcena. 1934. "Los últimos días del govierno de Grau." *Carteles* (Havana). February 4.

Crespo, Manuel. 1934. "Memorias." *Bohemia*. February/March.

Cuban Affairs Commission. 1935. *Problems of the New Cuba*. New York: Foreign Policy Association, Inc.

Diario de la Marina. 1933. Havana. August 25.

Diario de la Marina. 1933. Havana. September 3.

Diario de la Marina. 1933. Havana. September 4.

Diario de la Marina. 1933. Havana. September 5.

Diario de la Marina. 1933. Havana. November 5.

Diario de las Américas, Reloj Section. 1974. Miami. March 11.

"El Ejército es para mí la institución más querida; declaró el Presidente." *Diario de la Marina*. 1930. October 11.

El Mundo. 1933. Havana. September 5.

El País. 1933. Havana. August 22.

El País. 1933. Havana. September 5.

El País. 1933. Havana. September 16.

El País. 1933. Havana. September 22.

Embade Neyra, José E. 1934. *El gran suicida (apuntes de una época revolucionaria)*. Havana: Imprenta La Propogandista.

Fernández, Enrique. 1950. *La razón del 4 de septiembre*. Havana: Editorial Neptuno, S.A.

Ferrer, Horacio. 1950. *Con el rifle al hombro*. Havana: Imprenta El Siglo XX.

Foreign Relations of the United States. 1933. Vol. IV and V. Washington, D.C.: U.S. Government Printing Office.

Foreign Relations of the United States. 1934. Vol. V. Washington, D.C.: U.S. Government Printing Office.

García Bárcena, Rafael. 1952. "Razón y sin razón del 4 de septiembre." *Bohemia* (Havana). September 4.

Gold, Vic, and Paige Gold. 1986. "The FDR Diaries." *The Washingtonian*, December.

González Peraza, Carlos. 1933. *Machado; crímenes y horrores de un régimen*. Havana: Cultural, S.A.

Grupo cubano de Investigaciones Económicas. 1963. *Estudios sobre Cuba*. Miami: University of Miami Press.

Infante, Guillermo. 1974. *Vista del amanecer en el trópico*. Barcelona: Seix Barral.

Krogh, Peter Frederick. 1933. "The United States, Cuba, and Sumner Welles: 1933." Fletcher School of Law and Diplomacy. Thesis.

"La charla de despedida con Emilio Laurent." 1934. *Bohemia*. August 19.

Laurent, Emilio. 1941. *De oficial a revolucionario*. Havana: Imprenta Ucar, García y Cía.

"Los nacionalistas interpondrán recurso contra la resolución del gobernador Barceló." 1930. *Diario de la Marina*. April 13.

Machado, Gerardo. 1982. *Ocho años de la lucha*. Miami: Ediciones Historicas Cubanas.

Mañach, Jorge. 1942. "Destino del ABC. Remisión a la prueba." *Acción*. Havana.

Marías, Julián. 1967. *El método histórico de las generaciones*. 4th ed. Madrid: Revista de Occidente.

Miami News. 1933. Miami. June 19.

Miami Herald. 1933. Miami. July 16.

Miami Herald. 1977. Miami. April 26.

New York Times. 1934. January 19.

Organización Abecedaria del Exilio. 1977. *Cuba y el ABC*. Miami: Editorial Rex Press, Inc.

Ortega y Gasset, José. 1965. *En torno de Galileo*. Madrid: Espasa-Calpe, S.A.

Ortega y Gasset, José. [1931] 1961. *The Modern Theme*. Trans. James Cleugh. New York: Harper & Row.

Padrón Larrazábal, Roberto. 1975. *Manifiesto de Cuba*. Seville: Publicaciones de la Universidad de Sevilla.

Paz, Octavio. 1983. *Tiempo nublado*. Mexico City: Seix Barral, S.A.

Pensamiento Crítico. 1970. Vol. 39. April.

Pérez, Louis A., Jr. 1976. *Army Politics in Cuba, 1898-1958*. Pittsburgh: University of Pittsburgh Press.

Pichardo, Hortensia, ed. 1973. *Documentos para la Historia de Cuba*. Havana: Instituto Cubano del Libro, Editorial de Ciencias Sociales.

Portell Vilá, Herminio. 1934. *Cuba y la Conferencia de Montevideo*. Havana: Imprenta Heraldo Cristiano.

Portell Vilá, Herminio. 1969. *Historia de Cuba en sus relaciones con los Estados Unidos y España*. Miami: Mnemosyne Publishing Incorporated.

Roa, Raúl. 1934. *La jornada revolucionaria del 30 del septiembre de 1930*. Havana: Cultural, S.A.

Rosell, Mirta, ed. 1973. "Garantías ofrecidas por el gobierno de Machado a los representantes de los grupos de oposición durante la mediación." *Luchas obreras contra Machado*. Havana: Editorial de Ciencias Sociales.

Rubio Padilla, Juan. 1970. *Pensamiento Crítico*. April, 105-108.

Scheler, Max. 1961. *El Santo, el genio, el héroe*. Buenos Aires: Editorial Nova.

"The Secret Files of J. Edgar Hoover." 1983. *U.S. News and World Report*. December 19.

Soto, Lionel. 1977. *La revolución del 33*. Vol. 1-3. Havana: Editorial de Ciencias Sociales.

Suchlicki, Jaime. 1969. *University Students and Revolution in Cuba 1920-1968*. Coral Gables, Fla.: University of Miami Press.

Thomas, Hugh. 1983. *The Revolution on Balance*. Washington, D.C.: The Cuban American National Foundation, Inc.

Torriente Brau, Pablo de la. 1969. *Presidio Modelo*. Havana: Instituto del Libro.

Torriente, Cosme de la. 1938. "Antes y después del 12 de agosto." *Carteles*. August 14.

Disclaimers

1. None of the persons mentioned — with the exception of the co-authors Rubio, Armenteros, and Alvarez Tabío, and only in that which refers to their contributions (aportes) — is responsible for the events nor the critiques expounded by the author.

2. The emphasis and interpretations are the responsibility of the author.

Final Observation

The author understands the intense rhetoric which may result from this work. With respect to events, the author has been most severe in requiring accuracy and avoiding falsehoods. In regard to the interpretations of actual events related, the author graciously accepts criticism from true combatants in the fight for liberty; however, he refuses to respond to merchants of traditional Cuban politics.

ABOUT THE AUTHOR

Justo Carrillo, Jr., was born in Cuba. This Caribbean nation gained its independence from Spain in the latter part of the nineteenth century, following three wars of independence that spanned thirty years. All of Carrillo's immediate ancestors were involved in the long struggle, and three of them perished in its battles.

Carrillo's father, Colonel Justo Carrillo Morales, youngest of eight brothers and sisters, fought in the final war that led to Cuba's freedom in 1898 and was later a congressman. The oldest brother, General Francisco Carrillo, became a senator, governor of Santa Clara province, and vice president of Cuba. The wars of independence claimed the lives of three of the author's uncles: Andrés, Sixto, and Vicente. Carrillo's three aunts were in the military and became prisoners of the Spanish government. Their mother, Ana Joaquina Morales, was with her daughters during their imprisonment on the Isle of Pines.

Justo Carrillo, Jr., was born ten years after Cuba gained its independence and was raised in a tradition of love and sacrifice for his country. At age seventeen, he was one of the founders of the Directorio Estudiantil Universitario (University Students' Directorate) — the main opposition force to the dictatorship of Gerardo Machado. Four of its members lost their lives fighting against this first dictatorial government, and many went to prison, Justo among them.

During the years of democracy that ensued, Carrillo was undersecretary of the Oficina de Regulación de Precios y Abastecimiento (ORPA), the government agency that regulated prices and imposed rationing at the time of the Second World War. From 1948 to 1950 he was ambassador at large and director of international economic affairs for Cuba. He led the Latin American delegations to the early General Agreement on Tariffs and Trade meetings and obtained from the developed nations the concession of the "principle of non-reciprocity" that permits developing countries to begin the process of industrialization. He was awarded Cuba's highest decoration, the Great Cross of the Order of Carlos Manuel de Céspedes.

In 1950, Carrillo founded and became the first president of Banco de Fomento Agrícola e Industrial de Cuba (BANFAIC), Cuba's development bank, and vice president of the Central Bank. He resigned these posts after Fulgencio Batista's coup d'état, immediately prior to the elections of 1952. In 1959, after the downfall of Batista, he reluctantly agreed to assume, once again, the presidency of BANFAIC and the vice presidency of Banco Nacional de Cuba (the Central Bank). In disagreement with Fidel Castro's regime, Carrillo left Cuba in January 1960 to organize the Revolutionary Democratic Front and the Revolutionary Council, through which he directed early opposition to the communist tyranny of Cuba — an ideal to which he continues to devote his efforts from Miami, Florida.